# The Last 15-Minutes

## Living Life in the Choice Space

by

Douglas R. Templeton

# Acknowledgment

The list of those to whom I am indebted for the treasures of wisdom and knowledge contained in *The Last 15-Minutes* is a long one.  First, I have had many teachers over the course of years that have each contributed a piece or pieces of the puzzle. Most notable are Graham Cooke, Bob Mumford, and the books by Paul Bilheimer and Norman Grubb.  But I must make special mention and express overwhelming gratitude to my friend and long-time instructor in the way of life, Keith Lamb.  To each of these men, I say "Thank you," not only for your personal contribution to my experience, but for your long-term faithfulness of serving Papa to the best of your ability, and in both the measure of your faith and grace.

Second, I must humbly-yet-proudly acknowledge the contributions of my family, on whose backs the stripes for my learning have fallen much more than they deserved.  I am proud of their response to my weakness, and the suffering I have caused them.  They have demonstrated what unconditional love is about—making a place of repentance. To my wife of 46+ years, Susan, I say "thank you" for your steadfast commitment.  You could write a book about what the wedding vow words, "For better or for worse" mean! Thanks for simultaneously being my greatest support and toughest critic.  You have taught me that those are complementary actions, two sides of the same loving coin.

It is not false humility to say in this context that I am well-acquainted from where the wisdom in *The Last 15-Minutes* emanates—the Holy Spirit.  I have typed the words, but only as He has dictated them.  I love the way He works!  I love that He invests His genius in us!  I have read and re-read this manuscript many  times, and each time I learn some new aspect of His purposes in the earth, and of His plans for the Bride of Christ.  In the final analysis, that is the testimony of His authorship—He is still teaching, still revealing, still stirring.

Finally, I dedicate the pages of this book to those courageous believers who take the risk to see life in the Spirit in a different light than they have always been taught, and that is antagonistic to the flesh in which we are all so comfortable.  It is a risky business—at least it feels that way—when we leave the warm and snug confines of Independent Self and allow our viewpoint and understanding to be redefined in a different context.  I salute your courage to engage in the scary business of peeking behind the veil of the flesh and investigating with me the pilgrimage of heart that costs you everything, but that returns so much more than you could ask or even think.


Blessings, All!


Randy Templeton (2019)

# Contents

# Preface

*"Let us be glad and rejoice and give Him glory, for the marriage of the Lamb has come, and His wife has made herself ready."* **Revelation 19:7**

## Objective: Practical Discipleship

The thrust of this book will be practical discipleship. That is, every word, every concept should be affirmatively tied and translated to practical action. There will be theoretical thinking involved, however, because our ability to "see" the Kingdom at all is an exercise of being *born again*—Jesus' terminology for an awakening of spirit to unseen eternal realities. We must be able to see the Kingdom before we can enter (**John 3:3-5**). Such sight is not a function of any of our physical senses, but another sense entirely— a spiritual one. Our physical senses are more often than not a hindrance to knowing the Father, a barrier to be set aside and overcome when they become our absolute measure of what is *real* and what is not. So, by definition, every practical action toward the Kingdom must begin as an abstract concept perceived first in the eternal realm, then embraced and learned in the time/space/matter (T/S/M) dimension. The challenge of discipleship is bridging between these and turning abstract and unseen into the practical and visible. That sounds very similar to the definition of faith given us in **Hebrews 11:1**, and that is no accident!

"Unseen" does not mean "unreal," it just means we use a different sense organ to perceive. To see the Kingdom, we must imagine as a child imagines. But that does not mean it is "imaginary." The Kingdom of God is more real than our time/space/matter (T/S/M) world, if for no other reason than it will remain long after the T/S/M dimension has passed away. We access the Kingdom through the eyes of our spirit.

> **Hebrews 11:1**, "[1]Now faith is the substance of things hoped for, the evidence of things not seen."

There are important concepts about discipleship that you will not read between the covers of this book because they are beyond the scope of what I hope to accomplish. *The Last 15-Minutes* is not intended to be the definitive, complete reference book on the topic. I am convinced it takes a lifetime to barely scratch the surface of the treasures of wisdom and knowledge that the Father has for us. Instead, I will focus on practical actions that answer the question, "What do I do *today, this moment,* to be His disciple?" I have observed that many believers fail to make the discipleship progress they might otherwise make because they never get specific, and they never make a plan to grow in the most important responsibility in life: Faithfully transacting with the resources with which the Master has entrusted us (**Matthew 25:14-30**).

If I have done my job, what you *will* find in these pages is a model of discipleship action designed to provide a roadmap—a *plan*—for living your discipleship experience on a granular level. Failing to get specific allows us to fudge our estimate of success in the transformation-into-His-image-process—the process we will identify as *salvation*. We cannot evaluate our progress when our spiritual goals and objectives remain too general. "How can I be like Jesus?" is an entirely different question (in terms of likelihood of success) than, "What choices can I make today to overcome my anger?"

This life is not about you, that is, the physical you that you look at in the mirror. It is not about finding happiness, enjoyment, fulfillment, or your contentment in this body of flesh. It is affirmatively not about your possessions, importance, career, position, social status, and standing, or your command and control of circumstances. It is not about your influence, your witness, your religion, or your beliefs. ***It is not even about your ministry***. Your existence in this T/S/M world is for one overarching purpose and one alone: ***for your training***. There is nothing wrong with acquiring possessions, finding happiness and contentment, or enjoying life. But in His Sermon on the Mount in **Matthew 6:33**, Jesus commanded us to, "Seek first the kingdom of God and His righteousness, and all these things shall be added to you." The things we seek are put in perspective and appropriate priority by His words. They are a collateral benefit to a life expended in pursuit of righteousness, peace, and joy in the Holy Spirit.

If there is one Scripture that summarizes what we are to be about in this T/S/M preamble to our marriage to the Lamb, it is **Revelation 19:7**, "Let us be glad and rejoice and give Him glory, for the marriage of the Lamb has come, ***and His wife has made herself ready***." You ain't never seen a wedding like this one! It will not just be the social event of the season, but the greatest social event of every season from *before there were* social seasons! And, as the Bride of Christ, we will be at the center of the action and on display for adoration by our Bridegroom and the whole universe. In

> **Matthew 6:31-32**, "³¹Therefore do not worry, saying, 'What shall we eat?' or 'What shall we drink?' or 'What shall we wear?' ³²*For after all these things the Gentiles seek.*"

**Ephesians 5:31-33**, Paul declared the marriage relationship a "great mystery" involving Jesus and His Bride. We know mysteries are intended to tantalize and draw us into our pursuit of Him. As the Bride and the Bridegroom become one flesh through union and discipleship, our "me" becomes "we" (as **Galatians 2:20** declares His life alive in our container of flesh), and we become the visible manifestation and presentation of Jesus to the T/S/M world.

## The Elevator Speech

The challenge of any author (or hack, hoping to be an author!) is to condense the whole of the work into a few sentences that summarize: an "elevator speech." With that purpose in mind, I offer the

> No earthly activity *has any lasting value apart from its eternal effect,* and will not survive the transition from our present reality to the eternal.

following: Christians are placed on earth for a purpose, and our circumstances of life are intended to tutor us to take our inheritance, rule beside our Bridegroom in His Eternal Kingdom, and fulfill our responsibilities in the future Kingdom as He assigns them to us. The Father has given us a marvelous life coach in the person of the Holy Spirit. Our purpose in this life is two-fold, two overarching "Father's business" activities that we must be about: 1) Preparing ourselves to rule with Christ in His Eternal Kingdom (e.g., being regenerated, transformed into His image, and renewed in our mind); and, 2) Increasing the Kingdom by laying up treasure in Heaven through love and good deeds. *All* our experiences on earth are intended to constitute an internship/apprenticeship preparing us for the Kingdom. No earthly activity has any lasting value apart from its eternal effect, and will not survive the transition from our present T/S/M reality to the eternal Kingdom[1]. Later, we will identify this as the "Accumulated Value Principle."

We are fond of telling each other that, "God has a plan for your life"; I believe that statement is true, as far as it goes. Sometimes our consideration of Papa's plan is myopic and egocentric. Beyond the specific coaching of the Holy Spirit ("Turn right. Turn left here"; "Take this job"; or, "Don't trust that person") there is a level of planning in the Godhead that is the overarching framework for our T/S/M existence. Papa

---

[1] Throughout this book we will make the distinction between time/space/matter (T/S/M) reality and eternal reality as two separate dimensions with overlapping qualities and influences.

derived great pleasure from His creative activities recounted in **Genesis 1 and 2**, as His pronouncement that, "It is good," evidenced. However, the rest of the story ("His story") details a Plan that exceeds and supersedes pleasure and proceeds on to magnificent Purpose. His Plan, though in no way simple, can be simply stated: To restore the Kingdom to His Son. We are an integral part of the Plan, the Purpose, and the resulting Kingdom. As joint-heirs with Christ (**Romans 8:17**), we can legitimately claim to share Jesus' central place in history, but only as our glory reflects His. If we engage His suffering, we share His glory:

> [16]The Spirit Himself bears witness with our spirit that we are children of God, [17]and if children, then heirs—heirs of God and joint-heirs with Christ, if indeed we suffer with Him, that we may also be glorified together. [18]For I consider that the sufferings of this present time are not worthy to be compared with the glory which shall be revealed in us. [19]For the earnest expectation of the creation eagerly waits for the revealing of the sons of God. [20]For the creation was subjected to futility, not willingly, but because of Him who subjected it in hope; [21]because the creation itself also will be delivered from the bondage of corruption into the glorious liberty of the children of God. (**Romans 8:16-21**)

**Romans 14:17**, "For the kingdom of God is not eating and drinking, but righteousness and peace and joy in the Holy Spirit."

With the foregoing understanding as a rock-solid foundation, we begin to explore *our role* in *His story*. The first and most obvious conclusion is that God's Plan becomes the *context of life* for our own story. But not only our story, but the story of all creation between the foundation of the world to the return of the King. Our duty—our "Job One"—is to continuously and endlessly seek to conform our agenda and interests to our future position in His Kingdom as the Bride of Christ. No other effort is worthy of His majesty; indeed, no other effort will survive the transition from this reality to Eternal reality. Nothing else qualifies as faithfulness, and nothing else is discipleship.

## Which "You" is You?

If our precious life is destined to spend this T/S/M reality confined in a container of flesh, a legitimate question is, "Which me is the real me?" That is the central question of identity. I am reminded of the humorous saying, "Who are you going to believe, me, or your lying eyes?" In a very real way, that is the question asked of us by the Holy Spirit on a day-by-day, moment-by-moment basis. Our five senses do not give us an accurate appraisal of our true identity, mainly because they are designed for a world that is not the ultimate reality. Yet the immediacy and the power with which our senses press in on our consciousness gives them a faux legitimacy that we must struggle to suspend and overcome.

All understanding of what we should do in this life begins with who we are to be in the Kingdom, and who we are to be in the Kingdom begins with who we are and how we are known by Papa. Jesus told us in **Matthew 7:23**, "And then I will declare to them, '*I never knew you*; depart from Me, you who practice lawlessness!'" It seems that there is a *huge* priority connected with knowing and being known! Everything hinges on

**Matthew 7:23**, "And then I will declare to them, 'I never knew you; depart from Me, you who practice lawlessness!'"

an accurate understanding of, and investment in, our true identity. By identity, I do not mean your name or any of the other so-called "facts" that the world associates with distinguishing one person from another. When the world speaks of "identity theft," it is really addressing strings of letters and/or numbers that have nothing to do with the real you, or the real resources at your disposal. Your true identity does not depend on the various ways you represent yourself to the world, only the core essence of how you are known in heaven. *Identity theft happens to each of us every day that we allow the enemy to cloud our vision of how we are known in heaven!*

No believer can know or access their real self until identity with the flesh is cleaved, separated from our precious life.[2] The Fall of Man resulted in separation from the Spirit of God; in the void, the flesh steps in and becomes our identity, overwhelming the spirit of a man and making insistent, clamorous demands for the soul's attention. Soul ties and habits are formed over time and chain us to the flesh, and they give birth to the carnal mind. The ties of soul-to-flesh must be broken in order for us to see clearly the truth that God has pronounced concerning who we are; that is why the emotional healing process can be so helpful in our quest. Guided healing session(s) can be a key to uncovering soul ties, injuries, ill-advised vows, trauma, misbeliefs, and emotional scarring that hinders our ability to see and receive our Bridegroom's love and also the truth He pronounces about us.

One vital issue in our spiritual growth is our grasping of the *fact* of our identity—who God has made us, and how He currently views us. He has judged *all* sin, and it is no longer an issue. In order for God to continue to look at and account for sin, He would have to affirm that Jesus' death was somehow lacking in its atoning effect. He has completely eradicated all charges against us (**Colossians. 2:14**). We must begin to live in the reality of who He has made us, not only for the grateful acknowledgment of what He has done, but also to clear the way for our spiritual development into the person He already sees. The objective of accountability is not to condemn bad behavior in ourselves or others, but to encourage us to live in the reality of our eternal identity. It is a completely different orientation and focus for life, one that is preoccupied with positive and scorns the negative. The principle of **Psalm 115:8** is that we become most *like* what we *most look at*.[3] If we focus on our behavioral shortcomings, we will get more of the same. If we focus on Him and who He has made us and declares us to be, we will find ourselves walking in the Fruit of the Spirit—effortlessly, naturally, and being our silly self!

> **Psalm 115:4, 8**, "[4]Their idols are silver and gold, the work of men's hands...[8]Those who make them are like them; so is everyone who trusts in them."

In **1 Corinthians 13:12**, the Apostle Paul makes an interesting statement that exceeds its face value in meaning: "For now we see in a mirror, dimly, but then face to face. Now I know in part, but then I shall know just as I also am known." There is an "I" that is known differently, more completely than we can see in the dimly lit, darkly reflecting mirror that is this life, and that separates us from the reality of our true self. So, the answer to, "Which "me" is the real me?" is, "The man in the dim mirror!" In this present T/S/M reality, we struggle to perceive our true selves. But, when the veil of the flesh is completely taken away, we will completely see. Until then, our task is to continue to pursue the true self that lives through the looking glass in the eternal realm.

You will find that you—the real you—*does not exist* in this T/S/M reality at all. The *real* you is currently seated with Christ in heavenly places (**Ephesians 2:6**). Your *real* life is hidden with Christ in God (**Colossians 3:3**). The *real* you existed before the world began, and will continue after this T/S/M training and testing environment has served its purpose and is brought to an end. The *real* you will be present at the Bema Seat and will be judged for what you have done with the resources He has made available to you. At that

---

[2] The Greek word for "sanctify" is ἁγιάζω (hagiazō), meaning "to separate, consecrate; cleanse, purify, sanctify; regard or reverence as holy." Separation and consecration from our weak-but-dominant flesh is a prerequisite to knowing and being known.

[3] This is the principle that David recognizes in **Psalm 115:4-8**. Verse 8, "Those who make them are like them; *so is* everyone who trusts in them," tells us that when we establish other gods in life, we become like the ones we adopt.

point, the *real* you will be an integrated member of the Bride of Christ, and rule beside Him as a joint heir of the Kingdom—*or not*.

Your true identity is not the one subject to the whims, demands, follies, and foibles of your T/S/M flesh. The real you exists and thrives in another dimension that is so distinctive and divergent from the one we observe with our physical senses that it is unimaginable without the aid of the Holy Spirit; unattainable without concerted, intentional effort; unspeakable in the sense that our words are pitiful attempts to convey meaning; unknowable without Papa's revelation; unfathomable in the absence of the width, length, depth and height of Christ's love for us, and the fullness of God (**Eph. 3:17-19**).

> **Colossians 2:13-14**, "[13]He has made alive together with Him, having forgiven you all trespasses, [14]having wiped out the handwriting of requirements that was against us, which was contrary to us. And He has taken it out of the way, having nailed it to the cross."

## The Corner Pieces

Seeing and understanding life in the Spirit in terms of a jigsaw puzzle is an apt metaphor for spiritual understanding, because only by assembling spiritual mysteries can we discern the whole picture. The wisdom of God remains foolishness to the world because it cannot cross the spiritual threshold into discernment (**1 Corinthians 2:14**), and because there is a certain irreducible assembly quotient of pieces required before other actions can be undertaken, or even understood. Sometimes one has to make a beginning before being able to see the next step, and sometimes you must put together certain pieces to see others, and the pattern as a whole. It is a progressive revelation in a nutshell, and the "line upon line, precept upon precept" (**Isaiah 28:10**) school of thought. It is the way Papa speaks to us in the cave— digestible bites that *lead us* in the quest for wisdom, not *body slam* us into conformance.

If you have put together a jigsaw puzzle, you have a thought model for constructing the puzzle of life as prep for the Kingdom of God. Papa has hidden puzzle pieces in His Word, in our experience, in our study, in His creation, and in our meditation and discussions with Him. We will return over and over to Solomon's pronouncement of **Proverbs 25:2**: "It is the *glory of God* to conceal a matter, but the *glory of kings* is to search out a matter," because it portrays one of the factors that distinguish between some sheep and other sheep. Some sheep pursue hard after knowing Papa's mysteries, and some discount the existence of such mysteries as unknowable, or even as dark knowledge. But we are destined to be "kings and priests unto our God" (**Revelation 1:6**); and, as such, it is our *glory* to commit to assembling the pieces of His puzzle. We will see in a later section that in **John 15:15** Jesus declared the qualification for being called His friend: Knowing what the Father is doing. That means not only knowing what He is doing in the earth at this moment but also the goal of His Program from beginning to end. And, although we surely may not find all of the pieces alone, nevertheless we dedicate ourselves to the faithful pursuit of understanding His ways as well as His acts. We are dedicated to discover the pieces to Papa's puzzle and to put them into a discernable picture that matches the one on the "cover of the box."

The first step in assembling a jigsaw puzzle—after removing the pieces from the box and turning them all upright for viewing—is to locate the corner pieces (pieces with *two* straight sides). Next, the puzzler undertakes the exercise of locating and setting aside the straight-edged pieces that make up the frame. Locating the boundaries is always essential in any process because it determines the scope of our inquiries; our process of becoming a disciple is no different. After the corners are set, the frame is set apart (sanctified!), and all the pieces spread out for viewing, the puzzler is ready to embrace the work. I propose the following four corner pieces that will define the scope of our study:

- **Corner Piece #1:** Jesus is staffing His eternal Kingdom by training His Bride, the Church, to rule beside Him. He is growing His Kingdom in the earth from seeds, planted in the life of believers. The training process for ruling is the reason for the T/S/M experience and is the purpose of life. We will refer to this overarching purpose as "God's Program." Papa has constructed a perfect training and testing environment in this T/S/M world. He employs the mechanisms of suffering, trials, and tribulation to teach us obedience, accomplish our regeneration from the dead, transformation into His image, and renewal of our mind. The result of the salvation process is to grow His character, values, and ways in us.

> **Revelation 1:5-6**, "[5]To Him who loved us and washed us from our sins in His own blood, [6]and *has made us kings and priests to His God and Father*, to Him be glory and dominion forever and ever. Amen."

- **Corner Piece #2:** Jesus' death and resurrection *brought us into spirit-union* with God; we are *being brought into soul union* (mind, will, and emotions) through the processes of regeneration, transformation, and renewal as we submit to His discipleship. We are transformed into His image as we face life circumstances and choose the spiritual mind over the carnal mind (**Romans 8:6**). Our stony heart is regenerated as we learn to feel like Him; our mind is renewed as we learn to think like Him; our will is transformed and we learn to make His choices. There is no longer any separation between us, and our experience increasingly reflects His life in us as we learn to live, "Christ *in* me, *as* me" (**Galatians 2:20**).

- **Corner Piece #3:** Our true identity is in the eternal realm, not in Time/Space/Matter reality. Our *real* self is who Papa says we are, and how He sees us—and He sees us as perfect and complete, lacking nothing. We *have been* justified by His blood once and for all time. We are working out our salvation (**Philippians 2:12**) as a *process* in this life: We *simultaneously* have been saved, are being saved, and will be saved. We live in the paradox of the now-and-not-yet Kingdom. Papa has endowed us with three primary resources to transact life: our identity, time, and our prerogative to make choices. We redeem these primary resources in exchange for gold (that we may be rich toward God), white garments (that our nakedness might be covered), and eye salve (that we may see) (**Revelation 3:18**).

- **Corner Piece #4:** God has given us great and precious promises to serve as seeds of the Kingdom within. He has put everything into our hands with respect to our discipleship. He has placed in us, "all things pertaining to life and godliness" (**2 Peter 1:3**). We are "God's field...God's building" (**1 Corinthians 3:9**). As His field, we are organically growing the character of a joint heir and co-ruler with Christ. We are learning His ways and values and preparing ourselves to be Jesus' perfect helpmeet. As His building, we are increasing the Kingdom by the good works that He has prepared beforehand in which we are to walk.

Each of the four corner pieces has its own place in framing discipleship activities as Papa has ordained them, and it is up to us in our kingly role to locate and connect the rest of the frame and the rest of the pieces—the "guts"—that provide the complete picture.

## Saving Yourself for Marriage

The concept of saving one's sexual purity for the marriage celebration has its spiritual origin and roots in the marriage union of Christ and the Church; and, as such, never becomes an old-fashioned idea. Scriptures compare the marriage of man and wife to the union of Christ and the Church. When we speak spiritually about being saved, sometimes we seem to wax glossy-eyed and lose sight of the plain meaning of the word as it is used in everyday language. Typically, when we use the word "saving" in common-speak, we refer to one of three meanings:

1) Rescuing—sparing from destruction or degradation

2) Reserving—laying aside for future use, or delaying gratification

3) Repairing—to upgrade from a current condition to an improved condition of usefulness

The Greek word for "save" is sōzō, and its meaning incorporates all of our common meaning when we use the English word.[4] It is clear how God's saving work in us begins with our justification and spares us from destruction and eventual Hell; but, in addition to rescuing us:

- What if God meant for us to understand that His saving work is also about "reserving" (sanctification) and "repairing" (salvation) us?

- What if we are laying aside our precious life for future use as well by sending it ahead of us into the Kingdom?

- What if He is as concerned with growing the Kingdom within you as He is in keeping you out of the trash heap of Hell?

- What if, "Lay up for yourselves treasure in heaven" (**Matthew 6:20**), is as authoritative as a command from the Master as, "Love the Lord your God with all of your heart, soul, and mind" (**Matthew 22:37**)?

- What if securing reward in Heaven is tantamount to putting items away in a hope chest in preparation for our eternal life together?

- What if preparing for the Kingdom that we will occupy, rule, and build together is the practical expression of loving God with our entire being?

- What if the *emotion* of loving Him in the absence of *action* (caring about what He cares about, active engagement in building His Kingdom, and preparing for it now) is nothing more than human emotion that, like other temporal things, "perish with the using" (**Colossians 2:21-22**)?

- What if the exchange process of, "redeeming the time for the days are evil" (**Ephesians 5:16**)—that is, *trading "our life" for His life*—is the act of worship and preparation that John spoke of in **Revelation 19:7**?

"Saving yourself for marriage" in this context has nothing to do with sexual activity and everything to do with reserving our affections and loyalty for our Bridegroom. It means that forsaking all others, we press toward our high calling of being regenerated, transformed, and renewed to be a fit helpmeet for Him. It has to do with faithfulness and *fierce loyalty* to His Kingdom and our longing to be with, and rule beside, Him. Writing this book has changed me. It has altered my orientation to life. It has changed my priorities and perspective. It has changed my personality to a degree, or at least that portion the world sees. Nothing in my Christian experienced since I was justified at the age of eight and Baptized in the Holy Spirit at 17 years old has so profoundly impacted my understanding of exactly what our Good Father is

---

[4] *Mounce Concise Greek-English Dictionary of the New Testament* edited by William D. Mounce. Copyright ©2011 by William D. Mounce. To save, rescue; to preserve safe and unharmed; σῴζειν εἰς, to bring safely to, to cure, heal, restore to health, to save, preserve from being lost; σῴζειν ἀπό, to deliver from, set free from, in NT to rescue from unbelief, convert; to bring within the pale of saving privilege; to save from final ruin; pass. To be brought within the pale of saving privilege; to be in the way of salvation.

> **Ephesians 5:31-32,** "[31]For this reason a man shall leave his father and mother and be joined to his wife, and the two shall become one flesh. [32]This is a great mystery, but I speak concerning Christ and the church."

accomplishing on this earth, in this T/S/M dimension. If there is one thing I know professionally, it is that the real work in any disaster takes place in the recovery period. Rescuing victims, extinguishing the fire, running up and down streets with lights and siren—these may be the adrenaline-producing "sexy" aspects of the job of emergency services, but resilience—or lack thereof—comes to the forefront during the reconstruction. After your story is no longer the lead on the six o'clock news or doesn't even make the first section of the newspaper anymore, the grindstone begins that determines where we go from here.

## Our Two-Dimensional Purpose: Position and Reward

God has implemented a program (hereafter, "God's Program") in the earth that is the motivation for His design of history and creation. As marvelous and important as creation was, as phenomenal as His ongoing orchestration of history, God's Program is the reason for the other two. His Program is the blueprint for staffing, building, and training *the leadership component of Jesus' eternal Kingdom.* The interim period between Foundation of the World and the Return of Christ constitutes a T/S/M reality during which God is accomplishing the planting, growth, care, and harvesting of Kingdom components— and the Church stars in the pivotal and preeminent role as the Bride of Christ. Consider these Scriptures that tell of our future role in the Kingdom:

- **Psalm 110:1-2,** "[1]The Lord said to my Lord, 'Sit at My right hand, till I make your enemies your footstool.' [2]The Lord shall send the rod of Your strength out of Zion. ***Rule in the midst of your enemies*!**"

- **Matthew 24:45-47,** "[45]Who then is a faithful and wise servant, ***whom his master made ruler over his household***, to give them food in due season? [46]Blessed is that servant whom his master, when he comes, will find so doing. [47]Assuredly, I say to you that *he will make him ruler over all his goods*."

- **Matthew 25:21,** "His lord said to him, 'Well done, good and faithful servant; you were faithful over a few things***, I will make you ruler over many things***. Enter into the joy of your lord.'"

- **Romans 8:16-17,** "[16]The Spirit Himself bears witness with our spirit that we are children of God, [17]and if children, then heirs—***heirs of God and joint-heirs with Christ***, if indeed we suffer with Him, that we may also be glorified together."

- **James 2:5,** "Listen, my beloved brethren: ***Has God not chosen the poor of this world to be rich in faith and heirs of the kingdom*** which He promised to those who love Him?"

- **Revelation 3:21,** "To him who overcomes ***I will grant to sit with Me on My throne***, as I also overcame and sat down with My Father on His throne."

"Joint heir" (**Romans 8:17**) *does not* mean half for Him and a half for me. It means that both heirs share 100% of the inheritance and preside over it together. When Christ inherits a Kingdom and rules over it, the Church—His Bride—will be right beside Him sharing His throne, sharing His responsibility and authority. Preparation for rulership means that the Church is being tutored by the Holy Spirit to assume the duties according to the values, characteristics, and ways of the King. We are learning to overcome our

Independent Self[5]; to put our absolute trust in our Father and Bridegroom; to enter into the collective mind of Christ, and bear His image. In short, we are growing the seed of the Kingdom of God within us. Our Independent Self is not well-equipped to understand or embrace our union with God, but we continue to pursue an understanding of the process that results in "the assurance of things hoped for, and the evidence of things not seen" (**Hebrews 11:1**). Paul makes clear that it is the witness—the "seal"—of the Holy Spirit that declares our membership in the family of God as children:

> **21**Now He who establishes us with you in Christ and has anointed us *is* God, **22**who also has sealed us and given us the Spirit in our hearts as a guarantee. (**2 Corinthians 1:21-22**)

In **Galatians 4:1-7**, Paul locates us in a growth and development curve that begins with us as children under tutelage, and eventually taking our place of rulership as sons:

> [1]Now I say that the heir [us], as long as he is a child, does not differ at all from a slave, though he is master of all, [2]but is under guardians and stewards until the time appointed by the father. [3]Even so we, when we were children, were in bondage under the elements of the world. [4]But when the fullness of the time had come, God sent forth His Son, born of a woman, born under the law, [5]to redeem those who were under the law, that we might receive the adoption as sons. [6]And because you are sons, God has sent forth the Spirit of His Son into your hearts, crying out, 'Abba, Father!' [7]Therefore you are no longer a slave but a son, and if a son, then an heir of God through Christ.

Our task in life is two-fold: 1) Submitting to the tutelage of the Holy Spirit in preparation for rulership; and, 2) Simultaneously using the time on earth to lay up treasure in the Kingdom. The task of the enemy of our soul is to keep us persecuted, bound up and pre-occupied in our flesh, our eyes averted from the joy that is set before us, and to steal the seed of the Kingdom sown in our heart. His objective is to overwhelm our spirit by crushing our soul to the ground, as David indicated in **Psalm 143:3-4**:

> **3**For the enemy has persecuted my soul; He has crushed my life to the ground; He has made me dwell in darkness, like those who have long been dead. **4**Therefore my spirit is overwhelmed within me; my heart within me is distressed.

If the enemy can keep us crushed, in darkness, overwhelmed and distressed, then we cannot rise to the point we can be regenerated, transformed, and renewed. In other words, he—with our cooperation and ignorance—can thwart the preparation and training we are intended to experience. With our eyes fixed on ourselves, our problems, issues, and all of the circumstances pressing in to crush us, we cannot escape the darkness to position ourselves to lay up treasure and be transformed. Until we grasp that we are created for an *affirmative purpose* and not some non-descript "life for its own sake" animus, we are putty in his hands and pawns in the game as the enemy wreaks havoc in us. Learning to reign in life is rising above the crushing, illuminating the darkness, and defeating that which overwhelms and distresses. In **Matthew 6:22-23**, Jesus is not addressing the quality of our physical eyesight, but of our inner focus. The eyes to

> **Matthew 6:22-23**, "[22]The lamp of the body is the eye. If therefore your eye is good [single/healthy], your whole body will be full of light. [23]But if your eye is bad, your whole body will be full of darkness."

---

[5] "Independent Self" is a term to which we will return repeatedly. It means our identity separated, segregated, and unique; and existing as a being distinct from God and all other entities in our consciousness. It reflects the first lesson a newborn learns upon exiting the birth canal, the "me—other-than-me" (M/OTM) distinction. The M/OTM distinction is our first real lesson of life, and it is so pervasive and dominant in our thinking that it is one of the last illusions we must master to experience oneness with God and one another.

which He refers are the same eyes that David meant in **Psalm 25:15**—"My eyes are ever toward the Lord"—the inner eye of the spirit, and the gaze of the soul. The function of the eye is not only to admit light without restriction, but also to focus that light into a meaningful, unclouded, clarified image. Since we know that, "God is light, and in Him is no darkness at all" (**1 John 1:5**), a good eye is one that is focused on God, one that admits the light of God and focuses the understanding of Him, His ways, and His promises for us. It starts with a good eye, a focused eye, a single eye. That is what **Ephesians 1:18-19** means: "[T]he *eyes of your understanding* being enlightened; that you may know what is the hope of His calling, what are the riches of the glory of His inheritance in the saints, and what is the exceeding greatness of His power toward us who believe."

In **Philippians 3:13-14**, Paul writes,

> Brethren, I do not count myself to have apprehended; but *one thing I do*, forgetting those things which are behind and reaching forward to those things which are ahead, *I press toward the goal* for the prize of the upward call of God in Christ Jesus.

"One thing I do" is a *singleness of focus*. The enemy seeks to diffuse our singleness of focus with *double-mindedness*. **James 1:5-8** describes the role of trials in our perfection process; then tells us that a double-minded man/woman is unstable, all over the landscape in focus:

> [5]If any of you lacks wisdom, let him ask of God, who gives to all liberally and without reproach, and it will be given to him. [6]But let him ask in faith, with no doubting, for he who doubts is like a wave of the sea driven and *tossed by the wind*. [7]For let not that man suppose that he will receive anything from the Lord; [8]*he is a double-minded man, unstable in all his ways.*

The verses immediately preceding talk about what we have been addressing as the object of our learning and preparation for ruling: *trials, suffering, and testing*. James tells us that the thing that holds us back in the learning process is lack of wisdom, lack of patience, lack of faith, and doubt. The result is that a man or woman with these characteristics will not receive *anything* from the Lord, much less the full measure of our promised inheritance. The idea here is *not* that they are lost and going to hell; it is that they *cannot be trusted with their inheritance* because of distraction and lack of focus. With all that goes on around us these days, maintaining a good eye is pretty much a full-time job.

## Time to Begin

It will soon become evident that discipleship is the process of unlearning that which we have learned from this world and our Independent Self instincts, re-learning that which we have learned wrong in the context of the carnal mind, and, learning for the first time eternal realities that prepare us for the next phase of existence beyond T/S/M. We will find that a life lived on "cruise control" and for purposes that come easily and naturally to our flesh is almost assuredly based in carnal mind reality. It will soon be clear that paradoxical questions drive our quest to see behind the veil of the flesh, questions like:

- How can I be dead and alive at the same time?

- How is it possible to be in union with God so that there is no separation, no "space" between us?

- How can I operate in this reality while "seeing" what Papa is doing and hearing Him speak in the eternal dimension?

- How do I overcome my Independent Self when it comes so easily and naturally to me?

- When the flesh's overwhelming viewpoint is, "me/other-than-me," how can I live assimilated into oneness with God, as Jesus prayed for us to experience?

- How do I successfully pull off the "in this world but not of this world" dynamic?

This book is about plans and planning in a way you may have never considered their application. It is about making a plan to incorporate the skills, leadership knowledge, character, values, and understanding of the Father's ways to prepare you for ruling beside our Bridegroom. It's about organizing your discipleship efforts—both for yourself, and any others God has given you to disciple—using a practical, fresh approach. It defines making and using your Discipleship Plan as a portion of the time and effort sacrifice that **Romans 12:1** defines as our "reasonable service." It is not about working your way to Heaven, but it is affirmatively about preparing yourself to be equal to the task once you are there.

> **Romans 12:1**, "I beseech you therefore, brethren, by the mercies of God, that you present your bodies a living sacrifice, holy, acceptable to God, which is your reasonable service."

As we delve deeply into the most basic issues of life (e.g., why we were created and what has God given us to do; and what is His curriculum and syllabus for our training to rule with Him), we will necessarily probe our own weaknesses, and the traps and plans for ruin that our enemy has laid for us. As Sun Tzu wrote in his masterwork, *The Art of War*, self-knowledge, and knowledge of our enemy are equally essential to victory. These knowledge factors have long been recognized and acknowledged by soldiers and pilgrims alike. What is perhaps less known—but is a primary contextualizing knowledge in *The Last 15-Minutes*—is an over-arching and comprehensive knowledge of God's Program on earth. It is futile to attempt to make our way to His intended destination for us unless we first know what He is accomplishing, what our part in His Plan is, and why *He* has chosen both the Program and the people to carry it out.

We will consistently refer to the overarching framework of why God created mankind and placed us in this time/space/matter (T/S/M) dimensional universe as *God's Program*, and the "why" of our existence as the *Foundation of Meaning*. The problem of demystifying Papa's Program is both simultaneously, and paradoxically, simple and incredibly complex beyond imagination. The mission may be succinctly described as, "Restoring the Kingdom to His Son (Jesus)." As for the mechanics of the process of history, they remain intricately complex interworking of God's will in all aspects and events of history, which history includes the individual lives of the Bride of Christ—and that is where we enter the drama.

## Writing it Down...

A good use of the blank space throughout the book would be to make notes, record insights, ask questions, etc. Wherever you see the fruit graphic—like the one below—think about recording your thoughts. If this book—like your Bible—is too good to write in, you should put it away and get a different one!

# Part 1: The Theory of Everything

## "One Ring to Rule Them All"

For centuries science has been attempting to develop a single, unified master theory of the universe that explains our physical existence. While scientists search for the micro components that explain the "how" of our existence, believers have the information recorded in the Scriptures that give us the "why." We know from Scripture, for example, that God did not just create the universe and then walk away. His involvement in the affairs of creation implies that He has a plan—a purpose-filled Program of Operation—for the material universe. If He has a Program, then He most assuredly has defined a goal for successful completion. If we know what Papa has set about to accomplish in His Program, we can more effectively bring our portion and role into alignment with the big picture. If we know that His overarching purpose is to restore an Eternal Kingdom to His Son, and if we know we have an important role as His Bride, we can enthusiastically engage in learning what we need to know to rule beside our Bridegroom. If we know that this life is a classroom constructed and existing for a particular purpose—*to prepare the Bride of Christ to rule beside her Bridegroom in His Eternal Kingdom*—we have the context for understanding not only the life we experience but also the whole stream of history. If we know that transformation into His image is the class curriculum; that learning His ways is the classwork; that meditation, prayer, study, and assimilation are the homework; and the trials and sufferings are the tests, we can structure our efforts into a concerted master theory of our own plan and activity. Let's do it, *and let's call it "Discipleship."*

It may seem strange to feature quotes attributed to a notable *atheist* philosopher and a popular *deist* writer in this context. But even a blind hog finds an acorn occasionally—or so I am told—and that seems to be the case with the two quotes. At least philosopher Frederick Neitche got one thing right: "He who has a reason *'why'* can bear any *'what'* or *'how.'*" Mark Twain expressed a similar perspective when he wrote, "The two most important days in life are *the day you are born* and *the day you find out why.*" If these two men (neither notable for positive, Christian spiritual leadership) are correct, then "why" as a reason for our existence on earth, and understanding life's purpose is important enough to warrant considerable effort on our part to investigate. A reason "why," when powerful and compelling enough, is motivation to act. "Why" can be the jumpstart to overcome the inertia that is so prevalent and so limiting in the fulfillment of our full potential. It is the only way we may ensure our compliance and harmony with our Great Commission as Jesus gave it to us—to make *disciples* of all nations. Making disciples of all nations necessarily includes the initial step of making a disciple of ourselves as well; and to this goal, we dedicate ourselves and the following pages.

# Chapter 1—A Heart Set on Pilgrimage

[5]Blessed is the man whose strength is in You, whose heart is set on pilgrimage. [6]As they pass through the Valley of Baca [dryness], they make it a spring; the rain also covers it with pools. [7]They go from strength to strength; each one appears before God in Zion. Psalm 84:5-7

## *The Last 15-Minutes*

This is a book about how we get from where we are to where we will be. It is about my own pilgrimage from slavery to the Promised Land, from wilderness to a place to call home, from accidental tourist to intentional partner. It is about the methodology that has helped me find my way in dark places. But, while a book about me and my journey have been affirmatively worthwhile **to** me, **for** me, it does not seem like the kind of book I would like to read if I were you—just doesn't sound that interesting. But I am probably a guy (in the generic sense) pretty much like you; and so, the kicker is that it is just as much about you and your own road trip across the desert as it is about mine; and, of course, that *should* make it immanently more interesting. Make no mistake—life's pilgrimage *is* through a wilderness. The landscape and landmarks across *your* desert are different from mine, the temperature and climate may be different,

> "He who has a reason 'Why' can bear any 'what' or 'how.'"

and the path itself even very disparate—some rocky and steep, while others relatively level and smooth, each with its own difficult peculiarities. However, it is still a journey from *here* to *there*. If you are reading this (!), here is still here (today); and even if you sit down beside your path and refuse to budge at some point along the way in the future (as the Israelites did), your pilgrimage still had a point of embarkation (today) and will have a termination point yet to be determined—even if it doesn't make it all the way into the Promised Land as was its intent and potential.

Stephen Covey's 2nd Habit of successful people,[6] "Begin with the end in mind," makes perfect sense on every level of every meaningful activity. We plan for years for our retirement, make a list before going to the grocery store, and chart our course on a map before setting off on vacation. We plan our budgets and sacrifice to purchase that new car and other major expenditures. We plan for contingencies, for emergencies, and for a health crisis. We plan for the unexpected and insure our houses, our physical life, and our possessions. We make written plans for weddings, funerals, and even quinceaneras! We fuss and fret over birthday parties, Christmas parties, and anniversaries. In my field—emergency management—we make plans for every hazard we can reasonably anticipate—some jurisdictions even have a plan for the inevitable asteroid strike! In the context of so much anticipation, thoughtful planning, and focused attention, it is clear that we give appropriate attention to that which we *truly* value. That planning rightfully should include what our experience and character will look like when we get to our swan song, the final curtain, *down to the Last 15-Minutes.*

Imagine with me, if you will, yourself at a ripe old age—your body well past it's "use by" date, expiring, and 15-minutes away from your last breath, your final heartbeat. You are headed for the last roundup, and this time you will not escape. Let's assume for the sake of the exercise that you are not in pain. Let's assume you are fully conscious and alert. Let's assume that you are surrounded by family and friends and that this scene comes to pass in a place of serenity and peace. In other words, let's assume it is a "good day to die," and you are down to the last 15-minute stretch. My question to you is, "Who is **that** person

---

[6] Covey, Stephen R. The 7 Habits of Highly Effective People: Restoring the Character Ethic. [Rev. d.].

laying on **that** death bed?"  Not, "What is his/her name?"; not, "What was his/her profession, place of birth, or age in years"—we will get all of those facts from the obituary.  My question has everything to do with the essence—the precious life of soul and spirit—that will shortly "shuffle off this mortal coil."  What traits of character will you possess?  What elements of the Fruit of the Spirit (Galatians 5:22-23) will have been routinely presented for consumption by those around?  What values will you have embraced, those of the world or of the Kingdom?  What will have been the reach and effect of your influence?

Does *that* person on *that* bed even look like you today?  If not, is that a good or bad thing?  Would you recognize yourself if you met you on the street?  For believers, is the "branch" laying on that bed connected to the vine, and is fruit veritably dripping from it?  Or, alternatively, is the branch's substance shriveled and unfruitful?  Is there an air of royalty hanging like a mist, like an anteroom where the Crown Prince waits for his coronation to begin, or like a bride waiting for the first notes of the Wedding March?  Is there an undercurrent of excitement and anticipation that dispels dread and fear?  Is there a profound sense of satisfaction that is just short of palpable?  Is there a notable feeling of peace and lack of urgency as is consistent with a well and thoroughly completed task?

I think we can all pretty much agree that 15-minutes before you die, the fat lady is on her last few words of the final chorus.  At that point, you and I have most likely saved all of the world we are going to save.  We have likely made the last acquaintance we will make, had our last meaningful conversation, and sipped our last cup of delicious coffee or tea while catching up with friends.  We have endured our last trial, encouraged our last disciple, learned our last life lesson, embraced our last test.  We have stood and delivered—**or not**.  Now is the time for the "amen"—the last word—except the privilege of speaking it will not belong to you.  It will be said for you, on your behalf, and according to your pilgrimage performance.

None of us like to contemplate circumstances such as these.  Truth be told, we are all privately convinced that such an event, while unavoidably *in everyone else's future*, will never happen to us.  But think about this: unless you know *that* person lying on *that* particular future death bed, and if your current self was not intentionally involved in designing both the outcome and the process to reach it, you have no roadmap for crossing the landscape between you (present) and you (future).  That means, among other things, you have consented (or, at the very least, acquiesced) to the philosophy that one destination is as good as another, one grave as final as another, one destiny as fulfilling as another, and one legacy as impacting as another.  If I may be frank: You have punted on the 1st or 2nd down of life.  It is impossible to score until you have defined the goal, and made significant, intentional effort to reach it.  When every shot is from the hip, and without the precision of careful aim, the odds of hitting many bullseyes are remote.

What does all this talk of your *Last 15-Minutes* on earth bring up inside you?  If the former paragraphs strike you as morbid, I would remind you that the Book of **2 Peter** is the result of Peter "folding his tent and breaking camp."  In other words, he was contemplating final instructions considering his impending death. There is an appropriate time for considering one's transition through death into the eternal realm, and that time is while there is still time to influence the outcome and be intentional about what you hope to accomplish. There is coming a time in your and my experience when it will not be possible to further implement change, grow fruit or lay-up treasure for future access.  Even Jesus was limited in the scope of what He could accomplish in the time allotted.  He said in **John 9:4**, "I must work the works of Him who sent Me while it is day; the *night is coming when no one can work*."  **1 Peter 4:7** tells us, "But the end of all things is at hand; therefore, be serious and watchful in your prayers."  The point is this: Believers and non-believers alike will face the same issue of giving an account for his or her life.  The earlier we start being intentional about

> **2 Peter 1: 13-14**, "¹³Yes, I think it is right, as long as I am in this tent, to stir you up by reminding you, **¹⁴knowing that shortly I must put off my tent,** just as our Lord Jesus Christ showed me."

arriving at our desired destination, and the more organized our effort, the better we are bound to fare in reaching it.

## A Heart Set…

We began this chapter and our journey together into the Choice Space with a passage of Scripture from **Psalm 84**. What does David's phrase in **Psalm 84:5**, "Blessed is the man…whose heart is set on pilgrimage" mean? It means that there is a blessing associated with grasping the understanding that life is a journey by God's design, the course over which we are intended to change, adapt, and grow. But that change, adaptation, and growth should not be haphazard or left to chance. Determining our approach and organization of our pursuit is the *first* step in our growth process. We are fond of claiming that God has vested each of us with free will and that we are subsequently free moral agents. Nowhere is that concept more applicable than in our choices related to our regeneration, transformation, and renewal. With free agency comes great opportunity, but also a great responsibility—responsibility to blast ourselves out of the complacency with which we get so comfortable, and in which we so readily take our ease. When inertia becomes our momentum, we have fallen into a deep pit.

A heart set on something is a heart committed to a vision; and not just *any* vision, but a vision that understands and accounts for God's purpose in creating us in the first place. Later, we will discuss the "From-To Principle," and that we are travelers moving through the alien territory *from* glory *to* glory, *from* strength *to* strength, *from* pool *to* pool, *from* faith *to* faith. And while it is wonderful for us to live in *today's* place of glory, strength, refreshing, and faith, we do not get to set up a permanent camp and settle down, because tomorrow's challenge is still before us. Each day the Israelites had to go out and gather fresh manna because today's manna expires and rots. On the Mount of

> **Matthew 17:4**, "Lord, it is good for us to be here; if You wish, let us make here three tabernacles: one for You, one for Moses, and one for Elijah."

Transfiguration, Peter blurted out, "*Lord, it is good for us to be here*; if You wish, let us make here three tabernacles: one for You, one for Moses, and one for Elijah" (**Matthew 17:4**). Peter had a history when he didn't know what to say, of blurting out something inappropriate for the moment. At *this* moment, he wanted to set up camp and settle down in today's place of glory. But while the vision of transfiguration was what the Father was doing *at that time*, Jesus knew that at the bottom of the mountain was the demon-possessed boy in need of healing; and to set up permanent camp on today's mountain means missing tomorrow's opportunity. It means settling for "today's self" instead of pressing forward to become your *Last 15-Minutes* self.

A pilgrimage differs from any other road trip in that it is *frequently* long, *typically* votive (i.e., performed, undertaken, etc., in consequence of a vow), and *always* directed with a defined destination. The destination for our pilgrimage of heart is a Promised Land where we will dwell with our Bridegroom and will take possession of our inheritance and rule beside Him. This book talks about the trip across the wilderness, the role that our commitment to discipleship plays, and the fact that our loving Father has placed us in a wonderful learning environment and given us a path to walk to prepare us to step up and take our inheritance.

# My Dance with Bitterness

I am sharing my story with you in hopes that you may understand that I come by this knowledge "honestly." With a 35-year career in emergency services and another seven years as a planner in the field

> **Hebrews 12:15**, "Take care that no one forfeits the grace of God; and that no **root of bitterness** grows up and causes trouble and by it many are defiled."

of emergency management, I have come to understand that managing the chaos of life does not happen haphazardly, whether on the scene of a disaster or in one's circumstances. In fact, without a plan, control usually does not happen at all. But unlike the chaos of life, every fire eventually goes out when it runs out of fuel; every flood eventually recedes when the rain stops, and every tornado or hurricane eventually loses its wind speed and energy. Life's chaos, however, can continue unabated indefinitely until it is wasted—frittered away—and time runs out.

I know the foregoing because it was very nearly my experience. I was told from an early age that any person could achieve great success if he or she had some modicum of talent, and is willing to work hard—I did, and I was, and therefore I was "guaranteed" to accomplish all of my career and life goals, including leading my own department as Fire Chief. I was something of a golden boy, celebrated in sports, music, academics, and by my family as talented and expected to achieve. First in my immediate family to graduate from a university, I then continued on to get the first graduate degree. I was elected to class leadership positions through middle and high school, and even into college.

My father was legally blind and had a sixth-grade education; even with his physical limitations he was a really intelligent man, and he taught me how to *think*. My favorite memory of my dad is coming home at night with him sitting at the dining table, reading the Bible under a low-hanging pall of cigarette smoke. It was a scene I witnessed many times throughout my childhood and teens. That cigarette smoke would later shorten his life, ending it at a time when I needed him to lean on to guide me through the overwhelming blur of my 20's. That is what fathers are supposed to do. I knew he loved me and was proud of me, although I cannot remember ever hearing him say it. We rarely hugged in my family, but I did not miss it because—ostensibly by virtue of our English heritage—it was just not done. It must not have been important.

I was a credibly good high school football player, and my dad may have been my biggest—if quietest—fan. One of my early disappointments and shortfalls (pun intended) was that I didn't grow tall enough to garner much interest from college football programs, in spite of multiple years of all-district honors, and averaging 20+ tackles per game in my senior year as a linebacker. That remains my first recollection of what I later came to define (to my detriment) as the injustice of life—failure to be awarded and take possession of that for which you have worked hard and *earned*. Two other players on my team were given football scholarships to a major university, one of whom was not even a starter in high school—but his father was an executive at the university. On the occasions that a few colleges asked for my game films, my coach failed to send them. *That* was my first real lesson in the "benefactor principle"—that is, if you are not one of the "coach's boys," your well-being and success are of little importance. Later, I learned it was not just the coach that operated this way; it is common in the workplace and the Church as well.

Looking back, the two harsh realities of the benefactor principle and the injustice of life combined as a one-two punch that greatly enhanced the pain as I experienced them again and again in other venues, each time spiraling a little lower into a more earth-bound orbit, and being drawn ever-nearer to the atmospheric re-entry that very nearly burned me beyond recognition. These two misbeliefs, working together, were producing in me a self-reinforcing cycle of "effort—rejection—bitterness" that produced in me a cynical "not chosen" syndrome. I was *that* kid standing, waiting for the two team captains to pick me, and sinking further and further into despair as all around me joined their prospective team and I was left alone. From my viewpoint, I was the last man standing, but not in any good sense that the phrase might be employed.

Both my parents worked for the State of Texas in low-level jobs, so money was tight and extras were scarce. We were what would today be known as "the working poor." However, my parents ensured that I had the *huge* advantage of growing up in the Church—one that instilled in me a deep love and respect for the Scripture. But that huge advantage also turned to an unbearable burden as others' expectations concerning my future grew with each new Baptist success until they were woven into the fabric of my upbringing. My mother missed few opportunities to impress upon me my "specialness"; she knew this because she almost died in childbirth with me, and that made me a miracle baby. No pressure there, right? My older brother (by 11 years) took up where she left off, making sure that I was fully aware of *his* plans for my success. Part of the internal conflict that I would later face was that everyone had a plan for my life; but all of the plans, being different, were impossible to reconcile and ameliorate. Consequently, when I showed signs of thinking for myself with regard to my future, I was not-so-subtly told of the disappointment that I was both headed for and becoming to others. My brother went so far as to later tell other relatives that, by going *my* own way, I had ruined *his* life. *Vicarious much*?

Performance expectation—whether self-imposed or from others—is a demanding taskmaster that never takes a break. Consequently, in my career, I set about to work hard, obtain advanced educational degrees and certifications, and a significant resume of skills and experience. I knew that the phrase often mistakenly quoted as a Scripture, "God helps those who help themselves," was actually the words of Ben Franklin, *not* the Apostle Paul. Yet, they certainly rang true in my psyche as I exhausted myself by burning my candle at both ends. I was making sure that He would have no other option than to help me, given the level of effort I was expending! I continued to serve God and my church as an ordained minister, youth pastor, and elder while working a full-time job 56 hours per week and taking a full load in graduate school. For years, I turned off the television, neglected the kids and my wife to go to class, read books and wrote papers—all with the promise of the pot of gold at the end of my rainbow of effort. Yet, that which I was convinced I *had been promised* and had *earned* through personal effort continued to elude me.

With each new pass over for promotion, or unsuccessful attempt to land the big job, my frustration and the intensity of my pain grew, as did my anger with God for failing me when I had *clearly* lived up to my end of the bargain. The lessons I was learning in my career reinforced the ones I had learned in high school; that is, usually, the advancement I sought was handed to others who had not done the extra effort things I had made part of my routine. Often those appointments seemed sardonically to be nothing more than the result of politically-correct largess, some unfair system of patronage of which I was not a beneficiary or a club to which I had not been admitted. Once again, I had no benefactor, no Good Father, to intervene and make up the difference between what I had produced and what was required.

My experience in Church was far from the place of refuge, acceptance, and unconditional love that we advertise to the world. My wife and I served as volunteer youth pastors for our church for many years, and that was a source of pure delight as well as a lot of hard work and lost sleep (teenagers *love* lock-ins)! We have always had a knack for relating to teenagers, probably because we genuinely care for that age group, and we refuse to take ourselves so seriously that we become too grown-up and respectable. Every youth group must have a cool thing that gives them a common vision and purpose, and ours was to travel on protracted mission trips during the summer months. As you might be able to guess, the summer project stretched out to cover much of our time the rest of the year because fundraising to send 20+ teenagers on mission trips to various parts of the world is expensive. During this time, I was accumulating a lot of activity, experience, teaching, and street cred. Being Youth Guy was in my wheelhouse, and I was having a blast!

If being Youth Guy had been enough, I might have been okay. But, unfortunately, I had to relate to the adults in the world as well. Simultaneously—or perhaps consequently—I was also serving as an elder in our non-denominational church, a position that drained all of the life that shepherding the youth was inputting. "Elder" in this context is purely descriptive of an office and place of responsibility, and *not* descriptive of my spiritual or emotional development. Whereas I found relating to youth natural and life-giving, relating to my co-elders was hard work at which I experienced much-mixed success. My middle forties were a Jekyll-and-Hyde story of production and success coupled with confusion and bitter disappointment. I have learned that two of the *defining characteristics of a man* are how he deals with his disappointment, and how he dissipates his boredom. (I suspect them to be true of women as well; but, having never been one, I cannot declare it with authority.) It is an understatement to say that my ability to cope with disappointment did not match my role and responsibilities in the church. And, cutting to the chase, it is only appropriate for me to say that my relationship with the elders—both on a personal level and as a leadership body—was severed, and in a manner that both bewildered me and compounded my despair. I am not deprecating my role in the conflict, nor placing blame on others; but this is a book about regeneration, transformation, and renewal, so I am integrity-bound to report the steps *down* into the pit as well as the steps back up.

Susan and I left the church shortly thereafter, and my tropical disturbance continued to grow. A perfect storm was brewing; and, like the hurricane that draws energy from the warm waters over which the depression broods, my heated thoughts were agitating, exaggerating, exacerbating, and generally contributing energy to my internal disturbance. Other sources of embarrassment and frustration, some resident in my memory from childhood and high school, contributed to the accumulation of emotional pain and bitterness until I could bear it no longer without medicating it in the best way I knew how—drinking alcohol until it was numbed. *I knew better*, but I also knew *bitter*.

I should interrupt the negative flow here to affirm that, in the clear blue skies of hindsight, I was not only where I had placed myself but was also right where I needed to be—though that thought is in itself a painful one. Throughout this book, we will discuss reframing and contextualizing our suffering *as* we experience it. Reframing an experience in the context of God's word does not *erase* the experience, it just corrects the damage. There are choices that I am forced to own but would never choose today. That said, neither would I trade the experience of Papa's total work in me for a smooth, trouble-free life of uninterrupted accomplishment, especially if it meant missing the "eternal weight of glory" that we are promised in exchange for our "momentary light afflictions" (**2 Corinthians 4:17**). The contrast of the two previous thoughts seems to be a dissonance that is unresolvable. But it *is* resolved in this understanding of Papa's Program for us: We may not choose our own cross, neither are we to crucify ourselves; rather, we embrace and learn to value the suffering that comes to us, even suffering from our poor choices.

> > The wise learn from their mistakes;
> > The wiser learns from the mistakes of others;
> > The wisest of all foresees the evil and hides him/herself! (**Proverbs 22:3**)

The really debilitating thought—as I would cry out to God to remove my pain, preferably by giving me what I had *earned*—was that I *knew* that He could change my heart *with a single thought* but seemed unwilling to do it. That misbelief opened me up to the lie of the enemy that, since He would not help or change me, I must not belong to Him at all. Or, if I did, I was not one of His favored kids (i.e., "coach's boys"). I even twisted my theology to the degree that I assumed that, since God knew the end and the beginning of my life from His position in eternity, He already knew that I was not destined to finish life well and had, therefore, abandoned me to my own way to cut His losses. I continued to spiral downward, drinking heavily every day and suffering significant depression. My life proved the truth of **Proverbs 31:6-7**, and it was not a pretty sight; it never is.

My low point occurred as I was by myself, making a road trip home from out of state. I always experienced intensified distress when I had protracted periods to think and meditate on the negative, stew in the unfairness of life, and become immersed in self-pity. To deal with my boredom and pain, I had begun drinking immediately when I hit the road. No one needs to tell me how irresponsible and dangerous that was—I am well aware. After several hundred miles, I awoke to find my truck turned over on its side, on fire, and a stranger kicking out my windshield to help me get out.

> **Proverbs 31:4, 6-7**, "⁴It is not for kings, O Lemuel, it is not for kings to drink wine, nor for princes intoxicating drink...⁶***Give strong drink to him who is perishing, and wine to those who are bitter of heart. ⁷Let him drink and forget his poverty, and remember his misery no more***."

(To this day I think that my rescuer may have been an angel—He disappeared right after I crawled out.) My injuries were not serious, a blessing for which I am grateful. However, after an overnight stay in the hospital, complete with making distraught plans of how to end my suffering permanently, my wife had the good sense to tell me not to come home until there was some resolution of my issues. My sons picked me up at the hospital (checking out against medical advice) in my deplorable state, and skirted me off to the home of my friend of 40 years to detox from the alcohol; and, as it turned out, from the bitterness as well.

My friend is a wise man. He is also just about as non-judgmental as they come. He nurtured me for seven weeks, as I worked to drain the pus from my infected, inflamed soul. He led me through a series of exercises designed to explore deep inside my cave to uncover the root causes of my pain, not just the symptoms. After a long time of reflection, I wrote a list of 63 events—from minor to debilitating—that I could remember that contributed in some degree to my emotional trauma. My friend's prescription for my soul-sickness was for me to make the list; then, we sat down and discussed each incident, and prayed over it, asking God to heal everything and help me re-frame my thinking. After we spent several evenings going through the entire list, and discussing my re-framed perspective, we built a small fire in a barbeque pit and burned it.

I cannot explain why such a simple process should have such a profound effect, but the change in me was *immediate,* the healing instantaneous. The suffering of which I had made such a friend disappeared! The pain was gone, as was the need and drive to medicate it. That was more than ten years ago, and I have not had alcohol since. More importantly, I no longer live with the pain. The next step was, over time, to learn to correct the misbeliefs that I had embraced and made my constant monologue. I have learned that one of the most important issues in life is to keep one's accounts short when it comes to debilitating emotional pain, and the effects of

> **Hebrews 12:15**, "[L]ooking carefully lest anyone fall short of the grace of God; lest any root of bitterness springing up cause trouble, and by this many become defiled."

misbelief (that is, believing a lie). It *must* be dealt with as it appears, or its accumulation will cripple us. Emotional pain results in what **Hebrews 12:15** calls the "root of bitterness" that defiles us. It is pretty clear that the root cause is failing to access the grace that is available. Sometimes we fall short of grace; sometimes, we don't even try.

Life control, as we normally consider it, is both an illusion and over-rated. If the world—even the world in my immediate vicinity—depends on my ability to control it, all who come into my orbit are in dire peril! We delude ourselves with the thought that we are capable of handling life; however, since we intuitively know in our deepest self that such an assertion is not true, the illusory thoughts are neither comforting nor do they inspire deep-seated security. Even self-control as a Fruit of the Spirit (FOTS) is in a sense illusory.  Consistent self-control is not even possible unless we surrender control to the Sovereign God; and this act of surrender is for our benefit, not His.  So, our efforts at self-control are best employed at "control of self"—and there is a world of difference!  Discipleship is the process of surrender to Papa's Sovereignty, and directing the resulting power of the Spirit to align our soul's mind, will, and emotions with His Mind, Will, and Emotions.  It is an intentional process; but a passive one also in that we are not in control or bear responsibility for the results, only our attitude, receptivity, and inclination to learn.

## The Long and Winding Road Home

After my protracted absence from tranquility, I finally returned home from the relative safety and anonymity of my friend's home and hospitality.  Over that seven-week period, I had convalesced in my asylum and had done some serious business and really hard work in the presence of the Holy Spirit.  (And, we had gone fishing!)  I had looked long and hard in the mirror; and frankly, the person that I saw looking back was not a person I *ever* thought I would be, and a world away from the affable Baptist boy that grew up on Arcadia Street in Austin, Texas.  I had suffered severe, lasting damage to my pride, repeated body blows to my self-esteem, and inflicted major familial trauma.  The net effect was that I simply wanted to disappear from the radar; or, at least, be as invisible to the world as practical.  At that point, I had no idea if the damage was recoverable.  I had fantasies of being homeless and alone; and for the first time, based on my personal failures, I could truly envision how that can happen to a person.

In my mind, there had been no shortage of responsible parties for my persecuted and tortured condition—the fact that I had plenty of likely suspects was a major problem that I struggled to overcome for the next several years.  I *still* struggle with those thoughts even after the pain associated with them is gone, and still have to re-frame my perspective yet again.  In the perfect storm that is life, all flesh has this common characteristic: It always seeks not only to stir up the tempest in our teapot, but also to place responsibility on the ill-winds of injustice, the storm surge of others' abusive behavior, and the wave-swamping effect of the world's conspiracy against us.  But these are targets of convenience to assuage our guilt and wrath, because the inconvenient truth is that the teapot is ours, and the tempest is ours, and the disturbances become hurricanes because we have not learned to speak to the wind, "Peace, be still."

The truth I have learned in the interval between that day and this is that the suffering of life is a completely separate issue from *how I think about* the suffering of life, e.g., what it produces in me.  When I fail to separate the circumstance and the result, I lose my grasp on the process.  And, when I lose my grip on the process, I lose my ability to separate my flesh from it.  When flesh becomes mixed up with suffering, *no good thing can come of it.*  Further, the suffering is separate even from the product of the travail, just as the child birthed is separate and distinct from the suffering induced by its delivery process.  When the tempest is brewing large like a hurricane, it is difficult to contain my thoughts to the truth that I know.  It takes discipline, and just plain 'ol hard work to keep my thoughts between the ditches and on a road to transformation.  Whether the challenge is a difficult circumstance, some element of suffering, a profound loss, or a speed bump on the road of life, "momentary light affliction" is transformed into "life-changing (or even "life-ending") calamity" by how we think, or fail to think, about a thing.

I can hear the objections now, and I understand—you don't want that level of responsibility and accountability over the outcome of the process.  But it is yours none-the-less, whether you embrace it— or even accept it—or not.  Our experience is what it is, but our spiritual efforts to put them into life-giving context determines their long-term effects, and whether they become life-supplying roots or roots of bitterness.  The flesh and carnal mind default to the latter, the Spirit and spiritual mind to the former.

When my time of self-imposed exile came to an end, and it was time to re-enter the disaster zone and see what was remaining of my home, I made the trip with the dread that hurricane evacuees feel when coming home to the unknown in the storm's aftermath. I made the 400-mile trip mostly in silence because there were no words. I was *deep* in my cave, partly because I was ashamed to show my face; but also because I still had enough good sense to know that, though my mental health was in shambles, if I could keep my mouth shut and my weeping silent, if I could refrain from dropping the final straw onto the camel's back, I *might* retain a place to sleep at night that was not under a bridge.

I had inflicted major trauma, not just into my own life, but also into the lives of my wife and children. It is an understatement to say that I had obliterated their trust in me and erased any respect that I might have previously garnered. Arriving home and contemplating the long, arduous path of reparation before me—if indeed I *could* repair the relationships—was daunting and discouraging. Standing at the front end of a 10-mile-long tightrope and a 50 mile-per-hour crosswind, there seems to be no way to be successful. But there is no other acceptable alternative, so you just start walking and see what happens. To this day I do not know all that transpired in the dynamic of my family; they have spared me the details. I only know that the hurt I caused ran to the core of what bound us together, tested and strained even love that had previously been rock solid. Even unconditional love can be bruised and wounded; but the thing that makes unconditional love unconditional is that, even when you abuse and wound it, it makes a place for repentance. That is what my family did for me, and I was, and remain, determined not to blow it again.

At this deep subterranean level in my cave, the shame was palpable, and each inspiration drew in another breath of poisonous atmosphere (one would not be so charitable as to call it air). In that state, breathing comes in the form of a shallow, dog-like pant so as not to ingest a fatal dose of humiliation all in one fell swoop. My strategy was to try to prolong another moment of sanity by metering the poison over time and hoping my body adapted to the cave's environmental toxicity. There is no natural light at this level below ground. It is the kind of darkness that **Exodus 10:21** describes in the ninth plague over the land of Egypt as, "darkness that may even be felt." Not only can it be felt, but it also communicates, and there is no interruption of the flow of accusation pronounced by darkness in the abyss. Part of the humiliation of knowing I had done this to myself was the knowledge that I had forfeited the comfort (!) of self-pity, finger-pointing, or even deflection of responsibility. There, at the bottom of your cavern, all one can do is sit quietly in the accountability atmosphere of deep darkness, hope that no one notices you, and try to remain as small a target as possible while still maintaining a presence in the world. It ain't easy; and if you are a person who is there or has been there, know that there is at least one other in the world that gets it.

> **Exodus 10:21**, "Then the Lord said to Moses, 'Stretch out your hand toward heaven, that there may be darkness over the land of Egypt, ***darkness which may even be felt***.'"

## When Darkness Is Your Friend

King David told us in multiple of His Psalms that our Good Father also dwells in darkness. Here is a perplexing conundrum about God: He *is* light, but He *dwells* in deep darkness. **Psalm 139:7-12** clearly declares this:

> [7]Where can I go from Your Spirit? Or where can I flee from Your presence? [8]If I ascend into heaven, You are there; if I make my bed in hell, behold, You are there. [9]If I take the wings of the morning, and dwell in the uttermost parts of the sea,[10]even there Your hand shall lead me, and Your right hand shall hold me. ***[11]If I say, "Surely the darkness shall fall***

*on me," even the night shall be light about me; $^{12}$Indeed, the darkness shall not hide from You, but the night shines as the day; the darkness and the light are both alike to You.*

God is light, so wherever He goes, He takes His light with Him, so there is no difference. He seems to prefer—even specialize—in darkness, and I think it may be because He gets pleasure in watching it flee from His Presence. Also, I have it on good authority that *He makes some really faithful and committed friends there.* Darkness functions as a friend if-and-only-if it attracts and welcomes light.

There was a single ray of hope in my despair. Though I packed my suitcases full of belongings for the journey from my friend's home, I had left behind a heavy weight of emotional-pain baggage. That said,

> **Psalm 88:5-7**, "$^5$Adrift among the dead, like the slain who lie in the grave, whom You remember no more, and who are cut off from Your hand. $^6$You have laid me in the lowest pit, in darkness, in the depths. $^7$Your wrath lies heavy upon me, and You have afflicted me with all Your waves."

there was still an immense, colossal, gigantic, and monstrous amount of emotional and spiritual work to be done. Burdens can be laid down because they do not become a part of us. But shame, condemnation, anger, failure, and blaming—when they become part of one's identity—*cannot be merely laid down,* neither can they be ignored no matter how long you have lived with it. These things must be *overcome* and *replaced*; and replacement is a long, labor-intensive process. God does not do magic, and He does not do parlor tricks. He is not our pet god, at our beck-and-call to perform on demand. He *is* Sovereign, faithful, and purposeful—and *He moves at the speed of God.* Replacement is a pilgrimage, one that requires a certain "set of heart" as described in **Psalm 84:5-7**. Well-meaning others can proclaim the need to "just move on" or "get over it"; but that advice reveals a lack of understanding of pilgrimage. Sometimes sitting still in darkness is the only way *to move on*. The shark that has to keep moving to get its next breath ends up swimming in a *lot* of circles, and it is swimming in fast circles that stirred up your whirlpool in the first place.

It is a strange orientation to life when you spend your entire waking day *not doing* something. For me, the thing I was concentrating on *not doing* was drinking alcohol. That became easier, and eventually effortless—though admittedly, without the emotional pain, my drug seemed much less critical to my well-

> **John 20:29**, "Jesus said to him, 'Thomas, because you have seen Me, you have believed. ***Blessed are those who have not seen and yet have believed*.'"

being, and more of a habit to be broken. I get it that some have a chemical interaction with the substance that becomes a physical dependence. That did not seem to be my case—my dependence was emotional. During my seven weeks of convalescence, I attended Alcoholics Anonymous meetings and benefitted from the group interaction. I understand that some will disagree with this point, but I always internally resisted the, "Hi, my name is Randy. I am an alcoholic," pronouncement. The reason was not that I did not want to own my behavior; it was because I was learning that it is vital that I guard what vows I speak and which declarations I accept *as part of my identity*. Words have *power*! Papa is taking me through a process and re-making who I am.

I understand the spiritual damage that can be done by making and binding one's self to negative

> "It is *vital* that I guard what vows I speak and which declarations I accept as part of my identity."

vows. So, when required by the AA meeting process to declare myself an alcoholic, I complied—but was careful to correct and cancel the effect of negative words as I went along. It was a case of "sitting down on the outside, but standing up on the inside." Some may say that I, therefore, did not fully benefit from my participation. I would reply that I remain alcohol-free some 10-plus years later, without my drug and without the negative label as part of my identity. A huge part of the discipleship process is to come to a clear understanding of one's true identity, and how we are known to Papa. Since both my Sin nature and my sin behavior were obliterated by the blood that Jesus shed on the cross, nothing of my sin is part of my identity, and therefore does not merit any portion of my thinking.

I was jobless when I returned home, so I had hours on end to think and to be present *in reality* rather than a buzzed altered state. I knew that my immediate past had wiped out any possibility of continuing my career in the fire service because the behavioral standards are high. For eighteen months, I spent my days jobless, incrementally climbing out of my pit and getting healthy again. Most of the time was spent just being consistent and trustworthy. That was not a passive process for me—I had promises to keep to my wife, children, and myself, and I worked on it every day. Later, we will discuss at length the commitment to intentionality, and this is the time period when I learned it in practice. My wife was heroically working hard to undo the damage I had caused within her and our relationship. She had trusted, faithful friends to help her through her own healing. She proved to be resilient and steadfast, though, by declaring it, I do not in any way minimize the pain I caused or the monumental effort she devoted to her own recovery.

One of the difficult aspects of recovery is that there is no discernible point when it ends. We *feel* an affirmative need to declare victory so that we can take the victory lap to assert, in effect, "Yes, I failed, but at least I recovered!" This is a face-saving strategy at a point where saving face is the *last strategy* on which we need to depend. It is another way of making a last-ditch effort to preserve our Independent Self by preserving some vestige of our ability to *win*. Saving face is anti-humility, and it is CPR for the Independent Self when the appropriate response is to let it die. *Of course,* I understand it—I have felt it. But the only hope of not repeating the past is to first stop doing the dumb stuff—and continuing to do what we have always done, including preserving personal space or distinction between ourselves and Papa, is just dumb. There is no finish line to cross, no checkered flag to wave until the *Last 15-Minutes*. Then it will be time to declare, "I have fought the good fight, I have finished the race" (**2 Timothy 4:7**).

An impactful lesson I have learned through my struggle is that all of the days of life leading up to today—*this* day—are designed to produce in us the person we truly are and will be. I am speaking here about the person that God sees—"the perfect and complete, lacking nothing" person (**James 1:4**). That is one bedrock lesson of *The Last 15-Minutes*: it ain't over until it's over. The final result is still in play until we draw our last breath; however, we will not realize the fulfillment of our promises unless we envision and commit to intentionally *being* and *doing*. At the end of each day, we have fulfilled some percentage of that of which we were capable of producing in terms of total spiritual potential. Whether that percentage be large, small, or even a negative number is up to us. God supplies the learning environment; He has supplied the curriculum for instruction; He has even given us a brilliant coach. Like Jesus in **John 13:3**, Papa has put "all things into [our] hands," and it is up to us to embrace the learning. Transformation into the image of Christ is totally available and completely free—but it is not without tremendous cost.

There were two things I had proclaimed (read: complained about) for many years: 1) that God did not seem to speak to me, at least, not in a way that I readily heard, and not in ways that others seemed to treat as commonplace; and, 2) He did not give me original, creative revelation, but only second-hand knowledge delivered by some other teacher. One time, long ago, as I was complaining to Papa about the fact that I never feel Him as others in the Church seemed to talk about so readily, He asked this question in response: "What if you never do?" Immediately upon hearing His question, I knew *exactly* what He meant, and many things in our relationship made sense to me. In the past, as I would listen to others describe their ability to feel His Presence and His Love, I had succumbed to feelings of inferiority of relationship quality; this inferiority over time had morphed into a brooding conclusion that, though I was OK to have around and was at times useful to Him, I was not one of the kids that Papa preferred to spend time with (there are those "coach's boys" and "not chosen" things raising their ugly head again!). But His question to me put my experience into context. I remembered that years ago I had embraced **Job 13:15** as a life Scripture, "Though He slay me, yet will I trust Him." Then the Holy Spirit reminded me of Jesus' reply to Thomas after he made his, "My Lord and my God" declaration (**John 20:28**), "Blessed are those who have not seen [felt] and yet have believed" (**John 20:29**).

I have finally connected with the truth that hearing Papa's voice is neither the trick or the objective. He is constantly speaking in one form or another. When I fail to hear His voice, it is usually because I am looking for an incorrect manifestation of it. We are constantly in our conscious and unconscious minds personifying God; that is, assigning to Him characteristics, traits, and attributes true of human beings. Therefore, when we listen for Him to speak, we assume it would be in some form of communication that we would use when speaking to our own children, our friends, or a co-worker. But that is a wrong assumption, and it leads us to despair when we fail to recognize His communication while holding out for a form that fits our conception and separation. But God is not limited by separation as we are. The fix is to understand that He is simultaneously **not** us—that is human, employing human tactics and strategies— and affirmatively **is** us in the sense that we are inextricably in union with Him in Spirit. It is to become comfortable with the paradox of crucifixion and union, as Paul explained it in **Galatians 2:20**:

> My old identity has been co-crucified with Messiah and no longer lives; *for the nails of his cross crucified me with him*. And now the essence of this new life is no longer mine, for the Anointed One lives his life through me—*we live in union as one*! My new life is empowered by the faith of the Son of God who loves me so much that he gave himself for me, and dispenses his life into mine! (The Passion Translation)

If we are one with Christ, and He is One with the Father; and if we no longer live but "Christ who lives in me" (**Galatians 2:20**) and we live "by the faith **of** the Son of God," then **Galatians 2:20** is not a metaphor; it is literal, actual eternal-realm truth manifested in the time/space/matter dimension. The struggle of the Independent Self to relegate "Christ **in** me, **as** me" as an idyllic metaphor is a pitiful attempt to preserve some semblance of separation and independence.

All of foregoing brought me to the affirmative conclusion that hearing God speak is the manifestation of my choice to listen to the spiritual mind and its perspective, and the result of my acknowledgment of union with Him. I hear Him speak as I hear my true self, my Union Self, internally directing me in the spiritual mind. I can hear the alarm bells going off in some because deep down they believe that they cannot be trusted with acknowledgment of the Person of God expressed as themselves in the world. I get it—it sounds like some manifestation of mental illness as a delusion of grandeur. But that is only true in the context of an Independent Self maintaining and manifesting its separated-ness. When we finally see that it is Papa's purpose and Program to bring us into soul union with Him (as we are already in Spirit-union), we are able to set aside the false humility and self-depreciation and get on with the context in which He has ordained our experience. If we can grasp it, our union with Him enables a shared consciousness that both sees what He is doing and hears what He is saying in "real" time—the eternal.

I do not depreciate the experience of any who clearly hear the voice and physically feel the Presence of God; but there are others of us who, though perhaps less sensitive, struggle with the absence of what others seem to experience so easily, even glibly. But I have this encouragement for those who are, *like me*, less sensing/feeling, and more cognitive: There is a kind of purity in believing *without* seeing, and maintaining faith *without* the experience of touching His nail-scared hands and pierced side. Papa's relationship with each of us is custom-made *for us*; and while others experience Him in a way for which we apparently are not equipped, our faithfulness in the absence of goosebumps is yet precious to Him.

## Forsaking Christianity

Recovery started very slowly. First, the din of accusation from the voice of darkness began to abate. Next, I started to lose my desire to be invisible and fear of moving (lest anyone notice I was still alive). Finally, I began to hear Papa speaking to me, distinctly, lovingly, purposefully. *Now* His voice was clear, and He was in a talking mood. What began as a casual, exploratory conversation soon became a regular, daily download of instruction. The consequence of these daily meetings was that my cave soon became my *favorite place in the entire world*. Also, the nature of my retreat had changed—what had formerly been a sulky slinking away to escape scrutiny became a sprint to receive that day's gift.

The best way to describe the change in Our relationship is the migration—the pilgrimage—from being a Christian to being His disciple. Over the past ten years, Papa has encouraged me to forsake Christianity for discipleship. The distinction is illustrated by the saying, "*Present* Christianity to the world, and it will applaud; *be* Jesus to the world, and it will crucify you." Jesus never called anyone to be a Christian, but He invites His sheep to be disciples. He is teaching me that there is a difference, *and it is an important one*. A Christian accumulates: He or she accumulates knowledge, accumulates experiences, and accumulates truth—but also accumulates pain and injury that keeps us earth-bound and often disabled. But a disciple goes beyond accumulation; a disciple spends his or her time *contextualizing experiences, learning from life, and transferring the burdens to the One who offered to carry them for us*.

> Over the past ten years, Papa has encouraged me to forsake Christianity for discipleship.

Not all things that are *true* are *the truth*, and the exercise of contextualizing—that is, putting information and experiences into Scriptural context and the context of transformation—makes all the difference. The context into which we learn to put all experience is His Program, His purpose for us, our eternal identity, and our future in His Kingdom. We learn to reject the flesh-pressure to live life for its own sake. Learning to contextualize changes our orientation to life, to the Church and its teachings, and to our priorities concerning how we invest our time. He is teaching me to forsake labels, to abandon philosophy, and to embrace assimilation and union. He gently *insists* that I look first to the log in my own eye, and has assured me that there is plenty of cellulosic material there to occupy me for a lifetime. There is a lot of truth to the saying, "Fake it 'til you make it!"—just not in the way it is typically used. The *"truth"* way to say it would be, "Imitate until you assimilate!"

## "You Might Be a Pharisee If…"

When Papa set about to change me, He was not saving a murdering gang member destined to spend life in a brick-and-mortar prison. He was not transforming a serial rapist or hardened thief. No, even more miraculously and remarkably than either of those is that, in my case, He was transforming a Pharisee destined to be imprisoned in the impenetrable cell of Independent Self and religious thinking! Pharisees are a hard nut to crack, mainly because they either cannot or will not perceive their need. What makes my story compelling is that my pre-disciple self as a type is so common in the Church today. Jesus displayed a lot of compassion for people caught up in the entanglements of all kinds of sin. But the remarkable exception to His merciful attitude is that He reserved

> **Matthew 23:25**, "Woe to you, scribes and Pharisees, hypocrites! For you cleanse the outside of the cup and dish, but inside they are full of extortion and self-indulgence."

vehement criticism for those who would consider themselves religious, and therefore capable of meeting God's requirement by the strength of their own performance. That group also includes those whose words *claim* dependence on God's grace, but their *actions* speak otherwise. He castigated those who made a show of their righteousness, those who "cleaned the outside of the cup and dish" but made little or no effort to be transformed on the inside (**Matthew 23:25**). I have been unable to locate any account where Jesus expressed anything but disdain for such an attitude. I am profoundly grateful that Papa showed mercy and gave me the grace to repent, even after a multitude and lifestyle of pharisaical choices.

There is a common saying in the Church: "God has to convince you that you are lost before He can get you saved." There is truth in the saying; but it does not *just* apply to our justification, it applies to our *salvation/sanctification process* as well. Just as surely as we were a sinner in need of justification by the blood of Christ, we remain an Independent Self in need of the salvation of His life (**Romans 5:9-10**), and to be transformed into His image. We must be convinced of our need to submit to His salvation process to clean us up once we are justified. If we stop short of scrubbing our vessel on the inside as well as the outside, we rightfully deserve the same "woe" that Jesus pronounced on the Pharisees of His day. The religious world is full of Pharisees—I was one of many brethren that are "…like whitewashed tombs which indeed appear beautiful outwardly, but inside are full of dead men's bones and all uncleanness" (**Matthew 23:27**). That is not a pronouncement of judgment, but an "it takes one to know one" recognition.

One of the problems with being a Pharisee is that it is hard to know if you are one, especially when you live, work, and go to church with a group of other believers that are much like you. I have for many years enjoyed and appreciated the humor of Jeff Foxworthy, particularly his, "You might be a redneck if…" jokes. I think I enjoy his jokes so much because I *know* those people. Those people are my friends. I work with those people. Heck fire, I *am* those people! What if we devised a "Jeff Foxworthy-like" model that could help us figure out if we have pharisaical tendencies? For example:

- "You might be a Pharisee if you have prayed aloud for more than five minutes is a single prayer" (**Matthew 23:14**);

- "You might be a Pharisee if you have ever come two hours early to a service to reserve the best seats for you and your friends" (**Matthew 23:6**);

- "You might be a Pharisee if you have ever thought (or prayed!), 'God I thank you that I am not like other men'" (**Luke 18:11**);

- "You might be a Pharisee if you are more concerned about appearance than substance" (**Matthew 23:25-26, 23:5**);

- "You might be a Pharisee if you expect others to work, but refuse to lift a finger to help" (**Matthew 23:4**);

- "You might be a Pharisee if you have ever crossed the street to avoid passing by someone in need." (**Luke 10:31-32**);

- "You might be a Pharisee if you have ever refused to associate, or even eat a meal, with someone because of their sin or lifestyle" (**Matthew 9:11**);

- "You might be a Pharisee if you have prayed or fasted to be seen by others" (**Matthew 6:5**);

- "You might be a Pharisee if you *preach* to others and do not *do* yourself" (**Matthew 23:3**);

- "You might be a Pharisee if you constantly want to see a sign from God" (**Matthew 12:38**);

- Likewise, "You might be a Pharisee if you require a sign from God in order to prove who He says He is" (**Matthew 16:1-3**);

- "You might be a Pharisee if you rely on rules, tradition and ceremony" (**Matthew 15:1-3**);

- "You might be a Pharisee if you can quote the Scriptures and have them memorized, but do not understand what they mean in the context of life" (**Matthew 23:23-24**);

- "You might be a Pharisee if you love to be introduced and greeted by your church title in public (rabbi, teacher, pastor, deacon, elder, apostle, etc.)" (**Matthew 23:6-11**).

Good news!  There *is* life after death, and there *is* discipleship after delivery from Pharisee-ism.  If Papa can break through and convict us of self-righteousness, we have a good shot at overcoming it.  But like the Kingdom and new birth, until we *see* it, we have no chance of entering.


## Running Naked Through the Crowd

I am confessing my weakness to the world ("running naked through the crowd," as it were) for two reasons.  The first reason is that if you can see yourself in my story, even if it is not a precise fit in-kind for your own, then hopefully you will understand that I am a guy (in the generic sense) just like you.  Our weaknesses lie to us in two major veins: First, they tell us *we **are** unique in ways that we **are not***—even the Apostle Paul had his Choice Space (**Romans 7:15-20**), and we are not alone in our struggle.  That fact portends that if there are others like you, and *even one* has managed to climb out of the pit, then there is hope for you as well.  Second, our weaknesses lie and tell us that we are *not*

> Our weaknesses lie to us in *two ways*: First, they tell us that we **are** *unique in ways that we are not*.  Second, they tell us that we **are** *not unique in ways that we are*.

*special in ways that **we are***.  Scripture tells us that we have been (and continue to be!), "fearfully and wonderfully made" (**Psalm 139:14**) and re-made.  God's works *are* marvelous, and you are a chunk of that work.  One Hebrew word used in connection with the creation of Man in Genesis means to construct bit-by-bit, part-by-part, painstakingly assembled for a particular purpose.  That is you, and that is me—each wonderfully different in ways that make us special and qualified to occupy a unique place in the Church, and in the Kingdom of God.

Secondly, I tell my story to commend to you God's *genius* Program and present it as an example of "reframing"—a primary strategy that the Holy Spirit uses to renew our mind.  We will discuss reframing in detail later; but at this point, suffice to say that reframing is more than just happy thoughts; and it is *way* more than a positive mental attitude, although it includes aspects of both of these.  It is even more than **Philippians 4:8** "whatever things" thinking.  Reframing[7] is taking your circumstances—good and bad—and viewing them through the *Foundation of Meaning*[8] process filters.  Reframing and contextualizing are primary skills in regeneration, transformation, and renewal.  We learn to understand *everything* that happens to us and through us in terms of its impact on our preparation for the Kingdom.

One fundamental difference between reframing and positive mental attitude is that it does not jettison all of the struggles and negatives that we experience as something to forget or get over.  Instead, it uses each new shovel full of manure meant by the enemy for covering us in our pit (thereby making it a grave!) as a platform for bringing us back to level ground.  Reframing is putting each new shovel of manure

---

[7] I am indebted to Graham Cooke for, among many other things, introducing me to the concept of reframing.

[8] Throughout the book, I will make reference to Foundation of Meaning, or FOM, as a principal governing the interaction of God's Program in the earth and our reason for being.  The FOM may best be considered as the "reason why" for life, and the purpose that God intends for our existence, and more detail is added in following sections.

under our feet, tramping down and compacting it into a useful step for escaping from whatever pit into which we have fallen! I have found that the Holy Spirit is something of a specialist at compacting manure and making it a platform. Shovelful-by-shovelful, we rise back to level ground. The process smells *awful* to our flesh—it smells like death! But to the mind set on the things of the Spirit—and pilgrimage—it is the sweet savor of "life unto life" (**2 Corinthians 2:15-16**). Reframing and contextualizing skills are *integral* for learning to *reign in life* (**Romans 5:17**) and preparing to *rule in the Kingdom*.

## Life Lessons from the Cave

There may be no more tragic word in language than "wasting." "Waste" and all of its synonyms (e.g., dissipate, squander, misuse, deplete, etc.) epitomize futility and meaninglessness. A life environment of waste depends on a lack of knowledge and insensitivity, resulting in misplaced priorities. Paul Bilheimer

> **Philippians 4:8**, "Finally, brethren, whatever things are true, whatever things are noble, whatever things are just, whatever things are pure, whatever things are lovely, whatever things are of good report, if there is any virtue and if here is anything praiseworthy—***meditate on these things***."

wrote an excellent book entitled *Don't Waste Your Sorrows* (1977) as a sequel to his book, *Destined for the Throne* (1975). Together, these two bodies of work present a cosmology from which I have learned much, and are of such importance and fresh perspective that they are classics in my mind. If you are familiar with Bilheimer's writing, you may recognize the threads of his thinking interwoven with my own—he has had a great impact on my world view.

Both books begin with the assumption that the purpose of life and destiny of the Church is to prepare the Bride of Christ to rule beside her Bridegroom, our Foundation of Meaning. Both books also propose that this earth, this T/S/M reality, is a learning classroom, testing and training environment created and constructed meticulously to support God's eternal purpose. But each focuses on a different strategy in God's Program as a channel for accomplishing His objectives: *Destined for the Throne* concentrates on spiritual warfare and prayer as a medium in preparation for ruling, while *Don't Waste Your Sorrows* focuses on the role of suffering and its redemptive value in the transformation process.

Much of the time in my cave has been spent meditating on these concepts and contextualizing them to my own suffering experiences. Beginning from the infrastructure laid by Bilheimer to understand meaning and purpose, Papa has taken my thinking in a parallel direction as a supplement. To supplement prayer, spiritual warfare, and redemptive suffering, we will add the process mechanics for discipleship—the pilgrimage in the Choice Space. All life that comes before our *Last 15-Minutes* contributes to the person we are becoming. My decade-long daily visits to my cave have been occasions for Papa to peel back layers of mystery, and to once-and-for-all dispel the lies that He doesn't speak to me and that He does not give me creative revelation.

Ultimately, our grandest and highest purposes must be made practical by our efforts to reduce them to daily activity. Said another way, our faith must be at a level that is *actionable*. As long as an idea remains a theoretical construct, it does not become a meaningful part of us, one that influences action and enacts change. But, by converting *high ideals* to *everyday ordeals*, we experience the fresh reality of **John 1:14**: "[T]he Word became flesh, and dwelt among us." As we experience His life-transforming us into His image, we prove the truth of the Word over and over again, dwelling *among* us, *as* us.

# He Brought Them Out to Bring Them In

The cry of the Israelites when they faced adversity was, "Were there no graves in Egypt that you [Moses] brought us into the wilderness to die?" (**Exodus 14:11**). This collective whine conveniently blamed Moses and ignored the fact that they had signed up for the wilderness gig voluntarily by leaving their slavery! But even if they had a legitimate complaint (they did not), their vision was faithless and short-sighted. As one might expect from an all-powerful, all-knowing God, there *was* a plan, and not only to bring them out of Egypt (Sin nature) but to take them all of the way to the destination (the Promised Land and salvation). Christians today express a similar untrusting sentiment (*sin*-timent?) when we fail to embrace God's Program and complain about our circumstances. As in the case of the Children of Israel of old, Papa has a plan in operation to bring the Church out of both our Sin nature and out of our wilderness wandering, and to bring us into the promised land of transformation and into the glorious Bride of Christ, prepared and capable of fulfilling our destiny to rule beside our Bridegroom!

Israel's Exodus is applicable to the Church today as a picture of what Papa is accomplishing. He is not teasing, playing, or "just kidding." He brought Israel out of Egypt for a purpose, and He brings us out of our Sin nature for the like purpose of completing our pilgrimage all the way to a mature state of glory. In the moment when we feel like complaining about the pain and discomfort of the purification process, we need to remember that we signed up for this gig, and that our rebellious champing at the bit only prolongs the suffering and puts us at risk of God releasing us to our own way—as He did a whole generation of Israelites.

All they had to do was load up the wagons, herd the children together, and follow. They were even told to go into the enemy's houses and take with them whatever spoils they could carry—that is how badly the Egyptians wanted to get rid of these offensive people in their midst. Leaving Egypt was a no-brainer until the Red Sea appeared before them and an angry horde of Egyptian chariots was behind them. Then, as was revealed to be their custom many times over the next 40 years, the Israelites panicked and went into a full complaining mode. "Were there no graves in Egypt that you brought us to the wilderness to die?" was their pitiful "Why us?" question. It was the first of many instances where unbelief was dominant—even with all of the demonstrations of God's power that they witnessed—over the 40-year journey that should have taken weeks!

Like the pilgrimage on which God invites us to embark, the walk across the wilderness was supposed to be a time when the Israelites came to know their God, and prepare to occupy the kingdom He had promised them. He provided all the supplies that they needed to survive the journey and marked the way with a pillar of cloud by day and a column of fire by night. He was ever-present with them, providing evidence of His love and care, and purpose for them. But instead of *learning* and increasing in their level of trust and obedience, the Israelites made a pastime of blaming Moses and God for all of the discomforts of the journey. They succumbed to the insistent murmuring of their individual and collective flesh. Their grumbling and complaining prepared their negative hearts for the disobedience of refusing to enter the Promised Land—their inheritance. Consequently, a whole generation died in the wilderness, failing to fulfill both their promise and potential. There is no more avoidable or more shameful culpability than God's people refusing to place their whole trust in Him. It is *vital* that we learn from their negative example and not despise the journey He has placed before us. We are not invulnerable to "death by whining" in the wilderness. It's time to quit complaining and start walking!

## "Yeah, But It Hurts!"

Graham Cooke wisely says, "God doesn't actually care about your comfort zone. Why? Because He gave you a *comforter*! That means He jolly well *plans* to take you out of your comfort zone!" We spend much of our time seeking and enjoying our comfort and entertainment. We've built whole segments of our society around it! There is nothing wrong with comfort or entertainment, only when it overwhelms the true purpose of life. Our comfort zone is not where we grow, nor is it where we change (at least for the better). In fact, there is an inverse relationship between the two: the larger our comfort zone, the smaller our growth zone. God is faithful to take us where we *need* to go, not necessarily where we *want* to go. **Hebrews 12:5-7** says,

> [5]And you have forgotten the exhortation which speaks to you as to sons: "My son, do not despise the chastening of the Lord, nor be discouraged when you are rebuked by Him; [6]***for whom the Lord loves He chastens, and scourges every son whom He receives.***" [7]If you endure chastening, God deals with you as with sons; for what son is there whom a father does not chasten?

Temper the discomfort you feel and urge to complain during times of chastening with the comfort of knowing that God is dealing with you as a son and not an orphan. Without this understanding, we remain babies in the Spirit, fed with *milk*, and never graduating to the *meat* of the Word.

Our learned habit of negativity—negative outlook, negative thought, negative speech—is a visible expression of the carnal mind; and, it is a really difficult habit to unlearn. However, there is no activity in which we engage that keeps us wandering in the wilderness longer than our nagging complaining and cynicism. Even overt acts of sin (you know—the biggies) usually bring overwhelming guilt and repentance for believers. But negativity is so pervasive these days as to frequently pass unnoticed—or worse, as expected behavior! Sarcastic wit can be funny and harmless occasionally among friends; but as a lifestyle, it is a mind-renewal killer.

**Matthew 25:21**, "His lord said to him, 'Well done, good and faithful servant; you were faithful over a few things, I will make you ruler over many things. Enter into the joy of your lord.'" Looking back on a life full of decisions and choices, it becomes clear that the *big ones* may decide one's path, but the *little ones* decide one's character. And, since God is much more interested in your character development than the path you take to get to the destination, it stands to reason that small decisions are the ones that make or break us, particularly when they involve appropriating **Galatians 5** Fruit of the Spirit. Some of the most meaningful "small" decisions I have faced are:

> Do I forgive against my desire to punish being wronged, or cave in to my flesh and hold a grudge?

> Do I take responsibility for my mistakes, or do I produce that excuse that is so readily on my tongue?

> Do I complain when it's not going my way, or do I choose to see the big picture and rejoice in my suffering?

> Do I get impatient and surly, or do I remain at peace, joyfully content to flow with the speed of life?

> Do I intervene where I do not belong, or do I let God fight my battles for me (Meekness)?

> Do I remain faithful when it costs me something to keep going, mile-after-mile, step-after-step, day-after-day?

> Do I trust, or do I manipulate?

Faithfulness in small things is one of the keys to successful discipleship life. Attending to small things is the **Song of Solomon 2:15** process of "catch[ing]...the little foxes that spoil the vines." While you are dreaming big, do not forget to attend to small things—the fortress is only as strong as the individual blocks of stone from which it is built, and a pilgrimage is composed of many, many small steps.

> **Song of Solomon 2:15**, "Catch us the foxes, the little foxes that spoil the vines, for our vines have tender grapes."

## From Cave to Mountain Top (and Elevations Between)

The chances are that I am a guy pretty much like you. I do not spend hours or days on end in the glorious presence of Papa—but I feel His love every day. I do not bask in the glow of the Holy Spirit's goosebumps very often, but I experience His classroom every day and multiple times per day. I do not always respond correctly—or even well—to my life circumstances, but I have set my heart on pilgrimage and have made a commitment to faithfulness and life-long improvement. I do not have a clear understanding of all of Papa's ways, but I *know* some of them very well. I often do not know what I am doing tomorrow, but I know who I want to be when it comes time for my *Last 15-Minutes*!

> **Philippians 4:11-13**, "[11]Not that I speak in regard to need, ***for I have learned in whatever state I am, to be content***: [12]I know how to be abased, and I know how to abound. Everywhere and in all things, I ***have learned*** both to be full and to be hungry, both to abound and to suffer need. [13]I can do all things through Christ who strengthens me."

What I have learned about visiting the mountain top I learned in the depths of my cave—that is how it is supposed to be, how God has "ordained strength" (**Psalm 8:2**). I am convinced that the suffering of the cave is the only path to the mountain top and that there is no shortcut across the desert. That is how Jesus learned it (**Hebrews 12:2**), and that is how the Apostle Paul learned it. In **Philippians 4:11-13**, Paul summarizes what he had *learned* from experiencing need: contentment, flexibility, endurance, joy independent of circumstances, and the source of his strength. That is a pretty decent list and one to which I aspire. Those are some of the lessons of discipleship, and those are the lessons that Papa teaches us in the cave, and at every elevation and terrain, He takes us to on our pilgrimage.

"Looking unto Jesus, the author and finisher of our faith" (**Hebrews 12:2**), we "endure [our] cross" with hope, and we "despise [disregard with contempt] the shame" with understanding and patience. We visualize and hold tightly to the *Last 15-Minutes* person that we want to be—the spitting image of Christ, dripping with Fruit of the Spirit, the wife of the Lamb that has "made herself ready" (**Revelation 19:7**) to rule beside Him. We value the process of increasing the Kingdom, growing it inside us from the seeds Papa plants, and laying up treasure in Heaven from its produce. We begin each new day with the end in mind, and we intentionally act rather than being acted upon by the world. In each Choice Space, we exercise the choice that Papa has put into our hands and hearts—the choice to embrace the spiritual mind and forsake the flesh (**Romans 7:15**). And, in the meantime, we anticipate our marriage and coronation to the King of Kings and Lord of Lords. The pilgrimage is easy to summarize, but to do?—*not so much*!

# Chapter 2—Becoming A King!

God conceals the revelation of His word in the hiding place of his glory. But the honor of kings is revealed by how they thoroughly search out the deeper meaning of all that God says. **Proverbs 25:2**, *The Passion Translation*

## Kings and Priests

Humans are fascinated and tantalized by the prospect of knowing the future, a fact that accounts for the proliferation of all forms of occultic practice. But for believers, not only are these avenues of spirit knowledge out of bounds (*and* an affront to Papa—**Leviticus 19:26**), they are totally unnecessary because our Good Father is pleased to reveal to us our destiny. Prophetic Scriptures not only forthtell the truth of God, but they also foretell our destiny as the Bride of Christ.

Somehow, the full impact of **Revelation 1:5-6** and **5:9-10** seems to blow right past us without having the effect appropriate to their meaning. *Kings and priests to our God!* How could anything be better than that? There are many implications, not the least of which is debunking the idea of Christians sitting on clouds and playing harps, or singing in an angelic choir for all eternity (Frank and Ernie cartoons notwithstanding!).

> **Revelation 1:5-6**, "To Him who loved us and washed us from our sins in His own blood, ⁶and has **made us kings and priests** to His God and Father, to Him be glory and dominion forever and ever. Amen."
>
> **Revelation 5:9-10**, "⁹And they sang a new song, saying: 'You are worthy to take the scroll, and to open its seals; for You were slain, and have redeemed us to God by Your blood out of every tribe and tongue and people and nation, ¹⁰**and have made us kings and priests to our God; and we shall reign on the earth**.'"

There are other implications of **Revelation 1:5-6** and **5:10**. Learning to rule in the Kingdom is learning to choose the spiritual mind over the carnal mind, and the Spirit over the flesh here on earth. In my natural life, I am neither a king nor the son of a king! If I am to function as a king or a priest in God's service in the realm to come, I need to be trained to fulfill my responsibilities to the standard befitting the Kingdom. *What if good leadership on earth is the same thing as good leadership in the Kingdom?* What if, when Jesus prayed "on earth as it is in Heaven" in His model prayer, He was including the character and structure of leadership? God designed this life to be an internship specifically for the purpose of training His people to reflect the character of the King and to prepare them to rule in His Eternal Kingdom. That means that our time on earth should be first and foremost dedicated to a learning process—learning His ways, values, purposes and plans—in short, His Program.

I will take this thought one step further. Jesus reinforced this perspective—**Matthew 9:35** says, "Then Jesus went about all the cities and villages, teaching in their synagogues, preaching the gospel of the kingdom, and healing every sickness and every disease among the people." God instituted "kingdoms" in this T/S/M existence at least in part so that we may understand what they look like, and how they are organized and run. Kingdoms require subjects, and they require leadership. People in kingdoms have assignments and daily tasks. They have areas of responsibility and duties. There is no shred of Scripture that suggests that we will stand around the Throne and sing for all eternity. There will be coming and going. There will be commerce; and, yes, there will be taxation! Sometimes I am at a loss at how we arrive at our conclusions about the Kingdom, but **Revelation 21** gives a very different picture than many assume:

²⁴And the nations of those who are saved shall walk in its light, ***and the kings of the earth bring their glory [tribute] and honor into it***. ²⁵Its gates shall not be shut at all by day (there shall be no night there). ²⁶And they shall bring the glory and the honor of the nations into it. ²⁷But there shall by no means enter it anything that defiles, or causes an abomination or a lie, but only those who are written in the Lamb's Book of Life.

Solomon's Kingdom is, in many ways, a picture of Jesus' Kingdom. Nobody messed with Solomon. His glory far surpassed any that had ever come before (as Jesus' will), as detailed in the Book of **1 Kings, Chapters 4-10**. In Chapter 10 the wealth of his kingdom is given, in part, as:

¹⁴The weight of gold that came to Solomon yearly was six hundred and sixty-six talents of gold, ¹⁵besides that from the traveling merchants, from the income of traders, from all the kings of Arabia, and from the governors of the country. ¹⁶And King Solomon made two hundred large shields of hammered gold; six hundred shekels of gold went into each shield. ¹⁷He also made three hundred shields of hammered gold; three minas of gold went into each shield. The king put them in the House of the Forest of Lebanon. ¹⁸Moreover the king made a great throne of ivory, and overlaid it with pure gold...²¹All King Solomon's drinking vessels were gold,

> **Revelation 22:14**, "Blessed are those who do His commandments, that they may have the right to the tree of life, and may enter through the gates into the city

and all the vessels of the House of the Forest of Lebanon were pure gold. Not one was silver, *for this was accounted as nothing in the days of Solomon*. ²²For the king had merchant ships at sea with the fleet of Hiram. Once every three years the merchant ships came bringing gold, silver, ivory, apes, and monkeys. *²³So King Solomon surpassed all the kings of the earth in riches and wisdom.* ²⁴Now all the earth sought the presence of Solomon to hear his wisdom, which God had put in his heart. ²⁵Each man brought his present: articles of silver and gold, garments, armor, spices, horses, and mules, *at a set rate year by year*.

Solomon was renowned worldwide and greatly admired for his wisdom. He received tribute from the Kings of the earth, but, knowing human nature, we can safely assume that was not because they admired him so much or just wanted to share their stuff! He commanded tribute as a symbol of both respect and submission. Jesus will command that same respect on steroids. As His Bride, we will share in His glory, but some will be closer to the inner circle than others, depending on what you chose to do with your resources committed to you in this life.

What is the point of this nostalgic look back at the reign of Solomon? No doubt Jesus' Kingdom will be different from any other in the history of this world. But if we spiritualize His Kingdom to the degree that we lose the *literal sense of what a Kingdom does and is for*, we lose the ability to look around us in the earth and glean Papa's mysteries from our surroundings. Not everything in Scripture is a metaphor or a type. Sometimes it is a literal example. Sometimes the Holy Spirit is whispering, "You need to pay attention and learn something from this."

The description of Solomon's Kingdom is not a story thrown in just for fluff! God is actively staffing Jesus' Kingdom; and under the tutelage of the Holy Spirit, we are in training to take our place in "the Father's business." That is what an intern does. We are learning *now* what we will *need to know then*, and our "job performance" in this time/space/matter (T/S/M) dimension will translate to responsibility in the Kingdom. Jesus' words in **Luke 19:17-19** are a foreshadowing of how our discipleship performance may affect our Kingdom assignment:

<sup>17</sup>And he said to him, "Well done, good servant; because you were faithful in a very little, have authority over ten cities." <sup>18</sup>And the second came, saying, "Master, your mina has earned five minas." <sup>19</sup>Likewise he said to him, "You also be over five cities."

Jesus' message was not "be nice to one another" as some seem content to preach today. It was not "don't smoke, chew, or date girls that do!" He did not preach church attendance; His gospel was not about the Church at all, but about the *Kingdom*. **Mark 1:14-15** tells us that He "came to Galilee, preaching the *gospel of the kingdom of God*." Much of His message was in parable form, designed specifically to be a mystery to those for whom it was not intended. Jesus said in **Luke 8:10,** "To you it has been given to know the mysteries of the kingdom of God, but to the rest it is given in parables, that, 'Seeing they may not see, and hearing they may not understand.'" But about those who are the intended recipients of Jesus' message, Solomon says in **Proverbs 25:2**, "It is the glory of God to conceal a matter, but the glory of kings is to search out a matter." It is clear that it is to our glory *and* His glory when His kings dedicate themselves to searching out His concealed mysteries.

To be sure, there are a number of messages that should emanate from the Church, including "Be nice to one another," and "Do not forsake the assembling of [ourselves] together." But the central message Jesus preached concerning the nature of the Kingdom and our preparation for it must remain *preeminent*. In **Romans 14:17** Paul writes, "For the kingdom of God is not eating and drinking [e.g., physical activities or comforts], but *righteousness and peace and joy* in the Holy Spirit." These are characteristics of the King and the values of the Kingdom; if we intend to share His throne, we would be advised to share His compatibility in large measure. We must be intentional about acquiring the skills, values, and ways of a ruler. We must learn to lead with one eye on the flock, one eye on the lookout for the enemy, one eye looking to ourselves lest we are tempted to stray, and both eyes on the Master! I do not know about you, but I could use some "five-eyes" training before having to perform in service to the King.

## Learning to Lead

No one in the Church should *ever* say or think that they are not a leader. *To be in Christ is to be a joint heir to a Kingdom! To be in Christ is to be joined with Him in His office as Head over all principality and power* (**Colossians 2:10**)! *To be in Christ is to have a future leadership responsibility beyond what most of us can imagine!* Our future is God's current reality, and He sees us as already successful. Indulge me in some more "What if" questions pertaining to our leadership future:

- *What if* one of the core principles and tasks for the pre-Kingdom Church is to nurture and assimilate our seed of leadership potential within?

- *What if* the qualities and traits of a good leader are the same in our T/S/M reality as they are in the eternal reality?

- *What if* our future Kingdom responsibilities will be determined by how we respond to the leadership training environment in this world?

- *What if*, instead of constantly begging God to intervene in our circumstances, we finally grasp that He intends to use our circumstances to train us to rule beside Him? What if hard circumstances are *precisely* what we need to be trained?

- *What if* the Father has given all things pertaining to our own growth and development into our hands as He did Jesus (**John 13:3**)?  What if that means He intends for us to develop our identity and ability to stand up and represent Him and His interests?

- *What if* the highest and best use of our will is to make choices in life circumstances that teach us the character and conduct of "kings and priests unto our God" (**Revelation 1:6 and 5:10**)?

- *What if* the "in Jesus' name" that we tack onto the end of our prayers grew in our understanding until we realize that "in Jesus' name" means "standing in the place and authority of Jesus"?

- *What if* being regenerated, transformed, and renewed in Him means to become indoctrinated with His leadership style, values, ways, thought processes, abilities, judgment, and creative nature?

In **Matthew 22:34-40**, Jesus answers one of the most important questions that one could ask; too bad that the lawyer that asked it was trying to trap Him:

> ³⁴But when the Pharisees heard that He had silenced the Sadducees, they gathered together.  ³⁵Then one of them, a lawyer, asked Him a question, testing Him, and saying, ³⁶ "Teacher, which is the great commandment in the law?"  ³⁷Jesus said to him, "'You shall love the Lord your God with all your heart, with all your soul, and with all your mind. ³⁸This is the first and great commandment.  ³⁹And the second is like it: 'You shall love your neighbor as yourself.'  ⁴⁰On these two commandments hang all the Law and the Prophets."

For Jesus to give us the first and second great commandments is huge!  It is like getting the Cliff Notes instructions for handling all of life's situations and circumstances in one condensed presentation!  Our leadership role in the Kingdom is the reason God put us on earth; here we have the Father's most important marching orders.  Here, Jesus connects how we should conduct ourselves, on what principles should we concentrate, and what we should be learning to prepare for Kingdom rule.  *What if*, in giving us the important venues in which to concentrate our efforts in life, Jesus was also indicating the two most important leadership qualities for us to aspire to?  *What if* being in committed, loyal, loving submission to the King, and loving and laying down "our life" for those over whom we will rule qualifies us for "greatest among you" status (**Matthew 23:11-12**)?  *What if* life in the classroom is about these two great concepts?

> **Matthew 23:11-12** "¹¹But he who is greatest among you shall be your servant. ¹²And whoever exalts himself will be humbled, and he who humbles himself will be exalted."

## Growing the Royal Character: The "Add—To Principle"

Your Discipleship Plan (as we will see in a later chapter) is about charting the course for "getting from here to there."  It is about mapping a path across the wilderness and getting to where you want to be at the end of the journey.  It is about setting objectives, adopting strategies, and fleshing out (pun intended!) tactics that move you consistently forward, consistently upward, and sustain you in tough conditions.  The "Add—To Principle" is a solid strategy for planning your discipleship development given to us in **2 Peter 1:5-9**:

> ⁵But also for this very reason, giving all diligence, *add to* your faith virtue, [*add*] *to* virtue knowledge, ⁶[*add*] *to* knowledge self-control, [*add*] *to* self-control perseverance, [*add*] to perseverance godliness, ⁷[*add*] to godliness brotherly kindness, and [*add*] to brotherly

kindness love. [8]For if these things are yours and abound, *you* will be neither barren nor unfruitful in the knowledge of our Lord Jesus Christ. [9]For he who lacks these things is shortsighted, even to blindness, and has forgotten that he was cleansed from his old sins.

In addition to the specific character traits listed by Peter, we also find that it begins with a principle: Incremental progress over the course of a lifetime. The "Add—To Principle" has to do with building a character structure one component at a time on a rock-solid foundation. The character-building program is the curriculum of discipleship. Peter declares that the result of failure to employ the "Add—To Principle" with regard to the character traits and Fruit of the Spirit (FOTS) he lists results in short-sightedness to the point of blindness.

When we read this scripture, we may see a list of character rules that often add up to an inventory of our shortcomings. The attributes Peter lists *are important*, but so is the *pattern* that they constitute. Notice that Peter does not assume that your growth in the spirit will occur all at one time, and neither does Papa. Rather, he encourages us to add one thing to another—"Precept upon precept, precept upon precept; line upon line, line upon line; here a little, and there a little" (**Isaiah 28:13**). *This is the way the Spirit works in us:* He uses the *process itself* to build in us the fruit of patience, faithfulness, and self-control while He is building in us *the same Fruits of the Spirit! Genius!* He establishes a thing before building another upon it. That *does not* mean that He is only working on one area of your character—He frequently works on several simultaneously. It *does* mean that He aligns everything He is doing in you. Papa is not in a hurry, nor is He worried about your outcome. He knows what He has ordained for you, He knows the real person He already sees. He will not change His mind, *and He is able to bring it to pass!*

## Leadership Character: Perfected Love

If there is one term to apply to our discipleship quest to describe the character, nature, and values that we seek as a qualification to rule beside our Bridegroom, it is "perfected love." That is because when love is perfected in us, then we are perfected in the essence of God—because God is love (**1 John 4:8**). A would-be king that does not understand love cannot be perfected in it; and, a king who cannot love is a tyrant and unfit to rule in the Kingdom.

Love is not squishy emotion and goosebumps; it is, in fact, often the opposite. It is often saying hard things and doing hard things. It is changing poopy, stinky diapers—literally and figuratively—and having

> **1 John 2:5**, "But whoever keeps His word, truly the love of God is perfected in him. By this we know that we are in Him."

our own changed by others as well. In short, perfected love is action-based, not emotion-based. Of course, there is often great and positive emotion associated with it, but not always. Sometimes one has to hold his or her nose and dive right into the task of loving, and that is what the Holy Spirit does with us in teaching us to love perfectly. **1 John 2:5** tells us that perfected love is the measure that alerts us if we are abiding in Him, or merely dropping in from time-to-time. Further, the same verse tells us how we know if our love is perfected: by keeping His word. Keeping His word brings us into union with Him and perfects love in us.

Perfected love is the character of leadership in the Kingdom because it is the character of the King. It is the object of our quest for union (oneness) and is the result of the regeneration, transformation, and renewal (the Discipleship Triad) worked in us by the Holy Spirit. Therefore, we need to have a clear, unclouded understanding of what perfect love is—or rather, *Who* it is—without the pollution of carnal ideas from the environment in which we currently live. Paul gives us a good list of characteristics and guidelines we may emulate in **1 Corinthians 13**. But like all list of characteristics, they describe the thing but are not the thing. Further, we get a clue about how perfect love is developed in us by Jesus' words in **John 15:12-14**:

> ¹²This is My commandment, that you love one another as I have loved you. ¹³Greater love has no one than this, than to lay down one's life for his friends. *¹⁴You are My friends if you do whatever I command you.*

How could Jesus *command* us to love if love is an emotion? I cannot legitimately be *commanded to feel*; I can, however, be commanded to take actions that express love. We find additionally that there is a collateral benefit to following His command: In our obedience, we are transformed into His image. We overcome separation and *become* Him when we lay down our "right" to live an independent life. We become most like what we most look at; and when we intentionally look at Him and take our eyes off ourselves, we are changed from servant to a friend, a friend to a son, and a son to a king. Perfected love is a Person, not an emotion, an activity, or a religious goal. The principle is, "Imitate, Emulate, Assimilate." We *imitate* our teachers and we *emulate* our Master until we *assimilate* into union with Him. Our Independent Self gives way little by little until, "I...yet, not I" (**Galatians 2:20**) is the reality on earth in us, as it is in Heaven.

> **John 15:13**, "Greater love has no one than this, than to lay down one's life for his friends."

How do we apply the "Add—To Principle" to discipleship, leadership, and visioning? It does not change the principle contained in 2 Peter to rephrase it as the following: "Add to your **Vi**sion, **I**nsight, and [add] to your insight, **E**ndurance, and [add] to your endurance, **W**isdom. For those in leadership that lack these things are short-sighted, even to blindness, and have failed to lead themselves and their organization responsibly." I propose the following V.I.E.W.-point definitions:

- **V**ision: the ***exercise*** of creating a spiritual and mental image of the ideal future state of the organization. The ideal state is known as the "Goal."

- **I**nsight: **defining** reality in such a way that a bridge and pathway between today's circumstances and tomorrow's goals are clear and clearly communicated.

- **E**ndurance: the ***skill*** to embrace and learn from adversity, tolerate ambiguity, and prosper when others are fainting; and to encourage the heart of followers to inspire perseverance in mind, emotions, and will.

- **W**isdom: the **art** of blending *all* of the resources of the organization in such a manner as to produce the fruit of organizational success.

Finally, the difference between one who has *vision* and a *visionary* is the master-craft of communication. The most insightful strategy, the best cutting-edge direction, the finest inspirational nugget—all of these have no value unless they are skillfully shared. As Solomon writes in **Proverbs 26:8**, there is such a thing as the foolishness of "binding the stone in the slingshot"; and that is tantamount to the foolishness of devising a brilliant organizational strategy, then failing to communicate it.

## The Leadership Choice: Where Will You Eat Your Cake?

Jesus indicates that there is an inverse relationship between our earthly *choice* conduct of leadership and our *conferred* Kingdom leadership status. In other words, we may have our reward here on earth, or have it in full in the Kingdom. We cannot have it both ways! Note these three declarations by Jesus in **Matthew 6**:

- "Therefore, when you do a charitable deed, do not sound a trumpet before you as the hypocrites do in the synagogues and in the streets, that they may have glory from men. Assuredly, I say to you, *they have their reward*." (**Matthew 6:2**)

- "And when you pray, you shall not be like the hypocrites. For they love to pray standing in the synagogues and on the corners of the streets, that they may be seen by men. Assuredly, I say to you, *they have their reward*." (**Matthew 6:5**)

- "Moreover, when you fast, do not be like the hypocrites, with a sad countenance. For they disfigure their faces that they may appear to men to be fasting. Assuredly, I say to you, *they have their reward*." (**Matthew 6:16,**)

Perhaps this concept is the origin of the phrase, "You cannot have your cake and eat it, too!" In any case, the clear message is that our conferred position in eternity will have a great deal to do with where we choose to "eat our reward cake." Paul alludes to the principle in **1 Corinthians 1:26-27**:

> [26]For you see your calling, brethren, that not many wise according to the flesh, *not many mighty, not many noble, are called.* [27]But God has chosen the foolish things of the world to put to shame the wise, and God has chosen the weak things of the world to put to shame the things which are mighty.

It is natural to ask (from a human perspective), "Why do I have to choose? Why can't I have both?" The question itself indicates its origin: our separated, independent, self-centered nature. Paul gives us the answer in **verse 27**: to put to shame the things that are mighty. That is, He intends to contrast Heavenly reality with T/S/M reality for the purpose of glorifying the former and presenting the latter for what it really is—an *inferior* choice! The "where we eat our cake" choice also reveals much about us to the world and to ourselves as a clear indicator of linage and calling. Here are some of the clear characteristics revealed by "where you eat your cake" (WYEYC):

> ### The Parable of the Rich Fool
> **Luke 12:16-21**, "[16]Then He spoke a parable to them, saying: 'The ground of a certain rich man yielded plentifully. [17]And he thought within himself, saying, 'What shall I do, since I have no room to store my crops?' [18]So he said, 'I will do this: I will pull down my barns and build greater, and there I will store all my crops and my goods. [19]And I will say to my soul, "Soul, you have many goods laid up for many years; take your ease; eat, drink, and be merry."' [20]But God said to him, 'Fool! This night your soul will be required of you; then whose will those things be which you have provided?' [21]'So is he who lays up treasure for himself, and is not rich toward God.'"

- "Sheep" vs. "non-sheep" status
- "Wise" vs. "fool"
- "Weak" vs. "mighty"
- "Humble" vs. "noble"
- "Kingdom" vs. "earthly" citizenship
- "Sincere" vs. "hypocrite"

These are only a few conclusions by observing life from the WYEYC perspective. Earthly nobility and wisdom may actually be *contra-indicators of a heavenly calling* because to accomplish either typically requires total immersion in one kingdom or the other. Jesus told us we cannot serve God and Mammon (**Matthew 6:24**). That should be a loud-and-clear wake-up call for our motivations, affections, loyalties, priorities, and life goals.

**Luke 12:16-21** presents one of Jesus' lesser-known parables. Perhaps it is lesser-known because it hits a little too close to home to our "American dream" mindset. It conveys a critical warning to those who hoard their produce for their own benefit and ease. Notice that Jesus nowhere indicated that the Rich Fool's choice was not his to make—only that it was ill-advised in light of the eternal consequences. Jesus nowhere indicates that we are entitled to a lifestyle of ease. Finally, we are not told whether it was the

Rich Fool's ungenerous nature, his "life of ease" and "eat, drink and be merry" choices, his over-confidence in a guaranteed future of long life, or some combination of all of these that doomed his best-laid plans. We *are* told that the summation of the above is a futile strategy as a treasure laid up on earth and in the absence of "rich[ness] toward God." Combining this with the principle of **Matthew 6:20** ("Lay up for yourself treasures in Heaven"), and we may conclude that it is not the *accumulation of treasure* that is at issue, but rather the location of *where you will eat your cake!* As for me, I plan to have a really big slice of wedding cake at the Marriage Supper of the Lamb!

## Before the King is the Crowned

> **Galatians 4:1-7**, "[4]Now I say that the heir, as long as he is a child, does not differ at all from a slave, though he is master of all, [2]but is under guardians and stewards until the time appointed by the father. [3]Even so we, when we were children, were in bondage under the elements of the world. [4]But when the fullness of the time had come, God sent forth His Son, born of a woman, born under the law, [5]to redeem those who were under the law, that we might receive the adoption as sons. [6]And because you are sons, God has sent forth the Spirit of His Son into your hearts, crying out, "Abba, Father!" [7]Therefore you are no longer a slave but a son, and if a son, then an heir of God through Christ."

We have the capacity to read Scripture and skip right to the good stuff without noticing the conditions attached. The good stuff in **Galatians 4:1-7** is the promise of adoptions as sons, having completed some term of "guardians and stewards" tutelage. But to advance from "child" to "son" status (and therefore, from a servant to the master of household) we must first submit to growing up in the Spirit. The growing-up process is not a function of age, but of *learning*! The only way to possess your inheritance is to grow up and learn. There is no shame attached to beginning life in the Spirit as a child—that is by Papa's design. We are not supposed to remain in our milk-fed childish state, however. Child-like, yes; childish, no.

Life in this T/S/M reality is the classroom experience where we are intended to place ourselves under the teaching authority of the Holy Spirit. Each day, we present our bodies a living sacrifice. Each day, we roll out of bed and forge our way into the classroom of our environment and circumstances that are custom-made for training. Each day, we fulfill some percentage portion of the lessons available from that day's activity. This is the context from which we are intended to approach life—not, "Was this a good day or bad day?"; rather, the pertinent question at the end of the day is, "Did I squeeze all of the learning possible out of my experiences today?"

## Thinking Like A King

God has created us in a manner that our sense of self, our communication with one another, and our sense and understanding of community are all dependent on contextualizing events in an on-going, ever-expanding narrative—our "story." Shakespeare summarized it like this in, *As You Like It*: "All the world's a stage, and all men and women are merely players." One of the functions (dysfunctions!) of our Independent/Separated Self is to ensure that we are the central figure—the "star"—of every scene and every act of this play; so, we are not merely players, we are the quintessential prima donna, insisting that our whims be satisfied immediately and fully. Truthfully, we pretty much believe that everyone else's story should revolve around ours; some do a better job than others of concealing this underlying assumption, but we all have it—that, too, is a symptom of the Independent Self.

We accumulate pieces of our story from multiple sources, ranging from people and events to feelings and beliefs. As we learn of stories that have preceded ours, we learn to glom our story onto the chain of world history. We have no way of actually verifying that our understanding of history is accurate; yet, that inconvenient fact does not deter or even slow us down from writing and rewriting our narrative. The uncomfortable ramification of our inability to control the narrative of previous events is that we are in a position of relying on faith and trust to understand our place in the line of chronology. The most avowed atheist or agnostic among us still exercises faith many, many times a day, much less in their lifetime. Every time we believe a report of something outside of our immediate environment or observation, we exercise faith. And the facts in which we place our trust depend on the assumption with which we begin—we see best what we expect to see. We all do it—we *have* to. Psychology calls this our Confirmation Bias—that is, the tendency to search for, interpret, favor, and recall information in a way that confirms one's pre-existing beliefs.[9]

We will discuss Confirmation Bias in Chapter 7 as it relates to the assumptions we make and rely upon. Life is a great puzzle with complex and moving parts, and many of the movements are outside of our immediate vicinity. Yet, we are driven to assemble the picture as best we can according to the information we have. *That* is the kingly function at work in us: the drive to assemble and reassemble the story pieces until they make some sort of sense.

When we assemble the puzzle pieces of our story in context, the emerging picture is understood in terms of the roles of the two lead characters: you and God. When we speak of assembling the pieces with respect to us, the reference is to our broken, smashed, stony heart that is undergoing the rebuilding and regeneration process that constitutes our salvation; that is, the process that makes us "sōzō,"[10] whole and complete. But the puzzle pieces as they relate to God are those secrets, those mysteries, those understandings He reserves for the initiated, and that He has hidden for Kings to search out. And when our puzzle—our story—looks like the cover of the box, we know we are on the path of discipleship, and growing into sonship. The next chapter will add the richness of detail to our quest, and the mystery of discipleship should come alive.

Whatever challenges and tips over *my* container might not seem like any big deal to you—or yours to me. Nevertheless, the intent of each individual's pilgrimage is to exercise us in overcoming the independence and separated-ness inherent in our flesh by driving us into His arms; and enable our way back to union with Him through the life-circumstances with which we struggle and suffer. We learn to *reign* with Him as we master walking in the Fruit of the Spirit and learn to preside over our circumstances. We prepare to *rule* with Him as our dead parts are regenerated, our mind is renewed to His thought patterns and values, and we are conformed and transformed into His image—the image of the Immutable God. In short, we learn to think like the King, and we take on the nature, character, and values of the King.

---

9 Confirmation bias. (2017). En.wikipedia.org. https://en.wikipedia.org/wiki/Confirmation_bias

[10] Strong's #4982: sozo (pronounced sode'-zo) to save, i.e. deliver or protect, heal, preserve, save (self), do well, be (make) whole. https://www.bibletools.org/index.cfm/fuseaction/Lexicon.show/ID/G4982/sozo.htm

# Chapter 3—What Is Discipleship?

[65]And He said, "Therefore I have said to you that no one can come to Me unless it has been granted to him by My Father." [66]From that time many of His disciples went back and walked with Him no more. [67]Then Jesus said to the twelve, "Do you also want to go away?" [68]But Simon Peter answered Him, "Lord, to whom shall we go? You have the words of eternal life. [69]Also we have come to believe and know that You are the Christ, the Son of the living God." (**John 6:65-69**)

## "What's the Dif?"

Jesus had many people who followed Him—that is, followed Him around—that were not disciples. In this chapter, we will explore the difference between a follower and a disciple. One can only speculate who the people were in **John 6:66** who left Jesus and followed Him no more, or why they followed in the first place. Maybe they were bored or curious in the beginning. Maybe they heard He did miracles and wanted to see for themselves. Maybe they saw Him stir up a hornet's nest with the Pharisees in the temple and were drawn to a troublemaker. Maybe they heard He had turned water into wine and hoped He would be a source of free drink; or that He had fed five thousand and were looking for their next meal. Maybe it was because of the glowing reference from John the Baptist. Maybe their interest was political, and they thought He would run the Romans out. But whatever the initial reason, it was not substantive enough to outlast the day-in-day-out trudging after the Master one exhausting footstep after another. Their followership was *notional*, not *motivational*.

There is an inconvenient truth that hangs like a pall over life, and it is this: There is a very real distinction between *notional* and *motivational* belief. It is possible to believe something on which we would/will never act, simply because the belief is not deep enough to compel action. That is what a notional belief means— we hold it as a truth in our mind, but not so strongly as to compel our action in specific matters of life. For

> **no·tion·al** ˈnōSH(ə)n(ə)l/ *adjective*
> 1. Existing only in theory or as a suggestion or idea; existing only in the imagination.
> http://www.dictionary.com/browse/notional?s=t

example, everyone knows (notionally) that he or she will die someday, but a great many people do not act (motivationally) as if they *know* it. Conversely, some people routinely buy lottery tickets, because they are sure that, irrespective of the odds, they are the ones who will beat the odds to win. That is a motivational belief, and it is our Optimism Bias in its full glory!

There is a qualitative difference between beliefs that we hold as a notion, and those that inspire and obligate action on the scale of a life-directing force. Discipleship cannot happen in a notional environment—there simply is not enough strength of heart to push past the obstacle of the flesh. For our discipleship to outlast the pain of self-denial, the reality of disappointed expectation, the gut-wrenching torment of turning our back on our flesh, the loneliness of not belonging in this world, and the simultaneously crushing and invigorating effect of Papa's discipline in us (**Hebrews 12:11**), our motivation must be substantive, and it must reach to the core of our being.

## The Fudge Factor (TFF)

It is a fair question to ask: "Why do we need a separate book on discipleship when we already have the Bible?" The answer is, "*Theoretically, we don't.*" It is the gap between theory and practice that may make this book useful.  There is a common saying that, "The devil is in the details," and nowhere is that concept truer than in our spiritual walk.  The naked truth is that most of us give ourselves much more credit than we are due when considering our own virtue.  In our hearts, each of us believes that we are above average in many areas of life, including spiritual development.  It does not take a statistical expert (only a graduate of 4th-grade math!) to recognize that all of us being above average is impossible.  And yet, we persist in thinking that *we* are the ones with exceptional ability and are the exception to universal rule.  *That is why we need a book on discipleship!*

Psychology has a term for our unreasonable expectation of success, both past, and future: The Optimism Bias.[11]  The Optimism Bias simply says that people generally exaggerate their probability of success, generally exaggerate the quality of their effort, and generally exaggerate compliance with known measurable standards.  I will simply refer to the concept as *The Fudge Factor* (TFF).  "Fudging" is not just an episodic exaggeration of an event; it is a distorted view of life.  But mostly, it is a distorted view—a more generous view—of our own performance.  The Fudge Factor makes an accurate appraisal of our growth difficult, if not impossible.  Optimism is a wonderful thing when it pertains to hope for the future, but biased optimism is out of order when it is time for an accurate appraisal.  Not negative appraisal—accurate, honest self-appraisal.  TFF is one of the unconscious strategies that we employ to stave off the pain of our non-performance, the domination of our flesh over our spirit, and the stalemate of remaining unchanged year-after-year.  *That, also, is a reason we need a book about discipleship.*

> "In theory there is no difference between theory and practice; in practice there is!" Yogi Berra

As a child growing up in a Southern Baptist home and church, I was expected to attend a class called Training Union on Sunday evening.  The first order of business at each gathering was to fill out a slip of paper to record our adherence to specific tasks for the week.  Time has erased my memory of most of the boxes on the checklist; however, I will never forget the one labeled, "Daily Bible Reading," and the ingenious (for an eight-year-old!) strategy I devised to be in compliance (read: get to check the box), preserve my integrity (read: not technically lie), yet not to have to commit too much effort.  My method involved keeping a copy of my New Testament next to my bed.  Before closing my eyes, I would open the Testament to a random page, read a few words (on a good night, a whole verse), then slam it shut and drift off to dreamland.  Repeating this tactic at least five nights a week entitled me to guiltless "box-checking," the smile of God, and whatever reward was waiting for the compliant children (usually candy).  As can be readily seen, I learned to fudge (pun intended!) at a very early age.

> **James 4:17**, "Therefore, to him who knows to do good and does not do it, to him it is sin."

Fudging is about expectations and intentions coloring perceptions; that is, what one *perceives* to be their past performance, and *anticipates* being their future experience.  What TFF does not appraise accurately is our *actual* behavior, considered independently of our intent.  We credit ourselves with praise-worthy performance if we *intended* good, even if our delivery was something less.  We tend to "round up to the next higher digit"; and when we consistently overestimate, we accumulate error that distorts accuracy.  That can be problematic if we value continuous improvement, yet fail to accurately measure our current performance.  We tend to think we sinned less than we actually did, we gave more than we actually gave, we prayed more frequently than we actually prayed, acted out our integrity more often than we actually did, we studied longer than we actually did, and were nicer than we actually were.  If you have

---

[11] For a presentation of Optimism Bias, see https://www.ted.com/talks/tali_sharot_the_optimism_bias#t-238709

difficulty accepting my word for it, ask your spouse. *That, too, is why we need a book on discipleship.*

A life strategy (or habit) of fudging is the opposite of intentionality. If fudging our way through life is a strategy, we should also be able to identify the tactics that make the strategy tick. Such tactics *are* identifiable, along with a group of related behaviors, which serve to promote self-deception while maintaining plausible deniability. Here are a few of the tactics that comprise the art of moving through life with as little precision and as much ambiguity as possible:

- Keep your commitments general, and your promises vague;
- Always be on the lookout for a better offer even if you have given your word;
- Avoid accountability, and avoid getting too close to others;
- Never give permission for someone else to "get into your business," even if just to check in on you;
- Never commit your plans and goals to writing;
- Don't waste your time reviewing past performance;
- Keep a list of reasons at hand (i.e., excuses), and rehearse them regularly so that they flow readily, skillfully, and naturally on demand;
- Keep your conversations light, meaningless, and trite; declare certain uncomfortable subjects—like religion and politics—to be off-limits for discussion;
- Don't have fixed boundaries, but adapt your conscience standards to fit the circumstances;
- Rather than making plans, rely on your ability to live and act spontaneously;
- Assign the same or higher level of significance to your good intentions as your actual performance;
- Don't try too hard, and tell yourself you don't want to make others look bad;
- Embrace the "good enough for government work" standard.

Fudging depends upon generalization as a practice and perspective. Never getting specific is the key that allows us to escape unscathed with our claims of performance. As long as I am not required to be specific, I can escape accountability. As long as I am not held to account for any particular part, I can claim to be successful on the whole without a legitimate challenge. We all know the fantastic escape mechanism of never getting specific, never committing "it" to writing, and never asking someone to hold you accountable! In short, I can legitimately *claim to be a genius if I never actually have to prove I am one*, and if I can minimize evidence to the contrary. I can stake a claim to being Christ-like if I never have to accurately compare my behavior to the published standard (the Bible).

Along with generality also comes the negative consequence of loss of motivation. I am indebted to another friend for this gemstone of truth: *Without accountability, there is no motivation for change!* If we accept and embrace that Jesus' loving attention is primarily for the purpose of changing and transforming us into His image, then we must acknowledge that TFF is the enemy of that

> "Without accountability, there is no motivation for change!" --Scott Boss

change. To see accurately one must see specifically and in detail. *That is why we need a book on discipleship.*

Finally, to experience success in transformation, we must embrace a detailed view of life that supplements and completes our big-picture view. Self-examination is a routine practice of disciples. Consider the following Scriptures from the Apostle Paul:

- **1 Corinthians 11:28**, "But let a man *examine himself*, and so let him eat of the bread and drink of the cup."

- **2 Corinthians 13:5**, "*Examine yourselves* as to whether you are in the faith. *Test yourselves*."

- **Galatians 6:4**, "But let each one *examine his own work*, and then he will have rejoicing in himself alone, and not in another."

When we commit to a habit of examining ourselves, we have much less time to examine one another, and that is frequently a good thing. When we commit to self-examination, we fulfill Jesus' mandate to,

> Working Definition of Integrity: "What you *do* with what you *know*!

"First remove the plank from your own eye, and then you will see clearly to remove the speck from your brother's eye" (**Matthew 7:5**). The best definition of "integrity" that I have ever come across is, "What you do, with what you know." This definition requires self-examination. Integrity is about execution, not just knowledge. I cannot ensure integrity in my actions unless I regularly take the measure of both my actions *and* my motivations. Efficiency is doing things well; effectiveness is doing the right things right; but integrity goes farther—it is doing the right things right, *for the right reasons*! That is to what James was referring in **James 4:17**, "Therefore, to him who knows to do good and does not do it, to him it is sin." Execution is also the plain message of Jesus' words in **John 13:17**, "If you *know* these things, *blessed are you if you do them*."

The words "integrity" and "integrate" come from the same root. That alone should tell us that the true measure of our integrity is how thoroughly, how deeply, and consistently we have integrated truth

> - Efficiency is doing things well;
> - Effectiveness is doing the right things right;
> - Integrity is doing the right things right, *for the right reasons*!

into our dealings with ourselves and others. Integrating truth is also what life in the Choice Space is about. We cannot help but be conflicted—in a state of dilemma—when our flesh demands a self-interest reaction or behavior, yet our spirit is whispering the Word of Life. At that moment, in that response space, we have the opportunity to change, and to express that change to the world. When we do it consistently enough, and heartily enough, it soon becomes a rock-solid part of our ongoing transformation. "What you do with what you know" is personal, demanding, and objective. It requires that we know our own heart and motivation. At a very deep level, we are the only ones that can answer as to whether we are acting from integrity, rebellion, manipulation, or self-deception. We are still responsible for our "failure to know," but integrity failure only applies when we ignore or act contrary to the truth we know. *That is why we need a book about discipleship.*


## God's Field, God's Building

In **1 Corinthians 3:9**, Paul gives us two metaphors that summarize God's work plan for us. These metaphors neatly tie together two important concepts: being, and doing. As God's field, we organically produce fruit and a harvest (being). As God's building, we mechanically construct a temple in which the Holy Spirit may take up residence (doing). These are the two purposes of our internship on earth. As God's field, we are host to the seed of His Kingdom. The seed grows up in us, producing the character, nature, values, and ways that constitute our preparation for leadership. By submitting to His planting and the intrinsic value of the seed within, we learn to reign in this life under the tutelage and governance of the Holy Spirit. His rain waters our crop and covers the landscape with pools (**Psalm 84:6**) that take us from initial strength to mature strength, and from a state of initial glory to mature glory. His light shines on us, and from us, as we turn our faces and our gaze toward Him. His word speaks to us and fertilizes our understanding. We abide in His love, and by remaining attached to the vine, we produce fruit for the enjoyment of the husbandman (Papa) and all those around us. As His "good ground," our lives yield the crop foretold by Jesus, "some a hundredfold, some sixty, some thirty."

As God's building, we build our structure on the foundation that the Apostle Paul laid (**1 Corinthians 3:10-15**) by walking in the "good works for which we were created, and which God has prepared beforehand that we should walk in them" (**Ephesians 2:10**). Building on the foundation in this life has the effect of increasing the Kingdom in the eternal reality—at least when we use quality building materials! Papa does not allow the inferior structural materials of wood, hay, and straw! While those may be common construction grade materials for the present, God insists on only the best for His Son's Kingdom—gold, silver, and precious stones! Concentrating on the *quality* of building instead of merely the *activity* of building ensures future "fire safety" for one's work, and ensures that it will survive the transition from one reality to the next.

> Nothing that we do in this life has any lasting value apart from its effects on our development and preparation for our position in God's eternal Kingdom.

## Begin with the End in Mind: Accumulated Value

Unless we are actively guarding against it, we naturally fall into the trap of living life for the sake of life itself; that is, for no higher purpose than *to collect and enjoy day-to-day experiences*. Even believers get trapped in the habits of "life for its own sake" (LFIOS). Such a view is unavoidable when we depend on, and are dominated by, our body consciousness—it is the nature of the carnal mind. But any discussion about our mission and purpose should appropriately begin with this understanding: *Nothing that we do in this life has any lasting value (and therefore, no eternal purpose or meaning) apart from its effects on our spiritual development and preparation for our position in God's Eternal Kingdom.* This is the "**Accumulated Value Principle**" (AVP). Our experience has *only* the accumulated value of all the character qualities of our Bridegroom that have been transformed in us and the good works that we have sent ahead into the Kingdom. *Nothing*—not our occupation, relationships, or resources; not our pass times, habits, accomplishments, or choices; not our social standing, experiences good or bad, our spiritual or religious activities, or our organizational memberships, etc.—has *any* lasting value beyond the boundaries of our physical life except in consideration of their contribution to our primary purpose and preparation for the Kingdom. The AVP is *true* and is the *truth*, and acceptance of it obligates a compelling action response.

In His Sermon on the Mount, Jesus told us:

> [19]Do not lay up for yourselves treasures on earth, where moth and rust destroy and where thieves break in and steal; [20]but *lay up for yourselves treasures in heaven*, where neither moth nor rust destroys and where thieves do not break in and steal. [21]*For where your treasure is, there your heart will be also.*" (**Matthew 6:19-21**)

The principle Jesus articulates here is related to the Accumulated Value Principle—we will call it the "Lay-Up Principle." Basketball fans will recognize the collective groan from the hometown crowd that accompanies missing a lay-up in the final seconds of the big game with a close rival. However, the loss associated with missing the Lay-Up Principle is many magnitudes higher.

Our heart's true affections guide the bulk of our actions, direct our priorities, determine the way we spend our time, and ultimately establish the outcome of our efforts. Jesus placed emphasis on establishing lasting, secure treasure, safe from theft, deterioration, and destruction. He also clearly implied that we should have a *healthy self-interest* when it comes to eternal matters. In other words, we should take *active* and *intentional* interest in the eternal consequences (treasure, position, and authority) that result from our earthly activities.

A second Accumulated Value Principle Scripture is **1 Corinthians 3:10-15**. I know of no other Scripture that, for Christians, has the potential to be as incredibly glorious for some, and simultaneously terrifying for others! Jesus foretold our appearance before the Judgment Seat of Christ in **Matthew 16:27**, "For the Son of man shall come in the glory of His Father with His angels; and then He shall reward every man according to his works." Paul refers to this appearance as, "the Day" (i.e., Day of Christ). In **1 Corinthians 3:10-15**, he describes the setting and purpose of our appearing before (what is sometimes called) the Bema Seat Judgment:

> **2 Corinthians 5:10**: "For we must all appear before the judgment seat of Christ, that *each one may receive the things done in the body, according to what he has done, whether good or bad*."

> [10]According to the grace of God which was given to me, as a wise master builder I have laid the foundation, and another [that's you!] builds on it. But let each one take heed how he builds on it. [11]For no other foundation can anyone lay than that which is laid, which is Jesus Christ. [12]Now if anyone builds on this foundation with gold, silver, precious stones, wood, hay, straw, [13]each one's work will become clear; for the Day will declare it, because it will be revealed by fire; **and the fire will test each one's work, of what sort it is.** [14]If anyone's work which he has built on it endures, **he will receive a reward**. [15]If anyone's work is burned, **he will suffer loss**; but he himself will be saved, yet so as through fire.

The Bema Seat is the place of reward for the works done in the body. The most consequential factor is the subjection of each person's life activities to the test of fire. We will be evaluated by whether any portion of what we have built in life survives the purification effects of Papa's fire. The material we have used in the building process is the issue. Being a Master Firefighter by trade, I know fire and its effects on various building materials. But it does not take an expert to know that the fire burns and removes *all* of the building's structure that is flammable; that is, those components subject to deterioration and destruction. In its place, only ash remains. Our reward (read: Kingdom responsibility) is predicated on our having chosen quality, fireproof building materials in this life.

**1 Corinthians 3:10-15** is *the* definitive support for the AVP; it clearly declares that *only the things of value in the Kingdom* (the gold, silver, and precious stones used for building) will survive the transition process from the T/S/M world to the eternal! The temporary value will give way to lasting; the values and standards of men will give way before Kingdom values and ways. The very fact that the T/S/M world *will come to an end* makes it a poor investment. The cost/benefit comparison between this world and the Kingdom orders our priorities, shifts perspective, and reframes our assumptions of what is and is not time-worthy. Paul warns us to redeem our time—that is, exchange it as one would redeem a ticket or coupon—in a wise manner by walking and investing wisely (**Ephesians 5:15-17**).

**1 Corinthians 3:15** tells us that whoever's work is burned up will suffer loss, and this seems to be one of those grand understatements of Scripture. There is *no recovery* from this loss. There is no declaring bankruptcy, reorganizing your debt, and starting over. There is no collecting insurance and rebuilding. There is only living in the Kingdom for one thousand years knowing that, instead of investing wisely and laying up treasure when you had the opportunity, you myopically and selfishly squandered the Master's resources.

Much wistful comfort is taken by the Church from the promise of **Revelation 21:4** that, "God will wipe away every tear from their eyes." To be sure, His love and care for us *is* comforting; what is less wonderful is the answer to the question, "Why will God *need* to wipe away tears from His people's eyes *at the end of our Millennial Reign*?" The promised tear-wiping reference is contemporaneous with the coming of the New Jerusalem at the end of the Millennial Reign of Christ *after* we have ostensibly already been ruling beside, our Bridegroom on earth for one thousand years. The Revelation makes clear to those with ears to hear that some of His people going into the New Jerusalem will be subject to tears and sorrow in the Millennium immediately preceding. This will be the circumstance of those of His children who squandered the resources He has put at our disposal in this lifetime, and for those who have embraced the philosophy of "life for its own sake." It is no wonder that God will be in a position of needing to wipe tears considering that many will be living with the *full knowledge* of the time they squandered, and the inheritance that might have been theirs but for their preoccupation with this life and its faux rewards.

> **Revelation 21:3-4**, "³And I heard a loud voice from heaven saying, 'Behold, the tabernacle of God is with men, and He will dwell with them, and they shall be His people. God Himself will be with them and be their God. ⁴*And God will wipe away every tear from their eyes*; there shall be no more death, nor sorrow, nor crying. There shall be no more pain, for the former things have passed away.'"

A natural question is, "What are the gold, silver, and precious stones with which we should be building, and how are they obtained?" John records Jesus' advice to the Laodicean Church (the "Lukewarm Church") concerning their spiritual malaise**:**

> I counsel you to buy from Me *gold* refined in the fire, that you may be rich; and *white garments*, that you may be clothed, that the shame of your nakedness may not be revealed; and anoint your eyes with *eyesalve*, that you may see. (**Revelation 3:18**)

We see that the gold (and presumably silver and precious stones as well) with which to build may be *purchased* from the Lord Himself. The purchase process is the exchange of one thing of value for another—as in the exchange for our time, effort, and intention for the gold, silver, and precious stones of being conformed to the image of Christ, transforming our mind through the process of renewal, and gaining the wisdom and understanding of God's ways. This exchange describes the *core activity of discipleship*! Every one of us has the ability to make the exchange—He has placed the necessary resources in our hands, within our grasp. Consider the following Scriptures, through which God tells us a portion of the resources that He has provided:

- **Ephesians 2:10**, "For we are His workmanship, created in Christ Jesus for *good works, which God prepared beforehand* that we should walk in them."

- **1 Timothy 6:17-19**, "¹⁷Command those who are rich in this present age not to be haughty, nor to trust in uncertain riches but in the living God, who gives us richly all things to enjoy. ¹⁸*Let them do good, that they be rich in good works, ready to give, willing to share, ¹⁹storing up for themselves a good foundation for the time to come,* that they may lay hold on eternal life."

- **Proverbs 17:16**, "Why is there in the hand of a fool the *purchase price of wisdom*, since he has no heart for it?"

- **2 Peter 1:3-4**, "³[A]s His divine power has given to us *all things that pertain to life and godliness,* through the knowledge of Him who called us by glory and virtue, ⁴by which have been given to us *exceedingly great and precious promises, that through these you may be partakers of the divine nature,* having escaped the corruption that is in the world through lust."

Lust is *not* primarily sexual; it *is* primarily selfish.

- **Ephesians 5:15-17**, "[15]See then that you walk circumspectly, not as fools but as wise, [16]*redeeming the time,* because the days are evil. [17]Therefore do not be unwise, but **understand what the will of the Lord is**."

- **Matthew 25:16**, "Then he who had **received the five talents went and traded with them**, and made another five talents."

These Scriptures point to the transactional nature of life, and our responsibility to take what has been given and use it to enlarge the Kingdom and reserve incorruptible treasure. The treasure that we are ordained to take from this world into the everlasting Kingdom is prefigured in the example of Israel plundering the treasure of Egypt as Moses led them out of Pharaoh's clutches. We are to be about the Father's business of actively transferring the wealth of this world into the realm of His eternal Kingdom, plundering it, and returning it to the rightful Ruler from whom it was usurped.

Scripture gives us an indication of how pervasive the AVP is in all life, even in matters that seem incidental to us in the conduct of our daily affairs. Consider these examples of small, transient matters that accumulate to our benefit in the eternal dimension:

**Exodus 12:35-36**, "[35]Now the children of Israel had done according to the word of Moses, and they had asked from the Egyptians **articles of silver, articles of gold, and clothing.** [36]And the Lord had given the people favor in the sight of the Egyptians, so that they granted them what they requested. **Thus they plundered the Egyptians**."

- **Psalm 56:8**, "You number my wanderings; **put my tears into Your bottle**; **are they not in Your book**?"

- **Revelation 5:8**, "Now when He had taken the scroll, the four living creatures and the twenty-four elders fell down before the Lamb, each having a harp, and **golden bowls full of incense, which are the prayers of the saints**."

- **Matthew 10:42**, "And whoever **gives one of these little ones only a cup of cold water…**he shall by no means lose his reward.

These examples serve to illustrate a pervasive principle: *Our lives are lived on the micro-level, and faithfulness in even the seemingly mundane aspects have a glorious effect in the eternal realm*. Our tears are stored in His bottle and recorded in His book; our prayers are heard and stored up in bowls in heaven, and even acts of kindness as small as giving a cup of cold water to the thirsty are significant. Having such accumulated impact in the eternal realm, we ignore—or worse still, disregard—the AVP to our own peril. We *must* give serious attention to the resource that constitutes our opportunity to accumulate lasting value: our time.

## Making the Exchange: Redeeming Time

There are very few things in life that are inherently precious as a commodity, and fewer still that are truly ours to possess. The shortlist is 1) Identity, 2) Choice, and, 3) Time. Of this shortlist, time is one commodity that is of incredible value—not as a "life for its own sake" experience, but rather, *its exchange value for what it can purchase*. One thing that enhances a commodity's value is its limitation or scarcity, and it cannot be argued against that our time is both limited and scarce. We *must* understand that T/S/M life is for a purpose, and according to **Revelation 3:17-19**, the time that we are allotted has an infinite redemption opportunity value:

[17]Because you say, "I am rich, have become wealthy, and have need of nothing"—and do not know that you are wretched, miserable, poor, blind, and naked—[18]*I counsel you to buy from Me gold* refined in the fire, that you may be rich; and ***white garments***, that you may be clothed, *that* the shame of your nakedness may not be revealed; and anoint your eyes with ***eyesalve***, that you may see. [19]As many as I love, I rebuke and chasten.

When Jesus counsels us to, "buy from Me," a wise response would be to take inventory of our assets, understand the purchase price, do some market research in order to make the wisest, most efficient, most effective purchases possible, then dive head-first into the transaction and invest everything we have or can scrape together! It is beyond advisable to purchase from Him the future assets on which the Kingdom will be based and that will have true value when this life is only a memory if that. Those purchasable assets are obtained by making the exchange Paul indicates in **Ephesians 5:15**—*we redeem our time on earth wisely to purchase the treasure of heaven.*

> **Ephesians 5:15-17**, "[15]See then that you walk circumspectly, not as fools but as wise, [16]***redeeming the time***, because the days are evil. [17]Therefore do not be unwise, but ***understand what the will of the Lord is***."

The concept of wise redemption is interesting. It is about exchanging that which is of recognized value for other items of value. Often, in this world, the value of the thing given in exchange is not equal to the usefulness of the thing obtained. For example, paper money has no intrinsic value except as we have agreed on its value in exchange to obtain goods and services that *do* have intrinsic value. We go to the grocery store and exchange/redeem our paper money (or electronically swipe our credit card!) in order to obtain food that keeps us alive. Likewise, we redeem coupons from an advertisement for a discounted price. The discount is the thing of actual value, but the coupon provides the opportunity to access it. We cannot eat paper currency or coupons—and certainly not electronic bits of data—and expect to remain alive for long! However, by near-universal agreement, society accepts tokens of value for a thing of real value. Redeeming time for treasure is exactly the same idea. It could be said that the real value of anything is in our agreement in the exchange potential for a thing, *and also in the transaction itself!*

When it comes to Jesus' redemption of the Church, the item of infinite value exchanged was His life (for our salvation) and blood (for our justification); the thing of value purchased was the life of His Bride. Consequently, we have the incalculably valuable opportunity to exchange what we have been given—life, in terms of our time spent in T/S/M reality—to purchase commodities of eternal value, thus completing the circle! When we understand *exactly* what is at stake, it is a no-brainer to gather up every scrap of redeemable time, and trade it for as much eternal treasure we can transact. When we understand our transaction potential, we can also understand Solomon's bewilderment in **Proverbs 17:16**, "Why is there in the hand of a fool the purchase price of wisdom, *since he has no heart for it?*" While we may not all have the same total amount of time to exchange, it seems obvious that everyone reading this has *today*, and it should be exchanged for eternal value. Solomon tells us only a fool would fail to do so.

It is God's prerogative to assign meaning to existence, not man's. It is also His prerogative to assign value to the activities, exchanges, relationships, attitudes, and *choices* that comprise what we call life. God's ultimate judgment on His people (that is, the people that name Him as Father) is not Hell or destruction, it is *to let them go their own way*! It is to allow them to waste their lives wandering in the wilderness until they die. To be sure, He gives *us* the prerogative to decide how *we redeem our time*; but He retains His prerogative to decide what is and is not valuable in—and transferable to—the Kingdom. Throughout this book, we will refer to the Choice Space—the place of decision between the carnal mind and the spiritual mind, between union with the Spirit and immersion in the world; and ultimately, between life and death. It is the choice between the service of one of two masters, God, or mammon. We make that choice moment-by-moment, in the mundane and the spectacular, in the routine and the extraordinary.

To question God in the flesh is to find fault with Him. Paul's answer to those who would question His prerogative to conduct the affairs of the world and the Kingdom is in **Romans 9:20-21**:

> $^{20}$But indeed, O man, who are you to reply against God? Will the thing formed say to him who formed *it*, "Why have you made me like this?" $^{21}$Does not the potter have power over the clay, from the same lump to make one vessel for honor and another for dishonor?

There comes a point of line-crossing disobedience where God releases a people or an individual to go their own way and experience the consequences of fleshly choices. The end of such an undirected journey for us would be to wander in the desert until the resources and life available to us are squandered, just as they were for a whole generation of Israelites.

Finally, returning to **Ephesians 5:15-17**, we should note that Paul adds two key pieces of information to our time-redemption process. First, he writes, "$^{15}$See then that you walk *circumspectly*, not as fools but as wise." "Circumspectly" is not a word we hear or use a lot these days, so for clarity, here is a partial listing of synonyms:

- attentively
- conscientiously
- deliberately
- faithfully
- fully
- honorably
- meticulously
- precisely
- prudently
- thoroughly
- thoughtfully
- reliably
- dependably
- with forethought
- rigorously

"Walking circumspectly" has the idea of painstaking caution, and precisely matches the idea of an intentional pilgrimage. Walking circumspectly is to live mindfully, according to a plan, according to an understanding, and according to established wisdom. The second piece of information is in **verse 17** where Paul admonishes us to, "know what the will of the Lord is." In the next section, we will discuss that the difference between a servant and a friend of the Master is that the friend "knows what the master is doing," whereas the servant does not (**John 15:15**). If we intend to be in the "inner circle" of relationship with Jesus, it is required that we know both His ways and His acts. Knowing these begins with understanding His Program on the earth; and how our conduct in His Program results in, and translates directly to, our responsibilities in the Kingdom.

## A Discipleship Promotion—From Servant to Friend

Jesus' announcement to His disciples of their change of status in **John 15:15** was huge for them and huge for us today. Jesus' promotion of His disciples from *servant* status to *friend* status indicates that under His guardian/stewardship they had been taught what they needed to know about what the Father is doing in the earth (His Program). Paul refers to this relationship growth in his first letter to the Corinthians: "I fed you with *milk* and not with *solid food*; for until now you were not able *to receive it,* and even now you are still not able." (**1 Corinthians 3:2**) The principle of spiritual immaturity is in **Hebrews 5:12-14**:

> John 15:15, "*No longer do I call you servants*, for a servant does not know what his master is doing; *but I have called you friends*, for all things that I heard from My Father I have made known to you."

> $^{12}$For though by this time you ought to be teachers, you need someone to teach you again the *first principles* of the oracles of God; and you have come to need milk and not solid food. $^{13}$For everyone who partakes only of milk *is unskilled in the word* of

righteousness, for he is a **babe**. [14]But solid food belongs to those who are of **full age**, that is, those who **by reason of use have their senses exercised** to discern both good and evil.

Paul chides the Corinthians and the Hebrew believers in Jerusalem for not progressing from the milk (servant) to meat (friend) stage. And, if the disciples who sat with Jesus watching closely day-after-day had to reach a level of knowledge and experience to attain the level of "friend of the Master," what arrogance leads us to believe that we can attend church once or twice a week, spend precious little time otherwise learning what the Master is doing, and still sit and sing full-voiced, "What a *Friend* We Have in Jesus"? It takes beyond first-principles knowledge to qualify as His friend. Of course, we remain His servants; but friendship is another, a higher level of relational achievement.

Putting it all together in one visual, the two potential relationships look like this:

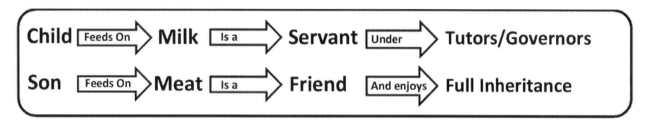

It is one thing to know what Jesus **did**, and quite another to know what He **is doing**! Knowing what He is doing applies not only to His immediate and current actions, but also to His overall Program, His goals for humanity, and His plans for our development. In other words, knowing what He is doing is to know the meaning of life! "Jesus loves you and He died for you" is *essential* first knowledge, but we are intended to take that knowledge and develop from it an understanding of the Master's *whole* program—and that is friendship and discipleship.

We have discussed the privilege of *kings* to search out the mysteries of the Kingdom. Addressing His disciples in **Luke 8:10**, Jesus said, "To you it has been given to know the *mysteries* of the kingdom of God, but *to the rest* it is given in parables, that, 'Seeing they may not see, and hearing they may not understand.'" The Scripture clearly draws a line in the sand between "you" and "the rest," indicating that there are two groups of people who hear His message: those *with*

> **Psalm 103:7**, "He made known **His ways** to Moses, **His acts** to the Children of Israel."

ears to hear, and those *without*. His message to the masses was veiled, but His disciples are expected to diligently apply themselves to deciphering the deeper meaning. *To fail to do so is to remain a servant, and one of the masses.* Failure for believers to understand the mysteries of the Kingdom is a tragic waste of opportunity. It really is impossible to overstate the value or the importance of visualizing and connecting with Papa's Program on earth. We transcend a lower dimension of relationship (servant) and access a higher dimension (friend) when we not only obey His commandments but *obey with knowledge*. Even better than knowledge is to internalize God's ways to the degree that your knowledge matures into wisdom, and finally, understanding.

> **The Learning Progression:**
>
> Knowledge (Information)
>
> ⬇
>
> Wisdom (Application)
>
> ⬇
>
> Understanding (Assimilation)

**Psalm 103:7** gives an indication of the difference between the servant level relationship and the friend level: "He made known **His ways** to Moses, **His acts** to the Children of Israel." It is one thing to see God's activities on the earth, and another to understand the purpose, nature, and goals behind the acts. We can pray, "Your kingdom come. Your will be done on earth as it is in heaven," from the servant perspective; but the same prayer from the friend perspective qualifies us for a higher level of partnership because we know *what that will is*, how it appears, and its effects are on people and events because we know what the Master is doing! We mature in the relationship status from child/minor to a son, ready and qualified to take our place in the Father's business and grow and extend the Kingdom. This higher dimension of interaction with the Father is not *uber*-achievement, but is, in fact, the *normal* Christian life as a friend of the Master. "To you it has been given to know the mysteries," implies that such knowledge and relationship is not only a gift but also a privilege of friend status. Jesus' announcement to His disciples of their change of status in **John 15:15** was a major change for them and remains so for us. Jesus' promotion of His disciples indicated that they had surpassed blind obedience and had replaced it with a cooperative partnership.

## What ~~Would~~ Did Jesus Do?

Modern philosophy says that to be enlightened, one must be cut loose from the anchors of past dogma, consider all truth to be relative, and be free to embrace new thinking that places man at the center of the universe and culture, not God. However, a society without an anchor is one adrift, and without direction or meaning. Modern philosophy devoid of God claims that life has no meaning, no grand purpose, other than its own experience and enjoyment. In that context, "Eat, drink, and be merry, for tomorrow we die!" is the logical, rational pursuit of "our" life.

While we speculate "What Would Jesus Do?" (WWJD), it is not necessary to speculate what His actions *actually were* because Scripture tells us in three places how He spent His time:

- **Matthew 4:23**, "And Jesus went about all Galilee, teaching in their synagogues, ***preaching the gospel of the kingdom***, and healing all kinds of sickness and all kinds of disease among the people."

- **Matthew 9:35**, "Then Jesus went about all the cities and villages, teaching in their synagogues, ***preaching the gospel of the kingdom***, and healing every sickness and every disease..."

- **Acts 1:3**, "[To] whom He [Jesus] also presented Himself alive after His suffering by many infallible proofs, being seen by them during forty days and ***speaking of the things pertaining to the Kingdom of God***."

We *must* recognize what was *constantly* on Jesus' mind—His Kingdom! Even the time between His resurrection and ascension—ostensibly His *last* opportunity to speak to them all directly—was dedicated to imparting information regarding the Kingdom to the disciples. If it was that important to Him, doesn't it make sense that it should command the center of our focus and attention as well? Any Scripture verse that begins, "The Kingdom of God/Heaven is like..." should immediately *snap to our grid of focus*.

Jesus knew He had a limited time of ministry on earth, and He did not waste any of it delivering extraneous messages. Even His healing ministry was for a targeted result: **John 10:38**, "[T]hough you do not believe Me, ***believe the works, that you may know and believe*** that the Father is in Me, and I in Him." For those with eyes to see, His whole orientation to life and ministry also reveals the purpose for ours, since, "it is no longer I who live, but Christ lives in me" (**Galatians 2:20**). It is unreasonable and illogical to think that He would live His life on earth with a particular intent and focus, and then continue that life *in us* with a *different* intent and focus! Many today pursue miracles as the main event, rather than seeing them for what they were/are: a warm-up band for the message of the Kingdom.

# What is Intentionality?

When I was a much younger man, I spent a period of time employed as a police officer. It was a wonderfully difficult time of chasing bad guys and struggling with my own imperfections. It left me with a permanent appreciation for the men and women that perform the service daily. One of my good friends that graduated from the police academy with me shared with me this story of one particularly priceless and campy service call—I will never forget it. It taught me the essence of being intentional in my pursuits (pun intended!). The call was dispatched as a "See the Complainant." This category was a sort of "other jobs as assigned" catch-all and meant that the dispatcher could not figure out a standard category into which to put the caller's request. The unpredictability of this call type made them frequently an adventure. This is the story he told:

When he arrived at the address—a quiet, modest and older residential neighborhood of single-story homes—the knock on the door was answered by a small, frail woman in her late 70's or 80's. She was obviously agitated and insisted that the officer come into the house immediately. Upon being asked how the Austin Police Department might be of service to her, the following conversation ensued.

"I want you to make those people stop having sex in their back yard," she said, pointing toward the house immediately across her back fence. This was a new one for my friend, and he must have looked somewhat dumbfounded as he stammered and searched for appropriate questions to ask.

"How do you know they are…ah…ah…doing that?" he asked lamely. The lady was matronly and grandmotherly, and it seemed inappropriate to be discussing such matters with her.

"I know because I can see them! I watch them!" she said, gesturing toward a sliding glass patio door leading into her own back yard. Still searching for appropriate questions and stalling for time, Dave (his name is David) walked to the sliding glass door and looked out toward the neighbor's house. There, running the length of her back property line was a six-foot privacy fence, in good condition, and blocking the view of her neighbor's property.

"Isn't this a one-story house?" Dave asked.

"Yes, of course, it is," said Ms. Stewart—we'll call her Ms. Stewart (not her real name).

"And you say you see them having se—ahh, relations—in their back yard?"

"Yes, it happens all the time, and I'm tired of it."

"But, Ms. Stewart, you can't even *see* into their back yard."

"That shows how much you know, young man."

What happened next taught me (and, I assume Dave—I haven't seen him in many years) a poignant lesson in intentionality that I will never forget. Ms. Stewart hobbled carefully over to the dining room table, grasped a massive dining chair, and slowly drug it into a carefully-positioned location, then adjusted it for precision. She then commenced to climb onto the chair—with great difficulty, and to Dave's alarm—and stand up on her tippy toes and lean far to her right.

"See? If you get up here and lean over as far as you can, you can see plenty!"

When Dave finished the story, we both laughed until we cried. He told the story to me as an amusing anecdote, but to me, it became a life-lesson—it was at that moment that I understood intentionality, with a side-serving of dedication!

# Intentionality and Connecting the Dots: It's Child's Play!

God's mysteries are by design of a nature that they must be sought after, studied, prayed over, and coached by the Holy Spirit. Mysteries are hidden for a reason, and our pursuit of His secrets and fulfilling the meaning of life must be *intentional*, not left to haphazard happenstance. There are *many* informational and actionable dots to connect:

- ☐ Scriptures to read
- ☐ Prayers to say
- ☐ Coaching to receive
- ☐ Thoughts to reframe
- ☐ Suffering to embrace
- ☐ Meditations in which to soak

- ☐ Wisdom to glean
- ☐ Ways to understand
- ☐ Interpretations to make
- ☐ Metaphors to contemplate
- ☐ Typology to connect
- ☐ Meanings to uncover

- ☐ Flesh to reject
- ☐ Wisdom to take in
- ☐ Attributes to imitate
- ☐ Discipleship plans to make
- ☐ Fruit of the Spirit to choose
- ☐ Good works to walk in

Papa has arranged our journey through the pilgrimage of life so that there is never a shortage of quests, any dearth of mysteries to solve, no lack of paradoxes to contemplate. There is always a new horizon rising before us, a new wrinkle of truth to conquer, and a new wavelength of His light to see for the first time. In fact, *if you are bored with life (or even aspects of life), that is direct evidence that you have yet to connect with life's eternal meaning.* It is expected that you and I will grow weary and need rest and refreshing along the way. It is predictable that we will become distracted and flag in our efforts toward intentionality. It is even inevitable that we will get lost from time-to-time. These are all contingencies for which Papa has planned and designed mechanisms to get us back on track. But boredom is a different issue; boredom is attitudinal, not structural. When we are bored, we suffer from a myopic vision: We are near-sighted to the degree that we cannot see beyond our immediate surroundings and interests. For believers that have connected with purpose and identity-driven life, boredom is a "red flag on steroids" that must never be tolerated without challenge.

> **Galatians 4:1-3**, "[1]Now I say that the heir, as long as he is a child, does not differ at all from a slave, though he is master of all, [2]but is under guardians and stewards until the time appointed by the father. [3]Even so we, when we were children, were in bondage under the elements of the world."

Most likely, we have all had the experience of playing "connect the dots" as children. Once the lines from dot-to-dot are drawn, a picture emerges that may then be colored in. The final objective of the activity—seeing the picture appear—is ostensibly the most important thing. But there is also value, challenge, and fun(!) in the process of dot connection. We use this exercise to occupy, educate, and stimulate our children. As we move on further in *The Last 15-Minutes*, I submit for your consideration that, as children of God, connecting the dots of His mysteries and secrets—hidden from all but those who would be kings—fulfills the same purpose in the Church. It is our privileged engagement as His children to "know what the Father is doing," and that takes some concerted effort. As we have discussed, Abba has set up His secrets and mysteries in such a manner that they must be searched for like one would search for gold or buried treasure. God bless our efforts to see behind the veil!

# Chapter 4—The Choice Space Explained

¹⁴For we know that the law is spiritual, but I am carnal, sold under sin. ¹⁵For what I am doing, I do not understand. For what I will to do, that I do not practice; but what I hate, that I do. ¹⁶If, then, I do what I will not to do, I agree with the law that it is good. ¹⁷But now, it is no longer I who do it, but sin that dwells in me. ¹⁸For I know that in me (that is, in my flesh) nothing good dwells; for to will is present with me, but how to perform what is good I do not find. *¹⁹For the good that I will to do, I do not do; but the evil I will not to do, that I practice.* ²⁰Now, if I do what I will not to do, it is no longer I who do it, but sin that dwells in me. (**Romans 7: 14-20**)

## The Nature of Choice

**Romans 7:14-25** gives words to the frustration that we all feel. It is a window into the basic conflict between the kingdom of this world and the Kingdom of our Lord and of His Christ as each individual believer experiences it internally. There are few more frustrating, more vexing, or more mystifying internal conflicts than the desire to do good with no ability to perform it. However, Paul gives us the key to our "wretched man" dilemma in **verse 25**. The answer is not behavior, it is a person—"Jesus Christ our Lord." It is not improving our appearance in the world. Jesus is not interested in making a nicer, more compliant, more polite, sweeter smelling version of your Independent Self. He *is* interested in taking over, and that requires your "self" to die. Our impatience and frustration with the process result from "right-hearted but wrong-headed" motivation. It is why our "heart set on pilgrimage" mindset is so important to grasp and maintain.

One does not typically just wake up one day and decide, "I think I will become a disciple today." If it were that easy, we could fit in several changes of life and genre every day—perhaps a little Christianity in the morning, Buddhism midday, and polish off the evening with Humanism, with a nightcap of Islam. Papa *could* transform us in that way, but He usually elects for a much more protracted process so that we do not come out of the oven half-baked. Our wrong-headedness is a lack of understanding of how permanent change takes place in us. The frustration associated with the Choice Space goes away—or is greatly mollified—when we finally get it that the pilgrimage is a *long-life* and *life-long* process. It is putting one faithful foot in front of the other over the course of a lifetime. The fix is not changing behavior, but rather changing the *source* of our behavior. The fix is regeneration, renewal, and transformation—and those things take time.

Life in the classroom is all about choices; the Choice Space takes place in the virtual space between the carnal and spiritual minds where we transact resources Papa has given us—time, identity, and choice. It is the place where we determine the degree to which we are transformed, and the direction of that change, positive or negative. A dilemma is a place of choice by definition and the daily exercise *workout* that *works out* our salvation. It is the struggle of our soul against the chaotic insistence of our separated flesh, and it is a contest that will be with us until our last breath. It is the power struggle for controlling authority between our Independent Self and our Union Self. If you are still battling against sin, you are fighting a paper tiger—an illusion—because Jesus has solved our sin problem. *Now* we struggle against the flesh—weakness—that inhibits our development into a mature Union Self Son of the Kingdom. One accurate *functional* definition of life is, "A series of conscious and unconscious choices that determine future Kingdom responsibilities." It is where the "will to do" and the "that I practice" are merged (**Romans 7:19**).

> **"When you come to a fork in the road, take it." Yogi Berra**

## Jesus' Priestly Prayer

I am pretty sure that, when Jesus prays for you, He gets that for which He asks. I am also pretty sure that whatever blessing He prays for me, I want! There may be no more precious words in the New Testament than Jesus' priestly prayer for His disciples, and also for us by extension.

> [9]I pray for them. I do not pray for the world but for those whom You have given Me, for they are Yours. [10]And all Mine are Yours, and Yours are Mine, and I am glorified in them. [11]Now I am no longer in the world, but these are in the world, and I come to You. Holy Father, keep through Your name those whom You have given Me, *that they may be one as We are.* (John 17:9-11)

It is really great to know that Jesus prayed for us right before He went to His death on the cross. So, what is the primary blessing that Jesus prays? Oneness. Oneness is a huge word with huge ramifications! However, there are several ways that oneness can be interpreted, and several ways it can be contextually understood. It is interesting to note what Jesus *did not* pray for them and us. He did not ask for faith; He did not ask for wisdom; He said nothing about works, or miracles, or anything "flash/bang." He did not even mention character traits, doctrinal correctness, or spiritual success. He prayed for oneness, with each other, with Him, and with the Father. *He knew that with oneness comes all of the other things that we need.* He prayed for oneness because Jesus understood that it is the foundation of all other activities and success. He prayed for oneness because He knew that achieving it would take all of our focus, effort, and attention; but success would bring all of the other spiritual results that we typically seek. Jesus prayed *strategically, and He prayed with the end in mind.*

My experience has been that when we hear messages about oneness, the context is usually "unity of thought, feeling, belief, aim, agreement; concord." That application is one that fits well within our western mindset. But that is *not* the meaning or context in which Jesus uses it. As is always the case, the most accurate definitions of words come from the Scripture itself; and "oneness" is defined in **John 17:21**, "[21]that they all may be one, as You, Father, are in Me, and I in You; that they also may be one in Us"; and again in **17:23**, "[23]I in them, and You in Me." When Jesus talked about being one, He was speaking about a union, about conjoining, and about shared identity. Oneness is about no distance between us: No separation in spirit, soul, and ultimately, in the body.

Oneness is the polar opposite of the Independent Self, as we will see in *Part 2—The Tool Chest* with the discussion of each of the Fruits of the Spirit. So, in asking the Father to make us one, *Jesus effectively spoke out of existence our Independent Self.* I recently attended a Trust-Based Relational Intervention course and was reminded how science confirms what scripture taught us long ago—that our connections to one another, our parents, our children, our friends, and ultimately the Body of Christ—are the most influential force for empowering security in human beings. Children without strong attachment skills and habits grow up with issues not experienced with those with strong skills. Adults that were children without attachment skills usually produce children without the skills to connect. Fortunately, there is hope even for the unattached and the seemingly unattachable, and that hope is found in Jesus' prayer.

The Greek word in **John 17** (all instances) is *heis*, and it means "one and the same" or "one virtually by union." *"Heis"* is also the word Jesus uses in **Matthew 19:5** describing the union of man and woman in marriage: "'For this reason, a man will leave his father and mother and be united to his wife, and the two will become *one* flesh.'" This meaning makes perfect sense when applied to the metaphor of Bride and Bridegroom reflected in Christ and the Church. We certainly should strive to be in agreement, in "one accord" as was reported of the followers of Jesus in **Acts 2:1**. We are right to pursue "unity of the faith" as Paul urges in **Ephesians 4:13**. Nevertheless, to depreciate Jesus' prayer for oneness by relegating it to harmony and agreement is to miss the essential nature of union, and risk misunderstanding the objective of the salvation process.

## Replacement and Union

There is another understanding that is *key* to the salvation process, and it is this: Papa is not interested in improving *you* because, in His eyes, you are already dead. Transformation does not result in some kind of weird mixture of Him and you. Transformation results in Him *replacing* the you that you know with the Him that He is—"I AM" replaces "you are." As He replaces you, the reality of "Christ in you, the hope of glory" becomes manifest, and the mystery is made plain for those with eyes to see. Our spirit union *was* accomplished *once and for all time* with Jesus' death on the cross; our soul union *is being* accomplished incrementally as a function of the discipleship process. In very real terms, our life quest as a believer is to be completely transformed—completely replaced—by the life of Christ in our body. *That* is "Christ *in* me, *as* me!"

> **Colossians 1:27**, "To them God willed to make known what are the riches of the glory of this mystery among the Gentiles: *which is Christ in you, the hope of glory*.

Consider these two Scriptures here side-by-side, and their relationship to our pilgrimage:

- **Colossians 1:27**, "To them, God willed to make known what are the riches of the glory of this mystery among the Gentiles: *which is Christ in you, the hope of glory*."

And,

- **Galatians 2:20**, "I am crucified with Christ: *nevertheless, I live; yet not I*, but Christ lives in me: and *the life which I now live in the flesh I live by the faith of the Son of God,* who loved me, and gave himself for me."

This the "Hope of Glory Principle," *Christ in me, as me!* Even believers well-practiced at taking Papa at His word have difficulty accepting the plain, literal meaning of the words of **Colossians 1:27** and **Galatians 2:20**. The resistance comes from our deeply-seated separated thinking and the fact that we have a difficult time wrapping our understanding around truth so different from our daily experience in the world. One need not be a mystic to hold the thought of union in one's mind; yet, it is a great mystery simply because it is an other-worldly concept. If we could grasp this *one* principle—the Hope of Glory Principle—the rest of this book (and the content of many other Christian books!) would be unnecessary. About the best we can muster is to acknowledge the truth of the Scripture, admit that we don't understand it, *but accept it anyway*. Then, over time, the Holy Spirit teaches us the deep mysteries of God—embracing always comes before understanding.

A central truth of the Kingdom is that, as believers, we are ***one spirit*** with Christ. In turn, He is one Spirit with the Father and the Holy Spirit. Therefore, by equivalence, we are *one spirit* with the whole Godhead! "One spirit" is mind-blowing! "One spirit" is astonishing, and so foreign to our thinking that unless we dedicate significant effort to meditating on and contemplating its meaning, we are likely to miss it altogether. Another way to say "one spirit" is to say that we are in *union*

> **1 Corinthians 6:17**, "But he who is joined to the Lord is *one spirit* with Him."

with Him. What are the implications of this Truth? They are staggering beyond comprehension, and so far beyond our finite minds that, if we study continuously for our entire biological life, we would only scratch the surface at best. Yet, as kings, we are driven to try to understand His mysteries and to seek to experience Union.

In **1 Corinthians 6:17,** Paul explodes our world with an astounding statement! Ready or not, here is an amazing truth: He (God) and I/you are the same being! That is, assuming you are a believer, you are an actual, *literal* expression of God in, and to, the world.[12] Union on the spiritual plane means "no separation." Not "small" separation, or "so-close-we-are-touching" separation—*no* separation! That is so difficult for us to contemplate because we fundamentally think of the world in "me/other-than-me" terms. The self-centric "me/other than me" awareness is the outcome of the fall of man in the Garden of Eden, and the first—and ongoing--casualty of that event.

We have no problem making **Acts 17:28** a metaphor, but we have difficulty wrapping our mind around how we literally could, in Him, "live and move and have our being." I am no different and have struggled with how **Acts 17:28** and **Colossians 1:17** can be anything other than a metaphor. However, I

> **Acts 17:28**, "[F]or in Him we live and move and have our being."

also know that, as in other paradoxes of Scripture, the fact that I cannot readily see the connecting bridge does not mean that there is not one. Therefore, I hold the assurance of the truth in my mind until I can see the bridge connecting the two ends of the paradox. **Colossians 1:17** tells us that, "in Him all things consist [hold together]." He is simultaneously bigger than the universe itself, and the microscopic glue that holds our atoms in their configuration. He holds galaxies in their orbit and electrons in theirs! In a very real sense, the concept of size is only human accommodation to give us a touch-point for relating to something familiar in our frame of reference. Knowing that, it is more easily imagined how we may lack the equipment and frame of reference to ever fully grasp His substance until we see Him face-to-Face.

The simultaneously tragic and wonderful result of man's Fall in the Garden of Eden was the initial cleaving of the spirit of mankind and the Spirit of God—to that point they had experienced perfect

> By His Sovereign act of sacrifice, our justification resulted in *full restoration of union in our spirit*; and, our engagement in the salvation process *is resulting in our incremental replacement by the life of the Lord Jesus in our soul.*

fellowship. We were severed in both our fellowship with Father and with our true self. The result was tragic in that so much was lost and ceded to the enemy. But it was wonderful in that it is God's Program in the earth to restore that which has been squandered. Sin nature is first and foremost *separation* as a root cause before it is *bad behavior* as a consequence. As a result of the Fall, every human being born from that day to this—save One, the Lord Jesus—has been born an Independent Self and the inheritor of a Sin nature. Independence in this context does not have the seductive and magnetic positive connotations that we often associate with the word. Without Him, we are so utterly alone, even if in a relationship with others traveling on this same starship through time and space. With Him, we are joined with the Majesty on High at the sub-sub-atomic level! Here is the distilled truth regarding our union with Papa: By His sovereign act of sacrifice, our justification resulted in the *full* restoration of union in our spirit; and our engagement in the salvation process is resulting in our incremental replacement by the life of Jesus in our mind, will, and emotions.

---

[12] An excellent discussion of this truth can be found in Bill Volkman's book, *The Wink of Faith*. See Volkman, Bill, *The Wink of Faith*. Union Life Ministries Publishers, Glyn Ellen, Ill. 1983. pp. 63-86.

To be in union is not the same thing as being in unity. Unity is agreement and likeminded-ness, with each party retaining their full autonomy. Union is total assimilation of being and essence. It is to be absorbed in the Divine. The word "assimilate" is a combination of two Latin words meaning "to make like" and "like, resembling." In the same context, consider the difference between a "conglomerate" and a "collective." A conglomerate consists of any aggregation of unlike

> **Corinthians 12:12**, "Now you are the body of Christ, and members individually."

substances that are in a relationship but retain their individual qualities. A collective, on the other hand, also consists of "members" (in the sense of "body members" or parts) whose relationship is the essential element of the dependency. In a conglomerate, pieces can be "bolted on"; in a collective, they must be absorbed in order to make their contribution to the whole. Their contribution organically changes the identity and quality of the organism. Paul clearly indicates this idea in 1 Corinthians 12:12-29. To be in a conglomerate body is to be a Frankenstein monster; to be a member of the collective is the Body of Christ.

I have struggled to discover *some* language, *some* analogy to describe the "no separation" truth. The best I can come up with is this example from my woodshop, and it is even grossly inadequate. I enjoy deluding myself that I am a woodworker; and, when I make a piece of furniture, I often join two or more pieces into a more suitable single board configuration to accomplish my goals. These boards are joined together edge-to-edge, or surface-to-surface using various bonding methods and high-quality glue. The obvious applications of our justification standing as joining surface, and the function of the Holy Spirit as "glue" are immediately apparent. Add the "clamps" of our love relationship to our Bridegroom to pull it all tightly together, and the curing effect of our salvation process to make it strong, and the result is not two boards in close proximity, but rather *one board* that is now useful for shaping and service.

The original identity of the individual board(s) becomes *almost indistinguishable* except for the qualities and nature of the individual boards. For example, I may join two boards, one mahogany, a darker species, and one maple a lighter species. They become one board of two components that maintain their individual contribution. The former separation is no longer relevant, only the rich tapestry effect of the diversity of gifting. Whatever space was originally between the planks has now disappeared as a function of the glue's bonding; and, the new joint is actually stronger than the individual pieces of wood previously were on  their own. Obviously, the analogy breaks down at some point, but it serves to illustrate how I can claim to be my silly self and an expression of the God of Gods simultaneously. "One spirit" means we cease to be an Independent Self, and we are assimilated into the collective Body of Christ.

## The Independent Self and the Collective Body

One has to wonder, in a prevalent conglomerate atmosphere of so many Independent Selves bolted on to one another, if there is any hope for the Body of Christ to ever come into oneness as Jesus prayed for us. Don't get me wrong—there are plenty of examples of the Body moving in *unity*. But as already noted, unity is not the same thing as union. A natural follow-up question in the discussion of eradicating the Independent Self in the Church is, "Is there any place for individuality in the collective which is the Bride of Christ?" The answer is, "Of course!"

One of the precious things about our eternal identity is that we are all known by Papa by highly specialized characteristics—gifting—that creates a niche for us. That is the lesson of **Proverbs 18:16**; and, it is also the lesson of **1 Corinthians 12:12-21**:

¹²For as the body is one and has many members, but all the members of that one body, being many, are one body, so also is Christ. ¹³For by one Spirit we were all baptized into one body—whether Jews or Greeks, whether slaves or free—and have all been made to drink into one Spirit. ¹⁴For, in fact, the body is not one member but many. ¹⁵If the foot should say, "Because I am not a hand, I am not of the body," is it therefore not of the body? ¹⁶And if the ear should say, "Because I am not an eye, I am not of the body," is it therefore not of the body? ¹⁷If the whole body were an eye, where would be the hearing? If the whole were hearing, where would be the smelling? ¹⁸But now God has set the members, each one of them, in the body just as He pleased. ¹⁹And if they were all one member, where would the body be? ²⁰But now indeed there are many members, yet one body. ²¹And the eye cannot say to the hand, "I have no need of you"; nor again the head to the feet, "I have no need of you."

> **Proverbs 18:16**, "A man's gift makes room for him, and brings him before great men."

Paul's writing to the Corinthian Church makes clear that the purposes of spiritual gifts are four-fold: 1) to ensure an adequate distribution of ministry across the geographically-separated Church Body; 2) to secure the advantage that "specialization of function" provides to the Body of Christ; 3) to ensure the *interdependence* (not *independence*!) of members of the Body on one another and on the Holy Spirit; and 4) serve as a source of individual identity for members of the Body that transcends fleshly traits/characteristics (e.g. Jew or Greek, slave or free).

When we learn to contextualize *everything* in terms of the meaning of life, we necessarily include our approach to ministry. Whatever Papa does both in and through us in a ministry setting always supports His overall work. *That* is why all members are indispensable; *that* is why we see what the Father is doing

> **Hebrews 2:10**, "For it was fitting for Him, for whom are all things and by whom are all things, in bringing many sons to glory, to make the captain of their salvation perfect through sufferings."

today in the context of what He is doing across time/space/matter and eternal realities. So, an important follow-up question becomes, "Is discipleship a topic for the individual acting alone, or for the whole Body acting together?" The answer is "Yes." We have emphasized the role of each believer coming into a disciple relationship with the Holy Spirit, and that is where the forward movement begins. Papa did not design the relationship to remain isolated but to function without a hitch across local groups, regional organizations, and even the world-wide Body of Christ. **1 Corinthians 12:20** emphasizes that the many members make up one body; and it emphasizes that for the Body to function correctly and as designed, each member must function in its intended role. That is where individual and personal discipleship comes in. It is evident that before the collective can function, the individual must be functional. So, when Jesus tells us in **Matthew 28:19** to "Go therefore and make disciples of all the nations," the process necessarily begins at home—with us and in me—living the life, doing the stuff, and being the "I AM." Then, once the individual members of any local expression of the Body of Christ are functional, they may be shaped into a discipleship force that carries the impact of genuineness and integrity. Recall that in **John 13:17** Jesus said, "If you know these things, blessed are you if you **do** them." He did not say "Blessed are you if you **teach** them"; nor did He only say "Blessed are you if you **know** them." Without functioning individual disciples, the Church is no more than a conglomerated, disjointed mess of dysfunctional body parts.

It is the intended purpose of the "captain of [our] salvation" to bring ***many*** sons into glory (**Hebrews 2:10**)! That can best be accomplished by a shaped and cooperative effort of local churches and in cooperation with extra-local organizations—each playing their own role. When disciples are taught to embrace their purpose of preparing for their role beside the Bridegroom and building the Kingdom in this life, they can band together to enjoy the synergy, momentum, and blessing of a collective effort that Jesus pronounced.

## When God Plays "Let's Make a Deal"

Perhaps many have watched the long-running, popular television game show, *Let's Make A Deal*. The game show, with its first host Monte Hall, was entertaining largely because it traded on the unknown and the human tendency to minimize risk and assume an optimistic outcome when considering our future circumstances. Mathematics has even given a name to the set of probabilities presented by the choice of "Door #1," "Curtain #3," or "keep the $1000 you have already won." It is called the *Monte Hall Problem*.

The heavenly version of *Let's Make a Deal* operates on a different premise and by a different set of rules. First, the heavenly show's host—the Holy Spirit—is totally on the contestant's side, and gives him or her all kinds of hints and coaching about which choice optimizes their good and beneficial outcome. He does that in a number of ways, not the least of which is that He opens the doors, pulls back the curtain, and lifts the box to *let the contestants see* what the outcome of their choice will be before they have to make it. That may seem to you like a rigged system. You are correct! It *is totally* rigged, and it is rigged *in your favor*! The truth is that you cannot lose if you are paying attention at all.

When the Holy Spirit calls a believer from their contestant's seat and into the aisle—onto the stage, as it were—we leave our place as an observer of life and become a full-fledged active participant and partner. There, He gives us three choices—"Choose you this day whom you will serve." This initial choice is, of course, crucial to determining future choices and actions. **Joshua 24:15** tells us our potential initial choices behind Doors #1, #2, or #3:

> Door #1: "The gods your father served that were on the other side of the River." The "god on the other side of the River" is a false god, a god of religion, a god of rules and laws and rituals that cover sin but are unable to remove it.

> Door #2: "The gods of the Amorites." The gods of the Amorites are neither the true God nor the god of religion. The names "Amorites" and "Amalekites" seem to be used interchangeably as a group of people descended from Cain (who killed his brother, Able, in a fit of jealousy). In typology, Amalekites stand for "the flesh," with which we will always be at war all of our days. Those that choose to serve "the gods of the Amorites" have chosen to serve the flesh, and enthrone themselves at the center of their life.

> **Joshua 24:15**, "And if it seems evil to you to serve the Lord, choose for yourselves this day whom you will serve, whether the *gods which your fathers served* that were on the other side of the River, or the *gods of the Amorites*, in whose land you dwell. But as for me and my house, we will *serve the Lord*."

> Door #3: "We will serve the Lord." For those who understand the Choice Space, Door #3 is the only rational choice and the only one that is in the contestant's best and highest interest. Choosing to serve the Lord over religion and self opens up endless possibilities of good, including all of the "exceedingly great and precious promises [by which we] partake in the divine nature and escape the corruption that is in the world through lust" (**2 Peter 1:4**).

God's deal is different than the world's deal in that He tells us plainly ahead of time what is the nature of our choice. He tells us the consequences. He tells us the potential and future of each. From that perspective, it is truly mind-boggling to think that any person of reasonable spiritual snap would make any other choice than Door #3, to serve the Lord, and to serve Him in each choice as it appears.

Our initial declaration to serve the Lord opens up many, many future selections and choices, each potentially greater and more marvelous than the last. Here is how it works: The Holy Spirit calls us out of our contestant's seat into the arena of choice to face the carnal mind/spiritual mind dilemma. Here, we face situations and circumstances that compel us to embrace the consequences of our Door #3 decision: choices that regenerate, transform, and renew us—or not; choices that move us further and deeper into the Promised Land or sentence us to another lap around the mountain in the wilderness. As we stand in the throes of choice, evaluating our decision, a myriad of voices from the studio audience crash in upon our conscious and unconscious mind. Some of the voices are friendly and helpful; some are destructive and deceptive, bent on misleading.

Just when it seems like the chaos will overwhelm us, the still, small voice—the voice of our Father—whispers in our ear, and suddenly, our choice is clear. I love this scene from *Indiana Jones and the Last Crusade*:

> Professor Henry Jones: "Junior, give me your other hand! I can't hold on!"
>
> Indiana Jones: [reaching for the Grail] "I can get it. I can almost reach it, Dad..."
>
> Professor Henry Jones: [speaking quietly, calmly] "Indiana."
>
> [Surprised, Indy looks up at his father]
>
> Professor Henry Jones: "Indiana...let it go."

At that moment in time, all becomes crystal-clear. We know our heritage, our role, and the Kingdom to which we belong. At that moment, when the Father is reaching out His hand and urging us to take it, and we look deeply into His eyes and see the love and the pride He has for us, we are strengthened to make the right choice, the Kingdom choice. At that moment we are pulled to safety and changed, little by little, bit by bit, inch by excruciating inch. After the right choice is secured in our experience hundreds or thousands of times, we begin to look like Him. We begin to think like Him. We begin to know Him, and He knows us. We begin to be Him.

## The Choice Between Two Gods

**Psalm 31:14**, "But as for me, I trust in You, O Lord; I say, 'You are my God.'" The older I get, the more clearly I see that there is one central issue in life: "Who do I/you serve as God?" Our answer to this question neither changes adds to, nor diminishes from the fact that Yahweh is God from eternity past to eternity future. Our answer does, however, change the quality of experience in this slice of eternity that we call time/space/matter, and determines positionally the place I/you will occupy in the Age to come. The wise have grasped that *God is currently staffing a Kingdom*, not with angels to sit on clouds and strum harps, but with active partners who share His values and continue to advance His Kingdom throughout eternity. He is a *King* who rules over a visible, literal *Kingdom* that exists for His will and benefit, not a glee club of spirits that recline at a table throughout eternity!

The ultimate answer to the, "Who do you serve?" question boils down to *whose voice you choose to obey*, not necessarily who you claim to serve—**Romans 6:16** is clear on that point. The choice is by nature one of two: Me as a god (in my carnal capacity of Independent Self); or Yahweh God (in our spiritual union with His Collective Self). If we fail to intentionally submit our Independent Self to our true God and Father, to obey His voice speaking through our spirit, it will always assert itself to be "...like the Most High," and to be enthroned "...above the heights of the clouds" (**Isaiah 14:14**). Perhaps you will recognize those words as Satan's aspiration in his rebellion against God. His goal has not changed, and he used it to his advantage in his manipulation of Eve in the Garden of Eden. The motivation to be "like God" was at the heart of Eve's deception; it also continues to be the critical question in our soul when facing a decision

> **Romans 6:16**, "Do you not know that to whom you *present yourselves slaves to obey, you are that one's slaves whom you obey*, whether of sin leading to death, or of obedience leading to righteousness?"

in Choice Space. The default answer—the one that happens in the absence of intentional action—is "self," or the carnal mind. But when a person is favored by grace to perceive that the life-giving spiritual mind answer is Abba Father it opens their soul to the process of salvation—the process of re-orienting our self-centeredness to a God-centered Person. It is imperative that we see that salvation is not a once-for-all-time decision, but a choice-by-choice decision of will in the Choice Space! Justification, yes, but salvation, no. When we give up our futile and evil attempt to be "*like* God," in the flesh and embrace union in spirit and soul, we have flipped the switch that enables His power to flow and fuse us into His "all in all."

The foregoing brings us to the heart of the paradox: When we choose to abandon our "be like God" pursuit, He begins to remake us into His image! Salvation transforms us into the image of Christ and instills the nature of the Father in us. Transformation is the objective of discipleship. It is more than a little ironic that we arrive at our destination when we embark on a pilgrimage 180 degrees out of phase with our flesh, our instincts, and natural inclinations. God confines His work to the willing, the weak, the incapable, the needy, the disenfranchised, and the desperate. The process reflects these paradoxical truths sprinkled throughout Scripture:

- Only that which dies ultimately lives (**John 12:24**);
- He who loses his life shall find it (**Matthew 16:25**);
- Give away whatever He has given to you (**Matthew 5:42**);
- When I am weak then I am strong (**2 Corinthians 12:10**);
- I am dead, nevertheless, I live (**Galatians 2:20**).

## The "Frustration-to-Focus Cycle"

One of the facts of the modern world is that frustration is rampant in daily life. The wonders of communication acquaint us with events and situations that cause our teeth to grind even if they are not in our immediate vicinity or do not directly impact us. Personal and business interactions have changed dramatically in the past generation, and the changes are both wonderful and maddening as the *competition* for our attention *consumes* our attention. Issues of faith that were unquestioned in previous generations are categorically rejected by many, and there is a strong push in our society to completely remove any residual. One result is a general increase in anxiety and all the ramifications that accompany it. Jesus' referral to the seed that fell by the wayside (**Matthew 13:22**) and was choked out by the "cares of this world and the deceitfulness of riches" has never been more real or more pressing than today.

But in addition to the dark side of frustrations, when our thinking is re-framed, they also have a spirit-boosting upside! Frustrations are designed by our Creator to motivate us to overcome our inaction. That means that frustrations, viewed appropriately, are the first step in accomplishing your mission! Frustrations are designed to drive us from complacency and goad us into action. To the trained consciousness, they bridge the gap between our "as is" and "could be" perception.

> ## The Frustration-to-Focus Cycle
>
> - God gives you frustration to inspire dreaming. *Frustration without a dream is **vanity**;*
> - He gives you a dream to inspire a vision. *A dream without a vision **is fantasy**;*
> - He gives vision to inspire you to set goals. *A vision without a goal is **purposeless**;*
> - He provides a goal to inspire you to make a plan. *A goal without a plan is **wishful thinking**;*
> - God gives you a plan to give you focus. *A plan without focus is **unworkable**.*
> - He gives you focus see your mission clearly and stay on task. *Focus without a mission is **myopia**.*

Frustration and contentment—though seemingly antagonistic—are complementary states and cooperate in this way: Frustration drives us and contentment is the enjoyment of the place of peace that results from making progress along our continuum of spiritual growth. A holy frustration is experienced in the emotions and intellect, but it is overcome as an act of will. It is the result of recognizing the need for change. Contentment is the settled result of successfully acting. It is not necessary to have completed the process to be content, only to know that we are making meaningful progress, that stagnation has been overcome, and that we are responding to the voice of the Spirit. If frustration is the beginning point of action, a razor-sharp focus is the intended result.

Frustration without movement results in exasperation—it must be transitioned to action to be effective. Without hope, frustration has nowhere to go. Many people confuse wishful thinking with hope,

> "Hope" and "wishful thinking" are not the same things!

but there are major differences. Both are initiated in a desire; but hope is active, going beyond desire to attach action; and hope operates on the *assurance* of the promise of the One who is able to accomplish all things. Hope is a catalyst; wishful thinking is a waste of time. The positive advantage of hope is revealed in **Romans 5:5**, "Now hope does not disappoint, because the love of God has been poured out in our hearts by the Holy Spirit who was given to us." Hope *never* disappoints us because its objective is assured in us by the Holy Spirit. Wishing carries no such assurance. Wishful thinking is easily discouraged and stops short of action. Wishing is initiated in our flesh and consumed with the *prospect of having* rather than the *assurance of attaining*. Hope has its origin in the Mind of the Spirit; Who, according to **Psalm 37:4**, is responsible for the initiation of our desires in the purposes of God (e.g., "He shall *give you* the desires of your heart" in the sense of putting them there in the first place).

In between frustration and focus is a planning process based on the input of the Holy Spirit, and

> **Psalm 37:4**, "Delight yourself also in the Lord, and He shall *give you the desires of your heart*."

prayerful consideration of component process and ordered steps. Spiritual vision is our window on the eternal realm and, therefore, what is possible. To attempt to accomplish something for God without accessing *His version* of the finished process is to waste our time with dead works, and that sounds a lot like wishful thinking. Dead works by definition do not comply with the Builder's specifications and plans and are fit only to be torn down or consumed by fire.

We are only as successful in completing the journey from frustration to focus as we are able to maintain our grasp on our purpose. There is *no mystery* about how and why Jesus was able to endure the suffering for which He was ordained. **Hebrews 12:2** tells us, "[L]ooking unto Jesus, the author, and finisher of our faith, *who for the joy that was set before Him* endured the cross, despising the shame." Meditating on the joy of His future Kingdom provided the context that gave Him endurance. His example makes the first principle of our endurance and perseverance in trials and tribulations to be ever and eternally to focus on *"Context, context, context!"*

# The Choice Space: The Discipleship Triad

If the meaning of life is to prepare believers to rule beside our Bridegroom; and if life is a dynamic learning environment complete with a curriculum, instructor/coach, learning objectives, tests, and homework, it makes sense that there would be a teaching strategy employed by the Holy Spirit to accomplish our learning. He has a three-part strategic approach for changing us from what we currently are into what we will eternally be. The three-part strategy is regeneration, transformation, and renewal. Each strategy is different to accomplish a different desired outcome.

## Strategy 1: Regeneration

Regeneration is about bringing life out of death, order out of chaos, and union out of separation. Death is not annihilation, it is disorganization, it is chaos, and it is separation. For example, **1 Timothy 5:6** presents the illustration of a widow who pursues pleasure in her widowed status, rather than living a godly life of prayer and supplication. Paul pronounces such a person, "dead while she lives." Her physical life had not come to an end, but her estate was one of confusion, chaos, and separation. If we could see death the way that Papa sees it, we would have a very different concept of its effect. We would

> **2 Corinthians 4:10** "[A]lways carrying about in the body the dying of the Lord Jesus, that the life of Jesus also may be manifested in our body."

learn that the physical death we fear so much is nothing more than a transition, a "putting off" of the body not much different than a beetle losing its skin or a hermit crab leaving one shell and moving to another when the original gets too confining. We would see that the areas of death remaining in us result in lives that are a mess. The regeneration effect restores life to the death we carry around in our bodies. It restores us to the order of life; we are regenerated to union with God in our mind, will, and emotions as we are washed with the word of His truth (**Ephesians 5:26**). Believers are intended to experience new levels of regeneration life daily—or, at least routinely. Jesus declared in **John 5:24**, "Most assuredly, I say to you, he who hears My word and believes in Him who sent Me has everlasting life, and shall not come into judgment, *but has passed from death into life.*" Passing from death into life is the regeneration effect.

Satan's "Plan B" is to keep us bound in a life of ineffectiveness, disorganization, and separation—in other words, a life that is "dead while [we] yet live." The cumulative heart-stomping effect of our tribulation in the world frequently leaves us a bloody mess, unable to feel (except anger!), unable to love ourselves or our neighbor, and unable to be a source of life. **In Romans 3:12**, Paul quotes King David's assertion in the Psalms that, "They have all turned aside; they have together become unprofitable; there is none who does good, no, not one" (**Psalm 14:3, Psalm 53:1-3**). Paul and David say that men have *become* corrupted, indicating a progressive, deteriorating slide. We are born dead, separated in spirit from God, and we become progressively "deader" in our soul as a result of our trespasses, sins, and cumulative emotional scars. "Why does it matter when and how we get there—dead is dead?" one might ask. Au contraire! Dead *would be* dead if it were not for the "power of His resurrection," about which Paul wrote in **Philippians 3:10-11**:

> [10][T]hat I may know Him and the power of His resurrection, and the fellowship of His sufferings, being conformed to His death, [11]if, by any means, I may attain to the resurrection from the dead.

Soul corruption is the result of both what we do and what is done to us. We are born into the world with a Sin nature, separated from God in spirit, and in need of a Savior. As we age, our soul suffers the trauma of life and separation and accumulates corruption through the process, ultimately to the point of searing. It is from this dead-while-we-yet-live state that the Spirit regenerates us. Paul tells us that this trauma is the result of death reigning over the world as a result of Adam's fall, but the regeneration effect of Jesus' life in us reverses the reign of death over us:

> [17]For if by the one man's offense death reigned through the one, much more those who receive abundance of grace and of the gift of righteousness will reign in life through the One, Jesus Christ)...[21]so that as sin reigned in death, even so grace might reign through righteousness to eternal life through Jesus Christ our Lord. (**Romans 5:17, 21**)

Our soul suffers much violence in the early years of life. Even those fortunate enough to have a good childhood, the process of socialization in this world's system is brutal and vulgar as we are pounded into conformance during our formative years. Children can be savage to one another while establishing the social pecking order. It does not take long for the emotional beat down to begin and have its cumulative effect. The result, even for the best of us, is a bloody, scarred mess, often barely functional. One outcome of our ability to know instantaneously of world-wide and ghastly incidents of man's inhumanity to man is that it creates a layer of calloused mental "tissue" as a defense mechanism over our emotions. It is painful to watch, and it is painful and damaging to live. John Denver's 1977 tongue-in-cheek song, *You Dun Stomped on My Heart*, facetious and humorous at the time, takes on a more serious and ominous tone as *taboos* give way to *tattoos*, *civility* is replaced by *civil suit*, and the *golden rule* is crushed under the feet of the *gold rush*.

---

**You Dun Stomped on My Heart** (John Denver, 1977)
You dun stomped on my heart, and you mashed that sucker flat.
You just sorta stomped on my aorta.
You started going out with guys, I felt us drift apart,
And every step you took was a stomp upon my heart.

I only hope someday you'll get them low down blues.
In some smoky honky-tonk you'll look down at your shoes,
You'll think about that tender heart that you crushed beneath them soles,
With your clod-bustin' stompers, you left my heart so full of holes.
https://www.youtube.com/watch?v=79FracPReK4

---

The irony is that those who seem to have best adapted to the world's system of relationship and relating are frequently those with the thickest, most calloused skin and toughest scar tissue. The natural process teaches us all the wrong lessons as they pertain to the Kingdom of God, and the acculturation process that we experience has to be reversed and healed as we come into union. The normal net result of the socialization process is mind, will, and emotions that have been conditioned to be:

- Resistant to grace;
- Unwilling to forgive, show mercy;
- Fortified against further injury;
- Angry at perceived injustices;
- Hardened by repeated abuse;

- Hope-fatigued, discouraged, despondent;
- Hyper-sensitive to criticism;
- Independent and isolated from others;
- Preoccupied with fleshly lusts;
- Self-centered to the point of narcissism.

Obviously, not every person has been conditioned to an extreme degree in all of these areas. The hope we embrace under the weight of our trauma is that the child-like estate that Jesus declared to be welcome in His Presence (**Matthew 19:14**) remains recoverable, even if dead and buried by layer-upon-layer of abuse and neglect. Our regeneration quest is to be exfoliated of dead works, the scars of trauma, and unlearn our worldly coping mechanisms. The pre-eminent questions in the Choice Space process are,

"How does the regeneration process work?" and, "What is my part?" According to Paul's letter to Titus, regeneration takes place in two phases: 1) washing, and 2) renewal.

Think of your soul as covered with a thick layer of dry, calloused, dead skin. Then imagine your soul being washed—"exfoliated"—of all the dead layers by a process of scrubbing by God's loofah! God generously pours out His Holy Spirit on us (**Titus 3:6**), and there is no better cleaning astringent on earth or in heaven than the water of His Word, and the Holy Spirit's ability to strip away the death from our soul! Jesus said it this way in **John 13:10**: "He who is bathed [justification] needs only to wash his feet [regeneration], but is completely clean [salvation]." Step 2—Renewal—follows the cleansing. Renewal brings back to vitality that layer of life that has laid dormant, latent, and suppressed for so many

> **Titus 3:5-6**, "[5][N]ot by works of righteousness which we have done, but according to His mercy He saved us, through the *washing of regeneration and renewing of the Holy Spirit*, [6]whom He poured out on us abundantly through Jesus Christ our Savior."

years! Paul describes the result in us as "[By His grace and mercy He has] made us alive together with Christ" (**Ephesians 2:5**). Our souls take on the healthy glow that follows the removal of all that is dead in us.

The washing of regeneration accomplishes the process that **Ezekiel 36** prophesied would be ours:

> [25]Then I will sprinkle clean water on you, and you shall be clean; I will cleanse you from all your filthiness and from all your idols. [26]I will give you a new heart and put a new spirit within you; *I will take the heart of stone out of your flesh and give you a heart of flesh*.

A heart of flesh is a good thing because it indicates a return to the intended function, a return to feeling, a return to life. Regeneration replaces the dead, calcified rock beating in your chest for a live functioning and feeling organ. Regeneration accomplishes resurrection, and it is to that resurrection to which Paul aspired in **Philippians 3:10**, "[T]hat I may know Him and the power of His resurrection." He understood that our hope of resurrection is two-fold: 1) We are being resurrected to new life as we experience His regeneration in this life; and, 2) We will be resurrected to a new life in the Age to come.

Heart disease is a leading killer in today's world. The common saying, "What doesn't kill me only makes me better," is not necessarily the case. Sometimes, in the case of the state of your heart, what does not kill you only makes you sicker, more dysfunctional, more broken than ever before. That which does not kill you *outright* may be killing you *by degrees*! In the absence of regeneration, a slow, tortured, incremental death is not only descriptive of the end of many people's lives but describes the whole process of life from beginning to end, from birth to cessation of biological function. The state of our *physical* hearts accurately reflects the reality of our collective and individual *emotional* heart. Nobody gets out of this life alive. And, nobody grows to any ripe old age without experiencing many, *many* potential heart-stompin', heart-scarring, heart-wrenching, and heart-hardening experiences. Of course, some have it much worse than others; and some appear also to be more tender-hearted—at least in the beginning until the calloused hardness sets in—and therefore more susceptible to injury. All of us have this common experience: We begin life with a tender-if-self-centered heart that quickly calcifies into a stony mass of dysfunction. The calcification metamorphosis is all but unavoidable, given the fallen and separated state of humanity, and given the vulnerability with which we enter the T/S/M world.

## Strategy 2: Transformed into His image

There is a saying that goes, "Imitation is the sincerest form of flattery." That is somewhat true, but there is a higher, more sincere form—emulation. Emulation does not just want to "be like," it wants to "be." Emulation is imitation on steroids! That is the bottom-line goal of all of our efforts in discipleship—

not just to be *like* Jesus, but to actually *become* Him by taking on His nature, instilling His values and ways. That is **Galatians 2:20's** "I, yet not I…" in practice and in fulfillment! It is Paul's declaration of the wall of separation taken out of the way in **Ephesians 2:14-16**:

> ¹⁴For He Himself is our peace, who has made both one, and has broken down the middle wall of separation, ¹⁵having abolished in His flesh the enmity, that is, the law of commandments contained in ordinances, so as to create in Himself one new man from the two, thus making peace, ¹⁶and that He might reconcile them both to God in one body through the cross, thereby putting to death the enmity.

**Luke 9:24** is one of the Scriptures we glibly quote without attaching its literal spiritual meaning to our circumstances: "For whoever desires to save his life will lose it, but whoever loses his life for My sake will

> **Luke 9:24**, "For who-ever desires to save his life will lose it, but whoever loses his life for My sake will save it."

save it." Losing one's life is transformation. In this context, it does *not* mean to die physically. There is no martyrdom involved here except in the soul— which is still considerable! "Lose his life" means to be absorbed into the collective life of Christ in mind, will, and emotions. It means that His life overwhelms and engulfs existence so that my physical presence in the world is an expression of His spiritual presence. He replaces the "me" that the world knows; the lesser is assimilated into the greater. His life lives through my body, *in* me, *as* me. Therefore, to "save [one's] life" is to preserve my fleshly life. It means to remain separated, to hold myself distinct and detached from His collective mind and will. *It means remaining an Independent Self.*

Losing "our life" is difficult for us to contemplate because of the "me/other-than-me" life filter. Additionally, Colossians 3:3 reminds us that we are dead and we have no life but His. Papa never has had any problem viewing you as part of Himself. Further, it is Jesus' express wish and prayer for us that we be one with Him and with the Father in the same manner that He modeled for us in John **17:21-23**. Becoming one with Jesus and the Father is not self-aggrandizement, it is to lose one's self in the Collective Self of God, to merge one's identity with His. Additionally, it is to lose one's self with a particular purpose: "[T]hat the world may believe that you sent Me [Jesus]."

The big lie foisted on Eve in the Garden of Eden was, "You shall be *like* God." The serpent's lie to Eve in **Genesis 3:5** mirrored his rebellious declaration in **Isaiah 14:14**, "I will be *like* the Most High." But Papa has never desired that we be *like* Him. The desire to be *like* Him is rebellious and separated thinking because separated thinking always preserves something of me in the transaction. His purpose is to push past separation into union, past "me-other-than-me" into "One." (**John 17:21**). It is another of the Spirit's paradoxical truths to grasp that, for all of its appearance of humility, separated thinking is, at its heart, the pinnacle of arrogance. The reason is that as long as we preserve a distinction between Him and us, we will always enthrone ourselves as god—we can do no other. We used to sing a song in church that goes, "He walks with me, He talks with me, along life's narrow way." The words to the popular hymn not only preserve the distinction of me separate from Him, but they also imply that "me" is the center of the walking and talking action, and "He" *is there as the assistant*. That is god-enthronement in practice.

In all of this talk of union, there is a central truth: Jesus does not intend to preserve any distinction between Himself and the Bride. Instead, He intends for us to grow up and get past the faux humility of preserving our Independent Self, and grow into the life we are intended to live, "Christ in me, as me." The Holy Spirit is teaching us that we are intended to view ourselves as one with the Bridegroom, just as Paul wrote in **Ephesians 5:31-32**. Wrapping our finite mind

> **Colossians 1:27**, "To them God willed to make known what are the riches of the glory of this mystery among the Gentiles: **which is Christ in you**, the hope of glory."

around His infinite mystery is a significant challenge, but the beginning of understanding is to see and embrace the truth long before we totally get it.

Paul plainly tells us in **Ephesians 5:30-32** that Papa gave us the marriage relationship on earth to learn to reflect the realities of our spiritual union with Christ:

> [30]For we are members of His body, of His flesh and of His bones. [31]"For this reason a man shall leave his father and mother and be joined to his wife, *and the two shall become one flesh.*" [32]*This is a great mystery, but I speak concerning Christ and the church.*

When we read this Scripture, it seems that smoke immediately begins to come out of our ears, or we start explaining away the plain meaning. One means "one." We are so used to thinking as an Independent Self that we cannot imagine anything different. That is actually okay to a point because the Holy Spirit is delighted to teach us what it means. In fact, Papa has designed a whole T/S/M classroom experience to teach us what it means. Our part is to grasp that there is such a thing as oneness, and collective, and allow our puny brain and

> **Romans 12:2**, "And do not be *conformed* to this world, but be *transformed* by the renewing of your mind."

parochial self-interests to concede the possibilities. "One flesh" in the T/S/M world is the companion equivalent to "One Spirit" in the eternal. Paul wrote in **1 Corinthians 6:17**, "But he who is joined to the Lord is one spirit with Him." That is the fact. Now what remains is for us to adjust our Independent Self *feelings* to the *facts*.

When I attended Baylor University at the tender age of 20-years old, I worked to support myself in a crisis psychiatric facility. It was always fascinating to me that such a large percentage of people in mental crisis express it in the form of thinking of themselves as, and claiming to be, Jesus or God (occasionally, you run across a Moses). The mystery persisted until I realized that, at the heart of every one of Satan's lies and counterfeits is an underlying truth. No counterfeiter in their right mind would produce a $7 bill for the obvious reason: immediate detection and capture! When the fake is obvious, it doesn't fool anyone except the most gullible, and those not paying attention. It is the same with Satan's lies, and the wise believer sees the counterfeit and immediately seeks out the underlying truth. In the case of aberrant psychiatric behavior, Satan attempts to discredit the truth that

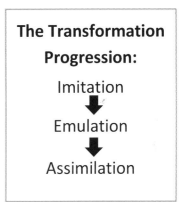

**The Transformation Progression:**

Imitation

⬇

Emulation

⬇

Assimilation

we are intended to progress in our understanding and view ourselves as one with God; and that oneness takes the form of "Christ in me, as me." That is transformation. That is the goal of discipleship.

To pursue the question, "What are the mechanics of the transformation process?" we return to the quote with which we opened this section: "Imitation is the sincerest form of flattery." To express this same modern idea in New Testament language, Paul introduced the complementary process components of "conformation" and "transformation." We may think about them in the complementary terms of imitation/emulation (conformation) and assimilation (transformation). Conforming is adapting or adjusting our Independent Self to the degree that we portray to the world the Life

> **Galatians 6:8**, "For he who sows to his flesh [chooses the carnal mind] will of the flesh reap corruption, but he who sows to the Spirit [chooses the spiritual mind] will of the Spirit reap everlasting life."

of Christ instead of "our life." But conformation in and of itself is an inferior response because it preserves some vestige of the Independent Self—though I conform *my* behavior to His life, it remains *my* behavior, attitudes, etc.

Conformed behavior is the correct *first step*; but if the next step of transformation does not occur, conformation has the potential of becoming rules and law, and "the pursuit of being nice." In other words, when we are satisfied with conforming our behavior without experiencing transformation, we stop making progress and lock in at a lower level. Then, that which was intended to be the path to life for me becomes death instead. It is a *great evil* when we turn that which is provided to be for our benefit into that which hinders our development.

What, then, is required to keep conforming from becoming death? It is to press on in the pilgrimage through conforming to transformation. As we keep on being faithful to imitate, at some point, we cease to imitate and we assimilate; that is, we become the change we are emulating. Often, it happens without our even noticing. The line between conformation and transformation can be understood as that point when the imitated behavior, attitudes, values, ways, etc. cease to become something I do and start to be something I am. That process can work for my growth *or in reverse* as I choose the carnal mind over the spiritual mind. The transformation has occurred when my T/S/M identity mirrors my eternal identity. The transformation has occurred when we can claim with integrity, "Christ in me, as me." We are transformed by the Life of Christ (**Romans 5:10**) in us because that life is active and effective in all that it touches.

> **Assimilate** (verb)
>
> 1. To take in and incorporate as one's own.
>
> http://www.dictionary.com/browse/assimilate?s=t

There are conditions that are prerequisite for transformation. The first is that our imitation of righteousness must not be possessed as our own or have its source in confidence in our own ability to conform. Conformed behavior in the absence of clear recognition of its source in the Spirit is law, and the law will never result in positive transformation. Paul expressed clearly where he found righteousness in **Philippians 3:9**, "and be found in Him, not having my own righteousness, which is from the law, but that which is through faith in Christ, the righteousness which is from God by faith." The second prerequisite is related to the first: We must be intentional about losing Independent Self and embracing the Collective Self. Finally, we must, "not grow weary in well-doing" (**Galatians 6:9**); this is the lesson of faithfulness, and of completing our pilgrimage without dying in the wilderness. Paul knew the dynamics of the process, and he understood the dangers of beginning the pilgrimage without finishing it. That is why he pleaded in **1 Corinthians 11:1**, "Imitate me as I also imitate Christ." Imitation is only the first step: We must press through all the way to transformation!

> **1 Corinthians 11:1**, "Imitate me as I also imitate Christ."

## Strategy 3: The Renewed Mind

We are, at times, very careless with guarding what comes into our mind, what goes out as speech and action, and what just hangs around in there. Our will and emotions play a large role in our transformation, but nothing influences our discipleship experience as much as what and how we think. In his writing, the Apostle Paul *assumes* that our minds need renewal—and for good reason. We live our whole T/S/M lives in enemy territory, and the assault of flesh-stimulating input is daily, if not continuous. Our "big lie" usurpation of God's prerogative to define truth is always at work in us. Reinforcement of the Independent Self is non-stop in our daily culture. The constant barrage leaves us in significant need of renewal if any progress is to be made toward

> **Ephesians 4:23-24**, "[23][A]nd be renewed in the spirit of your mind, [24]and that you put on the new man which was created according to God, in true righteousness and holiness."

replacing the world's attitudes, values, methodologies, and viewpoints. The enemy's influence is so pervasive in the world system that, unless countered by the truth of Scripture, even believers begin to adopt his ways as the "way things are done around here." A person of responsibility in the Kingdom must go into it with his or her mind having been overhauled to reflect the nature and priorities of the King.

Our mind is the center for a number of Kingdom-vital processes. First, truth resides in our spirit, but it is accessed for reference through our conscious mind. As a storage "cache" and communication access point to the Holy Spirit, our renewed mind is able to continuously compare our current situation and merge it with the truth of Scripture. My friends and I have adopted an "iron-sharpening-iron" system for encouraging one another. Frequently, some topic in our conversation will bring Scripture to mind; we pause our conversation and say, "That reminds me of a Scripture." We then share it and move on. Not a big deal; not a heavy teaching; just a light way to continuously direct our thoughts heavenward, and let our renewed mind keep us in the center of truth. By inputting God's word in our cache memory, a symbiotic relationship results as life reminds us of God's word and God's word informs us about life.

Second, our mind is the communication center between body and soul, and spirit and soul. When our body clamors for attention, it has a way of drowning out all other communication. But with a renewed mind, the word of life gets through. One of the skills of a renewed mind is the ability to put the flesh in its place. When Papa speaks to us, He speaks to our spirit; but our spirit communicates His words to our mind. Without at least some degree of mind renewal, the messages from our spirit meet a brick wall. It is like a radio that is tuned to a different frequency.

> **Romans 12:2**, "And do not be conformed to this world, but be transformed by the renewing of your mind, that you may prove what is that good and acceptable and perfect will of God."

Third, our mind is the center of our creative interaction with the Holy Spirit. New birth in the renewed mind looks like a childlike response that sees all things as conceivable, hopes all things as attainable, and believes all things as possible. When Papa speaks to our spirit, He creates faith; that faith is stored up in our mind, where it directs our response to the world. Creative thought is where the faith-to-action process begins. Revelation also takes place here, and that makes the renewed mind *the only legitimate way to know anything.* Until your mind experiences renewal, you can only know what others tell you is true—and that is a trap just waiting to spring.

Of all of the functions of our mind, none is more important than its role in allowing in or blocking out environmental stimuli. Our mind is the gatekeeper; and when our mind is ruled by the flesh or overwhelmed by worldly attitudes and priorities, the floodgates are wide open to whatever the enemy wishes to foist upon us. With mind-renewal comes a new values system, one that impedes or blocks the worldly tidal wave, but remains open to the whisper of the spirit. A renewed mind recognizes truth; that is, we learn to recognize lies because most often they are direct contradictions of truth that we have stored. Or, alternatively, they are $7 bills offered to us as legal tender.

Our renewed mind puts all of Papa's puzzle pieces together in some actionable form. It is not enough to have the knowledge, and it is certainly not enough to merely collect information—it must be fused into wisdom (knowledge of His ways) to ultimately be useful. Recall from Chapter 1 when Papa spoke and urged me to forsake Christianity for discipleship. A full-fledged renewed mind is what He was, and is, after. When wisdom is processed and contextualized through the filter of God's Program, it morphs into understanding—the highest form of mind-renewal to which we can attain! Our renewed mind is the fusion center that fights the confusion that is rampant in the world system. Confusion is a major weapon in the hand of the enemy. It keeps us bound behind enemy lines without a clear path home, or even forward. But our renewed mind thinks the thoughts of Christ, sees from His vantage point and evaluates according to His priorities. It sees relationships and connections between the moving parts in the spirit realm. Before renewal, the spiritual realm remains unreachable to the carnal mind. After renewal, understanding of God's ways and Program directs our spiritual interaction. That is what **1 John 2:27** means:

> But the anointing which you have received from Him abides in you, *and you do not need that anyone teach you*; but as the same *anointing teaches you* concerning all things, and is true, and is not a lie, and just as it has taught you, you will abide in Him.

This is the mystery of revelation: Before renewal, we need tutors and governors to teach and guide us. After mind renewal, as a mature son, we have no need for anyone to teach us because we are instructed by the anointing! Religious systems depend on keeping devotees as spiritual milk-fed children in order to maintain the pre-eminence of their teachers. But the "Holy Spirit School of Transformation and Mind-Renewal" puts religious systems out of business; or, at the very least, it equalizes the former instructor to truth-seeking peer status.

As we experience progress in mind-renewal, it directs and shapes our goals, values, activities, plans, and life mission. It changes our priorities, and how we allocate our time. A deep understanding of our purpose affects our assumptions, which, in turn, diminishes the pressure on us to conform to this world's way of thinking and definition of what is good, acceptable, and perfect. The unavoidable conclusion of all of this is that we cannot legitimately claim to experience the salvation process until, unless, and to the degree that our mind is renewed, and we no longer think as the world thinks. Nor do we define what is good, acceptable, and perfect as the world defines it.

There are two aspects in which we are to experience mind renewal in our salvation process: 1) To forsake the carnal mind and the default programming of the flesh in favor of the spiritual mind as a consistent choice; and, 2) To learn to think like our Bridegroom and anticipate His response in all circumstances. It makes perfect sense that, since we will spend eternity as Jesus' co-sovereign and helpmeet, we need to be conformed to *His* values, *His* thought processes, and *His* ways of governing.

My dad used to have a phrase I have heard many times: "You are majoring on minors!" By that, he meant the equivalent of dealing with symptoms without dealing with root causes. We spend our time "majoring on minors" when we concentrate on our sin, or the sin of others, as the major activity of the transformation process. The way you act is only part of our transformation process, and it is not even the most important part. The other 3/4 of our soul's transformation that prepares us for the Kingdom is what and how we choose (our will), what and how we feel (our emotions), and what and how we think (our renewed mind). The sinful behavior on which we spend so much time focusing flows from flaws in the other three components. Consider these three Scriptures from **Hebrews 10** in relation to one another:

- "For the worshipers, once purified, would have had no more consciousness of sins" (**Hebrews 10:2**);
- "For by one offering He has perfected forever [justified] those who are being sanctified" (**Hebrews 10:14**); and,
- "I will put My laws into their hearts, and in their minds, I will write them" (**Hebrews 10:16**).

Papa woke me one night recently with this phrase: "No more consciousness of sin." He has promised those who hear and trust in His Son a priceless change process the writer of Hebrews calls "sanctification," and the Apostle Paul in other places calls "salvation" (they are technically different-but-related). But He leaves it up to us to determine the degree to which we engage. The important take-away is that Papa's process for us results in our perfection before Him, His laws written on our heart and mind to the degree that we no longer even have consciousness of sin because it is no longer a "thing"! Many believers spend much of their consciousness dwelling on sin in themselves and others. The principle of **Psalm 115:8** is, "You become most like what you most look at." If Papa has declared, "Their sins and their lawless deeds I will remember no more" (**Hebrews 10:17**), what business do we have dredging them up over and over?

One of the more important aspects of transformation and the renewed mind is adjusting that which we hold dear. In **Psalm 115:4-8**, David reveals a principle in operation in the world that explains a lot about the direction in which our culture seems to be drifting:

> [4]Their idols are silver and gold, the work of men's hands. [5]They have mouths, but they do not speak; eyes they have, but they do not see; [6]They have ears, but they do not hear; noses they have, but they do not smell; [7]They have hands, but they do not handle; feet they have, but they do not walk; nor do they mutter through their throat. *[8]Those who make them are like them; so is everyone who trusts in them.*

Norman Grubb teaches this principle in his books: "What you take, takes you." King David reveals the practical outworking of worshiping the product of the work of your hands. We don't see a whole lot of gold and silver statues (except maybe the Oscar!) being worshiped these days, but there are plenty of idols! An idol is any material object that is venerated or held in high esteem. Another definition is, any person or thing regarded with blind admiration, adoration, or devotion. It has always mystified me when I hear a Christian adoring some celebrity or obsessing over some possession. If you fashion an idol, you become like it. Period. People are *not* impressive, no matter how talented or famous. God is impressive. Look upon Him, and you will become like Him.

## The Choice Space: Reflexes, Routines, and "Big Hairy Deals"

It may *sound* like a no-brainer, but often recognizing the choices before us is not as simple as it seems, or even that there *is a choice to make*! We go through life on auto-pilot, frequently by-passing conscious decision-making whenever possible—that is one role of our assumptions. "Auto-Pilot Bypass Mode" (APBM) is the strategy of those whose preferred method of aiming is to shoot from the hip and those who don't want to be bothered by the *business* of living so that they may enjoy the *entertainment* of living. In order to consistently choose the spiritual mind over the carnal mind, an early skill in which we must train ourselves is to recognize the choices that present themselves before us. That means living mindfully, intentionally, always on alert that we must be about the Father's business. For sons of the Kingdom, there is no recess, no snow days, no holidays, no vacations, no day off from being who we are born to be.

The visual that most appropriately depicts our dilemma is living in the space between the carnal mind on one side and the spiritual mind on the other. If we are to learn to recognize choices—even disguised as routine activities or things over which we have no control—the first question to answer is, "Where should we look?" The answer, as I see it, is "Yes"; in other words, we look everywhere and at all times. Think of the Choice Space as a long hallway with many twists and turns, whose end cannot be seen, and in which there are an infinite number of doors on the right and left. Each door represents a choice to make, and *not* going through any particular door is in itself a choice. Of course, the Choice Space is not a "space" at all in the literal sense; nor does it have a definitive structure as a hallway would have. However, I find it helpful to think about it in those terms because it perfectly symbolizes the separation between two different Kingdoms and destinations within each choice we make. It recognizes the "space" between our spirit and flesh (flesh as a system, not as a structural vessel) that resulted from Man's fall in the Garden of Eden.

We are very keen to assert our belief in freedom of choice. Sometimes, though, we are not so keen to understand the ramifications of having such freedom. Scripture says God chose us before the foundation of the world (**Ephesians 1:4**) and has written our names in the Book of Life *since* the foundation of the world (**Revelation 13:8**). God exercised His sovereignty in choosing us; we exercise our limited sovereignty by making choices that regenerate, transform, and renew us. His choice makes our choices possible and profitable. He predestined the process by which we are adopted as sons (**Romans 8:29**).

> **Ephesians 1:4-5**, "⁴[J]ust as *He chose us in Him before the foundation of the world*, that we should be holy and without blame before Him in love, ⁵having *predestined us to adoption as sons* by Jesus Christ to Himself, according to the good pleasure of His will."

Our choices in life come at us from all directions, at different speeds, and with different priorities and importance. Sometimes our choice-making requirement is instantaneous and evokes more of a reflex response than a well-reasoned, prayed-through decision. Sometimes life is like a batting cage, where we eagerly await the next pitch to whiff, foul off, or knock out of the park. Sometimes our decision-life is like working on an assembly line, making the same movements with the same parts and the same tools day after day—the very definition of faithfulness! Sometimes, our decision-life is like watching a train wreck in slow motion, but watching from inside the train! Whatever the reaction speed or effect of the choice, we know that "all things work together for good to those who love God, to those who are the called according to His purpose" (**Romans 8:28**). It behooves us, however, to understand the decision/choice dynamic, how it occurs, what it means, and what the various puzzle pieces teach us.

Reflex choice happens when we, for example, are cut off in traffic, or drop a heavy object on our big toe, or some other such quickly-evolving circumstance for which we have no time for "cool reflection." The reflex response serves the purpose of revealing the progress that the Holy Spirit has made in changing us from our carnal mind to the spiritual mind. It is the classic Holy Spirit "tipping over our container" revealing to us the mystery liquid that is in our heart. Our instantaneous reflexive response bypasses our conscious mind—thereby revealing to us what is really underneath. Our intent is that, over time, we incorporate the word into our soul and share union with Him to the degree that even our instantaneous reactions become regenerated life responses, fully reflecting the Fruit of the Spirit. Love, Joy, Peace, Patience, Kindness, Goodness, Faithfulness, Gentleness, and Self-control become our reflex responses, not an after-thought choice that follows yet another repentance session! Reflex Fruit of the Spirit is the sweet spot of the transformation process! In these displays of Papa's work in us, we can truly and rightfully take heart and hope. They are direct evidence of our sonship because these characteristics present proof of God's discipline in our training.

The second Choice Space I call the "batting cage," because it is the space where we make routine day-after-day decisions according to the tools, habits, attitudes, and assumptions we have collected over a lifetime. Habits are the autopilot of our conscious and unconscious mind. It is the place where we get dull because of boredom, disengaged as a result of non-challenge, and lethargic because of inactivity. Habits, when thoughtfully formed, are very useful. But more often than not, when we get locked into a habit it is

> We spend the majority of our decision space life in the batting cage, so it is imperative that we add to our tool set daily!

because it is the routine of the path of least resistance: the easiest way, the simplest way, the path of least conflict. Frequently, habits have formed as a result of our carnal mind having free reign. Spiritual learning *does* happen best in a place of peace, but peace does not imply "least resistance" because peace is an internal state, and not dependent upon external circumstances.

The tools of the batting cage are the skills we have honed to help us make solid and positive contact with the circumstance being hurled at us at 90+ miles per hour. Our skill set must be varied: the ability to hit a well-placed fastball, a wicked curveball, a tricky slider, and the ever-possible knuckleball. The tools, to whatever degree they exist in the believer's life, are made up in bulk of the Fruit of the Spirit character traits listed for us in **Galatians 5:22**. We spend by far the majority of our decision space life in the batting cage, so it is imperative that we add to our toolset daily! Increasing our tools for the batting cage Choice Space teaches us to reign over our circumstances, and enlarges our rulership ability for the Kingdom.

High-stakes Choice Space decisions are, thankfully, few and far between for most of us. This category is the "Big Hairy Deal" (BHD) Choice Space because the decisions made in this space are, well, big and hairy. They are important, and frequently life-changing. There is no script for this decision space, only a lot of prayer, often tears, hopefully supportive friends and family, and undoubtedly the comfort of the Holy Spirit. Here are some circumstances that I, family, or close friends of mine have faced:

- When the doctor announces, "You have cancer"

- When the police call to say your child has been arrested

- When someone close to you tragically loses their life, or your moment of distraction seriously injures or kills another

- When you are physically or emotionally abused by someone you trusted

- When your unmarried daughter sits you down and tells you she is pregnant

- When you develop a debilitating injury or condition that leaves you in pain and/or dependent on others

- When someone close relapses or refuses to get help for an addiction

- When you are betrayed by a good friend, or spiritually abused by a church leader

- When you are laid off from your job with little or no warning and no safety net

- When your husband/wife announces they want a divorce

- When you come home from vacation and discover your home burned to the ground

We could continue to list BHDs for pages, but this abbreviated list should be sufficient to get our attention. BHDs hurt—a lot! The surprise factor of BHDs is that, because of our optimism bias, we tend to believe that they only happen to others, making us unprepared and vulnerable when our turn for this degree of suffering comes around.

BHDs are the serious business for which all other situations work together to prepare you. Everyone gets their turn in the BHD space, and everyone has an equal opportunity to reign over, or be crushed by the circumstance. Experiencing a BHD is usually the occasion of experience of grief and all of the attendant feelings and questions accompanying it. The decision space for BHDs is usually as big and as long as you need it to be. And because the stakes are high and consequences are imminent, it is usually the best course of action to breathe deeply and prolong your response until we spend some time with the Comforter. The discipleship planning process is all about partnering with the Holy Spirit to tailor the strategies right for you to accomplish the transformation He is working in you and on which you will rely in the BHD Choice Space.

# The Choice Space: Flesh vs. Spirit

It is comforting to know that a man as venerable as the Apostle Paul experienced the same struggles in life as I do; and, I suspect, as do you. It is also interesting to note the progression of his humility in the chronology of his writings, from "least of the apostles" (**1 Corinthians 15:9**), to "least of all of the saints" (**Ephesians 3:8**), and finally to "chief of sinners" (**1 Timothy 1:15**). Though he was given a revelation of the Kingdom like no other in history, his chosen status as the bearer of the revelation of God did not inflate his estimate of his own importance. It is said that "Proximity to deity *always* brings prostration"; and that is precisely the reaction that Paul exhibits—the prostration of humility.

A prerequisite for understanding Paul's frustration is found in **Romans 7:16-18**:

> [16]If, then, I do what I will not do, *I agree with the law that it is good.* [17]But now, it is no longer I who do it, but sin that dwells in me. [18]For I know that in me (that is, in my flesh) nothing good dwells; for to will is present with me, *but how to perform what is good I do not find*.

Before the Choice Space can become a dilemma at all, there must be an understanding and acceptance that the "law is good." Without an agreement with the "good Law," there is no accountability standard against which to evaluate the practices of my flesh. The flesh begins as separation from God; it is not primarily sinning, it is primarily *weakness*, as confirmed by both Jesus and Paul:

> **Matthew 26:41**, Watch and pray, lest you enter into temptation. The spirit indeed is willing, but the *flesh is weak*.

And,

> **Romans 8:2-3**, [2]For the law of the Spirit of life in Christ Jesus has made me free from the law of sin and death. [3]For what the law could not do in that it *was weak through the flesh*, God did by sending His own Son in the likeness of sinful flesh, on account of sin: He condemned sin in the flesh.

| **Newsflash!!!** |
| :---: |
| You are **NOT** your body! |

Paul makes a clear distinction between the separation of flesh and soul. He also alludes to that part of our tri-part being that constitutes the *real us*. The "I" in the text "it is no longer I who do it, but sin that dwells in me," refers to his mind that agrees with the law that is good. Understanding who the "I" is in our study of the Choice Space brings us to a key concept completely foreign to many: **You are not your body**! You—the real you—are the precious life, the consciousness that lives in the flesh vessel; and that is the part that will return to eternity.

Our flesh container always *clamors* out of its greatest desire or need; our spirit *flows* out of our deepest security. Our soul, then, gets to choose which of the two we will follow, or more accurately, *wills* (as an exercise of will) to follow. That is where and when we make the carnal or spiritual mind choice. When Papa chastens us, it is to produce in us the "peaceable fruit of righteousness" (**Hebrews 12:11**). At these times, it is not helpful to pitch a fit, indulge in self-pity, or hold one's breath until passing out. When you quit acting out, you will still have a choice to make and a lesson to learn.

Since we have been given the *power* to be free from the compulsions of the flesh, the problem *de jure* now becomes **Romans 6:16**:

> Do you not know that to whom you **present yourselves slaves to obey**, **you are that one's slaves whom you obey**, whether of sin leading to death, or of obedience leading to righteousness?

Now, what was formerly a compulsion of the flesh becomes for us a discipleship choice. That is good news! It is good in that being free from compulsion enables us to respond to our true selves, and *responding according to our true self is the very definition of freedom.* Compulsion negates and removes choice from our repertoire of responses. While we are under compulsion of the flesh, therefore, spiritual mind selection in the Choice Space is not even possible!

Being free from compulsion enables us to grow, mature, and take responsibility for our discipleship progress. It enables us to act

> **Galatians 5:13**, "For you, brethren, have been called to liberty; only do not use liberty as an opportunity for the flesh, but through love serve one another."

intentionally. Paul adjures us to present our bodies as living sacrifices to God, not only as our reasonable service (**Romans 12:1**), but it is also the only way we can live in the freedom that Jesus has purchased for us. When we live in our freedom inheritance, we are an open channel of His love, mercy, forgiveness, truth, and every other spiritual blessing. We walk in liberty, but we do not use it as an opportunity to fall back into the trap of satiating the flesh. Instead, we use our liberty to serve one another and fulfill Jesus' Commandment to, "Love your neighbor as yourself" (**Matthew 19:19, Mark 12:31**).

## The Choice Space: Between *the* "Rock" and a Hard Place

There is something a little perverse inside of us that sadistically *enjoys*—or at least takes comfort in—the opportunity to complain and whine. Most of us have a childish first reaction of self-pity in our trials and tribulations, stemming from a *misbelief* that we are somehow *entitled* to a smooth, trouble-free life. This misbelief has its origin in Satan's lie to Eve in the Garden: "[Y]ou will be like God, knowing good and evil" (**Genesis 3:5**), a lie that inverts sovereignty and places separated, Individual Self at the center of the universe. This expectation of smoothness is at the core of all of our anger responses. Expectations are a prerequisite for resentment, and a predisposition to judge. Think about it—it is impossible to judge another or to resent your treatment unless you have first formed an expectation of what others should do, and what treatment you should receive. But it doesn't have to be that way. Whining, complaining, and self-pity is as much a *habit* as they are a genuine emotion within us.

Scripture tells us that Jesus was in all points tempted as we are, yet was without sin (**Hebrews 4:15**). He endured suffering as we do, and even learned obedience and was perfected in the process (**Hebrews 5:7-9**). The concept of Jesus being without sin and yet needing to be perfected creates a certain amount of dissonance in us. After all, if paintings by the great masters are to be believed, Jesus came out of the womb with a halo around His head, and a radiant light that made Him glow in the dark! In such a context, it is difficult to consider that He was anything less than fully capable, fully functional, and completely obedient from His first breath! In short, He was not a *regular* (I use that word carefully, instead of "ordinary"—He decidedly was not ordinary) infant, but instead

> **Hebrews 5:7-9**, "[7] During the days of Jesus' life on earth, he offered up prayers and petitions with *fervent cries and tears* to the One who could save him from death, and he was heard because of his reverent submission. [8]Son though He was, *He learned obedience from what He suffered,* [9]and once made perfect, He became the source of eternal salvation for all who obey Him."

was some uber-holy miniature adult whose body simply had to catch up with the rest of His being. There is only one problem with that line of religious thinking—it ain't so! If Scripture is to be believed, Jesus had plenty to learn just like us, the chief lesson of which was obedience to the Father and the complete subjugation of His will. His process of subjugating His will was a learned one, *just as it is for us.*

So, what is wrong with venerating Jesus to the point that we assume His "uber-ness" from the moment of birth?  The effect in the carnal mind is to erect a false wall of separation that enables us to excuse our failure to follow His example, considering it *super-human* or assisted by some external power not available to us, seeing that we are "regular."  It enables us to rationalize our failure to subjugate our will because we are somehow lacking in what it takes: *"Well, sure, Jesus could do it—He was God from the beginning! But I'm just a sinner, saved by grace!"*  The foregoing is true, but it is not *the Truth*—and there is a difference.  Our excuses beg the question of the subjugation of our will in all things as Jesus did.  Notice the sequencing in the Scriptures: **Hebrews 5**, *"He learned obedience...having been perfected"*; and **Philippians 2**, *"became obedient...Therefore."*  By the conjunction of these truths, Paul tells us that the sequence is that Jesus was perfected by His obedience; and that as a result of His obedience, He was exalted.  Finally, **Hebrews 2:18** says, "For in that He Himself has suffered, being tempted, He is able to aid those who are tempted," and we are the beneficiary of His aid.  Jesus did have one advantage (and it *was* huge!)—He and the Father were one, in spirit and soul.  It is the same oneness that He offers to us, and that is the challenge of overcoming our flesh through establishing our union in Him.

## The Choice Space: Sin is Separation

I am convinced that the temptation Jesus endured went way beyond the temptation to pass up the pain of dying on the cross; it spanned the whole gamut associated with living daily as a spirit being in this body of flesh.  Think of any and every temptation you have ever experienced, and Scripture says that Jesus also felt it.  Satan even made an appearance to make sure He felt temptation directly from him!  But there is a world of difference between feeling the temptation and entering into the transgression.  The fact that He was without sin in all of it tells us a great deal, not only about the strength of His will and character but also about how the "Flesh—Separation—Temptation—Sin" cycle works.  It also tells us how we may interrupt the cycle in ourselves and have the same success that Jesus did.

We are not separated from God because we sin; we sin because we are separated from God.  Norman Grubb says it this way: "What the Bible calls sin is, in one phrase, Independent Self."  The original creation of God was in perfect union with him, and separated thinking was not in the picture.  Adam and Eve experienced unbroken fellowship, and therefore sin was never an issue until separation happened.  The Independent Self is a self-centered self.  Independent Self seeks and acts in its own interests, its own gratification, and its own existence apart from the Creator.  It stands at the center of its own world, and that whole world revolves around it.  Independent Self has believed and invested itself in the lie, "You will be like God, knowing [in the sense of "defining"] good and evil."  It abandoned perfect harmony and fellowship, enthroned its interests above all others and became the carnal mind.  For the first time since his creation, Adam knew insecurity, because now there was a veil of separation between the source of his security and his heart; the source of his true identity and his spirit; and the source of deep understanding and what became his darkened mind, identified by Paul in **Ephesians 4:17-18**:

> [17][Y]ou should no longer walk as the rest of the Gentiles walk, in the futility of their mind, [18]having their understanding darkened, being alienated [separated] from the life of God, because of the ignorance that is in them, because of the blindness of their heart.

Man, in the Garden of Eden, was created in oneness with God.  In **1 Corinthians 15:45**, Paul connects the actions of Adam and the mission of Jesus: "And so it is written, the first man, Adam, became a living

> Reconcile: To bring into agreement or harmony; to make compatible; to re-consecrate; to restore.

being. The last Adam became a life-giving spirit." **Romans 5:12-21** also connects Adam and Jesus, and clearly explains that the process one started (Adam), the other finished (Jesus). That is the "It" to which Jesus was referring to on the cross when He said, "It is finished" (**John 19:30**). The mission on which Jesus embarked when He surrendered His position of equality in the Godhead and came to earth in the form of a bond-servant (**Philippians 2:5-8**) was to restore and reconcile the separation damage that resulted when Adam entered into the transgression with Eve, and Man fell from a position of perfect union with the Creator. Paul referred to Jesus' mission as "the reconciliation" in **Romans 5:11**.

"Operation Reconciliation" is what Jesus' mission and the discipleship process are about—first in our spirit with the Spirit of God, then in our soul with the mind, will, and emotions of Christ. One synonym for "reconcile" is "reunify." Jesus' death was about overcoming separation, and He accomplished His mission in two ministry dimensions: 1) The sacrifice of His blood presented on the altar for sin (that is, Sin nature) reconciled our spirit separation from the Father, resulting in *justification*; 2) The life He now lives in us overcomes and reconciles separation in our soul, resulting in *salvation*. It is inappropriate to interchange justification and salvation because they are two distinct ministries, one by His death, and one by His life. Paul refers to this two-dimensional process in **Romans 5:9-10**:

> [9]Much more then, having now been *justified* by His blood, we shall be *saved* from wrath through Him. [10]For if when we were enemies we were reconciled to God through the death of His Son, much more, having reconciled [a one-time event] we shall be saved [an ongoing process].

Alienation and separation are no longer a problem for us! Paul recorded the result of the end of separation in **Romans 8:35**: "Who shall separate us from the love of Christ? Shall tribulation, or distress, or persecution, or famine, or nakedness, or peril, or sword?" Once brought into union/oneness with God in spirit, we can no longer be separated in that portion of our precious life. We can, however, choose to our detriment and growth-stagnation to conduct our *soul-life as if still separated*, and in the life-context of the Independent Self. So, the choice boils down to this: Will you and I continue to live in the perverse illusion of separation, or will we make spiritual mind choices that regenerate, transform, and renew our soul, and thereby come into the same union of Spirit we already enjoy?


## The Choice Space: Living Life in Context

This may be the most important sub-chapter in this whole book because it describes at a very high level the task before believers throughout all of life. All that came before is preparatory, and all that comes after is for purposes of explanation and detail. We have established that Jesus has, by His act of sacrifice, bridged the separation of spirit between Man and God. He has brought us out of Egypt (Sin). Now, our quest, our purpose, and meaning of life is to overcome the separation in our soul—between our mind and His mind, our will and His will, between our emotions and His Love. Our daily activities serve as nothing more than to pursue this quest in whatever circumstance and venue we find ourselves. In this light and understanding, all "life for its own sake" motivation withers and dissipates.

To "live life in context" is to live it in a framework of understanding that filters all incoming stimuli and the outgoing responses. "Living life in context" is to understand "Why." It is to wrench our attention from the weeds of life and into a 50,000-foot strategic overview, from which vantage we can look far ahead, far behind, and all around for direction. I have a friend that says that life's short sprints of suffering—even intense ones—are not the most difficult circumstances we face; *the most difficult circumstance we face is "long obedience in the same direction."* "Long obedience," says, "I don't know what tomorrow's circumstances will bring, but I know how I intend to respond." Long obedience says, with Job, "Though He slays me, yet will I trust in Him" (**Job 15:13**). Life in context has this objective: To grasp and maintain the perspective that all that happens to and through us is intended to serve the purpose of changing us into His image.

It is often helpful in understanding other-worldly concepts by framing them in terms of not only what they are, but also what they are not. The polar opposite of living life in context is not *living without or out of context*. There is no such thing as living without context since our environment comprises a context for conducting our affairs whether we recognize it or not. The opposite of living life in context is existing in our environment *unaware* of our true contextualizing purpose. Just as the opposite of intentional is "accidental, unplanned, unwitting," the opposite of living life in context is living in a free-fall, subject to whatever stresses, whatever whims, whatever buffeting winds drive us along our path.

Sometimes we do not recognize that our day's activities are chocked full of choices between carnal and spiritual minds. You may never stop to think about the mechanisms that you use to make the world and life make sense. Perhaps you just go about your business day, week, and month-after-month until that day when you will arrive at your *Last 15-Minutes*. But if the common saying (attributed to Socrates) that, "The unexamined life is not worth living," is true, the first and highest examination criterion *must be* to figure out our contextual framework. It is not a matter of *if* we have a framework; the primary tool we use to make sense of life is *context*. Humans have a narrative bias that comes naturally to us; that is, we understand life and history in terms of a story to be told and retold. You understand me better—even if we have never met in person—because, in Chapter 1, I told you a story of highlighted events in my life that have led me to today.

The problem is that, by never examining *why* you do what you do, and making an affirmative decision about your intents and motivations, you default to your overriding programming—which is separated thinking, the flesh and its cravings, and living life for its own sake. Therefore, the default context—or filter, if you prefer—is to understand the world and our own actions from an Independent Self perspective. However, believers are intended to progress past independence to union with our Bridegroom and the rest of the Godhead. Union with Papa, by definition, brings us into union with the rest of His sons and daughters, all tuned to the same tuning fork. When one examines their own motivations and evaluates both their actions and experiences in the light of a framework of truth, it guides them on the choices that are consistent with where he or she wants to end up. Our contextual framework is the Global Positioning System (GPS) of sorts that directs us on the path of our pilgrimage.

In the old days, before satellites and GPS, surveyors recorded maps, established property boundaries, prepared legal descriptions of property and location—all by locating a fixed point and navigating from it. Often, the fixed point was an iron stake driven into the ground to mark a corner of the property. Once the fixed point was located, the surveyor could use their instruments to locate other boundaries. Sailors traversed the world's oceans and arrived at their desired destination by performing the same type of function—locating where they were on a boundary-less ocean by locating an ancient and fixed point—the stars—and navigating accordingly.

Our contextual framework establishes fixed points that do not easily change. For example, I have made an affirmative decision that the Bible is true. As God's word, I have established Scripture as the contextual framework for all decisions. There are parts of the Scripture that I do not fully understand. Still, that does not prevent me from navigating from the parts of Scripture I *do* understand. I continue along my life's pilgrimage, putting one foot in front of the other in the general direction that the

Bible (as my navigational aid) provides for me. Further, the Holy Spirit teaches and coaches me by whispering instructions that direct me to my destination—my *Last 15-Minutes* Self.

Context is a framework, an over-arching system of understandings and assumptions that color everything that we see and touch. It is the backdrop against which we view our story. It is the process by which we apply our assumptions—that is, what we perceive to be true—to our actual experience. Sometimes the process requires adjusting our initial responses to an event as we have time to reflect on what we believe. Ultimately, context helps us to evaluate what happens to us and through us, and in the world around us, *as it occurs*. When the Foundation of Meaning—that is, all of life is intended to prepare us for ruling beside our Bridegroom—is the context in which we view and evaluate all of our history, our experiences take shape in a manner that they will not otherwise. It changes our priorities. It changes *us*.

> Isaiah 30:20-21, "20And though the Lord gives you the **bread of adversity and the water of affliction**, yet your teachers will not be moved into a corner anymore, but your eyes shall see your teachers. **21Your ears shall hear a word behind you, saying, 'This is the way, walk in it,'** **whenever you turn to the right hand or whenever you turn to the left**."

Context serves to help us make sense of our story—past, present, and future—as we strive to make sense of life and our environment. The function of context when understanding our *future* is to facilitate our goal-setting, and goal-setting has *everything* to do with who we end up as in our *Last 15-Minutes*. The function of context with respect to our *past* is to 1) limit the damage caused by on-going emotional pain; 2) promote understanding that God is continuously at work in us; 3) provide proof that we are His sons as He works to discipline us; and, 4) transform us into the image of His Son as our suffering grows the Fruit of the Spirit in us. The function of context in our *present* is to harmonize what we believe to be true with what we are currently feeling, thinking, and experiencing. Context in our present helps us to understand our story *as it is being written*.

> We do not have a life, because we are already dead (**Colossians 3:3**). But we *do* have a story; and that story is the history of our reconciliation.

Context with respect to our future establishes a general direction and strategy by which we set off on our pilgrimage. It guides us in setting discipleship objectives. It also gives us an interim evaluation tool to know if we are being successful. For example, if I determine a goal to visit my children and grandchildren in Denver, Dallas, Phoenix, or here in Bastrop, TX, that intent serves as the context with which I select a road and/or a mechanism of travel. The context doesn't deliver me to my destination, but it helps me know if I am being successful, helps me make expedient and helpful decisions (e.g., "turn right or go straight"; "fly or drive"). If our goal is to prepare ourselves to rule beside our Bridegroom in the Kingdom, that context necessitates many choices to keep me on track. Note that context does not prescribe one particular way to arrive at the destination—there are many roads to get me there, some better and more expedient than others. Also, note that I am *not saying there are many ways to God!* Jesus is the narrow way and the straight gate. But once we have passed through the gate our path opens into many possibilities as King David wrote in **Psalm 18:19**, each requiring our exercise of spiritual mind choices according to life-context.

> Psalm 18:19, "He also brought me out into a broad place; He delivered me because He delighted in me."

I understand that this is a challenging concept, so here are a couple of examples of what I mean by "living life in context." Exercising perspective teaches us discipleship. And, context reinforces our faith rather than tearing it down as we experience the "bread of adversity…water of affliction" (**Isaiah 20:30**):

1) It is common for people, even believers, to cry out, "Why is this happening to me?" when they are in the middle of tough circumstances or some event that causes suffering in their life. But for believers, we have these contextualizing Scriptures:

- **Romans 8:28**, "And we know that all things work together for good to those who love God, to those who are called according to His purpose."

- **2 Corinthians 4:17**, "For our light affliction, which is but for a moment, is working for us a far more exceeding and eternal weight of glory."

- **Hebrews 5:8**, "[T]hough He [Jesus] was a Son, yet He learned obedience by the things which He suffered."

The truth we assume ("all things work together for good") provides a framework for us to evaluate our suffering experience beyond that of what feels good or bad to our flesh. Further, in context, we learn to understand that in the grand scheme (God's Program!) our suffering is both momentary and advantageous for us. We see that Jesus Himself was instructed in obedience through His suffering. In light of the Scripture, the dissonance is dissipated, confusion is organized, and discord is harmonized. We understand our past and present in terms of our future.

2) Sustaining life on the physical level doesn't get much more basic than bread and water. And, the association of basic life-giving substances with adversity and affliction in **Isaiah 30:20** indicate their importance as life-giving *to our soul*. The association is no accident! **Isaiah Chapter 30** establishes adversity and affliction to be the teachers of rebellious, headstrong people. To find such a person, one need only look in the mirror.

- **Isaiah 30:20**, "And though the Lord gives you the **bread of adversity** and the **water of affliction**, yet your teachers will not be moved into a corner anymore, but your eyes shall see your teachers."

- **Job 2:9-10**, "[9]Then his wife said to him, 'Do you still hold fast to your integrity? Curse God and die!' [10]But he said to her, 'You speak as one of the foolish women speaks. Shall we indeed accept good from God, and shall we not accept adversity?'"

It is difficult for some to embrace the notion that adversity and affliction can be from the hand of Papa, but the message of the Scripture is clear. Whether you say that He allows them or causes them, refusal to accept that adversity is a training tool in the hand of our Good Father is a clear and unmistakable sign of our living life entrenched as an Independent Self. It is also a hallmark of an attitude that refuses to live life in the context of its purpose and meaning. Training is the purpose of life, and to refuse to embrace adversity and affliction and learn from them is to reject God's Program as a contextualizing factor.

3). Some hallmarks of today's society and culture in America are discord, angst, factional hatred, and rampant self-interest, all of which result in a strong division. It would be easy to become overwhelmed and discouraged to the point of joining one faction or another to further sow discord. But we have (at least) these three contextualizing Scriptures that demonstrate that not only did Jesus foresee the events of the last days, but He also remains on the Throne and in control:

- **John 16:33**, "These things I have spoken to you, that in Me you may have peace. In the world, you will have tribulation, but be of good cheer, I have overcome the world."

- **John 15:15**, "[A]ll things that I heard from My Father I have made known to you."

- **Matthew 24:9-14**, "[9]Then they will deliver you up to tribulation and kill you, and you will be hated by all nations for My name's sake. [10]And then many will be offended, will betray one another, and will hate one another. [11]Then many false prophets will rise up and deceive many. [12]And because lawlessness will abound, the love of many will grow cold. [13]But he who endures to the end shall be saved. [14]And this gospel of the kingdom will be preached in all the world as a witness to all the nations, and then the end will come."

There are many more examples of contextualizing Scriptures. One way of contextualizing the whole body of Scripture is "truth that provides the context for how we view and evaluate life and prepare for what comes after!"

You will—you *must*—live life in some context. You cannot do otherwise, because it is how you were created, and it is how you are wired. You instinctively understand the events of life as a story to be told and retold—that is the way Papa made us. The context of our story has *everything* to do with its meaning. But the difference between a Christian and a disciple is that the disciple chooses the context in which they evaluate life experience, and submits him or herself to embrace the experience and be transformed by it.

## The Choice Space: Reframing Your Thoughts

In the process of renewing our mind, perspective is important. It is important to know that we have a choice of perspectives as it is to actually make the choice. The perspective one chooses determines what we see. Our minds are marvelous gifts from Papa designed to aid us in our pursuit of union with the mind of Christ. When we fail to see that there are alternatives when it comes to selecting a world view in general, and an interpretive perspective of any circumstance in particular, we essentially force ourselves into the same response patterns; and the same response patterns is stagnation, not growth. More often than not the single-choice reaction is the product of the carnal mind and the flesh working together.

The ability to envision multiple potential responses in any given circumstance is a gift from Papa! When we have the grace to slow our reaction to adverse circumstances, and delay flying off of the handle, we build into the choice process the time necessary to listen to the voice of the Holy Spirit, to review what we know to be true from God's word, and to discern the Fruit of the Spirit response applicable to the situation. This delayed response process is the essence of the Fruit of the Spirit Patience in a nutshell. At that point, we are "...complete, thoroughly equipped for every good work" (**2 Timothy 3:17**), and ready to make a spiritual mind response. Perhaps you have heard the common saying, "The issue is never the circumstance before you, but rather, your reaction to it!" The carnal mind focuses on problems associated with your circumstances. The spiritual mind concentrates on the lessons they teach us.

> **1 Corinthians 10:23**, "All things are lawful for me, but not all things are helpful; all things are lawful for me, but not all things edify."

When a person has not cultivated the ability to consider multiple perspectives, he or she has no choice between alternatives except whether or not to go down that one path or stand still—I guess that is at least something! But for that person who sees only one alternative and hasn't the self-control to stand still *or* keep their mouth shut, the outcome is usually more contention and strife. These are the people we describe as "always right," or, what is worse, "never wrong." Moreover, having the ability to hold only one perspective typically results in stubbornness, combativeness, or a wide range of intractability between the two. The reason is that when I have only one alternative, and it is challenged, I have no choice but to

# The Dilemma of the Cube

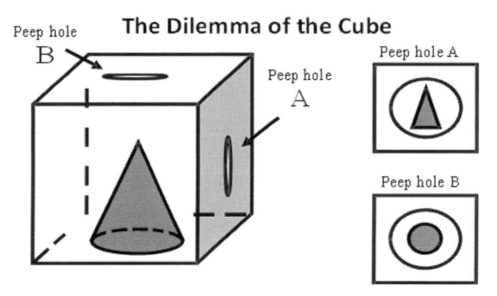

Peep hole B

Peep hole A

Peep hole A

Peep hole B

## Perspective = "The View from Where You Sit"

defend it in order to maintain my security. However, when my security is in Christ, and I am able to choose between multiple godly perspectives, I have no need to dominate, but can listen to you, listen to the Holy Spirit, and choose the most expedient and edifying path. That is the reframing process in one's choice-making. Intentionally cultivating the ability to choose between multiple perspectives and alternatives enhances our ability to live in unity in the Body of Christ and at peace in the world.

There is another aspect of reframing that plays an important role in our ability to get past abuse, emotional or physical. Our commitment to reframe our thinking allows us to disengage from the way we have always seen things, and the way we have always seen things is the binder that chains us to past mistakes and pain. Hurting people tend to hunker down around that which is familiar and known, even if not particularly safe or smart. It is the definition of crazy in action ("Doing the same things and thinking the same thoughts over and over and expecting a different result"), and makes a choice to examine events in a different light, see things from another perspective, and abandon unhelpful and unedifying thinking seem a lot riskier than it actually is. Choosing perspective change is particularly useful when the Holy Spirit is healing our wounded status and removing scar tissue from our emotional construct.

To be absolutely clear, I am not urging that we abandon Scripture when we consider multiple perspectives, nor am I urging situational ethics. Rather, we should reach beyond the same carnal mind thoughts that form our typical go-to habits. The Dilemma of the Cube[13] illustration above is a poignant demonstration of the effect that seeing from a different angle can produce. "Where you stand depends on where you sit" is another truth that illustrates the impact of perspective. The commitment to reframing our thinking allows us to choose a new context in which to understand our story, the accumulation of experiences, positive and negative, good and bad. Reframing gives us at least the possibility to "count it all joy"; without such a reframing commitment, our ability to see things differently is at best hit or miss.

---

[13] Marcus, Leonard J., et al, *You're It: How to Lead When It Matters Most.* June, 2019, Hatchette Publishing Group, New York, NY.  https://www.publicaffairsbooks.com/titles/leonard-j-marcus/youre-it/9781541768055/

# The Choice Space: A Mind Set on the Flesh

> **Romans 8:5-6**, "[5]For those who live according to the flesh set their minds on the things of the flesh, but those who live according to the Spirit, the things of the Spirit. [6]For to be carnally minded is death, but to be spiritually minded is life and peace."

The carnal mind is not primarily sinful (as we frequently think of it) but primarily obsessed with things pertaining to our flesh "container." Papa is not concerned with our sin—He dealt with our sin once-and-for-all at the cross (**Hebrews 7:27**). For Him to be wringing His hands about our sin now would require His acknowledgment that somehow Jesus' sacrifice was insufficient as atonement and that more is necessary. Nothing more *is* necessary—our justification depends on "grace-plus-nothing"! But God continues His work in us; once reconciled (justified) by Jesus' *blood*, He is engaged in transforming (saving) us through Jesus' *life*. They are two *distinct* ministries of the Lord Jesus. If Paul considered the topic worthy of separate treatment and some detail, we owe him the courtesy not to lump it all together in one gift basket.

If we limit our understanding of the carnal mind to what we typically consider sinful, we stop short of God's grace and limit our understanding of the scope of His work in us. The flesh is not sin; the flesh is weakness. Sin is separation, and Papa has dealt with our separation by bringing us into a union in spirit. If the flesh was equivalent to sin, and if it is Papa's Program to put our precious life into vessels of flesh in this T/S/M world, then His Program would be responsible for our sin! Hogwash! Once reunited in Spirit, He is bringing us into soul-union in order to transform us. Said another way, Papa dealt with our sin, now we deal with our weakness with His help and the life of Jesus.

If we focus on the carnal mind as primarily sinful, we spend our lives self-righteously attempting to fulfill the law that Jesus has already fulfilled; and that wastes precious time, time that can better be spent set on life and peace. The Holy Spirit is a genius at dealing with our sinful acts—He knows what He is doing. We, on the other hand, try to accomplish spiritual ends by employing fleshly means (including "self-imposed religion"), and it does not work. **Colossians 2:20-23** could not be clearer on this issue.

Some today embrace a prosperity gospel that claims that the mark of God's pleasure in His kids is a collection of fleshly things that will not even transition to the eternal realm. I find that rationale illogical, unscriptural, flesh-based, self-centered, and inaccurate. It *sounds* good to anyone who will embrace *any* philosophy to avoid pain. The problem is that it stands in direct opposition to the declaration of **Acts 14:21-22** (and other Scriptures telling us the role of trials) concerning the ministry of Paul and Barnabas:

> [21]And when they had preached the gospel to that city and made many disciples…[22]strengthening the souls of the disciples, exhorting them to continue in the faith, and saying, ***"We must through many tribulations enter the kingdom of God."***

Nothing gets our attention like a good tribulation! Nothing *focuses* our attention like a few momentary light afflictions! And typically, nothing elicits a stream of complaints, moans, and howls as does a good test or trial. Finally, nothing more accurately reveals what is in our hearts! Much of our culture and society today has as its epicenter the avoidance of trouble, striving, and pain in any form. From the products we sell one another to the pastimes in which we engage, discomfort avoidance, and comfort achievement qualifies as our principal objective of pursuit. It is no coincidence that trouble-avoidance may be the number one activity of the flesh. Neither is it a coincidence that the Choice Space frequently plays out on the stage of personal discomfort and self-interest. The path of least resistance always runs through the landscape of comfort and convenience. But, once again, quoting Graham Cooke: "God doesn't actually care about your comfort zone. Why? Because He gave you a *Comforter*! That means He jolly well *plans* to take you out of your comfort zone!"

## The Choice Space: Warfare!

We have been enlisted in God's army—this much we embrace. Beyond that, we sometimes lose a sense of what our enlistment means. We enthusiastically sing, "Onward Christian Soldiers!" Why, then, are we surprised when we are actually called upon to fight? *What exactly did you think the battles would look like?* In what army are the soldiers quivering blobs of emotion when they face hardship? **2 Corinthians 10:4-5** instructs us:

> ⁴For the weapons of our warfare are not carnal but mighty in God for pulling down strongholds, ⁵casting down arguments and every high thing that exalts itself against the knowledge of God, bringing every thought into captivity to the obedience of Christ.

Notice that Paul assumes the presence of strongholds unless, and until, we have taken action to intentionally pull them down. A stronghold is a place in our experience where the enemy has dug in and fortified his claim over aspects of our flesh and/or soul (mind, emotions, and will). If you think of God as a squishy, cute-and-cuddly stuffed-toy lion, and that all things in the spiritual realm are sweetness and light, then you are likely an undefended sitting duck for the enemy's attacks. One of the metaphors Scripture employs for such an indefensible strategy is a "city without walls" (**Proverbs 25:28**).

From within the stronghold, the enemy lobs mortar rounds into life's landscape to wreak havoc. That means that where strongholds exist, life likely bears the pockmarks, chaos, and rubble of exploding mortar rounds all over it. Unless strongholds are pulled down, the "high things that exalt themselves against the knowledge of God" are cast down, and "every thought is taken into captivity to the obedience of Christ" (**2 Corinthians 10:3-5**), then the chaos and scorched-earth disorder that accompanies an unopposed advance of enemy troops is inevitable. Sometimes believers become converted and make many changes, hoping for improved circumstances and Papa's favor to make their pilgrimage smoother. Certainly, Papa's blessing and favor are present; but until you pull down the stronghold and expose the enemy, chaos will persist even in the midst of blessing.

Upon the foundation of unbelief/misbelief, the enemy builds a fortified superstructure of deception, and together they constitute the stronghold. When the stronghold is ignored or left alone, Satan and "self" collude to make it more expansive and unyielding, and it usually becomes a dominant feature of one's life-landscape. Being rid of a stronghold is hard work, and it must be pulled down by confession, declaration, and application of Scriptural truths, including claiming our promised inheritance. Claiming our inheritance counters unbelief; confession and declaration neutralize deception. Once removed, the ground on which the stronghold once stood must be occupied, fortified, and defended to prevent enemy re-occupation (**Luke 11:24-26**). The replacement solution is usually one or more of the "Fruit(s) of the Spirit" (FOTS) (**Galatians 5:22-23**). More detail will be added about the process of building the FOTS in *Part 2: The Tool Chest*. Here are some common strongholds and the mortar rounds (attack forms) launched from them:

- Anger—The unbelief/misbelief on which the stronghold of anger is built is an expectation that *my life* should be smooth, trouble-free, undisturbed, and manifest all things just the way I want them. The misbelief is a lie because "our" life does not belong to us at all, but has been purchased by Christ (**Colossians 3:3**); therefore, we have no entitlement to expectations concerning it. Anger is an expression of an entrenched self and a forceful control orientation. We are often unaware that this software is running in the background of our soul. But when events occur in ways that disturb me, my comfort, or my wants and wishes, anger boils over in one of its mortar shell forms: passive-aggressive outbursts and tantrums, personal attacks on others, depression and withdrawal, vengeance, grudges, etc. The Fruit of the Spirit solutions for anger are Patience, Self-Control, Goodness, and Kindness. Patient endurance and Self-control fight against the lie that my life should be trouble-free. Goodness prevents engaging in behaviors that support and feed the anger. Kindness cancels the angry manifestations that present as slings, darts, and arrows directed at the people around us.

- Depression—Depression is anger turned inward. Clearly, I am not addressing the kind of depression that has a body chemistry etiology, nor am I addressing periodically being "down." Recurring episodes of depression are frequently the stronghold expression that we have fully embraced a lie from the enemy. Here is a bold statement: *It is impossible to experience depression when one has a clear understanding of their eternal identity.* A daily dose of who we are in Christ is the spirit-vitamin supplement that prevents anxiety and depression (common running buddies— see the next bullet point). **Proverbs 12:25** tells us the emanating source for this form of depression: "Anxiety in the heart of a man causes depression, but a good word makes it glad." The bulldozer that destroys the walls of a depression stronghold is the continuous habit of telling yourself the truth. That is the "good word [that] makes [our heart] glad." Anxiety stems from insecurity, and insecurity originates in a lack of trust and skewed self-image. We will see later that the FOTS solution for insecurity is Peace. A second FOTS solution for lack of trust is Self-Control, which we will define in a later chapter as "controlling your separated-self instincts." The FOTS Joy is the anecdote for the bitterness and self-punishment that often accompanies depression.

- Fear/Anxiety—The unbelief foundation for fear is the absence of love. **1 John 4:18** tells us, "There is no fear in love, but perfect love casts out fear...But *he who fears has not been made perfect in love*." The unbelief foundation for anxiety is separation from God, resulting in missing or wrong identity. The progression goes like this: God is love; perfect love casts out fear; therefore, the presence of fear is the absence of the spirit of God. Not being grounded in your true identity leads to not knowing where you came from or where you are going. It prevents understanding of the Father's care and provision and blocks accessing it. Some of the mortar rounds from this stronghold include worry; preoccupation with acquiring possessions; greed; inability to trust; stress, and inability to relax; lack of joy, gratitude, and thanksgiving; and imagining and dwelling on personal disaster scenarios. The FOTS solutions for fear and anxiety are Love, Self-Control, Joy, and Peace.

- Control—Control is a manifestation of its misbelief foundation, fear. "Control self" is also an expression of another devastating deficit—a deficit of trust. "Control self" insists on dominating others because they clearly cannot be trusted to produce the smooth, trouble-free result that "angry self" requires. "Others," in this case often extends to Papa as well. If anger is "self" personified, the stronghold of control is "god-with-a-little-g" personified—they are a matched set. Control is close-fisted; trust is open-handed. Jesus rejected His prerogative to control when He "did not count equality with God a thing to be *grasped*, but emptied Himself" (**Philippians 2:6-8, NAS**). The FOTS anecdotes for control are Love, Peace, Meekness, and Self-Control. When the stronghold of control is pulled down, it is imperative that it be replaced with the citadel of trust, and the fortification of forsaking self.

- Sexual sins—The unbelief on which all sexual sin is built is an immediate preoccupation with gratifying one's flesh, often through non-legitimate means. It is a baby's cry expressed through an adult body. Immediate gratification is paramount, often coupled with a strong self-destructive motivation. Some of the mortar rounds from this stronghold include addiction to pornography, lustful thoughts/fantasies, adultery and fornication, masturbation, and perversions. The FOTS solutions to sexual sin are Patience, Self-Control, and Faithfulness.

- Apathy/Laziness/Disengagement (A/L/D)—the foundation of unbelief on which the stronghold of A/L/D is built is double-mindedness, and is complicated further by lack of intentionality. This stronghold is the classic "double-minded man unstable in all of his ways" (**James 1:8**); and "tossed to and fro and carried about with every wind of doctrine, by the trickery of men, in the cunning craftiness of deceitful plotting" (**Ephesians 4:14**). A/L/D is often the behavioral manifestation of the root cause of insecurity, which is a form of fear. The stronghold's existence depends on a lack of vision and life-purpose because vision is a precursor to establishing goals and objectives which drive activity. Without goals, there is no energy or engagement. And, because apathy opposes love, the stronghold drains all love from life. The artillery from this stronghold usually falls in the form of excuse-making, dodging responsibility and accountability, isolation, no energy, existence without purpose, wandering, thwarted accomplishment, muddled thinking leading to wrong conclusions. The Fruit of the Spirit anecdote for the A/L/D trifecta is faithfulness, or "keeping on keeping on." Another anecdote is Hope. Although not a named FOTS, Hope is related to them as a precursor and precondition of their development. It is a "chicken-or-the-egg" question as to whether vision precedes hope or vice versa; in either case, they are co-dependent attitudes and conditions to pull down the stronghold of A/L/D.

- Negativity—The unbelief on which the stronghold of negativity is built is "clouded vision/wrong attribution." Often trauma, strong disappointment, or intensely painful emotional experience produces a "reject-you-before-you-reject-me" defensive response to the world. Negativity cannot exist except in an atmosphere where a person draws adverse, often worst-case conclusions; interprets meaning in a pessimistic and unfavorable light; exaggerates the significance of past events; or attaches jaundiced and unjustified interpretations. Often there is an exaggeration of circumstances in the negative person's mind. Another descriptive term for negativity is "anti-hope," and as such, interacts with the A/L/D stronghold—one rarely exists without the other. Negativity is often strengthened by a frustrated sense of perverted justice and a persistent preoccupation with the, "Why me?" question. The anecdote for negativity is the FOTS Faithfulness and Self-Control. The ability to re-frame one's thoughts is particularly important to pulling down the stronghold of negativity.

- Addictions—The unbelief foundation on which the stronghold of addiction exists is the urgent need to escape from pain, and a misplaced assumption of entitlement to comfort. Addictions are closely related to negativity and anger in that they often have the same originating events. They are an expression of anger because of an underlying assumption of entitlement to a smooth and trouble-free life. Behind every addiction is a backdrop of intense emotional pain, and an inability to face or confront the source. The internal conflict created when the strong emotional pain is met with the strong internal sense that we are entitled to a pain-free life swirls out of control into a full-fledged perfect storm. Addicts act to self-medicate and provide temporary relief from painful symptoms of abuse, disappointment, and shame. Non-substance addictions (e.g., sex addiction, cutting, eating disorders) are acting out emotional wounds and torment, with the accompanying deception of self-hatred. Addictions take the form of a drive—as opposed to a choice—because of the strength of the flesh's craving for the illegitimate substitute of an intrinsic right of the children of God—the Father's comfort. The tragedy of addictive behavior is that God has designed us in such a way that we are constructed to seek our comfort from Him. Addictions' mortar shell manifestations include shirking responsibility, refusal to cope, excuse-making, self-pity, skewed thinking and interpretation, preoccupation with the addiction, failure to perform even low-level life maintenance duties, and eventually a death spiral. As with negativity, re-framing is essential, particularly of events that resulted in personal trauma or shame.

- Selfishness—The most prevalent stronghold in man is selfishness, and it is near-universal. It is co-existent with all the others, and even remains as a stand-alone entity where others have been eradicated! The unbelief foundation upon which selfishness is built is the Independent Self. The selfishness stronghold produces a world view that considers events and circumstances first (and often, only) from the standard of, "How does this affect me?" Selfishness pushes aside Jesus' Second Commandment ("You shall love your neighbor as yourself," **Matthew 22:39**) and replaces it with, "You shall love your neighbor after yourself and if it works for you." The life circumstances of those hosting a stronghold of selfishness usually feature pockmarks and craters of failed relationships, loneliness, financial debt, and a host of other circumstances consistent with self-pampering, lack of stamina, anger, self-pity, and concentric rings of other strongholds that protect this inner sanctum of fortification. The FOTS anecdote for selfishness begins with Agape Love, features Agape Love in the middle, and ends with Agape Love. The reason for this is simple (as we will see in *Part 2*): Agape Love eradicates selfishness because the two cannot co-exist simultaneously. Agape Love in its role as the master Fruit of the Spirit includes the operation of the other eight FOTS to combat the mortar effects of selfishness.

There is more to say about pulling down each of these strongholds, and the mechanism of fighting them is the "stuff" of *Part 2: The Tool Chest*. The discipleship quest is often initially marked with combatting known strongholds and repairing the mortar damage. It is a victory when the stronghold is pulled down, but complete healing requires pressing on to repair the landscape damage and re-occupying the ceded territory as well.


## The Choice Space: Carnal Mind and Disbelief

Discipleship is all about the Choice Space; and the Choice Space is all about whose voice you elect to obey, carnal or spiritual mind. **Romans 8:7-8** tells us why the carnal mind is not an acceptable mindset for disciples: "Because the carnal mind is *enmity* against God: for it is not subject to the law of God, neither indeed can be. So then, they that are in the flesh cannot please God." Here Paul connects the "carnal mind" with the "flesh" and they are always a paired set—when you get one, you get the other. It is the nature of our flesh/carnal mind to relate to the physical world around

> **Romans 8:7-8**, "Because the carnal mind is enmity against God: for it is not subject to the law of God, neither indeed can be. So then they that are in the flesh cannot please God."

us *only* on the basis of our five senses—that is the flesh's reality. Likewise, that which can be observed, measured, and replicated is the approach of most science, if not all. Our bodies are hard-wired to depend on our senses for survival, and all that lies beyond the five senses (or six—some count balance as a sense) is suspect and non-reality as the flesh defines it. This strong bias related to our senses gives rise to disbelief—an *active bias/antagonism against* matters of spirit that cannot be measured or necessarily observed in the same manner. Here, I risk oversimplification, but this bias is the chief source of our internal spirit vs. flesh conflict at its most fundamental level. Scripture calls this conflict "enmity."[14] It is internally present in all human beings until, and unless, the person makes an affirmative decision to suspend disbelief. Said another way, no one can believe until the flesh's natural disbelief is intentionally counteracted and the carnal mind is transcended. This dynamic should not come as a surprise to any believer—it is the nuts-and-bolts of what Jesus described to Nicodemus as "born again." When we choose to circumvent disbelief, we can *see* the Kingdom; and when we see it, we can *enter*!

Unbelief and disbelief are two related-but-different concepts. Unbelief is the passive counterpoint to active belief. Disbelief is also active, like belief, but it is the *negative* counterpart of belief in that it *insists*

> **Ecclesiastes 3:11**, "Also He has put eternity in their hearts, except that no one can find out the work that God does from beginning to end."

on sensory confirmation to support a conclusion. Unbelief ignores or doubts; disbelief actively opposes. The difference between *disbelief/unbelief* and *belief* is the source where each obtains its information—belief from Spirit, disbelief/unbelief from the flesh/carnal mind. So, disbelief is affirmatively tied to the flesh in that, in the absence of sensory evidence, it is the flesh's default response. But Papa has put eternity (the eternal dimension) in our hearts (**Ecclesiastes 3:11**), and He intentionally designed His system so that eternal truths must be spiritually discerned, not observed by our five senses or measured by instruments. Solomon also tells us here "that no one can find out the work that God does from beginning to end"; but that declaration still leaves plenty of room for His kings to discover much of His mysterious "work" and intent in weaving together events, circumstances, dimensions, principles, and truths to accomplish His Program. The interface of T/S/M and the dimension of eternity/spirit is real, but it always occurs on the terms dictated by the greater reality—and that is the eternal.

If we are to embrace discipleship and choose wisely in the Choice Space, knowledge of the dynamic interaction of disbelief, unbelief, and belief is vital. *Passive unbelief must be overcome; active disbelief has to be intentionally suspended and rejected.* Both hinder faith, but disbelief opposes faith by requiring proof of spirit activity by taste, touch, feel, sight, or hearing where none can be demonstrated. Disbelief says, like Doubting Thomas in **John 20:25**, "Unless I see in His hands the print of the nails, and put my finger into the print of the nails, and put my hand into His side, *I will not believe*." Unbelief says, "I *cannot* believe"; disbelief says, "I *will not* believe." Understanding the difference, and how to stand against each, is to highlight the dilemma that disbelief creates between the carnal and spiritual minds.

**Ephesians 2:16** says that Jesus has put to death the enmity between flesh and spirit through the cross,

> **Ephesians 2:17-18**, "[17]And He came and preached peace to you who were afar off and to those who were near. [18]For through Him we both have access by one Spirit to the Father."

and there is, therefore, the potential for peace. However, to be able to even perceive the realm of the spirit—much less trust in it—we must first intentionally suspend our natural disbelief. Suspension of disbelief is not faith, but this first step does allow us to transcend our own story and enter another. The world calls this believing in "fairy tales." Paul points out in **Romans 8:7** that it is not even possible while our carnal mind rules. But intentionally suspending our disbelief opens up a new pervasive reality that is superior in every way. As we grow in maturity in the Spirit, the suspension of our disbelief becomes a habit and even our primary nature. Suspending

---

[14] Enmity: a feeling or condition of hostility; hatred; ill will; animosity; antagonism. https://www.dictionary.com/browse/enmity, last accessed 2/27/2019.

disbelief opens up the "eyes of our understanding" (Ephesians 1:18), a dynamic which we will discuss later as, "Learning to See."

**Mark 9:23-24** recounts the story of a father who sought Jesus' healing power for his child, and his cry to the Master is one we can feel rising within ourselves from time to time: "Jesus said to him, 'If you can believe, all things are possible to him who believes.' Immediately, the father of the child cried out and said with tears, 'Lord, *I believe; help my unbelief*!'" The father in this Scripture had tried all that he knew to find relief from his son's malady. Jesus offers him the key to relief: "If you can believe," was Jesus' admonition in **verse 23**. The father's response is *pivotal,* both for him and for us today: "Lord, I *believe*; help my *unbelief*!" If I may offer the following paraphrase, I think it captures the meaning: "Lord, I am a believer; help me overcome my habitual dependence on my five senses and my natural unbelief!" This father was poised on the cusp of entering the Kingdom because his declaration shows us that he had already suspended his *disbelief* ("Lord, I believe"), and merely needed some help from the Spirit to overcome his *unbelief* and the habit of defaulting to our T/S/M senses. Our faith, trust, and actions are imperfect; at any given time, we display both an overarching faith in Christ that justifies us, and the remaining pockets of unbelief influenced by our flesh and from which we are being saved. "Help my unbelief" is a legitimate prayer for all who dwell in this clay vessel but wish to clearly see the Spirit's work in us and in our world. "Help my unbelief" is a mantra of the heart set on pilgrimage. Abandoning disbelief is an affirmative act of will; it is up to us—not the Spirit—to first get past the disbelief that blocks our access to the birth canal through which entry is made into the spiritual realm. "Help my unbelief" is tantamount to crying out, "Make me childlike again!" It is like crying out to the Father, "Rebirth me into the place of a child."

**Hebrews 10:20** refers to our resident disbelief as the "veil of the flesh," which veil was torn from top to bottom in a figure when Jesus entered behind it into the Holy of Holies to present the sacrifice of His own blood. He forever changed the "Mercy Seat" to the "Throne of Grace." To gaze behind the veil requires an overt act of stepping beyond the finite limitations of our human senses to access our spiritual heritage. This is the meaning of Jesus' comparison for Nicodemus of those born of the Spirit to the wind in **John 3:8**:

> [8]The wind [Spirit] blows where it wishes [moves in the Eternal realm to accomplish His purposes], and you hear the sound of it [perceive the evidence of it in the lives of individuals], but cannot tell where it comes from and where it goes [cannot perceive with the flesh its coming and going]. So is everyone who is born of the Spirit." [Interpretation/Paraphrase mine]

Spirit birth requires a decision to intentionally expand beyond our senses-based reasoning into the realm of child-like imagination, trust, acceptance, and dependence. It is this world of spiritual imaging that Jesus declared that is the purview of children of the faith, and without which we may not *see* (perceive; acknowledge) the Kingdom. Suspension of disbelief is not faith; but this first step opens the door to allow us to transcend our own parochial, Independent Self story and enter another, a greater story concerning the Bride of Christ and the Bridegroom. It is the Great Story, a love story at the heart and motivation of all of God's creation. It is the story of the love between the King and the Shulamite Maid in the Song of Solomon! Again, the world calls this believing in fairy tales; but the truth is that these fairy tales are

> **2 Corinthians 3:16-17**, "[16][W]hen one turns to the Lord, **the veil is taken away**. [17]Now the Lord is the Spirit; and where the Spirit of the Lord is, there is liberty. [18]But we all, **with unveiled face**, beholding as in a mirror the glory of the Lord, are being transformed into the same image from glory to glory, just as by the Spirit of the Lord."

actual reality, not the temporary T/S/M placeholders! Setting aside our tendency to trust in only our senses opens up a new birth experience and the pervasive reality that is superior in every way. As we grow in maturity in the Spirit, the suspension of our disbelief becomes a second-nature habit. We learn to see that Papa's reality is more real than what our senses perceive because the veil of the flesh is passing away, but the eternal remains.

## The Choice Space: Momentary Light Affliction

The "light affliction" referenced in **2 Corinthians 4:17** refers to the whole gauntlet of human suffering, from the splinter in the finger to the prolonged torture currently experienced by some of our brothers and sisters. Why does God use the strategy of suffering to teach us His ways? In response to our perceived absolute need to know, we can make up answers; we can wail and thrash; we can nurse bitterness, hurt, and self-pity; we can pout, and meditate on the unfairness of life; we can conclude that the universe is a cold, unfriendly place. *Or, we can learn.* I have done all of the above in my pilgrimage, and my testimony is that the latter is better.

"Well, Mr. Wizard, what is there to learn?" Exactly. That question is everything. In fact, the question may have more value than any particular piece of the answer. Paul's **2 Corinthians 4:18** conclusion reveals the totality of the point to suffering: It yields for us a "far more exceeding and eternal weight of glory." If I may paraphrase Paul, he is saying, "the glory achieved by the processing of our suffering is disproportionately positive relative to our suffering's duration and discomfort...while we do not look at the things which are seen, but at the things which are not seen." "Look at" here means to contemplate, concentrate on, give undivided attention to, meditate on. When attempting to understand this, we *must* remember that *this life never has been and never will be the point*, except as it trains us to rule with Him in eternity; it is a training and learning environment, a classroom, the warm-up bullpen.

> **2 Corinthians 4:16-18**, "[16]Therefore we do not lose heart. Even though our outward man is perishing, yet the inward man is being renewed day by day. [17]For our light affliction, which is but for a moment, is working for us a far more exceeding and eternal weight of glory, [18]while we do not look at the things which are seen, but at the things which are not seen. For the things which are seen are temporary, but the things which are not seen are eternal."

The exercise of learning is to concentrate on the things that are unseen rather than the noise that our physical self and environment press upon our precious life. In short, suffering is designed to train us to think in terms (and in the manner of) the Kingdom. That is infinitely more than "thinking positive thoughts!" We have the *capacity* to discern the difference between Spirit and flesh, but no chance of *being successful* unless we learn to tune out the clamor of the flesh, tune in the still, small voice of the Spirit, and ask the right questions in our soul.

**2 Corinthians 4:18** continues, "For the things which are seen are temporary, but the things which are not seen are eternal." How does one "look at" the things that are not seen? Obviously, Paul is talking about looking with some sense organ other than our physical eyes. Likewise, when we hear God's voice, we do so with something Jesus called "ears to hear." It is equally obvious that not all people have ears to hear, otherwise, Jesus would not make the distinction between those who can and those who cannot.

> **2 Corinthians 4:18**, "For the things which are seen are temporary, but the things which are not seen are eternal."

After establishing ears to hear and eyes to see, the next thing for a believer to address in order to see and hear into the spiritual (eternal) realm is **TO LEARN TO FOCUS** *ATTENTION* AWAY FROM THE CLAMOR OF THE

WORLD and onto the quiet voice of the Spirit. Notice how I got your attention by shouting at you with **ALL CAPS** and drew your focus with a variety of fonts? That is the way that the world comes after you; and unless we intentionally turn it off, we will be distracted. That is the way the world clamors for our attention. Some ministries have pursued the "flash/bang!" strategy even in the light of the declaration of **Colossians 2:23**, "[23]These things indeed have an appearance of wisdom in self-imposed religion, false humility, and neglect of the body, but are of no value against the indulgence of the flesh." Paul's declaration here is, in effect, "You cannot accomplish spiritual ends using fleshly methodology—it is a conflict of worlds and dimensions." The objective is not to recreate a "Jesus version" of T/S/M norms. It is to learn to hear and see (discern) Him in the middle of battle, in chaos and clamor, with the world clawing at us for our attention, with society going crazy and trying to drag us down with it, with anguish and outcries all around, keeping our inward eyes and ears focused on Him for both our sustenance and instruction. Nothing to it, right? Such is the leadership training program for the Kingdom.

## The Choice Space: Happy Talk

**Philippians 4:13** tells us, "I can do all things through Christ who strengthens me." Anyone who knows me well knows that I do not do "happy talk." Happy talk in the way I mean it is for a person to ignore one's environment and experience, and work their emotions into a state of faux happiness or excitement by repeating platitudes and inspirational messages or posters. Happy talk is what motivational poster-makers depend on for financial survival. It is stirring up the flesh with fireworks, smoke, and turning up the bass so loud that we can feel it impacting our chest. That

> **Philippians 4:13**, "I can do all things through Christ who strengthens me."

may well work for others, but living in a perpetual emotional hype doesn't work for me. The rush of inspirational thought, to be useful, must be followed by inspired action. I find that, like medicating pain and problems with alcohol (or one's drug of choice), when one returns to earth from a whipped-up emotional high, T/S/M reality is still there to greet us. Jesus said a little phrase in **John 14:2** that means a lot to me: "In My Father's house are many abiding places; *if it were not so I would have told you.*" While most concentrate on the "abiding places" part, I am comforted by Jesus plainly declaring that his words are not "happy talk," and His word is not the text of a motivational poster, but spirit and life.

So, why contrast **Philippians 4:13** and happy talk? Because, although many people glibly rattle off the words of Scripture motivational poster-style, those who struggle with addictions (and that is most of us in one form or another) *cannot afford* for **Philippians 4:13** to be happy talk. We know that today and **Philippians 4:13** are all we have on which to base our hope for the future. On the other hand, neither can we afford fatalism and depression. Our enemy comes to us and says, "Others can, but you can't." When we lose sight of the "all things" God promises we can do, we dive head-long onto that slippery slope that dumps us inevitably at the bottom in a heaping mess. So, for many, **Philippians 4:13** is never quoted with a silly grin on our face and superficial lilt in our voice, but with an effectual seriousness associated with fighting for life.

"Momentary light afflictions" come to us in a myriad of natural and unnatural forms. As my body deteriorates to reflect my chronological age, I find myself taking comfort in the conversion of my dependence from outward man to inward man, as Paul described:

> **2 Corinthians 4:16-18**, "Therefore we do not lose heart. Even though our outward man is perishing, yet the inward man is being renewed day by day. For our light affliction, which is but for a moment, is working for us a far more exceeding and eternal weight of glory, while we do not look at the things which are seen, but at the things which are not seen."

One morning recently, as I sat on the side of the bed feeling the aches and pains of my 66+-year-old body, my first thought, my first communication in the Spirit was,

"You are *not* your body. You are the person-consciousness in this body, this shell, this vessel. Your aches and fatigue do not define you. The strength and energy you have lost to the passage of time do not define you. You are not defined nor hindered by the fog of mind that is so new and unfamiliar to you. What *does* define you is the identity I have has given you as a gift. You are defined by the sum of your spirit and soul interacting to become the better, future you. You are not defined by what you can no longer do, but by what I say about you, by the *'all things are possible'* you."

This was a fairly unusual experience for me to have such a clear voice of the Holy Spirit in my spirit out-of-the-blue, and especially before I had my coffee. But it was a message—a personal prophecy—that greatly encouraged me. The day before had been spent in rigorous work, the kind of work I love, and with which I have challenged my body my whole life. But these days there is a significant price to be paid for the same pleasure of engagement. I suspect that there are other friends reading this in the same category of past their physical prime; but you have a sense that you have never been more cognizant of who you are, who God has made you, and what you are to be about.

Make no mistake: Our outer man *is* perishing. (I count myself among those who have formerly considered themselves as bulletproof!) But the wise exchange/redemption of time ("redeeming the time," **Ephesians 5:16**) is for a renewal of the inward man that experiences the promise of "an eternal weight of glory." We do not look to things that can be seen—it ain't pretty, especially the view in the mirror! Instead, we fix the gaze of our soul on the unseen reality which is everything. What is there to lose heart about? As my dad used to say, "If you let things get your goat, it just proves you've got one!" In the same sense, if you let things cause you to lose heart, it just proves you need to refocus on the inward man—and the promised weight of glory!

## The Choice Space: You Are Dead—Get Over It!

All journeys begin with a point of departure—the first step if you will—and end with a terminal objective or destination. Our pilgrimage of spirit is no different. Random travel without beginning and end is difficult to conceive, much less understand. Yet it seems to be the common lifestyle of those who are acting outside of the eternal realm. One of the affirmative signs of life in the Spirit is *movement*, and that movement is intended for us to be ever upward and ever onward. Paul called the process, "press[ing] toward the goal for the prize of the upward call of God in Christ Jesus" (**Philippians 3:14**). I *love* that Paul had identified a process and that he had a goal, a prize that would motivate and urge him onward, especially in times when he did not particularly feel like it. I love it because I have those days, and I suspect that you do, too. Paul called his goal "the upward call." A pilgrimage without a gate of departure is not a journey at all, it is drifting, and a journey without a destination is aimless meandering.

We took some care in Chapter 1 to define our pilgrimage destination and reason for existing in this

> **Colossians 3:3**, "For you died, and your life is hidden with Christ in God."

time/space/matter world. To complete our trip planning then, it remains for us to define the departure gateway, and it is found in **Colossians 3:3**. In case you missed it, *you are dead.* You were born dead, and despite physical evidence to the contrary, your flesh remains dead. That is the gateway from which we begin our journey: dead. Lifeless. Deceased. Muertos. Dod. Wrap-it-up-and-go-home. The fat lady sang. Tot. Whatever language(s) you speak, whatever phrase you apply, your demise is a current reality, not a future probability.  We have said that every human being—save One—born from the sixth day of creation (Adam and Eve were not born, they were created) until this very moment have been born *separated* from union with the Father, and that means we are born dead.

Recall also that sin is not primarily bad behavior, it is separation, only one of the consequences of which is bad behavior.  Sin = separation, and sin = death, therefore separation = death.  For believers, *physical death is no more than a waypoint in the journey, not the end.*  The passing of our physical body and the transition to our resurrected body has nothing to do with the cessation of life, only the shedding of an unnecessary vessel with its accompanying limitations.

> - Sin = Separation;
> - Sin = Death; therefore
> - ∴ Separation = Death.

Travel brochures are written and serve the purpose of guiding and enhancing a journey.  Usually, they provide descriptions of waypoints and tell of the significant monuments and sights to experience at points along the journey.  We, too, have a spectacular travel brochure for our pilgrimage across life's wilderness.  The Scripture describes the point of departure, the destination, and the activities in which to engage along the way.  It tells what we may expect to see, the best viewpoints for observation, and even gives us warning of the dangerous pitfalls.  It tells where we may find sustenance, fuel for our travel, points at which to stop and rest, and directions to where we may find traveling companions.  It is a complete travel guide, and we neglect to consult it for our journey to the detriment of our experience and to our own peril!

If the Apostle Paul gave us no other gift, he left with us a priceless perspective of how to grace-fully and successfully wrestle with affliction.  Consider these two passages in the context of where we fix our thinking in the midst of momentary light affliction:

> For the love of Christ compels us, *because we judge thus*: that if One died for all, then all died; and He died for all, that those who live should live no longer for themselves, but for Him who died for them and rose again. (**2 Corinthians 5:14-15**)

And,

> *Set your mind* on things above, not on things on the earth.  For you died, and your life is hidden with Christ in God." (**Colossians 3:2-3**)

I recently watched an impactful episode of the television series, *Band of Brothers*.[15]  The episode was centered around the paralyzing effects of fear in war, and it told the story of Pvt. Blythe and his struggles to overcome his fear.  The memorable quote is from Speirs (the quintessential soldier, seemingly without fear), who tells Blythe:

> The only hope you have is to *accept the fact that you're already dead*.  The sooner you accept that the sooner you'll be able to function as a soldier is supposed to function: without mercy, without compassion, without remorse.

This quote pretty much encapsulates what I hope to convey, minus the "no mercy/compassion" part; for that part of the quote we should substitute "without regard to Independent Self."  The cogent message is short and sweet, and it is the same message of **Colossians 3:3**: You are dead.  Any life that you think you have is in Christ and never belonged to you in the first place.  I am consciously, intentionally making an attempt to eliminate the phrase, "my life," from my vocabulary and substitute, "my experience."  When a Christian carelessly talks about "my life," one of two possibilities exist: 1) He or she has temporarily lost focus on the fact that they no longer possess a life; or 2) he/she has never come to terms with the *fact*

---

[15] Episode 3—"Carentan"

that they have died, and therefore inevitably continues to operate in the world as if they are the central character, and that the whole of creation revolves around him/her. When we lose "our life" (or, more clearly, our *right* to live for ourselves) the *fact* of our death separates us from not only fear (as Speirs tells us), but also our faux central position as the most important being in the universe, with all other beings in orbit around our self-centered world. And, in losing our separate-ness (not individuality—there is a difference), we are joined in union with the true Central Being of the universe. Jesus said it this way in **Matthew 10:39**, "He who finds his life will lose it, and he who loses his life for My sake will find it." The conflict we often see and experience around us is less of a difference of perspectives as much as it is a collision of worlds.

What are the characteristics of a Christian in category #2 (above) who has never come to terms with their death? I focus on just one, one central to our discipleship quest: When a person—believer or unbeliever—is the center of their own universe, everything else (people, objects, events, etc.) become collectibles with value in proportion to their effect on "my life." We collect family, we collect friends, possessions, memories, and experience. We collect "religion," and yes, we collect an appropriate measure of "Jesus." Like charms on a bracelet, the stuff in orbit around us serves all of "my" egocentric goals and experiences, Jesus among the rest! When we never embrace the fact that we are dead, and therefore possess nothing, we remain oriented to acquiring, and all of its trappings: maintaining, appearing, possessing, and coveting. These activities are tantamount to "arranging the deck chairs on the Titanic"— they are going down! Until we come to terms with the fact of our death, Jesus remains one collectible among all the rest, along with our pet rock and Mickey Mantle autographed baseball. As Speirs so eloquently put it, "The *only* hope you have is to accept the fact that you're already dead."

## The Choice Space: The Faithfulness Standard

> Whoever can be trusted with very little can also be trusted with much, and whoever is dishonest with very little will also be dishonest with much. So, if you have not been trustworthy in handling worldly wealth, who will trust you with true riches? And if you have not been trustworthy with someone else's property, who will give you property of your own? (**Luke 16:10-12**)

The measure of integrity is micro-level adherence to the right things one knows to do. It is foolish self-deception for a man or woman to think that they will perform differently in their stewardship once they have "made it." It is equally foolish to believe that one's behavior in private, out of the public eye, will be different than their false public persona; or that whether in the public limelight or behind closed doors makes any difference at all except the size of the audience. The behavior may be different, but the integrity level remains the same since we are not allowed one integrity level for public activity and one for private behavior. **Matthew 6:4** assures us that our Father sees in secret and rewards (that is, brings to-fruitfulness that which is sown, both good and evil) openly. The "Audience of One" is always present.

In **Luke 16:10-12**, Jesus presents a principle in both the positive and negative, so we also know that the positive converse of the last half of the verse is also true: "He who *is* trustworthy in handling worldly wealth **will be** trusted with true riches. And, if you *are* trustworthy with someone else's property/responsibility, you *will be given* property/responsibility of your own" [*paraphrase and emphasis mine*]. The Faithfulness Progression Principle emphasizes how God has designed our spiritual growth process to mirror natural processes with which we are familiar. The natural progression, in this case, is, "First you demonstrate the ability to be responsible, then you get your own area of responsibility." The area of responsibility to which Jesus is referring—the "true riches"—is our future role in ruling with Him in the Kingdom of God.

**Luke 16:10-12** correlates to **Luke 19:11-27**, the "Parable of the Minas." In the parable, Jesus makes an affirmative connection between our faithfulness in transacting the Father's business in this life and using the resources He has put at our disposal and our position and responsibilities in the Kingdom. **Matthew 25:14-30** gives an account of this same principle/parable from a slightly different viewpoint. The Faithfulness Progression Principle is counter-intuitive from the carnal mind's perspective, which can be summarized as "give-to-me-regardless-of-proof-of-responsibility."

Worldly wealth and property are not Jesus' true interest, but rather the training mechanism and resource that He uses to teach us the larger, more pervasive eternal meaning. The most important takeaways from **Luke 16:10-12** are two-fold: 1) Our future role in the Kingdom of God is entirely dependent upon our faithfulness in this life; 2) As we learn and prove our faithfulness, we are progressively given responsibility pertaining to the Kingdom, and these responsibilities become our own. They also constitute a portion of the promised inheritance that we share with our Bridegroom.

It is a Kingdom principle that consistent performance of stewardship—faithfulness—is the standard by which all activity is judged, not the worldly standard of success or failure. In **2 Timothy 2:2**, Paul writes, "And the things that you have heard from me among many witnesses, commit these to *faithful men* who will be able to teach others also." Paul's guidance for Tim's School of Ministry was that Timothy should select those that had already proved their faithfulness in little things before choosing them for advanced responsibility. Paul's advice returns us to **Luke 16**, and the following "Faithfulness Progression Principle" may be articulated: "If a believer aspires to possess an expression of responsibility that is their own, they should first train, hone, and prove their faithfulness by supporting the work of another." Those already doing the stuff should look around for those aspiring to join their ranks and help them in the process. **Zechariah 4:10** encourages us not to despise the day of small beginnings. If you wish to have that which is your own, begin small by joining others in their work and so prove your faithfulness.

These days there is an interesting practice that totally flies in the face of Scriptural teaching: the "participation trophy." It is the practice of awarding a trophy to every player based on showing up and irrespective of their contribution. The theory is that we must take care not to damage the self-image of children by teaching them that there are winners and losers in life. Instead, "we are all winners by virtue of playing." That may be a nice humanistic philosophy, but it is neither Scriptural nor in the child's best interest to instill that lesson. Instead, if we take care to teach our children that their worth and identity is based on what Papa says is true about them, then their self-image will not be so fragile as to be damaged by failing to be the best at any one thing. The opportunity to excel is motivating, just as "sameness" and uniform reward is demotivating, and eventually extinguishes effort. When I was a fire chief, I had a saying to coach my firefighters competing for promotion: "Seniority is not a job skill, and showing up is not a job qualification." If you want to earn a promotion, you have to expand your knowledge and faithfulness base.

"Participation Trophy" thinking from the world has also had an impact on the Church. There is a common understanding that our inheritance in its entirety automatically accrues to our spiritual account. That is true with respect to our justification, but it is contrary to Jesus' words in terms of our Kingdom responsibility and reward. There *is* a performance aspect that is integral to our experience of the Kingdom and the development of our inheritance, and Scripture indicates that those that fail to use their lifetime on earth to develop themselves in this manner *will suffer loss* (**1 Corinthians 3:15**). Please do not misunderstand—I am *not* saying we are justified by works, and I am not anti-grace! Far from it! We are justified by nothing other than the Blood of Jesus. But, as we commit ourselves to learn and perform faithfully in working out our own salvation, we prepare ourselves to rule with Him, and qualify ourselves to receive "that which is [our] own."

## The Choice Space: The "Helpfulness Context"

Citizens of all countries must adhere to the laws and standards of the country in which they reside. Failure to do so usually results in confinement and punishment. Given that we are citizens of an other-worldly Kingdom, the decisions that we make and the standards to which we adhere *have importance as they impact our eternal destiny of citizenship in the Kingdom*. Some of the frequent choices we are called upon to make are our behavior toward others, choices that affect our own well-being and balancing the impact of the two. Perhaps you recognize this context for decision-making to be consistent with Jesus' Second Great Commandment: "You shall love your neighbor as yourself" (**Matthew 22:39**). The Apostle Paul gives us two more verses that serve as the standard for our behavior toward one another. In these two verses—**1 Corinthians 6:12 and 10:23**—Paul addresses our choice of actions and on what basis they should be evaluated:

> **1 Corinthians 6:12**, "All things are lawful for me, but all things are not *helpful*. All things are lawful for me, but I will not be brought *under the power* of any." And,

> **1 Corinthians 10:23**, "All things are lawful for me, but not all things are *helpful*; all things are lawful for me, but not all things *edify*."

In both verses, he declares, in effect, that the Jewish Law no longer applies to the Church. While we are exempt from the requirements of the Law, he adds a *conscience* standard that is a higher road—even if less specific—than the Law. By the phrase "not all things are helpful [expedient]," he intentionally sets a new standard: Our Choice Space actions should be evaluated by the standard of helpfulness to the spiritual life of the church, and of the believer (including yourself). By removing the parameters of the written Law and placing evaluation of our actions in the realm of conscience, Paul establishes the principle of governance of the Church by internal principles of the Spirit and by conscience, and not the flesh and external edict (Law). The standard becomes a part of us, not bolted on.

Paul then clarifies what is helpful by giving us two further evaluation criteria: "brought under the power of any," and "edification." Being "brought under the power" means to be controlled by, or addicted to. Edification means to build up, as compared to tearing down; it means to encourage, and not judge or criticize. The sum of his guidance is that our choices should no longer be subject to the dictates of behavioral rules, but rather be guided by a *higher standard*: The Holy Spirit interacting with our conscience. The Helpfulness/Edification Principle leaves no place for judging one another.

Expediency as a standard for conduct requires a layer of consciousness of the needs of others. It means more than simply being awake and aware of one's environment; it is aware of the specific effects of my behavior on myself *and* others. Such awareness implies evaluation and projection of consequences *before* executing a particular action. The implication of expedience and helpfulness is that we *slow down* our reactions to others and to situations in order to give our conscience and spirit time to come to peaceful terms with an appropriate response.

> **1 Corinthians 8:9**, "⁹But beware lest somehow this liberty of yours become a stumbling block to those who are weak."

For consistent "upward call" progress, our discipleship choices must be helpful, not a hindrance to growth, or even destructive. They must have the effect of building up those around us rather than tearing them down. Paul enjoins us not to allow our liberty to become a stumbling block to others (**1 Corinthians**

8:9). Adhering to this "building" standard results in the positive benefit to the Body of Christ, and a safe atmosphere for all of us to progress.

Finally, we should set as a goal not to be controlled by *anything* but the Spirit of God—no habit, no rule, no expectation. This is Romans **8:21's** "Glorious Liberty of the Children of God Principle." Jesus said, "My yoke is easy and My burden is light." Here, Paul reveals what that yoke is—the yoke of conscience. The helpfulness context must be well defined in us by consistent experience if we are to understand how individual choices are impactful to our ability to reign, and ultimately rule.

## The Choice Space: Contentment and Need

Standard thinking informs us that carnal mind decisions made in the Choice Space flow from our motivations; and our carnal mind motivations are usually prompted by our perceived needs. That means that our choices are often a product of our contented or discontented status. Contentment, satisfaction, and peace are friendly companions. Discontent attracts anxiety, striving, restlessness, unhappiness, and comparing ourselves to others. Choices made from a motivation of discontentment usually end badly.

Contrary to standard thinking, Philippians 4:11-12 contains a life-changing principle that explodes the myth that we cannot be content when we are in need. In a few words, Paul separates need and contentment, indicating that there is no cause-and-effect relationship:

> Not that I speak in regard to need, for I have learned in whatever state I am, to be content: I know how to be abased, and I know how to abound. Everywhere and in all things I have learned both to be full and to be hungry, both to abound and to suffer need.

You and I can have needs, and still, rest in a state of contentment because being content is not need-based, but attitude and decision-based. Any cause-and-effect relationship that exists between our ears concerning need and discontentment is learned; and, anything that has been inappropriately learned can be unlearned or re-learned with Papa's help and Holy Spirit's coaching. That is spiritual mind decision-making in action.

Another interesting element of this Scripture is that Paul seems to indicate that the competing states of *abased* and *abound* are not the opposite ends of a continuum as we tend to see them, but rather companion states—just different points of development. For example, we may be in physical need in one area of life, and be abounding in another and have leftover to share. If we allow circumstances to govern contentment, all of the stars will never align to bring us to that settled state. Paul learned that these external factors are irrelevant to the internal environment of peace and contentment. We simply need to unlearn the lie, and re-learn the truth—and that is where the Choice Space enters the picture.

In **1 Timothy 6:6-10**, Paul gives his adopted son, Timothy, some fatherly advice about that which is important in this life. Remember, this advice is from the guy who was caught up to the 3rd Heaven to see in person the Kingdom of God in operation:

> 6Now godliness with contentment is great gain. 7For we brought nothing into this world, and it is certain we can carry nothing out. 8And having food and clothing, with these we shall be content. 9But those who desire to be rich fall into temptation and a snare, and into many foolish and harmful lusts which drown men in destruction and perdition. 10For the love of money is a root of all kinds of evil, for which some have strayed from the faith in their greediness, and pierced themselves through with many sorrows.

The love of money is synonymous with the love of self because of all of the self-pampering, self-comforting, self-promoting, and self-stimulating items money buys. These days, with so many possessions to crowd and overwhelm our spiritual senses, the line between need and want has been obscured-if-not-obliterated. There are many interests pressing in from the outside to encourage and cultivate a drive to consume that goes *way* beyond need. Marketing has become a science, and science has become a god. In the prevailing economic climate, consumerism is implied to be one's duty, and the pressure to live up-to-if-not-well-beyond one's means is constant. Consumerism is another form of slavery; and as such, greed and consumerism are two sides of the same fleshly coin and currency. It is another voice in the world that, if obeyed, creates a master/slave relationship. The relationship is insidious because the "gotcha" consequences are not apparent until the hooks are well set, and many years of Choice Space pain to remove them is inevitable.

## The Choice Space: "It's Not Fair"

In the pursuit of our discipleship Choice Space, there are two characteristics that are *always* a trap. These two traps *never* meet the helpful or expedient standards of behavior. They are self-pity and victim-ness. These two are rampant in our society, and they serve one, and only one, purpose—to take our eyes off God's process and put them on 1) ourselves, that is, our flesh; and, 2) situations and circumstances that we perceive to be unfair. Fairness is a human concept that does not have any bearing on our response in the Choice Space except as dwelling on the concept distracts from and hinders our development. There is no such thing as an objective fairness standard. In order to decide about whether

> **Ezekiel 18:25**, "Yet you say, 'The way of the Lord is not fair.' Hear now, O house of Israel, is it not My way which is fair, and your ways which are not fair?"

or not something is fair or unfair, one must place him or herself in the position of judge, and ultimately the arbiter of that which is good (fair), and that which is evil (unfair). In order to decide whether a situation of unfairness with respect to themselves, one must first decide that they somehow deserve—entitled to—better or different circumstances. One functional definition of grace and mercy is that "Grace is getting *what you don't deserve*, and mercy is *not getting what you do deserve*." Self-pity and victim-ness depend on a beginning position that you deserve something better than your current circumstances, which attitude precludes mercy according to the foregoing definition! That is a lie and a major deception strategy of the enemy. If God treated us according to what we deserve, we would all be obliterated.

Fairness is not an issue in our circumstances because our circumstances are like test questions: They are what they are. Test questions may be hard or easy; they may be multiple-choice, essay, or true-false. They may be ten questions, or 2000! However, it is the Teacher's prerogative to make the test; and when God makes up a test for you, it is precisely fitted for your knowledge base, and serves the purpose of growing us in areas of need. The Holy Spirit is a tenured, experienced, *genius* professor that knows both His subject matter *and* His subject. You are not a mystery to Him, and His circumstantial tests are for your benefit. Fairness is irrelevant, and the standards by which you judge it are skewed by your filters and flesh.

Another emotional reaction that often follows on the heels of an "it's not fair" determination is our desire for revenge. "Somebody's gonna pay" is the natural carnal mind response to unfair circumstances. Of course, this is an ill-disposed and uncooperative response—that much is evident. But it also ignores the fact that *Somebody has already paid!* Jesus has already paid the price for all sin, for all time. The lesson of the unforgiving servant in **Matthew 18:21-35** reveals the personal peril of the servant who depends on the Master's mercy for their own debt relief but refuses to extend mercy to others.

"Somebody's gonna pay" is illegitimate as an expression of a fleshly thirst for revenge. We are promised a day of vindication, and we may legitimately morph our fleshly thirst for *revenge* into a patient desire for *vindication*:

- **Job 13:18**, "See now, I have prepared my case, I know that I shall be vindicated."

- **Psalm 26:1**, "Vindicate me, O Lord, for I have walked in my integrity. I have also trusted in the Lord; I shall not slip."

- **Psalm 35:24**, "Vindicate me, O Lord my God, according to Your righteousness; and let them not rejoice over me."

> **Matthew 18:21-22**, "[21]Then Peter came to Him and said, 'Lord, how often shall my brother sin against me, and I forgive him? Up to seven times?' [22]Jesus said to him, 'I do not say to you, up to seven times, but up to seventy times seven.'"

- **Psalm 43:1**, "Vindicate me, O God, and plead my cause against an ungodly nation; Oh, deliver me from the deceitful and unjust man!"

Vengeance is payback; vindication is an expression of God's Justice. Vengeance is a prerogative of God, and when we exact it, we usurp His authority (**Romans 12:19, Isaiah 63:4**). Our desire for vindication is a trust position in which we unwind our desire to lash out and retreat into the peaceful confidence that our Abba sees and knows our pain and suffering. He will vindicate us at the appropriate time—not just against the "deceitful and unjust man," but against the enemy of our soul, and against a world system that has conspired with him to keep the Bride from reaching her full potential. For that, we patiently wait.

### Writing it Down...

A good use of this space would be to make notes, record insights, ask questions, etc.

# Chapter 5—Learning to S.E.E.

*I counsel you to buy from Me gold refined in the fire, that you may be rich; and white garments, that you may be clothed, that the shame of your nakedness may not be revealed; and **anoint your eyes with eyesalve, that you may see.** Revelation 3:18*

## Mining Gold

Jesus was a master communicator who chose His analogies, metaphors, similes, and other tools of language intentionally; and left it to another (the Holy Spirit) to coach and guide us as we plumb the depths of the meaning of His words. **Revelation 3:18** is a portion of the prophetic letter to the Laodicean Church—the "lukewarm church." As the last of the seven letters (corresponding to seven church ages), and given the time in which we live, it is reasonable to examine the text for direct application to us, both individually and the full Church. When I read in **Revelation 3:14-19** that Jesus' people make Him want to "vomit [them] out of [His] mouth," I sit up and take notice so as to avoid that particular fate:

> ¹⁴"And to the angel of the church of the Laodiceans write, 'These things says the Amen, the Faithful and True Witness, the Beginning of the creation of God: ¹⁵"I know your works, that you are neither cold nor hot. I could wish you were cold or hot. *¹⁶So then, because you are lukewarm and neither cold nor hot, I will vomit you out of My mouth.* ¹⁷Because you say, 'I am rich, have become wealthy, and have need of nothing'—and do not know that you are wretched, miserable, poor, blind, and naked—*¹⁸I counsel you to buy from Me gold refined in the fire, that you may be rich; and white garments, that you may be clothed, that the shame of your nakedness may not be revealed; and anoint your eyes with eyesalve, that you may see.* ¹⁹As many as I love, I rebuke and chasten. Therefore, be zealous and repent."

We have addressed different aspects of Jesus' shopping list for us from **Revelation 3:18** because buying commodities that transfer to the eternal dimension is *crucial* to discipleship. Jesus' letter to us councils that we obtain three categories of items to avoid the "vomiting" fate: *gold, white garments, and eye salve.* These are metaphors for characteristics that repair our state of being "wretched, miserable, poor, blind, and naked" (**verse 3:17**). Note that the Laodicean Church suffered from self-deception that resulted in an over-confidence; and, in their deception, declared their need for "nothing" (i.e., "I need nothing from God"). Could there be any more bold and reckless expression of Independent Self than to thumb one's nose in the face of Deity? The declaration is made all the more poignant when we remember it is from the Church, not the world!

I was not present when gold—especially refined, pure gold—was chosen as *the* universal commodity signifying wealth, royal standing, and luxurious desirability, so I cannot account for all the reasons. I *do* know that its significance and value have their origins in the eternal realm. I know that it is symbolic of incorruptibility, renowned for its investment potential, and desirable as an adornment. I know it is a metaphor for intrinsic value and goodness. For most of history, it was the definitive standard for exchange value: The value of anything compared to gold. When Jesus says, "buy from Me gold," He is saying, "Sell every lesser thing to obtain that which is of true bedrock and lasting value: The largest stake and portion of the Kingdom you can obtain."

White garments speak to the purity of our standing before Him—our "wedding garment." **Matthew 22:11-14** gives us the context to understand the importance of proper attire when it comes to the Wedding Feast of the Lamb:

$^{11}$ But when the king came in to see the guests, he saw a man there who did not have on a wedding garment.$^{12}$ So he said to him, "Friend, how did you come in here without a wedding garment?" And he was speechless.$^{13}$ Then the king said to the servants, 'Bind him hand and foot, take him away, and cast him into outer darkness; there will be weeping and gnashing of teeth.' $^{14}$ For many are called, but few are chosen.

There are several things to notice about this account of the feast. First, the King called the guest, "Friend." The unattired guest was not a stranger, not a pagan, not a heathen, but one who was seemingly both known to the King and invited to the celebration! Therefore, the presumption is that the guest should have known better than to show up having made no effort to prepare. Second, the unattired guest was cast out of the King's presence, into "outer darkness." Outer darkness is not hell, it is obscurity! It is the same outer darkness Jesus referenced in **Matthew 25:30** destined for the

> **Revelation 19:7**, "Let us be glad and rejoice and give Him glory, for the marriage of the Lamb has come, and **His wife has made herself ready**."

wicked and lazy servant that buried the Master's resource in the ground—again, making no effort to prepare for His return. Scripture makes it clear that in the Kingdom there will be those who serve in the presence of the King and others who dwell in obscurity; and when the full impact of what *they could have had* is realized, it will be the place of much "weeping and gnashing of teeth." This is the "suffer[ing] loss" to which **1 Corinthians 3:15** refers, "If anyone's work is burned, he will suffer loss; but he himself will be saved, yet so as through fire."

The purpose of eye salve is to heal eyes that are afflicted, and therefore, cannot see. Dr. Jesus' Eye Salve serves to remove the scales that obscure our vision of the eternal. His eye salve targets, not our physical eyes, but the eyes to which Paul refers in **Ephesians 1:18**—the "eyes of [our] enlightenment." Jesus' told Nicodemus (and us!) in **John 3:1-21** that "see[ing] the Kingdom" is a prerequisite to "enter[ing] the Kingdom." To be able to perceive it one must be "born again." New birth is the process of regeneration; that is, bringing life to those who have already been born dead. Eye salve is for the regeneration/restoration of our child-like vision, enabling us to see the "there-but-not-there" Kingdom.

We frequently quote **Revelation 3:19-20** in the context of initial surrender to the Holy Spirit to "accept" Christ, e.g., "open the door of your heart to Him": "$^{19}$As many as I love, I rebuke and chasten. Therefore be zealous and repent. $^{20}$Behold, I stand at the door and knock. If anyone hears My voice and opens the door, I will come in to him and dine with him, and he with Me." The fact that we associate Jesus standing on the outside and offering to come in *with a message to unbelievers* is an interesting example of Confirmation Bias—that is, seeing and

> **Luke 24:30-31**, "$^{30}$Now it came to pass, as He sat at the table with them, that He took bread, blessed and broke it, and gave it to them. $^{31}$Then their eyes were opened and they knew Him."

interpreting information within our assumptive context, and what we already accept as true. Over the course of my Church life, I have heard **Revelation 3:20** preached as an evangelistic message to non-believers many times. But notice that Jesus' message was *not directed to unbelievers*, but rather to a lukewarm church who already ostensibly "knew" Him! In **Matthew 7:7**, we are the ones encouraged to "Ask...seek...knock." But here, Jesus is the one knocking *asking for entry to lives that believe that they "have need of nothing."*

> **Matthew 7:7**, "Ask, and it will be given to you; seek, and you will find; knock, and it will be opened to you."

The context of Jesus' message indicates His objective: to "warm-up" His lukewarm church by personal visitation and sharing a meal at wisdom's banquet table. During these times of "breaking of the bread," we recognize Him, we know Him for Who He is. That is the message and practice of discipleship. It is not a great leap form **Revelation 3:20 to Matthew 7:23**, "I never knew you; depart from Me, you who practice lawlessness." Could it be that our response to Revelation 3:20's knocking in our discipleship efforts will determine our **Matthew 7:23** future? What if by continually ignoring His soft knocking we are earning His "depart from Me" pronouncement? What if the supper we share in those moments when we open the door to Him are the occasions when He knows us, and we get to know Him? What if His importunity to be admitted is the "calling," and those times of communion and fellowship are when we become the few that are "chosen" (**Matthew 22:14**)?

## What is S.E.E.ing?

We are learning to wrap our brain and spirit around the fact that the full work of God has already been accomplished, both in the world, in the Church, and in our individual pilgrimage. Our true self already lives in our "perfect and complete, lacking nothing" (**James 1:4**) state in the eternal dimension. It is the "we have been saved, we are being saved, and we will be saved" paradox. That is, He has already given us all things that pertain to life and godliness (**2 Peter 1:3**), yet we still struggle with discipleship daily. Learning to see in this context means learning to embrace Papa's mysteries and grow comfortable living in the alternative reality of the eternal. It means to see what God has done, is doing, and will do in the context of the whole span of our personal story, and the history of the world. It is developing a vision beyond physical eyesight and encompasses your inner eyes, the "eyes of your understanding" (**Ephesians 1:18**). It means becoming aware of His Program on earth, and what He both intends and is accomplishing in T/S/M reality; and how His Program in this reality has an infrastructural purpose in His eternal Kingdom. It means understanding how His *work* is connected to His *Person* and attributes. It means learning to see beyond the flesh, behind the veil, and into the eternal. It means "see[ing] what the Father is doing," and doing it (**John 5:19**); "hear[ing] what the Father is saying," and saying it (**John 12:49**), as Jesus did. It means nurturing the seed of the Kingdom within myself and within the Body of Christ, and cultivating it until it grows a tree in whose branches others come to rest (**Matthew 13:31-32**). Ultimately, it means living an other-worldly existence.

**Revelation 3:18** is a direct and personal word to the Church today. As the last in the line of seven Church Ages, the Laodicean Church has the potential to follow the Master's investment advice, rise up from its lukewarm state (Jesus' words, not mine) and break the finish line tape of history strongly, victoriously, with a tumultuous welcome by the cloud of witnesses. Alternatively, we can whimper, cry and lick our wounds, and stumble around until we are carried across the finish line by a wave of lukewarm self-pity. The differences between the "write your own ending" mystery novel before us hinges on our embrace of discipleship. But not just any ol' discipleship—discipleship that concentrates on Kingdom value ("gold"), Kingdom fitness (the covering of "white raiment"), and Kingdom vision (eye salve). In this chapter, we concentrate on the task of S.E.E.ing, or "*Seeking the Eternal Essence*." Yeah, the acronym may be cheesy, but the task itself is incredibly important. Remember, the principle is, "Sight before entry."

Learning to S.E.E. means we learn to view all things from His perspective. It means that we learn that in our carnal mind status we are "wretched, miserable, poor, blind, and naked," and that the Independent Self confession, "I am rich, have become wealthy, and have need of nothing," makes Him nauseated. It means perceiving that our *self*-confidence is not the badge of honor the world says it is. Satan has peddled his snake oil to the world, and we have snapped it up and applied it generously to the eyes of our understanding, only to experience the blindness of our separated self. But Dr. Jesus stands at the door and knocks, ready to sell us His "Super-S.E.E.ing Eye Salve"! Applying His heaven-made remedy means we learn to experience everything in the T/S/M dimension in terms of its eternal context and not "life for its own sake." It means that Jesus' eye salve dissolves the scales from our eyes and veil over our heart that blinds us to, and separates us from, our true self. Learning to S.E.E. brings our home into view, and gives us a promised land destination for which to fight.

My favorite short story is Hans Christian Andersen's, "The Emperor's New Clothes." Recall that the story is about a ruse perpetrated on the emperor and the whole town by two charlatans claiming to be weavers, and boasting that they will make the emperor a new set of clothes made from "the most magnificent fabrics imaginable. Not only were their colors and patterns uncommonly fine, but clothes made of this cloth had a wonderful way of becoming invisible to anyone who was *unfit for his office*, or who was *unusually stupid*."[16] The weavers, of course, were not weaving anything at all but air, and pocketing the money given for non-existent supplies and services. But those called upon to witness their craft did not want to admit their inability to see lest they be thought unfit or unusually stupid (which fear was, itself, unusually stupid!). The ruse comes crashing down around the emperor when the baffled honesty of one little boy denudes (pun intended) the swindler's ruse. The little boy's blurted pronouncement, "But he hasn't got anything on," (he didn't know any better!) is the function of childlike vision at its finest—revealing the world *as it is*, not as our blindness, filters, biases, and fears portray it.

The application of the story's moral is that the source of the power of the charlatans is the same power source *our flesh* and *our carnal mind* (two charlatans!) wield against us today. It is the power of the fear of rejection, the fear of being found out, the insecurity of being found wanting. It is the power wielded by the serpent as Adam and Eve cowered in the forest, and weaved fig leaf aprons for themselves. The little boy's declaration, "But he doesn't have anything on!" are the same words that strike fear in the hearts of those propagating the lie that we need to cover ourselves and hide from Papa. It is the same underlying message God conveyed to Adam and Eve with His question, "Who told you that you were naked?" (**Revelation 3:11**). Do we really think that Papa didn't already know the answer to that question? I think the point of His rhetorical question is, "The same kind of dysfunction and accusation will follow every time you listen to and follow the voice of the serpent." He was reinforcing the source of our separated and cowering insecurity, and by contrast, His own acceptance and unconditional love.

Learning to S.E.E. is returning to our pre-fall vision. It is rejecting the voice that tells us we are naked and have to do something about it. It is forsaking the accusation that we have to be something or pretend something to avoid the charge and society's rejection as being "unfit" or "unusually stupid." It is purchasing Dr. Jesus' eye salve and slathering it generously over our eyes to cure our flesh and carnal mind-induced blindness. I get that Eve was deceived in the transgression and that Adam entered into it so that Papa could redeem them both out of it. But it is significantly more difficult to understand why we would listen to the same voice today *knowing* the outcome.

## Eating the Elephant—Really?

I do not know how "Eating the elephant" has become the go-to analogy for engaging a complex, ginormous project. Most of us, upon hearing the words, "The best way to eat an elephant is…," would respond, "…one bite at a time!" ("One bite at a time," though it is one way, is not at all the *best* way to eat an elephant. The *best* way is to throw a party, invite 100 of your hungriest friends, and serve elephant!) Discipleship is a life-long, intensive effort—and is a ginormous undertaking. Eating the elephant one bite

---

[16] http://www.andersen.sdu.dk/vaerk/hersholt/TheEmperorsNewClothes_e.html

at a time focuses on the process, as does our transformation into the image of Christ. Complexity requires patience, commitment, and endurance. It requires intentionality and faithfulness. It requires vision, knowledge, and understanding. It requires a strategic perspective and tactical focus. It requires learning to accurately see into the eternal realm and appraise the T/S/M path ahead.

One career lesson I have learned from working at thousands of emergencies, and from all of the incident management teams of which I have been a part of over the years: Collective effort (team) is *always* better than individual effort when the task is ginormous. And yet, collective effort is comprised of quality "one bite at a time" individual contributions. It is not either/or, but rather each/and. There is plenty of opportunity for individual gift contributions within the Church while maintaining our strategic view of collective effort in union with Him. I think that is the meaning of Jesus' scathing admonition to the unfaithful, fearful servant of **Matthew 25:26-27**:

> [26]'You wicked and lazy *servant*, you knew that I reap where I have not sown, and gather where I have not scattered seed. [27]So you ought to have deposited my money with the bankers, and at my coming, I would have received back my own with interest.'

What do we know about a bank from experience? It is a place where individual investors deposit and pool their resources with others to leverage them for larger projects than may be out of reach for most individuals. They do so with an expectation of an interest return. Spiritually speaking, the bank in our T/S/M reality is the Church. God gave *us the Church*–marvelous comrades to encourage and support us in our pilgrimage–and gave *us to the Church* to support and encourage others. Accomplishing our discipleship in this environment and assisting others in theirs is a goal worthy of collective effort.

Believers who deposit their resources in the Church are joining their efforts to the collective good being accomplished by the Body of Christ; and, to be sure, such investment yields interest. But that is not the whole story. Jesus' words indicate that, while good and beneficial, such an investment strategy *when it represents the sum total of the believer's investment efforts* is an unbalanced portfolio. Jesus' use of the phrase "at least" indicates that a greater benefit is possible, if not desired. The lesson is this: Believers who count on church membership and/or attendance as their entire investment of Kingdom resources transactions, *in the absence of personal investment and involvement in the transaction process*, have chosen a less-than-ideal strategy. In the words of Solomon, "It is good that you should grasp the one without letting go of the other" (**Ecclesiastes 7:18**). That is not to say that church involvement cannot be the vehicle of investing in the Kingdom—*it absolutely can!* But membership and attendance do not presuppose involvement, and therefore investment. It may well be sufficient to prevent being "cast into outer darkness," but there is no indication in the Parable that depositing the money in the bank *as a minimal response* would have yielded, "Well done good and faithful servant" praise from the Master.

## Giftings, Mindsets, and World Views

I think structurally. I do it naturally, and I do it easily. I deconstruct and reconstruct easily. I see relationships between parts, which enables me to fill in missing pieces and bridge many large and most small gaps. I imagine easily, and I see more easily than many what is not there in time/space/matter reality, but is present in the eternal dimension. *Mechanically*, I have learned that the process of discipleship can be distilled into a relatively simple iteration of steps: 1) See what is; then, 2) Envision what can be; then, 3) Declare what will be; then, 4) Do what you saw.

Of course, the mechanics of the process are only part of the story, but they are an important part that is often unseen and unpracticed by many believers who are otherwise gifted. For the longest time, I thought everyone viewed the world in the same structural manner. I was *so* wrong. But because I view the world from a structural and relational perspective, I hope to help others who do not have the same world view to build their Discipleship Plans. It is an expression of the "That Which Every Joint Supplies Principle" pertaining to the Church (**Ephesians 4:16**). You have your strengths to contribute, I have mine to bring, and together we make up the "manifold wisdom of Christ" (**Ephesians 3:10**).

| The Mechanics of Discipleship |
| --- |
| • See what is; then, |
| • Envision what can be; then, |
| • Declare what will be; then, |
| • Do what you saw. |

Our discipleship development is so important that it deserves our *first* and *best* effort. It deserves prominence, deference, planning, and continuous attention. By the foregoing, I do not mean every ounce of energy, concentration, and attention we can muster *after* we have taken care of other obligations. The flesh will always insist that its interests be put first. But the Father in whose house we dwell, the Bridegroom to whom we are betrothed, and the Spirit who gives us such loving care and most excellent comfort deserve our *first* and *best* effort. *They* put us here for a reason. *They* engage us for a reason. When we leave our spiritual relationships to our spare moments and weekend services, our growth to unstructured fiat, our precious life to undisciplined, unprioritized and undefined free-fall, we are making a statement to God. We are also making choices concerning our role in the future Kingdom with which we will live through all eternity. When we squander growth opportunities and dissipate the time He has gifted to us, we display how little we understand about the process and purpose of life.

Like He has in me, Papa has assembled in you a particular and unique set of spiritual gifts, talents, mindsets, and world views that come together in an expression of Him in the world. He has made you who you are that you might be an exclusive expression because no one individual (except the Son) can be all that He is. But we can be *part* of what He is, in all the fullness we can muster; and as a member of His body, you and I get the privilege of representing His glory to all of creation. Because of union with Him in the Spirit, and increasing union with Him in my soul, I am the *Randy Templeton expression of God to the world*. In the same manner, you are the _____ (fill in the blank with *your* name!) expression of God in the world. That is what it means to understand **Colossians 3:3**, "For you died, and your life is hidden with Christ in God." That is what **Galatians 2:20's** "I, yet not I" means. And that is what it means to abandon the Independent Self and lose one's life in His life for His sake.

## Learning to S.E.E. from the Child's Perspective

One of the things I remember from my early childhood is the Sunday School flannel graph stories, complete with drawings of Jesus hugging and kissing children. The lesson subject matter was something like, "Jesus loves the little children; the Bible tells me so." Childlike-ness is to us a mystery of the first order, mainly because we have outgrown our innate childlike vision and viewpoint. Our childlike-ness did not leave us—we abandoned it, and recovering our childlike perspective is a high priority of discipleship!

**Matthew 19:14** says, "But Jesus said, 'Let the little children come to Me, and do not forbid them; for *of such is the kingdom of heaven.*'" Again, in **Chapter 18:2-3, Matthew** tells us, "²Then Jesus called a little child to Him, set him in the midst of them, ³and said, 'Assuredly, I say to you, unless you *are **converted** and **become** as little children,* you will by no means *enter* the kingdom of heaven.'" What is it about children that prompted Jesus to set them as *the* example when one is ambitious and determined to grow up in the Kingdom of God? It is one thing to read and go, "Awww, Jesus loved kids." It is quite another thing to wonder, "Hmmm, what is it about a child's approach to life that I should be assimilating?"

What is it about little children that qualify them to see and enter the Kingdom? Is it their cuteness? Innocence? Their kindness? No way! Children are often as scheming, manipulative, and mean as any adult. Their purity? Not that either—you do not have to teach a child to lie, you have to teach him or her *not to*. Their selflessness? Nope—children are born into the world *totally* self-centered and self-focused. The two qualities that a child has—at least, until they become old enough for them to become veiled—is that they are totally dependent, and have the ability to "see" (in the sense of "imagine") what is not visible to the eye, *and to experience it as real*. At some point in our journey from childhood to adult, we lose the ability to imagine without attaching the negative value of "imaginary." Our rational mindset considers that which we designate as imaginary to be non-existent; or at the very least, inferior to that which we can see, touch, and manipulate. But just because that which we see from a child's perspective is not perceivable by our physical senses does not mean that it is not real; nor is it inferior to the visible, rational and tactile world. It is the "of such" of **Matthew 19:14** that opens our vision to the Kingdom.

The thing that makes a child able to see the Kingdom is their *paidion vision*, their ability to perceive and enter into a world that is "there-but-not-there." *Paidion* is the Greek word for "child" that Jesus uses in this text (there are others He could have chosen). It indicates not just chronological age, but an ability to gaze (literally, "see through") on a world unbounded by space, time, senses, or filters—bounded only by their ability to create in the spirit. For example, my three-year-old granddaughter is able (without breaking a sweat or a great deal of planning) to take a few raw materials—some plastic cups, saucers, teapot, and a little water—and produce an entire cotillion! When my sons and grandsons were younger, all we needed to do was release them to the outdoors and the whole world came within their purview. Every stick became a firearm. Every bush concealed an enemy soldier. Their imagination *became* real in the important sense that *it became experience-able*. A favorite phrase among kids is "play like"; "Play like we are army men," "Play like we are ninjas," "Play like we are princesses," or some such. Then they set out to fulfill whatever mission opens up within their wide-open *paidion* world. Perceiving the there-but-not-there world is far beyond what we call imagination—it is assurance and belief that what we perceive is real in some reality beyond time and space; and that assurance of "things hoped for" and "things not seen" that Paul tells us in **Hebrews 11:1** is the essence of faith and the entrance into the eternal. "*Play like*" becomes *be like*! Peter said it this way in **1 Peter 4:11**: "If anyone speaks, let him speak as the oracles of God." In other words, be God's mouthpiece. There is no way one can be an oracle without accessing the *paidion* vision within.

But with the encouragement to imagine beyond the boundaries of T/S/M reality comes a warning that the gift can be misused. Recall that early in His ministry, Jesus delivered a message that we call, "The Sermon on the Mount." From this sermon, we get many important and enduring lessons. I do not diminish the importance of any portion of the Sermon on the Mount, but I would like to simply point out that a big chunk of **Matthew Chapter 6** is devoted to a single topic: *Worry*. Worry is a *misuse of the paidion imagination* because it focuses on negative possibilities. One may even argue that it causes many of the negative potentials to be realized. Think about it: If our paidion imagination is how we access faith, yet we devote that spiritual energy to thinking about all of the bad things that may happen, is it any wonder that we can create a negative environment as well as positive faith and hope?

In **Romans 4**, Paul tells us the role of the paidion vision in Abraham's life and his faith response in obedience to God:

> [16]Therefore it is of faith that it might be according to grace, so that the promise might be sure to all the seed, not only to those who are of the law but also to those who are of the faith of Abraham, who is the father of us all…[17]God, who gives life to the dead and *calls those things which do not exist as though they did*; [18]who, contrary to hope, in hope believed, so that he became the father of many nations, according to what was spoken, "So shall your descendants be." (**Romans 4:16-18**)

Here is the critical lesson we must glean: Our paidion vision—the ability to "see that which is not as though it were"—is our viewing portal into the eternal! It is the means by which we _Seek the Eternal Essence_. Accessing our paidion vision is a prerequisite for exercising faith. Far from merely child's play, our spiritual imagination is an *attribute of God* and the aptitude to which we return as we mature in the Spirit! *God gives life to the dead (regeneration) and calls those things that do not exist as though they did!* He speaks into existence by the power of His Word. As those who will rule with Him, we must also develop the ability to access faith to create as He does!

## Paidion Vision and the Rational Mind

Rationality and logic are Kingdom-killers, not in the sense that they do actual violence to the Kingdom of God, but in the sense that they limit our capability and capacity to see and enter. Jesus acknowledged God's system of prerequisites for Kingdom discovery, and He rejoiced—I like to think He enjoyed the delicious irony:

> At this time Jesus was filled with joy by the Holy Spirit, and said, "I thank you, Father, Lord of heaven and earth, that you have *hidden* these things from the *wise* and *understanding* [rational and logical] and *revealed* them to little *children*; yes, Father, for such was well-pleasing in your sight." (**Luke 10:21**)

Working definition of *"genius"*: The ability to hold two seemingly—conflicting thoughts in your mind at the same time, yet consider them equally true. —Graham Cooke

There is a time and a place for rationality and logic in exploring Papa's mysteries, just not in our initial perception of the Kingdom. There, they often only get in the way, because, unless they are recalibrated, they only accept cues from this world as input. Once recalibrated to Kingdom sight, they can be invaluable in searching Papa's mysteries and formulating questions that Papa delights to answer.

Jesus tells us very plainly in **John 3:3-5** that the Kingdom of God must first be seen before it can be entered. Accessing the paidion in us unlocks both the seeing and entering possibilities: First, we see, *then* we have the *option* to enter. In discussing the concepts with Nicodemus, Jesus tells him (and us) that the prerequisite for both is a rebirth. Nicodemus' confusion is understandable when one begins with the assumption that Jesus is speaking about physical birth. But Jesus clarifies that He is viewing life from a different vantage. Nicodemus' default assumption was flesh—much like ours today, but Jesus' default was always the spiritual realm. If we are wise, perhaps we can connect the dots and understand that a large part of the transformation-by-mind-renewal process that Paul discusses in **Romans 12:2** is along these very lines—reframing our default responses and understandings to His paidion perspective.

Besides accessing our paidion vision, why is it so important that we be reborn in order to see and enter the Kingdom? I think we get a clue to the answer to this puzzle when we examine Jesus' words in **John 3** in the context of **Matthew 18:3**, "Assuredly, I say to you, unless you are converted [reborn] and *become as little children*, you will *by no means enter* the kingdom of heaven." The importance of rebirth is not "starting over with a clean slate," it is to become a child again—to unlearn the Independent Self to which we cling. Notice it is not enough to act like a child—we have to *become one,* and there is a difference. Also, it is important to see that Jesus said we must both be "converted" and "become." In other words, the metamorphosis from an adult to a child has a beginning point (conversion), but it also has an ongoing process of development (becoming). These two ideas have their direct antecedents in "justification" (beginning event) and "salvation" (an ongoing process).

> **Matthew 18:3**, "Assuredly, I say to you, unless you are converted [reborn] and become as little children, you will by no means enter the kingdom of heaven."

## Reversing the Aging Process

Considering the positive child reference we just looked at in **Matthew 18:3**, how do we reconcile Paul's seemingly pejorative reference to child-ness in **1 Corinthians 13:11**: "When I was a child, I spoke as a child, I understood as a child, I thought as a child; but when I became a man, *I put away childish things."* How do we reconcile that Paul ostensibly presents "put[ting] away childish things" as a thing to be desired, or at least grown into? It seems that is the way **1 Corinthians 13:11** is most frequently interpreted—that growing up by putting away the purview of children is a good, mature thing. Therefore, if we accept the words of Paul and Jesus both to be authoritative, the question becomes "How do we grow up and put away childish things (Paul) concurrently with being converted and becoming little children (Jesus)?"

The bridge connecting these seemingly conflicting truths is in the difference between "childlike" and "childish." There are at least three characteristics that children develop as a product of a nurturing relationship with a caregiver(s): trust, dependence, and veneration (love + respect). Obviously, not all children live in a circumstance that breeds these positive attributes. However, when a nurturing atmosphere exists, children thrive in these three primary characteristics, and they lead to other positive qualities: security, happiness, contentment, caring for others, peacefulness, and respectful demeanor, to name a few. Where a nurturing relationship with a caregiver is not present, egocentric behaviors quickly develop and are predominant—behaviors that can generally be classified as "childish."

Although we are born separated from the beginning of life, the process of becoming a fully formed Independent Self is progressive over the early years until it reaches the "put away childish things" status. The putting away process is not a function of chronological age, and some never seem to reach it and remain childish well into their elderly adulthood! We learn that each stage presents new opportunities and new lessons to perfect our self-dependence and independence, as we develop physically and mentally from newborn to infant, to toddler, to child, to adolescent. *This learned process is the very thing that we must unlearn to enter the Kingdom.* Discipleship is reversing the soul's aging process! It is reversing through rebirth our learned self-dependence and independence. It is systematically becoming a dependent child again. The requirement of unlearning is an apt description of our pilgrimage of heart in a nutshell, and it is the continuous challenge of the Choice Space.

Even those that grow up in a nurturing environment experience enough contact with the world that results in the calcification of our heart. Therefore, *all* of us need regeneration, not just those with a difficult childhood. Our stony heart is replaced with a heart of flesh through the process of regeneration. Jesus' admonition that we must be "converted to become" (**Matthew 18:3**) as a prerequisite to enter the Kingdom indicates that at some point in life, we all cross over a line of independence and self-dependence that necessitates rebirth and re-starting of the childlike process. Many of us cross that line when we pack up our childlike-ness and childishness in the same bag and throw it all away together in one bundle. Even believers, who often reject childishness, sometimes fail to embrace the rebirth of childlike-ness. The world and our culture conspire to urge us to be independent islands of stand-alone strength. What they *do not* tell you is that independence is an illusion: you were neither *designed* to operate that way nor are

> **Romans 6:16**, "Do you not know that to whom you present yourselves slaves to obey, *you are that one's slaves whom you obey*, whether of sin leading to death, or of obedience leading to righteousness?"

you even *capable of sustaining* independence (**Romans 6:16**). Our nature is that we are slaves that do the bidding of one kingdom or another; and by making the choice of whose voice to obey, we choose to whom our independence is surrendered.

With whom are we to be relating in our childlike-ness? Who is to be the object of our trust, dependence, and veneration? These core characteristics of becoming like a child are directed "Father-ward"— that is, we display our childlike state toward the One whose child we

> **John 8:44**, "You belong to your father the devil, and your will is to carry out the desires of your father."

are. If I were the progeny of Satan, my trust, dependence on, and veneration would be toward him; that is happening all around us. But as a child of God, my pilgrimage is to return to the trust in, dependence on, and veneration of, Him who has purchased me by His blood, and who calls me and sets me in His Presence to learn His ways.

## If You Can *S.E.E.* it, You Can *Be* it!

Collective mind is a difficult concept for us to embrace because the Independent Self is so much a part of us, and separates us from everything including our true identity. If we could *easily* understand and engage, there would be no need for renewal, only re-education! However, re-education does not equate with renewal any more than memorizing Bible verses makes them part of one's character, and going to church does not make you a disciple any more than hanging out at a gym makes you an athlete.

Jesus addressed our need for rebirth with Nicodemus in **John 3**; to be reborn is to start over fresh and new, not reshape and improve what is already there. But beyond a clean slate, it is the beginning of the reversal of the soul's aging process. Nicodemus did not get it any more than we do in our carnal world view. To be renewed in the "spirit of [our] mind" is an incremental rebirth. Re-birthing (regeneration), renewal, and transformation are the Discipleship Triad we discussed in Chapter 4. Paul, in his concern for the Galatian Church (**Chapter 4, verse 19**), wrote, "¹⁹My little children, for whom I **labor in birth again until Christ is formed in you**." In the language of Discipleship Planning, re-birthing is the strategy, and transformation and renewal are the tactics. And, as Paul indicated, it is an iterative process.

The objective of mind renewal is initially to change the way we think by changing the *source* of our thoughts from the Independent Self to our Union Self. Across the Body of Christ, mind renewal should standardize the way we stand together and present the gospel to the world. However, *even beyond that*, mind renewal changes the way we see and perceive life. Paul talks about the mind of Christ as the connection by which we are joined as members of His body:

- **Romans 15:6**, "that you may with *one mind* and one mouth glorify the God and Father of our Lord Jesus Christ."

- **1 Corinthians 2:16b**, "But we have *the mind of Christ*."

- **Philippians 1:27**, "Only let your conduct be worthy of the gospel of Christ, so that whether I come and see you or am absent, I may hear of your affairs, that you stand fast in one spirit, *with one mind* striving together for the faith of the gospel."

There is a not-so-subtle temptation when we read "one mind" and "same mind" to receive the meaning as "having a mind *like* His," or "a mind that *agrees* with His." That temptation results from our inability to understand union and our determined clinging to Independent Self. But each of the Scriptures quoted above employs the Greek word *heis* to indicate oneness of mind, and means "one and the same," and "one virtually by union," not to be independent/separate-but-alike.

> **Ephesians 4:23-24**, "²³and be renewed in the *spirit of your mind*, ²⁴and that you put on the new man which was created according to God, in true righteousness and holiness."

Because of the days in which we live, we have a model for understanding the collective mind dynamic better than has any portion of the Church throughout history. Though an inelegant example, we understand computer networks today as a collection of connected machines, and the collective network we call the internet. By accessing an internet search engine, we access the whole collective "mind." You may be physically sitting alone in your study, but your connection brings you into touch with a web of others for good or ill all over the world—and potentially even beyond. Because we have access to the connected network, we have at our fingertips an overwhelming amount of information, and very nearly the sum total of all of man's learning over centuries. We have instantaneous communications systems at our fingertips. Of course, all examples ultimately break down, and this one is no different: The internet is vastly inferior to the "network" of the Spirit because it is external, and not a part of us. We access it as an Independent Self, seeking answers from an outside source. But as Union Self, we have access to all of Papa's knowledge and wisdom through a source that is resident within and continuously speaking.

> **James 1:5**, "If any of you lacks wisdom, let him ask of God, who gives to all liberally and without reproach, and it will be given to him."

Because He abides in us, as us, and we in Him, we know that the mind of Christ is resident in us as well; and if His mind lives in all of us as believers, that makes it collective, accessible to and by the whole body of Christ as individual members and as a conjoined body. Our experience in this life as an accessor of the collective mind of Christ is *part of our training for ruling with Him*! One can easily imagine the mind of Christ as a vast, superior spirit-based communication organ as we rule with Him in the millennium. That may seem a little "science fiction-ish" for your tastes, but it does not change the reality of our need to hear and communicate with Him as we rule "in His Name" for one-thousand years. We can spiritualize the necessary concepts to the degree that we obscure their meaning and confuse ourselves; or, we can access our paidion vision and understand the future, and our role in it, in terms that we can wrap our minds around.

## S.E.E.ing All There Is

Is there any more on-point description of public dialogue these days than **Proverbs 18:2**? Foolishness abounds all around us as people, each from their own parochial corner of worldview, attempt to shout each other down. This is nowhere more evident than on television "discussion" shows where commentators and discussion panels constantly talk over one another in an attempt to express "their own heart." One of the most revealing characteristics of the collective wisdom and maturity of our society can be understood by sampling the way people communicate in their personal conversation and their public presentation. But it is also evident around the water cooler at work, and around the dinner table at home. The quest to S.E.E. is to understand, not just collect facts that agree with my perspective.

**Proverbs 18:2**, "A fool has no delight in understanding, but in expressing his own heart."

The collective mind is about learning to get beyond what is in our own heart and mind and connect with the heart and mind of God. It is about seeing that we connect to one another and everything else. It is learning to see and hear the Father's heart and mind, and imitating it— then doing it all over again. The discipleship challenge is learning to see the world *as it is*, and not the way our fleshly bias and carnal mind present it to us. The question, "What is reality?" is one at which we are at a huge disadvantage to answer because we are limited in our means and mechanism to view it accurately. When we are fully engaged in life with our carnal mind, our assumptions and biases confirm themselves according to what they *expect* to see, as we stand by and watch. We become interested in understanding *only* if it agrees with us. *We* are the fool expressing our own heart; *we* are the foolish ones dumping our limited perceptions, assumptions, and filters on the ears of anyone who will listen, and those who will not. *We* are the ones that insist that the louder we shout, the more authoritative and accurate our words.

There is a concept in psychology called "naïve realism" that is pertinent to our *Seeking the Eternal Essence* efforts. Leonardo Da Vinci has been credited with the admonition that we must, "Learn how to see. Realize that everything connects to everything else." The sight that Leonardo urges us to learn is the precise idea in S.E.E.ing. I do not know what was actually in his brain when he wrote it—the implications, the assumptions, the "everything" to which he refers. However, Da Vinci has in part described our challenge to grow in union with God. Naïve realism must be overcome because it assumes that we see and perceive all that there is to see and perceive, yet excludes the "most real" reality: *the eternal*.

## Me/Other-than-Me

From birth, we form the unconscious habit of viewing the world through a "me/other than me" lens, and we apply that same lens to our relationship with God. But what may be true in other venues of life in this physical world is an illusion when it comes to the eternal realm and a believer's relationship with God. There is no separation! We are in union with Him in spirit on the sub-atomic level, and He literally holds the molecules of our container together. "In Him, we live and move and have our being" (**Acts 17:28**) is a physics problem of the first magnitude for the T/S/M world, but it is also more than that: it is a metaphysical truth in which all of life is submerged. We may think about, "By Him, all things consist (i.e., 'hold together')" from a chemistry perspective as a system of positive and negative particle attractions; or we can see the meta-chemical application of the Holy Spirit as our life-force. When we understand this truth, it changes how we relate to Him in our oneness.

I suspect it takes a lifetime to approach any measure of understanding of this abstract, but I also suspect it is so worth the pursuit! I have set a personal goal of wrestling with this concept for the rest of my life, or as long as it takes to gain clarity about our union relationship, and what it means to be assimilated into His collective Being. To be "in Christ" has both an eternal and a time/space/matter meaning. As we contemplate the mystery of union, we must keep in mind that the physical body "me" is not the real "me." The real me is an eternal being that existed in some form before the foundation of the world (**Ephesians 1:4**) and will continue long after this body is rotted away in the grave (or meets Him in the air!).

> **Hebrews 10:19-20**, "[19]Therefore, brethren, having boldness to enter the Holiest by the blood of Jesus, [20]by a new and living way which He consecrated for us, *through the veil, that is, His flesh.*"

Consider these two Scriptures as they relate to our pursuit of union with God:

- "And there are diversities of activities, but it is the same God who works all in all." (**1 Corinthians 12:6**). And,
- "And God said to Moses, 'I AM WHO I AM.' And He said, 'Thus you shall say to the children of Israel, I AM has sent me to you.'" (**Exodus 3:14**)

What information can we glean from a God who calls Himself "I AM," and Whose activities constitute "all in all?" It is really difficult for us to think about—much less understand—that success in the spirit realm means abandoning our independence and all of that which makes us separated and being absorbed into the collective I AM. Your identity, your life-source, your persona, your activities, your "stuff," and more become assimilated into Him—our Independent Self gives way to His Collective Self. Therefore, that which we call "our" life becomes an expression of Him in this time/space/matter world. Think about it this way: As long as we are still trying to be "like Christ," we maintain a separated mindset that limits our development. He has no intention for you to be like Him; He is God, and He is taking over. We can resist, we can fail to understand, or we can surrender and work to facilitate our assimilation into the I AM.

Our brain struggles to understand union because the concept is so foreign to our T/S/M dimension and our self-awareness orientation. Union challenges our Independent Self! Child Development experts tell us that when we are born into the world, one of the first things we learn is the distinction between my person and other persons—"me/other than me." Another thing we learn very early is that we have needs, and to us, those needs come first. That gives us an expectation and world view that we are not only separate, but we are primary, first in line to be attended to get our needs met, and to receive all the attention and accolades of which we feel deserving. To be born into the flesh container is to inherit Adam's separation and his me/other-than-me orientation. It is the first thing a newborn learns, and the last thing the departing spirit unlearns. If you are skeptical, as an interesting spiritual exercise, sample the language you hear in the church at a typical gathering of believers and count the number of references to "God-as-other-than-me," or God as "out there" and "separate from me." Take note of our invitations to the Father to "Come and be with us"—then consider that the Scripture tells us that we are one spirit with Him, joined at the sub-atomic level—He is already with us! Consider that the word says that without Him (Holy Spirit) holding us together, atoms and molecules would literally fly apart. His people have a general lack of understanding of our union with Him as the Bride of Christ, and that is problematic. We assume He is in "our" life to serve us, not the other way around.

I recently had an interesting experience that illustrates how our Independent Self world view colors every experience, even our mundane work, and even our worship. So, I am out painting my house, right? While working away and minding my own business, I had this vision: One of the wasps building a nest under the eaves began buzzing me as if to send an ominous message. Then, he flew up in front of my face and started speaking. "You are not welcome here!" he said, "You need to back away from my nest!" I was taken a little aback, but managed to reply, "You *do* know, don't you, that it *is my house*? *I* built it, *I* maintain it, *I* pay the taxes. You just invade and act like it is yours." The wasp replied, "I have no idea what you are talking about! I was hatched right here, and spent my whole life right here! I've never seen you before!" Getting a little annoyed at the wasp's ignorance and presumption, I shouted, "I was here first!" Right then, in my Christian music headphones, the singer sang these words: "Holy Spirit *you are welcome here*, come flood this place and fill the atmosphere." I distinctly heard the Holy Spirit chuckle, and say, "You *do* know that the Church is *my* house, right? I built it, I maintain it, and I paid for it." Then I heard a belly laugh and, "I was here first!" Got it. Message received. Lesson learned. God forgive us for our ownership, our assumption of preeminence, and our arrogance.

In God's eternal reality, union is pervasive. T/S/M physics says matter cannot occupy the same space at the same time. Eternal reality says, "I and the Father are One." T/S/M thinks of union as being "right next to," or, "in agreement with." In eternal reality, union is intertwining to the point of assimilation. The carnal mind seeks to resolve the paradox by rationalizing Jesus'

> **1 John 4:8**, "He who does not love does not know God, *for God is love*."

reference to oneness as "oneness of attitude," or values, intents, actions, etc. But as we mature, we learn that separation in any degree and on any level is an illusion; it does not exist in eternity, the ultimate reality. The only thing that could separate us (sin) has been done away; now we live in the new eternal reality of **Romans 8:38-39**:

> [38]For I am persuaded that neither death nor life, nor angels nor principalities nor powers, nor things present nor things to come, [39]nor height nor depth, nor any other created thing, shall be able to separate us from the love of God which is in Christ Jesus our Lord.

To fully understand and appreciate the foregoing in the context of no separation, one must recall that **1 John 4:8** tells us that, "God is love," in unequivocal terms. So, when **Romans 8:39** says we are inseparable from the Love of God, we know that we are also inseparable from the Person of God. That is not trivial or incidental knowledge—it is heart-challenging and life-changing wisdom!

# Chapter 6—The Problem of Pain

³For consider Him who endured such hostility from sinners against Himself, lest you become weary and discouraged in your souls. ⁴You have not yet resisted to bloodshed, striving against sin. ⁵And you have forgotten the exhortation which speaks to you as to sons: "My son, do not despise the chastening of the Lord, nor be discouraged when you are rebuked by Him; ⁶ For whom the Lord loves He chastens, and scourges every son whom He receives." ⁷If you endure chastening, God deals with you as with sons; for what son is there whom a father does not chasten? ⁸But if you are without chastening, of which all have become partakers, then you are illegitimate and not sons. ⁹Furthermore, we have had human fathers who corrected us, and we paid them respect. Shall we not much more readily be in subjection to the Father of spirits and live? ¹⁰For they indeed for a few days chastened us as seemed best to them, but He for our profit, that we may be partakers of His holiness. ¹¹Now no chastening seems to be joyful for the present, but painful; nevertheless, afterward it yields the peaceable fruit of righteousness to those who have been trained by it. **Hebrews 12:3-11**

## Like You, I Dislike Discipline

You knew we would get to this chapter eventually—at least, you should have known. My flesh, like yours, hates discipline. *It is vitally important*—as the Apostle Paul pointed out in **Romans 7:20**—that we learn to see ourselves as a different entity from our flesh, reflecting the container reality. Again, *you are not your body*; the real you is the precious life (soul + spirit) that lives in a flesh vessel—much like a hermit crab inhabits a shell, but is not part of, or attached to, that shell. "What I do" (obedience to the flesh) and "what I want to do" (obedience to the Spirit) may start out as two disparate outcomes; but as we undertake to submit ourselves to God's discipline in the Choice Space, over time, we are regenerated, transformed, and renewed to the degree that the disparity begins to disappear.

> **Romans 7:20**, "Now if I do what I will not to do, it is no longer I who do it, but sin that dwells in me."

Applying and embracing the Father's discipline process is pertinent on multiple levels, some obvious and some not. Some are downright subtle! It is helpful in our discipleship planning to consider multiple genres into which to separate our pursuit of healing and the Discipleship Triad (regeneration, transformation, and renewal). A genre is defined as, "a class or category of artistic endeavor having a particular form, content, technique, or the like." Truly, discipleship is more of an *art* than *science*, but there are aspects of each that promote success. Embracing the Father's discipline requires a disciplined approach; and breaking the elephant-sized problem of becoming a disciple into daily cross-bearing bites.

## Suffering is Not Optional...

The importance of dealing with emotional pain in our lives *as it comes up* cannot be over-emphasized. There are observable symptoms of letting pain accumulate in us. Growing up in church, we used to sing a hymn, *Must Jesus Bear His Cross Alone?* that goes like this: "Must Jesus bear His cross alone, while all the world goes free? No, there's a cross for everyone, and there's a cross for me." **Luke 9:23** is a favorite quotation for many, but we seldom stop to think about what it means. The idea of "taking up [your] cross daily" has romanticized connotations that somehow gloss over the pain and go straight to the glory.

> **Luke 9:23**, "Then He said to them all, 'If anyone desires to come after Me, let him deny himself, and take up his cross daily, and follow Me.'"

To understand this Scripture, we must first understand that each one of us has a custom-made path to walk in this life, with all of its trials, tribulations, and challenges. That path is synonymous with our "cross." When I say custom-made, I mean that the Holy Spirit knows us better than we know ourselves, and He knows precisely what circumstances to arrange, what buttons to push, what frustrations to present, and what experiences will challenge us at our deepest level to grow to our greatest possible potential in the Spirit. Taking up your cross daily is to live daily your custom-made circumstances, and embrace them as God's dealing in you—not for the purpose of punishment or penitence, but as an opportunity for the "practice of the presence of God," as some have called it. *We do not acquiesce to circumstances*; we value the chance to fight and reign over them in the power of the Spirit, not lament them in the weakness of the flesh.

There are (at least) five observable symptoms of letting emotional pain accumulate in us that are pervasive, near-universal, and absolutely indicative of its presence:

- Anger
- Guarding
- Fear
- Excuse-making
- Addictive behavior

Anger, when it flows from emotional pain, is not just episodic; it becomes our go-to response to whatever does not go my way and becomes the dominant response to life. Anger often flows from an indwelling subliminal feeling of entitlement to a smooth, trouble-free life! Think about it—angry outbursts only emerge when obstacles and obstructions present themselves. It is some people's most prevalent response to anything that slows them down from their rush to appease the flesh. Guarding is an avoidance behavior to keep anything from

> Challenge, suffering, and emotional pain are not optional, but learning from the experience of them is!

reaching our soft emotional underbelly. Included in this defense mechanism are hardness, external and internal, and avoiding others. Guarding is sometimes seen in a cynical "I'll reject you *before* you reject me" attitude toward others. Fear needs little explanation, except to say that it manifests in some surprising ways. Excuse-making rears its ugly head when it hurts too much to admit that I am anything less than perfect. Excuse-making is inseparable from, and a reliable indicator of, someone under the bondage of performance expectation oppression. Finally, addictive behavior in whatever form eases the pain by distracting and numbing our feelings. *Any* of these (and others) can be *"friended"* when we embrace them as the way we carry our cross without collapsing under the weight. The result is obvious— our "friend strategy" with emotional pain is itself a form of collapse often worse than the disease. The alternative—the fix—is connecting with the grace that is sufficient (**2 Corinthians 12:9**) and letting the cleansing and regenerating waters flow over your broken heart and soul.

## ...But Learning from It Is!

When we understand that we have a cross to be borne, and borne successfully, we begin to scratch the surface of understanding that emotional pain is for our good—though not to be allowed to accumulate! Pain's proper processing in our soul is an incredible blessing opportunity. That is not *happy talk*—God has established His system so that suffering is essential. Even Jesus learned by the things that He suffered (**Hebrews 5:8**). However, here is the real rub: *Challenge, suffering and emotional pain are not optional, but learning from them is!* Learning must be chosen. Though learning from the experience of pain is non-compulsory, inclining ourselves toward embracing and learning from our experiences—including suffering—is the only way to successfully do discipleship.

When we grasp that God has placed us right where He wants us, that He has prescribed circumstances that are just for us and our salvation, and that He has provided all that we need, not only to be successful

> **Hebrews 12:11**, "Now no chastening seems to be joyful for the present, but painful; nevertheless, *afterward* it yields the peaceable fruit of *righteousness to those who have been trained by it.*"

*but also to triumph*, we have the spiritual infrastructure to make the most of struggle. When we understand His purposes, we have the context to value our pain. The saying, "God allows in His wisdom what He could easily prevent with His power," (Graham Cooke) is a good descriptor of His dealing in us. Life truly is a classroom designed to transform us into the image of Christ.

Struggle and discipline are the fertilizers that sustain and nourish the growth of the seed of the Kingdom within us. Even Jesus learned obedience through the things that He suffered. I am convinced that the suffering referenced in **Hebrews 5:8** included much more than His suffering on the Cross—great though it was. Being "other-worldly" like Him, we experience a certain antagonism-of-spirit just by being in proximity to the flesh and the kingdom of this world. Paul called this the suffering of anticipation, intense longing, and earnest desire:

> For in this we *groan, earnestly desiring* to be clothed with our habitation which is from heaven, if indeed, having been clothed, we shall not be found naked. For we who are in this tent *groan, being burdened*, not because we want to be unclothed, but further clothed, that mortality may be swallowed up by life. (**2 Corinthians 5:2-4**)

If we groan in anticipation of full union with the Father, how much more did Jesus suffer "in the days of His flesh" (**Hebrews 5:7**)? His was the kind of suffering experienced by a Kingdom spirit being confined

> **Hebrews 4:15**, "For we do not have a High Priest who cannot sympathize with our weaknesses, but was in all points tempted like as we are, yet without sin."

to the limitation of a mortal body. In **Philippians 3:10**, Paul expressed his desire to experience the fellowship of [Jesus'] suffering. I am convinced that to fellowship in His suffering is to develop the vision to see our eternal home so clearly and experience the reality of it so vividly, that the longing ("earnestly desiring") constitutes a kind of suffering induced from being absent from beloved others and the place we belong.

Jesus experienced on steroids what we experience daily, yet He was without sin. He was successful against all of the "like as we are" temptations because He knew union with the Father on both the spirit *and* soul levels. Still, He felt things intensely, and He used that which He suffered as a springboard to learn obedience and subjection to the Father's will. His oneness with the Father was that hope of union that He prayed for us in **John 17:21-23**:

> [21][T]hat they all may be one, as You, Father, are in Me, and I in You; that they also may be one in Us, that the world may believe that You sent Me. [22]And the glory which You gave Me I have given them, that they may be one just as We are one: [23]I in them, and You in Me; that they may be made perfect in one, and that the world may know that You have sent Me, and have loved them as You have loved Me. (**John 17:21-23**)

It is clear that Jesus was praying for us to know oneness while we are yet in our flesh container; that oneness is the progressive process of salvation that we experience as we submit ourselves to be taught by the process of life; and that reigning in life is the result (**Romans 5:17**).

Jesus tells us the practical result of the Oneness that He experienced with the Father:

- Then Jesus answered and said to them, "Most assuredly, I say to you, the Son can do nothing of Himself, but **what He sees** the Father do; for whatever He does, the Son also does in like manner (**John 5:19**).
- I can of Myself do nothing. **As I hear**, I judge; and My judgment is righteous because I do not seek My own will but the will of the Father who sent Me (**John 5:30**).
- For I have not spoken on My own authority; but the Father who sent Me gave Me a command, **what I should say and what I should speak**. (John 12:49)

Jesus did what He saw the Father do, and He said what He heard the Father say. *That* was the visible T/S/M expression of His eternal union. We are being trained to do likewise—learn to do what we see the Father do and say what we hear the Father say. Pursuing union is sensitivity training where we learn to tune our T/S/M consciousness to His eternal voice and activities. We aspire to grow in our sensitivity to the degree that the "still, small voice" (**1 Kings 19:12**) sounds like thunder in our ears! We will (likely) never suffer the shame, rejection, and pain of being hung on a cross. Yet we struggle against the same separated condition that He experienced in His crucifixion. He entered into separation from

> **1 Kings 19:11-12**, "[11][B]ut the Lord was not in the wind; and after the wind an earthquake, but the Lord was not in the earthquake; [12]and after the earthquake a fire, but the Lord was not in the fire; and after the fire a still small voice."

the Father so that He might lead us back to union. His episode of separation ("My God, My God, why have you forsaken me?") made possible our transformation and union that is the objective of our internship.

The biggest obstacle to faith in God for many people is the fact that they cannot confirm His existence by exercise of their physical senses. Faith that is seen is an oxymoron by God's wisdom and design, not some limitation on His communication ability. We cannot access the knowledge of Him the same way we can of, say, our cat or a lamppost. He may only be heard by those who interrupt life-as-usual to shut up, sit still, calm themselves, and listen intently with the heart. After a time of learning the sound of His voice, a running conversation in the middle of activity is not only possible, it is the norm. But these days, we want flash! We want bang! We want wind, earthquake, and fire! In short, we want a rock concert! Instead, God offers us a quiet meadow. Make no mistake—He can do flash/bang like no other! But He routinely chooses the still, small voice because that is what we need, even if not what we want.

The most difficult thing is not the short, ultra-intense sprint. It is long obedience in the same direction, putting one obedient foot in front of the other, day-after-day, year-after-year, through heartache, suffering, joy, and celebration. It is pressing through what we'd hoped for and what disappointed, and all the emotional gradients between. It is being taught by life. It is picking yourself up over and over, whether your fall was from hilarious laughter or a punch in the gut. The promise of Scripture is that the process *will* work for our good, and we *will* learn and grow.

## Passing Through the Fire: Purification Through Suffering

You may just have to take me at my word here: *There is not one Gnostic bone in my body.* I do not own a hair shirt, nor will I ever flagellate myself to induce suffering! Bob Mumford, a favorite Bible teacher of mine, makes this comment concerning our self-induced suffering: "Do not crucify yourself, because when we crucify ourselves, we tend to use rubber nails. Let Jesus do it for you—He was a carpenter and He knows what kind of nails to use." But though I do not relish suffering, my constant prayer is, "Perfect me, Lord, by whatever means necessary."

Long ago when I was young and foolish—before I knew what I was saying and the implications of the words—I selected **Job 13:15** as one of my life Scriptures. Since then, I have gained more wisdom, but only enough to understand that it is a dumb prayer for anyone wishing to live their own life, go their own way, and develop their own Independent Self! But for anyone longing to possess their full inheritance, it is a mantra and the way of life.

> **Job 13:15**, "Though He slay me, yet will I trust Him. Even so, I will defend my own ways before Him.

Elizabeth Elliot, herself no stranger to pain, is attributed with the following quote:

> *Our vision is so limited we can hardly imagine a love that does not show itself in protection from suffering. The love of God is of a different nature altogether. It does not hate tragedy. It never denies reality. It stands in the very teeth of suffering. The love of God did not protect His own Son. The cross was the proof of His love–that He gave that Son, that He let Him go to Calvary's cross, though "legions of angels" might have rescued Him. He will not necessarily protect us—not from anything it takes to make us like His Son.*

There is a brand of Christianity that rejects all pain, suffering, and obstacles. Some go even further to point to the presence of these as evidence of God's displeasure—or at a minimum, our lack of faith. Such beliefs are immature and reject the one most valuable tool in transformation into the image of Christ. Further, they deny the Scriptures, display a "life for its own sake" mentality, and a soul that is chained to the flesh.

I do not know why Papa selected fire as His purification tool of choice. I do not know the reason it is necessary for the people of God to experience suffering as the purification mechanism. Frankly, I have passed beyond asking, "Why?" because it serves no useful purpose. I like Graham Cooke's take on the "Why?" question: "'Why?' is an invalid question that makes you an invalid!" I cannot explain in detail *how* pain purifies us when it seems that with a few design tweaks by the Creator, eating candy and ice cream might bring about the same positive results! I just know that candy and ice cream cause cavities and weight gain; and suffering, when I embrace and learn from it, leads to my purification and growth. In case there are those who doubt the purification effects of fire, consider the following prophetic Scripture from **Zechariah 13:9**,

> [9]*I will bring the one–third through the fire, will refine them as silver is refined, and test them as gold is tested.* They will call on My name, and I will answer them. *I will say, "This is My people"*; and each one will say, "The Lord is my God."

I may not be able to articulate the particular mechanism by which suffering, chastening, and scourging change us, but I can articulate the effects it has when embraced:

- ***Suffering humbles us.*** We have a habit of slopping our way through life and getting more and more ego-centric and selfish until something stops us in our tracks. That something often is the realization that we do not operate in the level of control that we think we have. Believers come from the born-again factory with a system of "default settings." We know these settings because they are the ones we feel and operate in at that moment we are first convicted of our sin, and we humble ourselves before Christ, admit our need, and ask Him to justify us. At that moment, we are powerless to help ourselves and totally dependent on Father's love and mercy. We remain that way until we start to think we know something; then the "puffing up" process begins. Suffering returns us to our default setting and lets the air out of our inflated ego. The humble man or woman's response to suffering is always, "Father knows best."

- *Suffering gets our attention*. Suffering induces a "burst of focus" toward that which is important. We often are so distracted, so scattered by life, so busy with urgent activities that we "blur out," and end up ignoring important things. Even if we retain partial focus on spiritual development, we tend to prioritize it in the context of many things competing for our attention. One of my favorite sayings is, "Nothing focuses the attention as well as the hangman's noose!"[17] That may be a little dramatic, but it is no less true that when I begin to hurt, I begin to pay attention. Distractions blur into the background, and I begin to search for means to alleviate my pain. Most often, the answer to that search is found in some life lessons (or life-giving lessons) that Papa is teaching at the time.

> **Proverbs 18:10-12**, "[10]The name of the Lord is a strong tower; the righteous run to it and are safe. [11]The rich man's wealth is his strong city, and like a high wall in his own esteem. [12]Before destruction the heart of a man is haughty, and before honor is humility."

- *Suffering causes us to cry out.* The Psalms are full of examples of the response of "a man after God's own heart" (King David) to suffering. David's first response to his suffering was always to "cry out," "call out," or "shout out," often with tears. There is no shame in calling for help. It is the voice of the Independent Self that tells us that we are the Rock of Gibraltar, standing alone as a fortress against the world. *But we have a fortress*, a Strong Tower, and suffering alerts us to the need to run to it (**Proverbs 18:10**)! And while we are running, we are crying out with our whole being for Papa's loving care and attention!

> **Proverbs 17:1**, "Better is a dry morsel with quietness, than a house full of feasting with strife."

- *Suffering tunes us into the "God frequency."* This is another way of saying that we become more receptive to listening in those times when we feel the burn. The world is a manic, hysterical place that is in a state beyond uproar. From politics, to economics, to social interaction, to organizational and personal conduct—name any sphere of human endeavor and you will find an activity that clamors for attention and tumultuously insists that we take up its particular cause and feel its particular offense. But God's voice is not in the wind, fire, or earthquake. Suffering has a way of teaching us to still our inner man, tune our ear to the "still, small voice," and wait for instructions.

- *Suffering reminds us of where to find bread.* Solomon knew feasting. No one could throw a party like the King of Israel. All of the best people would come, and there was no lack of the most sumptuous of delicacies! And yet, this man who could party with the best knew best where to find sustenance. In **Proverbs 17:1** and in **Ecclesiastes 7:2,** he tells us to avoid the house of feasting, for in the celebratory atmosphere is strife, disorder, and clamor. Suffering teaches us this lesson over and over again: *Bread is found in quietness, and daily bread is earned by the sweat of our brow (in all of its forms).*

- *Suffering reminds us of who we are.* If you have ever been told by a defiant child, "I don't have to do what you say—you are not my boss!" then you have the equipment to understand that we

---

[17] The actual quote by Samuel Johnson is, "Depend upon it, sir, when a man knows he is to be hanged in a fortnight, it concentrates his mind wonderfully."

intuitively know those in authority over us. We know in our hearts that we are not accountable to those not in a position to discipline us. Now, I fully recognize that good parents teach their kids when they must and must not obey others. But the principle remains that parentage conveys authority, and that is the principle we see in **Hebrews 12:7-11**. So, if we can find no other comfort in our suffering, we can at least embrace that God's "spankings" are proof that He has embraced us, that He retains authority over us, and that we are members of His household.

- ***Suffering proves we are on the right path.*** When God judges His people as a lost cause, He lets them go their own way. **Hebrews 12:6-7** confirms that, as long as we are feeling the pressure of suffering, we may be assured that our paths are directed and ordered by the Lord (**Psalm 37:23**). **1 John 2:5** gives us precious information: *"By this, we know that we are in Him."* When He deals with us as sons, He teaches us His words and ways. And, as we see His perfection being duplicated in us, we know we are on the path to life.

> **1 John 2:5**, "But whoever keeps His word, truly the love of God is perfected in him. ***By this we know that we are in Him***."

In all of this, remember that God never teases, spoofs, picks on, harasses, or "bait-and-switches" us. His discipline is not hazing to be able to join His fraternity. What He promises, He delivers. He is unwaveringly faithful to fulfill His word. Settling this deep in our spirit enables us to assert with confidence, "It is written, 'Man shall not live by bread alone, but by every word that proceeds from the mouth of God'" (**Matthew 4:4**), when the tempter shows up and suggests that we take action to circumvent the work of God. *Then* we can claim the endurance that the writer talks about in **Hebrews 10:35-39**:

> [35]Therefore do not cast away your confidence, which has great reward. [36]For you have need of endurance, so that *after you have done the will of God*, you may receive the promise: [37]"For yet a little while and He who is coming will come and will not tarry. [38]Now the just shall live by faith; but *if anyone draws back, My soul has no pleasure in him*." [39]But we are not of those who draw back to perdition, but of those who believe to the *saving of the soul*.

Admittedly, it feels wrong to be quoting Karl Jung when my interest is life in the Spirit. But here, Jung highlights a truth independent of his humanistic insight: When we get our eyes off of the problem, and on to something and Someone bigger than ourselves, problems tend to diminish and even fade into obscurity. They become irrelevant except for the lessons they teach:

> All of the greatest and most important problems in life are fundamentally insoluble...They can never be solved, only 'outgrown.' Some wider or higher interest appears on...the horizon, and through this broadening of his or her outlook, the insoluble problem lost its urgency. [They are] not solved logically, but [fade] when confronted with a new, stronger life urge. (Karl Jung)

Nothing is ever as bad or as good as we make it out to be. Whether temptation or daunting problem, God (through Paul) promises in **1 Corinthians 10:13** that, "No temptation has overtaken you except such as is common to man; but God is faithful, who will not allow you to be tempted beyond what you are able, but with the temptation will also make the way of escape, *that you may be able to bear it*." Notice that the "way of escape" is not provided for us to be rid of the trial, but rather that we may be able to "bear it." God is creating, not a Kingdom of escape artists, but a Kingdom of bearers—able to bear and forebear—and that not in our own strength! True strength is not measured in how few problems one experiences, or how many problems one can carry. True strength is measured in how quickly and completely we are able to transfer our load to the One who "has borne our griefs and carried our sorrows" (**Isaiah 53:4**).

## What About Abuse?

One of the most elegant aspects of the Discipleship Triad is its application to the problem of abuse to which we have been subjected. Please hear me carefully on this point: Your suffering in any past or ongoing abusive situation(s) *is not trivial,* and I would never suggest such. Abuse is the "gift" that keeps on giving; it will continue to do so whether or not we subject the experience to the regeneration/ renewal/transformation process. The choices we make in the Choice Space are not whether or not abuse changes us, but the quality (positive or negative), effect, and duration of that change. Abuse is by definition traumatic to our soul in at least five major ways:

- Abuse feeds our fear;

- Abuse erodes our trust;

- Abuse has the potential to negatively define who we are and how we see ourselves;

- Abuse leaves scars, often in the form of vows and filters that affect the way we see the world;

- Abuse never goes away.

When the memory and continuing damage of abuse is active in one's soul, thus chaining him or her to the past, he or she cannot live up to their future potential. Abuse is like a strong acid eating away at our thought and feeling processes. And, like any acid, it will continue to burn and destroy until it is neutralized. The destructive effect continues whether or not we are conscious of its working, whether or not we feel affected, and whether or not we have forgiven the abuser. Forgiveness is an important step in the neutralization process. But until the Discipleship Triad process is applied, the damage continues. The good news is that I know, as a former HazMat Technician, even the strongest acid can be neutralized, and so can abuse.

The foregoing makes it appear as if it is my intent to paint a dark picture, but that is not the case. I present the information in stark terms because of the importance of the neutralization process, and to emphasize the redeeming value of processed memories/experiences. If abuse *always* produces damage, the converse is also *always* true: When the memories of abuse are regenerated, renewed, and experienced in a transformational environment, they produce life. It is a Scriptural principle—a *fact*—that life flows out of death. That is one of the corollary meanings of Jesus' declaration in **John 12:24**, that, "[U]nless a grain of wheat falls into the ground and dies, it remains alone; but if it dies, it produces much grain." Jesus was primarily addressing His upcoming death in His reference in **John 12**; but His death *must have,* and *does have,* profound effects on our experience. They are the same effects that transform abuse that is "meant for evil" into that which "God mean[s] for [our] good." It is challenging to attach any hope to a situation that inflicts so much emotional and/or physical pain. I can imagine that someone reading this might be offended by the idea that any good could come out of their abusive suffering. The flesh certainly wants us to place our trust in our anger and shame as the support system to power us through the debilitation. But my own experience is that the only remedy for abuse is the discipleship process. There are no magic words (although there are helpful prayers, like the Trauma Prayer[18]), no instantaneous healing, only a lot of hard work reframing our thoughts and choosing the spiritual mind peace and growth over our carnal mind condemnation.

> **John 12:24,** "Verily, verily, I say unto you, except a corn of wheat fall into the ground and die, it abides alone: but if it dies, *it brings forth much fruit.*"

---

[18] House of Healing Ministries, https://www.youtube.com/watch?v=31-o0EzLl7g

Joseph is the Old Testament poster child for familial abuse. The favored child of his father, Joseph was abducted by his brothers, thrown in a pit, and sold into slavery to a passing caravan—all because of the abusive jealousy of his siblings. Then, they reported to Joseph's father that he had been killed, and presented his blood-soaked, many-colored coat as evidence of the tragic accident. Like most abusers, they disavowed responsibility and covered up their dark deeds. The effects of Joseph's abusive experience were not temporary, and they were life-changing. He spent the rest of his life dwelling (eventually ruling!) in a foreign land, separated from family, and dead as far as his father knew—at least, until God restored the connection. And yet, after years of processing, Joseph was able to make this incredibly mature and healing statement to his brothers:

> ¹⁹Joseph said to them, "Do not be afraid, **_for am I in the place of God_**? But as for you, you meant evil against me; but God meant it for good, **_in order to bring it about as it is this day, to save many people alive._** (Genesis 50:19-20)

We are not told what mental and emotional processes Joseph struggled through to be able to arrive at his settled experience of healing from his brothers' abuse. What we *do* know is that he got there; and what we *do* know is that the outcome made the journey worthwhile, even if not one to be chosen. What we *do* know is that when he arrived at a place of truth and blessing, he brought others with him. What we *do* know is that Joseph had learned the secret of contextualizing his abuse in the framework of the work of God in his life.

**Romans 8:28-29** provides a New Testament context for our consideration of abuse and all other experiences in life:

> ²⁸And we know that all things work together for good to those who love God, to those who are the called according to His purpose. ²⁹For whom He foreknew, He also predestined to be conformed to the image of His Son, that He might be the firstborn among many brethren.

**Romans 8:28** is another one of those Scriptures that seems to roll off of our tongue while bypassing our brain! If we count ourselves among those who are called according to His purpose, we are obligated to *find/identify the good* that all things are working in us. But taking the principle further, we are obligated to *work the good* until it matches His purpose in our experience. The first response is one of a *servant*; the second is the response of a *mature son*. The first brings us to a place of peace; the second to a place of discipleship. By *finding the good,* we arrive at rest. By *working the good*, we arrive at understanding.

By experience, we know that some physical injuries leave a scar and others don't. Abuse comes to us in many forms, but one of the characteristics by which abuse is known is by the scar that it *always* leaves. Some experiences, particularly those in the self-abuse category, may have their beginnings and underlying cause in other forms of abuse perpetrated by others—they are seldom found as single incidents, but clusters of events. All abuse causes trauma, but not all trauma is from abuse. Some clear life experiences that routinely can be categorized as abuse are:

- Physical abuse/beating
- Sexual abuse and rape
- Marital infidelity and adultery
- Spiritual abuse, including many of the other acts within a religious or spiritual context
- Belittling, de-humanizing verbal treatment
- Bullying, and degrading exertion of one's power over another

- Public humiliation

- Categories of self-abuse, including cutting, eating disorders, drug use, promiscuity, self-loathing

- Rejection by important others

- Certain employment experiences, including sexual abuse, or "power humiliation"

The world today is capable of inventing new and more exotic forms. It is not my purpose to list or categorize all abusive behaviors, but only to point out the effects of certain behaviors that are common in our soul-destruction. Neither is it my purpose to detail the specific treatments pertinent to a particular form of abuse—there are many far more capable writers and practitioners than myself to guide one through the minefield leading to healing. My intent with this difficult topic is to assert that, like Joseph, we too are capable of arriving at a place of healing that confesses, "You meant it for evil against me, but God meant it for good." It is the recognition that, as we find ourselves in a pit with the manure being shoveled on top to bury us, we use that same manure as a platform to rise back to level ground. Changing manure into a step stool is a particular specialty of the Holy Spirit. If you have been on the receiving end of another's abuse (as I have) the Discipleship Triad was designed by our Good Father for you.

How does one know when past abuse has been transformed into the FOTS, and from death into life? I am tempted to say, "You just know," or "I know it when I see it." But from observing Joseph's story in **Genesis 45:1-9**, I can be more specific than that:

> Then Joseph could not restrain himself before all those who stood by him, and he cried out, "Make everyone go out from me!" So, no one stood with him while Joseph made himself known to his brothers. [2]And he wept aloud, and the Egyptians and the house of Pharaoh heard it. [3]Then Joseph said to his brothers, "I am Joseph; does my father still live?" But his brothers could not answer him, for they were dismayed in his presence. [4]And Joseph said to his brothers, "Please, come near to me." So they came near. Then he said: "I am Joseph, your brother, whom you sold into Egypt. [5]But now, do not, therefore, be grieved or angry with yourselves because you sold me here; for God sent me before you to preserve life. [6]For these two years the famine has been in the land, and there are still five years in which there will be neither plowing nor harvesting. [7]And God sent me before you to preserve a posterity for you in the earth, and to save your lives by a great deliverance. [8]So now it was not you who sent me here, but God; and He has made me a father to Pharaoh, and lord of all his house, and a ruler throughout all the land of Egypt. [9]"Hurry and go up to my father, and say to him, 'Thus says your son, Joseph: "God has made me lord of all Egypt; come down to me, do not tarry."'

How do you know when abuse has completed its course and has served as a transforming work in you? You know when:

- You can stand alone in the presence of your abuser(s) and declare your true identity;

- You can weep aloud in the house of your captors and not be intimidated;

- You can *articulate* the purpose and context of your suffering, and discuss the good that is has birthed in you;

- You can preserve life when death manifests itself all around;

- You can look with hope to the future and know that every step that has led you to this point in your experience is God-ordained;

- Finally, when you rule in and reign over, the house of your former captor, and when the former slave has become the friend of the King.

When you can do these six things, there is no abuse that can hold you in captivity—no matter how unjust, how heinous, how undeserved it is or was. You have broken its power.

## Our Emotions Under the Whip of the Flesh

Our emotions are fully one-third of our consciousness; but when under the predominant influence of the flesh, our emotions dominate and influence our soul beyond a balanced proportion. Our emotions *were not designed* or intended to lead the way on our pilgrimage. They *are* intended to provide richness and flavor in the dry and tasteless wilderness.

> **Matthew 24:43**, "But know this, that if the master of the house had known what hour the thief would come, he would have watched and not allowed his house to be broken into."

Emotional upset creates an open door for the enemy to waltz unimpeded into our unguarded thinking. When emotions are in an uproar, we are particularly vulnerable to deception. Emotional stimulation floods our body with chemicals that cloud judgment, block perspective, obliterate context, and command action. Emotions are not bad, nor are they to be avoided; they are to be guarded. Solomon tells us in **Proverbs 4:23** to, "Keep your heart with all diligence, for out of it spring the issues of life." Paul tells us in **Philippians 4:7** that it is the peace of God that "guard[s] [our] heart and mind through Christ Jesus." "Heart," in this context, does not mean emotions, it means the sum of all our consciousness. Our consciousness is what we are guarding with all diligence, and out-of-control emotion is one of the things we are guarding against.

Why is it necessary to "guard," "keep," "watch over," "stay alert," or other actions that urge diligence concerning our soul, and particularly our emotions? The need to guard and keep our inheritance has been with us from the beginning. Recall that God commissioned Adam in **Genesis 2:15** to "guard and keep" the Garden of Eden, the necessity for which we see in the temptation of Eve and the resultant Fall of Man. There are three primary reasons why we cannot go on cruise control for our emotional well-being:

1) The admonition to "guard" *presupposes* that there is an enemy present;

2) The enemy of our soul has "legal" standing to access our flesh at will; and,

3) Because of reason #2, our flesh has an affinity for, and an attraction to, the temptation that attacks through that portal.

Spiritual warfare can be waged in both offensive and defensive modes. The essence of defensive spiritual warfare is to watch these entry portals and rebuff all approaches by the enemy. But even without enemy intervention in the realm of temptation, our fleshly lusts operate on a near-continuous basis unless and until we built our union with the Father through discipleship training.

## Accessing Comfort for Life-Sucking Problems

You have them, I have them, we all have them—friends, family, and acquaintances that just suck the life right out of you. This is the "Life-Sucking Problem" (LSP). How is it that two groups of people can see the same facts and circumstances and come up with two so completely opposite responses and attitudes? One group sees problems as rejoicing and trusting opportunities, and the other sees them as yet another beat-down. None of us solely occupy one of these groups; we tend to oscillate based on our mood. Some days, others are the source of the LSP, some days that "honor" belongs to me. Some days, you are the bug, and some days you are the windshield.

The LSP is only a problem for us when we become disconnected from the life-supply. We are all vessels (**2 Corinthians 4:7**) connected in series to one another; and when our supply gets low, it draws a vacuum on those vessels around—it is simple physics! *All the stress* that we experience is the result of becoming disconnected from the supply.

The distribution equality Paul addresses in **2 Corinthians 8:13-15** may be thought about as an equalization of the pressure of life by an *interconnected and looped* supply. A looped system is one that is fed from multiple directions and sources, i.e., a water main fed from two or more directions (my firefighting experience becomes valuable in understanding water supply problems!). We are called to lay ourselves down for others, i.e., "get the life sucked right out of us" (**John 15:13**). For that reason, we *must* stay connected to the life

> **2 Corinthians 8:13-15**, "For I do not mean that others should be eased and you burdened; but by an equality, that now at this time your abundance may supply their lack, that their abundance also may supply your lack—that there may be equality."

supply or a vacuum and stress will result. We need to get it through our heads and hearts that LSP is *really* an acronym for "Life-*Supply* Problem." When there is a fresh inflow of continuous life-giving Spirit, the vacuum never develops, and there can be no such thing as negative pressure or stress. If you feel stressed, the outflow is not the problem; the problem is a choked-off supply. Jesus called it, "abiding in the vine."

The issue in all supply problems is sufficiency for the demand. In **2 Corinthians 12:9**, Paul addresses the problem of supply and demand from his own experience:

> And He said to me, "My grace is sufficient for you, for My strength is made perfect in weakness." Therefore, most gladly I will rather boast in my infirmities, that the power of Christ may rest upon me.

In this verse, Paul is introducing the Corinthians to the, "My Grace is Sufficient for You Principle" (MGISFY). Staying connected to the supply is a two-step process. Step One is, "Understand and embrace your cross." The MGISFY Principle is Step Two in preparing yourself for the daily cross-taking-up ritual that keeps us connected and supplied. The ultimate goal of emotional pain processing is our growth; Papa has allotted grace for us to ensure our success. In addition to "waves of grace never ceasing" that Papa sends, there is a measure of grace available to us that is person-specific and circumstance-specific, and our calling is to locate and stand in it (abide) in every situation we face.

## Dealing with Emotional Pain

Jesus took so much more than our sin with Him to the cross. As if our sin were not enough, He also took with Him our griefs, sorrows, affliction, frustrations, agitations, distresses, and discord—and that is the shortlist! Debilitation and devastation come to us through the vehicle of emotional pain more pervasively than any other vehicle. When pain is physical,

> **Isaiah 53:4-5**, "[4]Surely He has borne our griefs and carried our sorrows; yet we esteemed Him stricken, smitten by God, and afflicted. [5]But He was wounded for our transgressions, he was bruised for our iniquities; the chastisement for our peace was upon Him, and by His stripes we are healed."

most find a legitimate method of either dealing or living with it. However, we seem powerless to deal with the pain that comes from emotional wounding. There is *no other issue in life* except your justification in Christ that is as important as learning to be free from emotional pain. The reason is simple: *emotional pain keeps us bound*—bound to our flesh and its works, bound to our self-pity, bound to our anger, bound to past behaviors and transgressions, bound to our carnal mind, bound to our frustration, discontent, and anxiety. There are only four ways of which I know to deal with emotional pain, and three of the four are not solutions, but only make it worse: 1) Ignore it; 2) Make a friend of your pain—that is, nurture, coddle, think about, dwell/fixate on, identify with, and carefully guard it; 3) Medicate it—to medicate is to numb the pain by means of one of the substances that serve to temporarily cause us not to feel; and, 4) Be healed at the source and root.

The last phrase in **Isaiah 53:5** is an oft-quoted Scriptural promise. We have heard, "and by His stripes, we are healed" prayed many times as a claim/promise for physical healing. But if you will notice, the promise is given to us also in the context of *emotional* issues such as griefs and sorrows. It seems believers are quick to struggle against physical affliction; but when it comes to emotional pain, we tend to put off accessing the remedy Jesus has provided for us. Maybe we are ashamed because we are not *supposed* to be debilitated by our emotions. Maybe we think there is no healing and we just have to bear it. Maybe we get so wound around the pain axle that we fail to see what it is doing to us. Maybe we have grown up with terrible examples of how to access the cure. Maybe we live with it long enough that we call a truce and accommodate/incorporate the pain and its devastation into our identity and personality. Those of us who have experience in this area can testify to the spectrum of life-trauma that accompanies the failure to embrace healing from this peculiar life-sucking problem.

Stopping everything to deal with emotional pain *as it comes up* takes courage and discipline. Continuously growing in maturity and Kingdom power is all but impossible while dragging around the chains of the past. Remember, before Paul could claim to "press toward the mark of the high calling of God in Christ Jesus," he first had to "forget those things which lay behind" (**Philippians 3:13**). Accessing *as a routine* the emotional healing that Jesus' stripes purchased before the pain progresses to observable symptoms not only makes sense, it is a principal mechanism in our tool chest of discipleship growth.

**Luke 9:23-24**, "²³If anyone desires to come after Me, let him deny himself, and take up his cross daily, and follow Me. ²⁴For whoever desires to save his life will lose it, but whoever loses his life for My sake will save it."

**Luke 9:23** is a favorite for quotation, but Christians sometimes fail to stop to think about what it means. The idea of "taking up [your] cross daily" has romanticized connotations that somehow gloss over the pain and go straight to the glory. It also appeals to a certain resignation of self-pity that is *not* healthy or conducive to growth. A common sentiment seems to be, "Jesus suffered, so you have to suffer; Jesus *earned* His crown, *you have to earn yours." The words are true, but they are not the truth!* Jesus does not advocate carrying the *same* pain day after day until we are debilitated or destroyed by it—quite the contrary! He disciplines us with struggle and challenge that we may become adept at overcoming. *He did not stay hung on His cross, and neither should you!* We *are* commanded to take up our cross daily, but I have come to learn that it is supposed to be a *new cross each day*! New day, new cross! And, the cross we are to take up is the cross of self-denial in whatever form is appropriate for the moment.

God is not a sadist; He does not enjoy pulling the legs off of frogs or wings from flies, and He certainly takes no pleasure in watching us twist in the wind at the end of our emotional pain rope. We must remember each day that this world is a theater of operation for war and a training environment (in the truest and largest sense of that term) for preparing us to take our rulership place in the eternal Kingdom. We are not *earning* our crown, but we are preparing the head that will wear it to *be worthy and capable*.

To advocate that we are called to carry the same cross day after live-long day is to say that **Isaiah 53** is a nice idea, but doesn't work in the real world. Obviously, based on Paul's testimony, some crosses are life-long parameters that serve to keep us dependent on His grace; but debilitating emotional pain does not fall into this category. We are told to take up our cross for the purpose of learning to lose "our life" in Him and for His sake! We take up a new cross each day so that we *gain practice at getting rid of it*, and can look forward to tomorrow's challenge! That is the essence of the discipleship curriculum—to learn to be as free as Jesus is from the destruction of life! In the process, we are made

> **Luke 14:26-27**, "²⁶If anyone comes to Me and does not hate his father and mother, wife and children, brothers and sisters, yes, and his own life also, he cannot be My disciple. ²⁷*And whoever does not bear his cross and come after Me cannot be My disciple.*"

Christ-like, we learn to think as He thinks, and He regenerates our dead parts. As we gain practice and skills, we may develop a certain "Bring it on!" attitude, and that is a pretty cool place from which to live.

The corollary problem to holding on to one's pain is rejecting it altogether without acknowledging its presence or effect. But it doesn't work that way any more than a woman can birth a child without the labor and delivery process. Emotional pain's proper processing in our soul is an incredible blessing opportunity and the environment for rapid growth. That is not *happy talk*—God has established His system so that suffering is essential, but it is designed to teach us, and then come to an end. Learning to get rid of it *is* the lesson!

## Making Vows

In the diagnosis of emotional pain, *it is critical* to understand the effect and recognize when we have made a vow that binds our soul to the wounding. There is an excellent example of vow-making reported to us in **John 20:24-25**:

> ²⁴Now Thomas, called the Twin, one of the twelve, was not with them when Jesus came. The other disciples, therefore, said to him, "We have seen the Lord." So, he said to them, "***Unless*** I see in His hands the print of the nails, and put my finger into the print of the nails, and put my hand into His side, ***I will not believe***."

What was Thomas thinking?!? For this vow, recorded in Scripture, he will forever be known as "Doubting Thomas." There are several lessons here; the first of which is, "Be careful of the vows you make—they could end up determining your identity for a very long time."

> **John 20:25**, "***Unless*** I see in His hands the print of the nails, and put my finger into the print of the nails, and put my hand into His side, ***I will not believe***."

I hear Christians make ill-advised vows frequently. It must be because they fail to recognize that vows carry with them a power that binds us to the words. Call it soul-power, call it psychology, or whatever—the vows you make *remake* you. Be especially careful of sentences that begin with "I/You *never*..." or "I/You *always*..."! Here are some common vows that I hear frequently:

- "I will never trust another man/woman!"
- "No one will ever hurt me like that again!"
- "I will never again make myself that vulnerable!"
- "You can't trust anyone these days!"
- "You/I can't do anything right!"
- "If you _____, you are just asking for hurt!" (fill in the blank)
- "People/You are so _____!" (fill in the blank, with a negative of course!)

There are many more—but you get the idea. Notice that vows do not necessarily commit a person to action; frequently they commit you to a *mindset*. Also, you don't even have to speak the words yourself—if you agree with someone else's vow, you bind yourself to the words as well. Again, words have power and effect. Jesus said that we will give account for every word spoken in the day of judgment (**Matthew 12:36**). Until then, we still carry the burden of their effect until and unless the power is broken.

The second lesson occurs just four verses later in **John 20:29** when Jesus said to him, "Thomas, because you have seen Me, you have believed. Blessed are those who have not seen and yet have believed." Because of his vow of disbelief, Thomas missed out on a blessing that would otherwise presumably have been his as well. It seems so unlikely because Thomas was probably present when God, through Jesus, brought at least three people back from death to life. How could he doubt Papa's ability to do the same to His Son? I think that the lesson is that Thomas was hurting and profoundly disappointed after the death of Jesus—so much so that he avoided the other disciple's company and was not present when Jesus first appeared to them. Then, his outburst was a childish tantrum flowing from his hurt and disappointment in the fact that recent events had not occurred as he imagined and expected that they would. His intransigence and tantrum earned him a mild rebuke from Jesus and changed his identity forever. There is a lesson for us in Thomas' response: It is wise to set a guard on our mouth and be very careful of our words—*especially* when we are hurting, disappointed, or events do not transpire according to our expectations.

Lesson #3 stems from the fact that Thomas, in his pain, was unwilling to accept the testimony of his brothers and sisters, but insisted on the personal proof. Separating yourself and retreating into doubt, unbelief, and your emotional pain when you are frustrated and disappointed is equally unwise, because you never know when the Lord will show up, and you *do not* want to miss that!

## Disappointment…

Though this book is not *primarily* about emotional healing, the downstream problems associated with hurtful events in life cause enough challenges to our discipleship progression (or lack thereof) to warrant targeted attention. There is one cause (disappointment) and one result (fear) that deserve specific discussion because of their prevalence and devastating effect.

A friend once told me that, "Expectations are a predisposition to judge another, and a precursor to resentment." Even if not a particularly positive perspective, one has to admit that my friend's evaluation is somewhat true, as far as it goes. It is impossible to judge another's behavior or feel resentment unless one has set an expectation as a standard against which to evaluate. There are obviously positive aspects of setting expectations; we are focusing on the negative collateral damage that they inflict when thwarted, and they become the focal point of loss, shame, profound disappointment, failed performance and potential, deferred hope, tragedy, abuse of trust, and on and on.

Managing expectations is important, as is our *response* to the disappointment that they cause. With disappointment, judgment is usually not far behind in the string of cause-and-effect. If we wish to engage in consequence management, a good start may be to manage our expectations to prevent disappointment from resulting in a judgment of others, of life circumstances, and even of those closest to us. Managing our expectations is a precarious balance—we do not want to ditch them altogether and miss the benefits of positive expectations!

Disappointment cannot occur unless there is first a pre-existing expectation that is thwarted. The takeaway is that carelessly establishing an expectation is playing with fire. I know what you are thinking, and *of course,* there are expectations that are right and good. But it is also impossible to judge another person's behavior or experience resentment unless there first exists some expectation of treatment or performance; and often, those expectations originate in our self-interest. Depending on nature, strength, object, and life assumptions connected with them, disappointments can be minor, profound, or even devastating and crippling. One of the attendant attitudes that frequently accompanies "life for its own sake" is an expectation of a smooth, trouble-free life. It manifests as an underlying standard against which we evaluate (read: judge) others' behavior toward us and those about whom we care. Scripture clearly admonishes us to maintain a steadfast hope, both in this life and in the one to come. It would be hard to argue that hope is not an expectation. Obviously, then, all expectations are not bad. The question becomes, "When do we cross the line between expectations that are right and good and those that provide the fodder for judgment and resentment?" Discerning between maintaining hope and guarding against ill-advised expectations is the work of sons; spiritual children are incapable of such high-level skills and mature transactions.

> **Proverbs 4:23**, "Keep your heart with all diligence, for out of it spring the issues of life."

Managing disappointment involves what we: 1) accept as our underlying assumptions concerning our expectations of how we are *entitled* to be treated; and, 2) manage our tendency toward ill-advised expectations of other's behavior; and, 3) manage our response to events that do not match our expectations. Notice that all three actions fall into the "guard your heart with all diligence" category, but two of the three actions necessarily must occur before a disappointing incident occurs. In other words, numbers 1 and 2 are "pre-disappointment management strategies."

Rejection is a form of disappointed expectation that feels quite personal; but sometimes, it is not personal at all. Sometimes you experience the same rejection Jesus did because you are from the same place of origin—the eternal Kingdom. The only way we can guard against the pain of this kind of rejection is to disinvest our expectations from this world and reinvest it in the eternal realm. We do that by contextualizing our experience according to the words of Jesus and John:

- **John 15:19**, "If you were of the world, the world would love its own. Yet because you are not of the world, but I chose you out of the world, *therefore the world hates you.*"
- **John 7:7**, "The world cannot hate you [i.e., those that disbelieve], *but it hates Me because I testify of it that its works are evil.*"
- **1 John 3:1**, "Behold what manner of love the Father has bestowed on us, that we should be called children of God! Therefore, *the world does not know us, because it did not know Him.*"
- **1 John 5:19**, "We know that we are of God, and the *whole world lies under the sway of the wicked one.*"

Here is a hint for future reference: When Jesus cautions us about our treatment by the world, in the world, it is for a reason; and that reason is so that we will not be surprised nor be swept along in the negative feelings associated with rejection. Remember Solomon's admonition in **Proverbs 16:1a**, "The preparations of the heart belong to man"; and **Proverbs 22:3a**, "A prudent man foresees evil and hides himself." "Preparation" and "foresee[ing]" mean that we should read Jesus' and John's words and use them to devise strategies to guard our hearts and prevent the day-to-day damage that accumulates in us as emotional pain.

> **John 15:19**, "If you were of the world, the world would love its own. Yet because you are not of the world, but I chose you out of the world, ***therefore the world hates you***."

## ...And Fear

Fear is one of those antiquated incongruities in a believer's life that defies logic, reason, and even faith. It is antiquated in that if it ever had a legitimate place in life, it was before we placed our trust in God. Our trust in our good and loving Father is the basis for our being; and yet, because it is a staple of the carnal mind, fear manages to slither its way into our thinking, into our praying, into our feeling, into our willing, and into just about every other aspect of daily life. We tell ourselves that it is normal and natural to have fear—we are, after all, only human. Precisely. That is what I mean by illogical and unreasonable—if you *know* that you are only human, and if you *know* that you are in the hands of a good and loving Father that intends your best in all circumstances, a fear response to anything in life is *inappropriate*. Fear is only the logical response if we maintain our Independent, Separated Self and know we are on our own and inadequate. In that case, we *should* fear!

Fear, when and where it exists, is a portal into our soul that belies and bypasses the story we tell ourselves. Its existence is the sodium pentothal—"truth serum" of sorts—that causes us to know the unvarnished state of our soul. Its presence is a litmus test that confirms the carnal mind in control. In that sense, fear can be a useful tool when it is "just passing through," and when we are able to see it clearly for what it is. But, when it settles in for the long haul (or worse, we make it our friend) it is as damaging to our spiritual well-being as any self-destructive behavior because it often unlocks and opens the front door and invites in a host of companions. It is a drug that targets specific areas of our soul and spirit:

- It targets our peace in its function as tormentor;

- It sabotages our trust in its function as liar and underminer of truth;

- It undercuts our security in its function of isolating us from those around and from Papa Himself;

- It distorts our vision in its function as a deceiver;

- It confuses our clarity of purpose in its function as an imposter;

- It dilutes our resolve in its function as discourager;

- It drives us to strive even harder in its function as taskmaster;

- It disparages us for not being enough in its function as accuser;

- It encourages us to build walls and false fronts in its function as a pretender.

Here is the pertinent question: Believers all over the world who would never consider listening to the voice of Satan are regularly deceived by fear. Why? What is it about fear that waltzes so easily past our spiritual defenses? The answer is that fear is a permanent resident of the carnal mind and has been since the Garden of Eden when the serpent cast doubt on God's word with his question, "Has God really said that?" It is a lie—and we all know who is the father/originator of all lies.

The Apostle John gave us some frank words that put the presence of fear in a believer's life in stark perspective: "There is no fear in love, but perfect love casts out fear because fear involves torment. But he who fears has not been made perfect in love." (**1 John 4:18**). "Wow, John, cut us some slack. After all, *we are only human*!" If you believe (as I do) that all Scripture is God-breathed, clearly Papa takes a very dim view of our practice of making room for—much less coddling—pockets of fear in life. We know that God is love, and we know that He is perfected love and He loves us perfectly. If by its very nature and presence, perfect love (read: God) casts out fear, and if we know that "he who fears has not been made perfect in love," what does that say about our claims that God lives in us? What does it say about our dearth of spiritual energy to root about every vestige of fear anywhere lurking in darkness within us?

The concept is so foreign to our flesh and the carnal mind, it is appropriate to ask, "What does 'no fear' even *look* like?" Does it look like a dually pickup truck with a "No Fear" bumper sticker, tobacco streaks down the side, gun rack and a "Come and Take It" sticker on the back window? Does it look like defiant bravado and over-confident knowledge that I can shout-down and intimidate anyone who opposes my version of the truth? Does it look like recklessly throwing one's body into all manner of dangerous circumstances to prove that he or she has no fear? None of the above. It looks like **Psalm 131:2**: "Surely I have calmed and quieted my soul, like a weaned child with his mother; like a weaned child *is* my soul within me."

"Surely *I* have calmed and quieted my soul," speaks volumes to the listening ear. "Surely *I* have calmed and quieted my soul," tells us that hosting *fear is a choice*, just as casting it out is a choice! And, here is the kicker: There is no escaping the choices that *we* make! If fear has a permanent place of residence in the carnal mind (and it does), and if the Choice Space is the place of choosing between the carnal mind and the spiritual mind (and it is), then it is clear that a disciple must consistently reject the clamor of fear in the Choice Space! The pilgrimage to be free from fear *begins* with the settled understanding that fear is a choice. Only by consistently choosing the spiritual mind and rejecting the fear resident in our carnal mind can we become a "weaned child" (weaned from our fear addiction!) and rest against our Papa's breast.

If fear is a carnal choice, it stands to reason that there is a polar opposite preferred spiritual mind choice for every potential situation. We equip ourselves to be successful when we root out fear consequences within us and identify the spiritual mind remedy. Earlier, we identified a few of the consequences that choosing fear brings. So, then, it remains to name the spiritual mind choice appropriate for each of its carnal mind functions:

- In place of torment, we choose peace;
- In place of lies and suspicion, we choose truth and trust;
- In place of isolation, we choose union and security in Papa's love;
- In place of deception, we choose the clarity of how Papa sees us;
- In place of an impostor, we choose our true identity and Papa's purpose for us;
- Instead of discouragement, we choose faithfulness and perseverance;
- In place of striving, we choose rest;
- In place of accusation, we choose grace and Papa's fullness;
- In place of walls and false appearances, we choose genuineness and heart fellowship.

One final note on this topic: When I say that fear has a permanent residence in the carnal mind, that does not mean that we are always subject to its bidding. It just means that as long as we are in the flesh, fear will be a constant battle. But just because we battle it does not mean that it becomes part of our identity, and it certainly does not mean that we are destined to be overcome and accept its consequences.

## There is No "Fix," But There is Healing

Fixing people and attempting to fix one's self is ill-advised. First of all, it is highly unlikely to work, and the best that can be hoped for is a stalemate with pain that incorporates it into a quasi-functional life arrangement. The alternative that is light years better, and beyond fixing, is connecting with the "grace that is sufficient" (**2 Corinthians 12:9**) and letting the healing waters flow over your broken heart and damaged soul.

Jesus came and dwelt among us for at least three reasons: 1) To redeem His Church to Himself through His death and resurrection; 2) To show us the Father; and, 3) To reveal to us the character and nature of the Kingdom. It is this last purpose that was the subject matter of what we call the Sermon on the Mount, and it is a portion of that Kingdom revelation with which **Matthew 5:4** deals. One night, not long ago, the Holy Spirit awakened me and made this statement: "There is no more important skill central to our experience of the Kingdom on earth than to learn how to receive His comfort and abide comforted." This skill connects us to the topic of our healing from emotional pain. It seems obvious that in order for there to be a need for comfort, mourning in some form must exist, which we then experience as pain. We have discussed the nature and effect of emotional pain and how it connects to **2 Corinthians 12:9**, "My grace is sufficient for you, for My strength is made perfect in weakness." It is now time to connect the concepts of our mourning, and His grace *appropriated* in us, resulting in our experience of His comfort.

> **Matthew 5:4**, "Blessed are those who mourn, for they shall be comforted."

My infant granddaughter visited for a few days recently. I love watching her and letting the Holy Spirit teach me about being a much-loved child of the Father. She doesn't know *what* she needs, she just knows *that* she needs. We come into this world unable to comfort ourselves, only able to convey to our caretaker that we need. As we grow and mature spiritually, we are intended to learn to seek out the source—the "Father of mercies and God of all comfort" (**2 Corinthians 1:3**)—on our own. That ability is one barometer of our maturation in the Spirit. Babies lay there, cry out and get comforted; but at some point, we learn to seek out and access His comfort ourselves. If we fail to do so, or if we select something less than the appropriated grace of God, we pitch a fit and cry and mourn without effect, and it results in the emotional pain we experience in our adult-body-but-infant-soul.

> **Jeremiah 21:8**, "Now you shall say to this people, 'Thus says the Lord: Behold, I set before you the way of life and the way of death.'"

Accessing comfort has *everything* to do with connecting with the grace He has provided for the situation at hand. His grace is an umbrella providing us a general covering; but it is also a raincoat to provide us specific, situational covering for our pain. His promise, "My grace is sufficient for you," is that which turns the *illusion* of emotional pain into the *reality* of sufficiency. Accessing His comfort and grace happens by entering behind the veil into His Presence. It is in the Holy of Holies that we first know His comfort, and then carry it with us into the T/S/M world.

## The Defilement Death Spiral

There are only two choices in the dilemma Choice Space—the spiritual mind (life) and the carnal mind (death). But the choice we make has consequences that last long beyond our momentary light affliction. Our response to pain and the causer(s) of pain can shape our personality, world view, and our ability to embrace and receive Papa's love. Living things do not stand still or stay stagnant in life for very long; mostly they either grow or deteriorate. This change *for either positive or negative* may be thought of as a progression or regression—one change building on another change, forming a new structure with each new level of development. Our choices also build on one another to constitute an upward climb ("upward call," **Philippians 3:14**) or a death spiral ("defilement," **Hebrews 12:15**). In this chapter, we have examined the effects of, and our response to, suffering/pain. Often the death spiral occurs so imperceptibly as to be invisible to us until we wake up one day (or not) to an inability to perceive Papa's love for us, to feel His Presence, to hear His voice, and to see His glory. At that point, we have entered into defilement.

It is possible to return from defilement because Papa is a Good Father and restoration specialist by nature, and He is able to raise even the dead! However, it is far better to recognize the spiral and avoid it in the first place. Here is the death spiral in all of its negative glory:

**Expectation + Disappointment + Resentment + Judgment + Bitterness =_Defilement**

In a later section, we will look at a slightly different downward spiral related to grief and choosing the carnal mind options. But for now, note the slide down the proverbial slippery slope once the spiral develops! Some of the lessons we learn in the classroom of life are those we are to imitate, emulate, and assimilate. Some lessons are those we are to stay away—or even run—from. Recall that **Proverbs 22:3** presents a lesson in wisdom for all who will hear and pay attention: "A *prudent man* foresees evil and hides himself, but the simple pass on and are punished [suffer punishment]." "Prudent" is not a word we hear used a lot these days, mainly because it is a characteristic not greatly valued in our culture; it means "wise or judicious in practical affairs." The lesson for the

> **Proverbs 27:12**, "A prudent man foresees evil and hides himself; the simple pass on and are punished."

wise is so important that it is repeated again in **Proverbs 27:12**. I am pretty sure that the duplication is not an editing error on Papa's part; rather, He repeated it to make sure we do not miss it! **Proverbs 22:3/27:12** are Papa's "No Trespassing" signs adequately posted and on display to keep us from evil, including the defilement death spiral.

## Epilogue to Pain: The Joy of Birthing

Jesus' master storyteller skills, including His parables, metaphors, similes, and analogies serve to provide context for us to understand our path through our pilgrimage. He is careful to give us clues to His mysteries from experiences with which we are familiar so that we may squeeze every ounce of truth from each one. Such is the metaphor He gives us in the birthing process, rich in contextual meaning and depth of understanding:

> [20]Most assuredly, I say to you that you will weep and lament, but the world will rejoice; and you will be sorrowful, but your sorrow will be turned into joy. [21]A woman, when she is in labor, has sorrow because her hour has come; but as soon as she has given birth to the child, she no longer remembers the anguish, for the joy that a human being has been born into the world. [22]Therefore you now have sorrow, but I will see you again and your heart will rejoice, and your joy no one will take from you. (**John 16:20-22**)

In this instance, Jesus is addressing His imminent death, the subsequent suffering that the Disciples would experience, but joy upon His rising. It is also a promise to us, those believers born after His ascension and before His return. The pregnancy—birth metaphor foreshadows His return, and the joy that will be ours when the Bride completes the gestation period and travail, and we see Him "coming in the clouds with great power and glory" (**Mark 13:26**).

Jesus also conveys another broader lesson applicable to all of the nuts and bolts of our gestational travail, the Birthing Principle: Preceding each new birth, each new growth advancement in the Spirit, there is a period of travail and pain. That is the purchase price of our learning. The converse is equally true: Each period of travail/pain that we experience *births something*!

> The Birthing Principle: "Without travail, there is no birth. Where there is travail, something is always birthed."

But unlike in natural childbirth, it is up to us in the Choice Space to ensure that what is birthed as a result of our travail of the soul is a live, joy-giving growth result, and not wasted on a negative effort that must be repeated over and over.

Here, Jesus is saying the equivalent of, "Look at this metaphor with which you are all familiar, and understand something about the Kingdom." The first lesson is that eventual joy is inextricably linked to initial suffering. But the converse is also true: "Where there is suffering, something is always birthed." If we are overcome and defeated by the pain process, we birth bitterness, anger, and self-pity. If we respond to the labor process with hope, with grace, with rejoicing, and understanding, we give birth to righteousness, peace, and joy. In other words, we birth the Kingdom. It is no trick to revel in joy after the child is born; the trick is to understand that suffering eventually comes to an end, that Papa's promises to us *do* get fulfilled, and therefore choose joy in the midst of pain!

Jesus has put all things into our hands with respect to our choices and growth. With so much power over our own destiny at our fingertips, it is sobering to think that Papa has entrusted spiritual children with so much responsibility. It is daunting to think that it is possible to birth something that does not contribute to our advance in the Spirit. Rather, we have the ability by our choices to limit, cap, and even arrest our growth altogether. Conversely, though, where there is a great risk, there is potential for a great reward! On the positive end of our growth pilgrimage continuum is "rejoic[ing] with joy unspeakable and full of glory" (**1 Peter 1:8**).

To prevent any negative effects and hindrances in the Spirit, we do well to conduct life in the context of the Birthing Principle, and in the context of **Galatians 5:24**, "²⁴And those who are Christ's *have crucified the flesh* with its passions and desires." But even with the knowledge to act, the intent to crucify the flesh, and the determination to take up our cross daily, we bump up against Paul's dilemma of **Romans 7:18**, "For I know that in me (that is, in my flesh) nothing good dwells; for to will is present with me, but how to perform what is good I do not find."

> **Galatians 5:22-24**, ²²But the fruit of the Spirit is love, joy, peace, longsuffering, kindness, goodness, faithfulness, ²³gentleness, self-control. Against such there is no law. ²⁴*And those who are Christ's have crucified the flesh with its passions and desires.*

While we may not feel equal to the task, or even to begin, we recognize that Papa has put us here "for such a time as this," and that our instructional charge of Bridal preparation is to "make [ourselves] ready" (**Revelation 19:7**). As we approach the end of *Part 1: The Theory of Everything*, it seems that the "sweet spot" may be **Philippians 2:12**, "work out your own salvation *with fear and trembling*." That is, the effort to "work out" arises from within, but it occurs in the knowledge of our own inability to perform without Papa's strong help, and in the humility and meekness of fear and trembling. Clinging to all that is good, and forsaking any vestige of religious motivation, we now move into *Part 2: The Tool Chest*. There, we will explore some job aids that can help us be intentional, alert, and engaged in birthing the Fruit of the Spirit, against which there is no law.

# Part 2: The Tool Chest

## Navigational Aids for the Pilgrimage

We have discussed aspects of the Choice Space with the hope that you may visualize its usefulness in your spiritual perception as an instrument of Papa's transformation process. Remember, Jesus told Nicodemus in **John 3:3-5** that before being able to enter the Kingdom, we must be able to *see* (perceive) it. Further, in **verse 10** of the same chapter, He marveled that Nicodemus had risen to the level of a teacher in Israel and had not developed the sight to perceive the Kingdom. Some believers may think that their profession of faith was the only action necessary to enjoy the benefits of Kingdom citizenship. While new birth opens the door of entry to us (justification by His blood), it remains for us to dive heart-first into the salvation process (salvation by His life) that transforms us and prepares us to rule beside Him. Now we turn attention to tools that help us ensure that we do not persist throughout life in a place of spiritual stagnation, having accessed the Kingdom without taking positive steps to enter and claim as much of our transformation inheritance as we can in our time in the classroom.

Our efforts to be regenerated, transformed, and renewed in the Holy Spirit are most effective and efficient if they are intentional, and not haphazard. And they can only be consistently intentional if they are planned, organized, and clearly understood in our thinking. Such understanding is facilitated dramatically by a thought framework that enables us to study our own motivations, evaluate our progress, and focus our attention on areas of greatest growth potential. Our discipleship organizational efforts reflect the life-priority we assign to our spiritual growth. Christians often glibly proclaim our priorities to be some iteration of, "God first, family second, everything else in good order." These are easily proclaimed, but without the requisite time, planning, attention,

> **John 13:15-17**, "¹⁵For I have *given you an example that you should do as I have done to you*. ¹⁶Most assuredly, I say to you, a servant is not greater than his master; nor is he who is sent greater than he who sent him. ¹⁷If you know these things, *blessed are you if you do them*."

and effort devoted to them, and in the order that we claim to prioritize them, we are likely deceiving ourselves (fudging). The Fudge Factor kicks in and our execution of actual priorities looks significantly different than our words. However, there is no better measure of our priorities than what we actually *do* and how we *spend our time*. That is why Jesus' words "blessed are you if you do them" (**John 13:17**) are poignant to the point of being haunting.

There are tools to help us navigate through the Choice Space (and successfully be transformed into our desired *Last 15-Minute Self*) as it is described in **Romans 7:15**, "¹⁵ I do not understand what I do. For what I want to do I do not do, but what I hate I do" (NIV). The navigational aids I am talking about are ways to help us think about, plan, and focus our discipleship efforts. A complete tool would not only identify the "what I want to do" activities that help us, but also the "what I hate I do" activities that oppose and hinder growth. I find it very helpful to capture abstract ideas into visual representations that I can *study*, and on which I can *meditate*, and turn my study and meditation into *prayer*. My guess is that you are a lot like me in that regard.

## Writing it Down...

A good use of this space would be to make notes, record insights, ask questions, etc.

# Chapter 7: Discipleship Planning

[10][T]hat I may know Him and the power of His resurrection, and the fellowship of His sufferings, being conformed to His death, [11]if, by any means, I may attain to the resurrection from the dead. [12]Not that I have already attained, or am already perfected; *but I press on*, that I may lay hold of that for which Christ Jesus has also laid hold of me. [13]Brethren, I do not count myself to have apprehended; but one thing I do, forgetting those things which are behind and reaching forward to those things which are ahead, [14]I press toward the goal for the prize of the upward call of God in Christ Jesus. (**Philippians 3:10-14**)

## A Discipleship Plan Shapes Our Progress

I hope it is becoming clear that life is less about adventures to be experienced as it is time and resources to be shaped. What we call "our life" is not our own—we have been bought with a price (**1 Corinthians 6:20**). But our cumulative discipleship efforts *do* belong to us (or, more accurately, accrue to our account), and are the only thing we will take from this life into the Kingdom. In **1 Corinthians 3**, Paul describes our responsibility to build a temple on the foundation of Christ, and the manner that the quality of effort of our work will be judged:

> **1 Corinthians 6:20**, "For you were bought at a price; therefore, glorify God in your body and in your spirit, *which are God's*."

> [9]For we are God's fellow workers; you are God's field, you are God's building. [10]According to the grace of God which was given to me, as a wise master builder I have laid the foundation, and another builds on it. But let each one take heed how he builds on it. [11]For no other foundation can anyone lay than that which is laid, which is Jesus Christ. [12]Now if anyone builds on this foundation with gold, silver, precious stones, wood, hay, straw, [13]each one's work will become clear; for the Day will declare it, because it will be revealed by fire; and the fire will test each one's work, of what sort it is. [14]If anyone's work which he has built on it endures, he will receive a reward. [15]If anyone's work is burned, he will suffer loss; but he himself will be saved, yet so as through fire. [16]Do you not know that you are the temple of God and that the Spirit of God dwells in you? [17]If anyone defiles the temple of God, God will destroy him. For the temple of God is holy, which temple you are.

Paul employs the metaphor of constructing a building and tells us when our work will be evaluated (the Day, or The Day of Christ). It is an appropriate model because a building captures the result of intentional, purposeful, coordinated, and focused activity that reflects the vision and plan of the architect. That is how our discipleship efforts are supposed to be—with the resources placed at your disposal, with the knowledge that you have accumulated, with the time you have been given, and with the plan that you compose and execute, and with God's Program in mind as context.

My career in emergency services and management has taught me that formulating a plan of action directs our attention to specific issues and tasks that are unlikely to be addressed otherwise. I have worked on plans from single-page simple, to complex Emergency Operations Plans for large operations, and even an entire state for multiple disaster scenarios. Planners have a common saying: "*Plans* are nothing, but planning is *everything*!" While this saying understates a plan's usefulness as a reference tool, it conveys the message that the planning process *itself* is vital to performance. That is absolutely true with respect to discipleship planning as well. Regardless of its scope and complexity, a plan sitting and gathering dust on a shelf somewhere does little good. But when thoughtfully and carefully prepared, reviewed and updated regularly, it becomes a roadmap for successful action.

It may seem to some that mixing professional planning tools, processes and techniques is at least odd (if not downright out of place!) in the realm of spiritual development. I respectfully disagree, and for three primary reasons:

1) Any *reasonable* methodology (strategy) that works, promotes ownership responsibility for our growth, and organizes our effort is a good thing. I emphasize reasonable because I recognize that planning, taken to an extreme, can have the effect of returning us to the Law.

2) Planning techniques force us to see both the *whole* picture *and* focus our attention on the details of daily Choice Space decision-making. In a word, planning gives us *context*. There is an old anecdote about the "cowboy that ran out of the saloon, jumped on his horse, and *rode off in all directions*." Without focused direction, we *are* that cowboy.

3) We, at times, fall into the trap of separating and isolating the spiritual from the profane, religious from secular life, and compartmentalizing our existence into "church," "family," "career," and "everything else" boxes. In doing so, we fail to consider the cross-discipline tools and best practices available, and thereby lose the opportunity to profit from their use.

A friend recently said to me, "I do not want you to teach me—I want you to make me think." I love that! That resonates with me! *I can do that!* I will apologize readily for any transgression of which I am guilty, but never for making you *think*.

We experience life chronologically, consecutively, moment-by-moment and choice-by-choice. Doesn't it make sense, then, to pursue the most important issues of life with the same approach and strategy, guided and assisted by a Discipleship Plan? Shouldn't that Plan be carefully and prayerfully considered, constructed, and written down? The process of consideration, construction, and recording are essential elements of *intentionality*. We are told in Scripture of several Books in which God records His important information (Book of Life, Book of Remembrance, Book of the Covenant, etc.). **Revelation 20:12** tells us of the role for God's Books at the future Day of Judgment:

> And I saw the dead, small and great, stand before God; and the books were opened: and another book was opened, which is the book of life: and the dead were judged out of those things which were written in the books, according to their works.

If God uses the process of recording His important information in books, doesn't it make sense that we, His people, should do likewise and record our important goals, objectives, strategies, tactics, and action plans in a written plan for our own discipleship? If you have embraced the need for an intentional plan and an organized effort for advancing your discipleship, a natural question is, "In the face of such an insurmountable challenge, where do I even begin?" i.e., "How do I eat *that* elephant?" Before taking any action steps, it is essential that we do some prep work to establish the values, assumptions, and attitudes that provide the raw material from which the goal—and all that follows—is shaped. Any planner worth his/her salt knows that the first step in making a plan is evaluating the status quo; the second is doing research. Then we gather information and envision the goal, the, "What it looks like if we are completely successful." In our context, we have described this goal generally as our *Last 15-Minute Self*. Then, taking the information of our current status and comparing it to the ideal state (goal), we can get a sense of the gap that exists between current performance and future optimized growth; the resulting Gap Analysis gives us some concept of the magnitude of the task ahead, but it also gives us the beginnings of a roadmap. Of *course*, it is a ginormous undertaking; it is supposed to be! It is *supposed to occupy you for a lifetime*!

# Examining Assumptions and Misbeliefs

A *really* important prep step for assembling your Discipleship Plan is to spend quality time uncovering your assumptions. Knowing what is in your heart is one aspect of the discipleship research component, and knowing the assumptions you have embraced as "the way things work" is critical to understanding your way (**Proverbs 14:8**). Sometimes, our assumptions about the gospel are incorrect (that is, not accurate according to the Word of God) because they are based on someone else's

> **Proverbs 14:8a**, "The wisdom of the prudent is to understand his way."

assumptions being taught as "gospel." In this way, misunderstanding and error can be propagated through generations, especially if the error becomes the official teaching of an institution. We have said that the only way we can really know anything is by revelation and that by the Holy Spirit. Even those things we hear from our teachers can only be known when verified by the Holy Spirit to our spirit. But that does not mean we cannot embrace error and misbelief—we absolutely can! We begin to be vulnerable when we elevate and separate clergy and laity. Leadership with an honest heart and intent to exalt God only will agree with that position.

The Word of God reveals the Word of God, and the Holy Spirit is the Teacher and official spokesperson for interpretive truth. Examining assumptions requires carefully comparing the expectations we accept, the inferences we draw, and the data sets to which we give credence. Informational credibility is a commodity we assign *individually*, not en masse. Our leaders cannot assign credibility for us, and leaders with integrity will not try to do so, but encourage you to, "Be diligent [study] to present yourself approved to God, a worker who does not need to be ashamed, rightly dividing the word of truth" (**2 Timothy 2:15**). A so-called "fact" is not credible (e.g., worthy of belief, confidence, and acceptance) because someone else says it is, only because the Teacher says it is. I am convinced that the Holy Spirit has revealed the contents of this book to me; but I am not your teacher, only truth-seeking peer. You should only accept them as accurate if, and only if, He confirms the same word to you.

Today's world continuously floods us with more information than we can possibly process. In order to deal with the glut and prevent melt-down, we have had to develop methods to choke-down the flow and economize on the active processing required from our minds to conduct even simple tasks. Every person alive makes assumptions about the world and how it works on a daily, even minute-by-minute, basis. If we did not, we would have to start from square one for each decision we make. It is the nature of an assumption to:

- Shortcut decisions to enable more efficient (not necessarily more effective or accurate) response to multiple, simultaneous stimuli
- Filter extraneous information to limit overload
- Limit time needed to make certain decisions by relegating them to "settled" status, and therefore enabling an automatic response
- Serve as points of agreement for like-minded people
- Serve as a gatekeeper to let in information with which we agree, and keep out information with which we disagree
- Helps us form expectations that serve to interpret facts (e.g., "We see best that which we expect to see," and, "We understand most what we have already accepted")
- Be invisible (work in our subconscious or unconscious mind) unless and until the host sets about to uncover their own assumptions.

The value of examining and writing down our assumptions in a discipleship planning process is that our behavior and activities are often herded in predetermined directions by assumptions running in the background of our mental programming.  When they are contrary to the intent of our conscious mind goals—especially when we are attempting to make intentional changes to behavior and attitudes—the dissonance that results can hinder our progress.  By uncovering assumptions in the early stages of the plan-building process, we uncover those that need to change, those that need to be reaffirmed and reinforced, and we align them with goals to ensure that our plan is consistent from beginning to end.

I like to think that Solomon endorsed the practice of self-knowledge research, including assumptions, schemas, presumptions, and bedrock truths.

- **Proverbs 14:8**, "The wisdom of the prudent is to understand his way, but the folly of fools is deceit."
- **Proverbs 20:24**, "A man's steps are of the Lord; how then can a man understand his own way?"

"Understanding [your] way" is tantamount to knowing yourself.  **Proverbs 20:24** asks a rhetorical question, and implies the answer: If a man's steps are known by the Lord, we have to ask Him about them! **Proverbs 14:8** says that self-research is prudent, but he also adds the zinger implication that the person that fails to understand their own way is foolishly subject to deceit.

"Be[ing] transformed by the renewing of your mind," (**Romans 12:2**) includes all parts of our mind (conscious, unconscious, subconscious) and well as the more overt and obvious thoughts, determination of will, and misbeliefs.  Misbeliefs are the points in our journey where we have embraced that which is contrary to God's word, and that is the spiritual definition of a lie.  A critical starting point for embarking on a serious discipleship pilgrimage is to search the Word and identify as many of our misbeliefs as we are able, knowing that more will be brought to the light as you progress along your path.  Misbeliefs are the "strongholds" identified by Paul in **2 Corinthians 10:4-5** as "high thing[s] that exalt themselves against the knowledge of God":

> [4]For the weapons of our warfare are not carnal but mighty in God for pulling down strongholds, [5]casting down arguments and every high thing that exalts itself against the knowledge of God, bringing every thought into captivity to the obedience of Christ.

> **Romans 12:2**, "And do not be conformed to this world, but be transformed by the renewing of your mind, so that you may discern the will of God, what is ·good and acceptable and perfect."

"That which exalts itself against the knowledge of God" is a decent supplemental definition of a lie and the virtual job description of the enemy.  In contrast, a working definition of healing is to bring every thought into the captivity of discipline and reframing all life events in the context of Papa's meaning and purpose.  We experience God's healing of our mind and emotions when we are able to embrace His meaning and program of transformation.  The process helps us reframe and understand all of our past abuses, pain, and torment as the travail that births His image in us.

## The Gap Analysis: The FOTS Graphic Equalizer

Starting with a clear idea of where we currently stand compared to where we want to be (*Last 15-Minute Self*) is vitally important.  The gap then becomes our area(s) of concentration and can be crafted into objectives for our Discipleship Plan.  Notice that I use the terminology "gap" rather than "weaknesses."  I do that intentionally for three reasons: 1) Identifying something as a weakness attaches it to my identity (similar to declaring myself an "alcoholic"), and that skews our view of who we are and how we function.  2) A gap is a transitional state, but a weakness is more permanent.  3) A weakness is structural, part of the fabric of our being. A gap is a space to be closed, lessons to be learned, and a series of choices to make.

Determining our Fruit of the Spirit (FOTS) status is not an easy task. We do not come from the factory with easy-to-read digital gauges that measure our levels of Love, Joy, Peace, etc. So how does one measure the unmeasurable? How do you arrive at an accurate picture (sans "fudging") of that which is not tangible to our five senses or measurable by instrumentation? This is similar to a question with which we wrestled my entire fire service career—"How do we measure the impact of our fire education and prevention efforts?" "How do we measure that which we have prevented?" The answer lies in figuring out what would likely have happened but for your intervention; and, on perceived performance versus desired and comparing the new reality with the old.

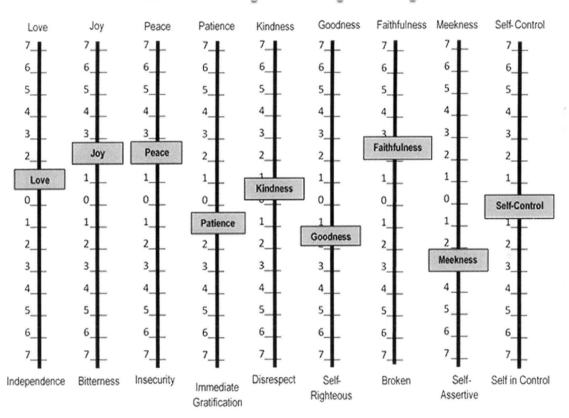

Likely, no one has followed you around recording your instances of Goodness, Faithfulness, when you displayed Self-Control vs. self-in-control, etc. You probably do not have a database indicating your Kindness and Meekness. So, where does one get the data to make an accurate self-assessment? If you have made a regular practice of journaling, that can help. Otherwise, it has to come from your own brutally honest best-estimate, based on identified criteria, and after requesting Holy Spirit guidance and revelation. Many years ago, Bob Mumford (Bible teacher extraordinaire!) used to teach this prayer: "Father, anesthetize me with your Presence, then reveal my heart to me." **WARNING!** It is unwise to pray so recklessly if you do not want to know the answer! The art of self-knowledge is painful-but-necessary— but only if you yearn to progress from servant to friend, from spiritual child to mature son of the Kingdom. Another source of status quo information is to ask friends and family that are close and know you best. **WARNING!** Do not try this at home if you are not willing to hear honest answers! Dishonest answers do no one any good, and it would be better not even to ask than to get fudged answers (we do enough fudging on our own!). If you determine that questioning friends and family is a wise move, I suggest a structured process that ensures everyone is employing the same definition of the concepts involved. For example, if you are asking friends about your "Joy level," and they are thinking "happiness," your evaluation will be fatally flawed. Another potential flaw in this method of information-gathering is the "Halo Effect," that is, one characteristic or one event that overshadows and colors the perception of actual objective evaluation. It is letting, "Remember that time when you made me furious?" and, "You really saved my life when you___" instances that come back to haunt—positively or negatively—and prevent objectivity.

What do you do with information that is conflicting? The world handles this eventuality by throwing out the highs and lows and averaging the remaining data. When the task is FOTS status quo measurement, highs and lows are important information because both show that of which you are capable, for good or ill. Some people bring out the best in me, and some the worst. But that is all useful information as I access Papa's comfort for my strikeouts and give Him glory for my home runs. The mediocre middle is only to be sought if that is where we belong, bringing us to another trap: the "Central Tendency." Central Tendency is the natural fudge that wants to throw out the extreme possibility of perfection and the abhorrent, of sublime and the ghastly, and land in the safe middle. In those cases where you suspect you are getting "Halo Effect" or Central Tendency-tainted information, I submit that suspicion is your inner voice correcting what others have not the courage to tell you. "Why don't they feel comfortable just being honest with me?" might be another uncomfortable-but-instructive question in that case.

Another source to answer the, "From where do we obtain 'identified criteria' information to help with our estimate?" question is found in the next chapter, Chapter 8. There, we will spend detailed time on each FOTS element (Love, Joy, Peace, Patience, etc.), with a continuum identifying positive and negative behaviors that move us toward or away from the nine FOTS. The behaviors listed in each continuum make a good tool for helping with our evaluation.[19] For example, if for our Gap Analysis we wish to gauge our development in our ability to flow in Agape Love, we may be aided by consulting the Continuum for the FOTS Love and considering the component behaviors associated with it. The information we seek comes by considering our Love response (the Master Fruit) to the world, and that comes from comparing our best estimate of what percentage of our responses in life-circumstances match those in the "Tendency Toward Love" column versus the "Tendency Toward Independence" column. You might even consider assigning a number to the comparison of each factor, based on some scale, say, 1 to 10. For example, "How independent am I (80%) versus child-like dependence on Papa (20%)?" Or, "What percentage of my time is spent characterized by 'Entertain me!' (50%) versus 'Teach me!' (50%)?" By repeating this exercise with each factor for each FOTS, we should arrive at a good estimate of our current status. For example, the factors on the following table are from the Love Continuum.

The FOTS Graphic Equalizer (FOTSGE) is a display tool to help remind us and help keep our, "Mind stayed on [Him]" (**Isaiah 26:3**). It is "My spiritual life at a glance," or computer dashboard of sorts. Hopefully, most are familiar with the role of a graphic equalizer in balancing various frequencies of sound in audio production. By manipulating the slides upward or downward, it is possible to enhance certain frequencies and mute others. Of course, when it comes to the FOTS, our ultimate objective is to blast *all* of the slides *all* of the way to the top of the scale and keep them there! More realistically, however, we can use this visual representation of the result of our Gap Analysis to remind us what specific Fruits we are targeting for improvement.

---

[19] There are other characteristics and traits in Scripture that are appropriate for the Continuum Model format, but are not included in the list of nine FOTS. Some examples are hope, perseverance, trust, honesty, integrity, serving, selfless, etc.

The slides on our two-dimensional equalizer can be adjusted as we grow, and perform update evaluations from time to time. My personal FOTSGE is part of my Discipleship Plan that I review and update regularly.

Every tool has some function to which it is specific. You may be familiar with the saying, "When the only tool you have is a hammer, every problem looks like a nail." Don't make the mistake of forcing a tool function that does not fit just because we have a need and we possess a tool. When we have a range of functions represented in our toolbox, and we know how and when to use each tool, we have greatly improved the chances of getting the job done.

| Tendency Toward Independence | VS. | Tendency Toward Love |
|---|---|---|
| • "My life" | ➡ | • "I live…yet not I" |
| • "Life for its own sake" | ➡ | • Life engaged in God's Program |
| • Independence | ➡ | • Child-like dependence |
| • Maintain my identity | ➡ | • Identity-based on my Eternal Self |
| • Isolated | ➡ | • Lose myself in Papa's Oneness |
| • Insecure | ➡ | • "God has put all things into my hands" |
| • Thirst for recognition | ➡ | • Hunger and thirst for righteousness |
| • The pursuit of happiness, possessions, etc. | ➡ | • Life is a classroom for learning to reign |
| • Identity = sum of all earthly factors | ➡ | • Identity = who God says I am |
| • "Self-made man" | ➡ | • "God-formed vessel" |
| • Engaged in self-pleasing, a life of ease | ➡ | • Engaged in good works |
| • Professes to love others, loves self above all | ➡ | • Loves others and self equally |
| • Refuse to sacrifice or compromise | ➡ | • Self-sacrifice, "be all things to all men" |
| • Rejoices when evil triumphs | ➡ | • Rejoices in the good |
| • Stingy, withholds self and goods | ➡ | • Generous with self and resources |
| • Grasping | ➡ | • Trusts in God's provision |
| • Eyes on the world | ➡ | • Eyes fixed above |
| • Seeks comfort | ➡ | • Seeks maturity |
| • "Entertain me!" | ➡ | • "Teach me!" |

## Discipleship Has Rules, Too

It is not enough for believers to believe. Moreover, it is not your or my prerogative to define the requirements of "believer" status. I do not get to make up the definitions and rules in the Christian life, or I would be living the **Genesis 3:4-5** lie ("You will be like God knowing good and evil"). French philosopher Rene Descartes first published his famous "I think, therefore I am" in 1637 as his "first principle" of philosophy. In essence, his principle employs an activity—thinking—to validated existence. So, the principle could be restated as, "Because there is enterprise, there is being." Some Christians seem to adopt a similar line of thinking, a "I identify as a believer, therefore I believe" philosophy, defining their believing activity by their believer standing. This circular argument most frequently manifests when church members claim to be a Christian and give their church organizational membership as evidence ("I go to church, therefore I am a believer"). Please hear me carefully at this point: Your faith in Christ combined with His grace is all that is necessary to get you into Heaven! However, to fulfill your purpose and your life mission of "preparing the head to wear the crown"—your discipleship—requires much, much more. It requires intentional, focused effort, an effort that goes against the natural grain of the flesh and the carnal mind. It requires engaging in the salvation process and experiencing His regeneration, transformation, and renewal. Your Father put you here for a more extensive reason than to "live a good life," a life of happiness, ease, and a three-car garage. It is not even our prerogative to determine what a "good life" is.

So, what is wrong with believing in God and calling that good enough? What makes us think that we can live in God's world, yet play by our own rules? Think about it like this: I like baseball. I never was any good at it, but I like to watch it nonetheless. What if my Texas Rangers or Houston Astros all decided that hitting singles is good enough to win the game? What if, as a team, they all decided that it is too much work to run all the way around the bases; and what if they decided to get to first base is a good faith effort and enough to prove that they are good players? What if the whole starting lineup did their best to hit a single, and once accomplished, would walk back to the dugout and slap "high-fives" all around? Of course, as soon as they left the base for the dugout, they would be tagged out; but no matter—the point was just to reach base in the first place, right? Once each member of the team hit a single—or maybe a double on a really good day—they would all congratulate one another and head for the showers. Though they may technically remain a baseball team, it is pretty safe to say that their effort would only be good enough to be in last place.

> **2 Timothy 2:5**, "And also if anyone competes in athletics, he is not crowned unless he competes according to the rules."

It seems so ludicrous as to be unthinkable. Clearly, these Rangers/Astros would be playing *some* game, but it *would not* be the game of baseball. Paul tells us that in order to win the game, one must play by rules. None of us are exempt from the requirements of God's Program. In **James 2:19**, the Apostle wryly tells us, "You believe in God? *You do well*." The next phrase should cut us like a knife: "*Even the demons believe and tremble*." So, if a believer stops at the point of believing (justification) and fails to press on to the goal of salvation (**Philippians 3:12**), he/she has attained the demon-level of belief. At least the demons respect His power enough to tremble!

> **James 2:19**, "You believe that there is one God. You do well. Even the demons believe—and tremble!"

Though we are unequivocally free from the requirements of the Law, we are not free from reaping the consequences of broken law; neither are we exempt from manifesting universal principles that Papa has established as the way things are done in His creation. And although we are not bound to a rule set to govern our behavior, discipleship best practices exist that enhance or deter our effectiveness:

1. **Be Intentional.** Discipleship activities are largely about crucifying the flesh, and that does not happen by accident. In the absence of intentionality, it likely doesn't happen at all. "Haphazard" is the enemy of "organized," and "disengaged" is the opposite of "committed." If we have a targeted goal (our *Last 15-Minute Self*) it makes no sense *not* to have an intentional, targeted path by which to reach it.

2. **Stop Doing Dumb Stuff.** Cause-and-effect is alive and well in spite of rampant denial in today's world. Also, alive and flourishing is a general feeling of exemption from negative consequences for actions. It is natural for us to feel that we are the exception to known negative consequences (that is the Optimism Bias we discussed in Chapter 3), especially when we occupy the central ruling position in our universe; that feeling is a subconscious version of the doctrine of sovereign immunity—a feeling that we *cannot* commit a wrong, or that we are immune from any prosecution to which we have not agreed.

Two types of immunity that we irrationally feel are "immunity from jurisdiction" ("Circumstances and consequences have no authority over me") and "immunity from enforcement" ("I can do whatever I want without consequences"). Doing dumb stuff *always* indicates who is seated on the throne of life because the spiritual mind does not do "dumb," it only does "wise"—that, *too*, is cause-and-effect.

> **Discipleship Best Practices**
> 1) Be Intentional
> 2) Stop Doing Dumb Stuff
> 3) Start Doing Wise Stuff
> 4) Listen to Your Coach (Holy Spirit)
> 5) Search for Root Causes
> 6) Deal with Emotional Pain ASAP
> 7) Review Your Discipleship Plan Often
> 8) Begin with/Keep the Big Picture in Mind
> 9) Be Accountable to Yourself and Others
> 10) Write it Down!

3. **Start Doing Smart (wise) Stuff.** Choice is one of the most precious gifts Papa has given us, but one common mistake is that we often equate the ability to make a choice with freedom, and they are not the same thing. Notice I did not say "freedom of choice," because unless we intentionally counter the effects of flesh, we are bound to it, *anything but free*, but are under compulsion. We are not free to choose wisely; we choose wisely and that sets us free. However, in those instances where we recognize and make wise choices according to the truth Papa has revealed to us, we prove His liberating work in us. Wisdom is *always* a function of revealed truth.

4. **Listen to Your Coach (Holy Spirit).** **Proverbs 16:25** and **Proverbs 14:12** present identical Scriptures that deserve attention: "There is a way that seems right to a man, but its end is the way of death." There is no stronger case for listening to our coach than the fact that our natural, normal instincts are exactly the wrong thing to do when the objective is experiencing life! The Holy Spirit's perspective is not bound based on a body of flesh and limited vision. Jesus described the Holy Spirit's role this way in **John 16:13**:

> However, when He, the Spirit of truth, has come, He will guide you into all truth; for He will not speak on His own authority, but whatever He hears He will speak; and He will tell you things to come.

And John, in **1 John 2:27**:

> But the anointing which you have received from Him abides in you, and you do not need that anyone teach you; but as the same anointing teaches you concerning all things, and is true, and is not a lie, and just as it has taught you, you will abide in Him.

The foregoing is why I wrote earlier that I have no desire to teach you, but rather to make you think. Then, the Holy Spirit can take what is presented and make of it whatever He wills, and what you can receive. The Holy Spirit is the storehouse of sound wisdom, and listening to Him causes us to dwell in safety, security, and without fear of evil (**Proverbs 1:33**).

5. **Search for Root Causes.** In the body, pain is a manifestation of some underlying condition that is out of the boundaries of the Designer's composition. Emotional pain is the manifestation of dysfunctional emotional conditions. There are common symptoms that alert us to pain's presence, and observable signs of letting emotional pain accumulate in us. We have discussed these five in Chapter 6 that are common: 1) Anger, 2) Guarding, 3) Fear, 4) Excuse-making, and 5) Addictive behavior. Treating symptoms is a superficial and unsatisfying attempt to be rid of problems, ranging from pesky to debilitating. It is also an avoidance technique for the heart surgery that we need and a temporary relief at best. When we settle for superficial solutions, we are sentencing ourselves to a repeat performance. When we establish a lifestyle of seeking superficial relief, we place a lid on our growth

that would otherwise not exist. Root causes often run deep, and they spread unseen until popping up in unexpected places. It takes commitment, it takes perseverance, and it takes intentionality to trace and remove the roots of pain, dysfunction, and bitterness —to their *bitter end*!

6. **Deal with Emotional Pain *Immediately, and as it Comes Up.*** Chapter 6 was devoted to the Problem of Emotional Pain. I have claimed that there is *no other issue in life* except your justification in Christ that is as important to our growth as learning to be free from emotional pain, and I bear the scars in my body to prove it. Dealing with emotional pain makes the "Top Ten Discipleship Best Practices" list because it is potentially *that* devastating. When allowed to accumulate over a lifetime or even a period of years, it artificially stunts and caps our growth. It is hard for us to see it in ourselves unless the manifestations are dramatic (as they were in me). Once free from pain, we may be able to look back and see the more direct path to the Promise Land, sense its crippling effect of pain in terms of what we could have otherwise accomplished while under its influence. I have a friend with whom I used to do construction work, and he would admonish me frequently: "Every chance you get, hurry up. You are burning daylight." Why wait until the pain appears overtaking you in the rear-view mirror? Or worse, runs you into the ditch? Address it ASAP and you will enjoy that much more life free from it!

   Having said the foregoing, I must be quick to add that Papa is never late, always redemptive, and our development is always right on time. Today represents the accumulation of learning from every day until this one, and it all works together for good. Even if we wimp out for years in facing our pain, Papa can still redeem the time. That is not a reason to procrastinate, but it is a path to the future and hope He has for us.

7. **Review Your Discipleship Plan Frequently.** Your Discipleship Plan should do *one* thing if it does nothing else—it should reveal and remind you of your true identity. I learned **2 Timothy 2:15** in Vacation Bible School as a child, "Be diligent [study] to present yourself approved to God, a worker who does not need to be ashamed, rightly dividing the word of truth." "Rightly dividing the word of truth" is a key phrase. "Dividing" means "to separate from." Not coincidentally, the Greek word for "sanctification" also means "to separate from, set apart." The study process that Paul recommends to Timothy is, "be diligent to separate the truth from the lies and misbeliefs that come at you in the world by concentrated and consecrated effort." No power in this world can overcome the combination of the Spirit of God in us in concentrated and consecrated effort! The outcome of that process is the ability and standing to live in the truth of your *eternal self*—without shame, without blemish, without stain. Here is the heart of the mystery: When you connect with your *true* self (eternal, Union Self), you are able to let go of your false self (Independent Self). That is the whole discipleship process in a nutshell. You are then free to be who you already are. If carefully prepared, your Discipleship Plan will be a compilation of truth concerning you. By frequently reviewing and updating it, you build connection, ownership, and self-knowledge. Your self-talk and thinking are renewed in an appropriate way and less and less (over time) influenced by the fallen world. You come into agreement with Papa, and agreement is the gateway to union.

8. **Begin with and Keep the Big Picture in Mind.** We have previously discussed the "Begin with the end in mind" principle, so here I will only enshrine the concept in the list of Discipleship Best Practices. The big picture of discipleship is God's Program on earth, my role in it as student of Kingdom principles in preparation of my future as the Bride of Christ; my availability as "God's field, God's building" production medium; my growth and development into the head that will be capable and worthy to wear the crown.

9. **Be Accountable to Yourself and Others.** Remember, without accountability, there is no motivation for change. I like to think that I do everything because it is the right thing to do. That is largely true, but it wasn't, and isn't, always so. The Independent Self is so named for a good reason—it likes to slink away and hide when it comes under pressure from the Spirit. It likes to distance itself from others in hopes that they can't see its true state—that is, its true *false* state! Hiding in darkness is totally ineffective and completely the wrong strategy—our God sees in secret, and even darkness is light to Him (**Psalm 139:12**). The only truly effective solution is to *run toward the light*—it shortens the time we have to live with our stinking self!

> **Psalm 139:11-12**, "¹¹If I say, 'Surely the darkness shall fall on me,' even the night shall be light about me; ¹²indeed, the darkness shall not hide from You, but the night shines as the day; the darkness and the light are both alike to You."

Accountability to others is a real thing, but we also have to be very spiritually alert and our "spidey-sense" (discernment) active and honed. Not all who appear to be His sheep are, and some proclaiming to be wheat are actually tares. And not all sheep are holding you accountable for the pure reason of "helping your joy." Be careful not to trade one jail cell for another, one of someone else's choosing, and be careful not to be the fodder for someone else's ego and kingdom-building.

10. **Write it Down! (What gets recorded, gets done).** Look, present work notwithstanding, I do not like to write either. Truth is, I do not like to think hard, especially when it requires denying my flesh. I would rather be playing with my grandchildren, working in my shop, fishing, or any of 1000 other things. But the unvarnished truth is that if I don't write it down, I cannot study it. And, if I don't study it, I will not make progress. And, if I don't make progress, I may as well "eat, drink and be merry" (**Ecclesiastes 8:15**) and forget about discipleship. "Wait! Did he just say that if I don't write stuff down, I can't be a disciple?" Well, yes and no. I said *I* can't be a disciple without writing it down because I am pretty average when it comes to managing life. You may be above-average. You may be able to hear it once and immediately proceed to successful implementation. You may have a photographic memory that doesn't have to study. You may be the exception to the overwhelming preponderance of the "Rule of the Flesh"; which, succinctly stated, is, "Entertain me *now*!" If you don't fall into one or more of the above-average exceptions, the likelihood is that you may as well devote yourself to **Ecclesiastes 8:15** and be successful at *something*—because discipleship probably ain't happening.

Writing it down is pretty much all about growing up—growing up in the sense of making actual spiritual progress (not the fudged kind!), and growing up in the maturity sense. Recall the working definition of maturity: "The ability to endure present suffering for future good." Children pitch a fit with suffering in any form, but the mature are able to see past present discomfort and choose patience, choose work, choose to concentrate, choose to put off entertainment for learning.

## Time to Build!

I like to build things. I helped my father build my "growing up" home as an early teen, and my wife and I built the home by the sweat of our brows in which our family grew! We continue to live in it and modify aspects from time to time. When I undertake a new remodeling project, I use a process that has served well over time. Long before the first two boards are nailed together, preparation begins. The initial phase in the building process is to have an idea or to perceive a need that inspires further contemplation and dreaming. In this phase, questions beginning with, "What if...?" are prominent. "What if I make a room there?"  "What if I take out this wall to open things up?"  "What if I redesign this kitchen to flow better and be more up to date?"

The second phase after the initial idea is to count the costs and compare my estimate to that which I am willing to pay.  Counting the costs associated with discipleship is not monetary, but they are tangible and real none-the-less.  Jesus addressed this phase of the building process in **Luke 14:28-30**; His words indicate that there is a price for short-cutting the "Can-I-afford-this-and-am-I-willing-to-pay-the-price?" step.

> **Luke 14:28-30**, "28For which of you, intending to build a tower, does not sit down first and count the cost, whether he has enough to finish it—29lest, after he has laid the foundation, and is not able to finish, all who see it begin to mock him, 30saying, 'This man began to build and was not able to finish'?"

After making the decision to proceed, it is time to adopt a plan that fits your resource level.  This process accesses your spiritual vision to imagine what is possible, and what your *Last 15-Minute Self* will look like.  Once a vision is secured, making a plan begins.  The plan is the central location where abstract vision becomes a concrete action, and ideas are translated into achievable steps.  There is also a form of self-accountability of formally making a plan.  As nebulous ideas take shape, it becomes more difficult to procrastinate. Building plan blueprints (like your Discipleship Plan) consists of multiple parts—e.g., floor plan, site plan, electrical, HVAC, flat conceptual drawings, or "elevation," that show the projected appearance, etc.—each part serving a particular detail-revealing purpose.

Your Discipleship Plan should also have multiple components because the different parts add richness and detail.  In a Discipleship Plan, the minimum components should be:

1) A goal
2) Written assumptions on which your efforts are based
3) A concept of important guiding principles
4) Relevant legacy Scriptures
5) An identity statement
6) Objectives you hope to accomplish, complete with detailed tactics
7) Some form of "My life at a glance" representation/diagram
8) Any relevant support and encouragement material

If any of these terms are unfamiliar, no worries!  We will address what each looks like in the coming sections.  The point of gathering all of this information in one document is so that it may be reviewed regularly—even daily—in a time of prayer and meditation, with Bible reading.  Making your Discipleship Plan review a part of a daily devotional time greatly enhances your potential for success, and decreases the time for real change to take hold.  It is the "What you take, takes you" principle in practice.  Peter acknowledged in his second epistle (**2 Peter 3:1**) the principle of "stir up your pure minds by way of reminder," and that is what regular review of your Discipleship Plan does.

Before remodeling an existing structure, it is often necessary to implement a demolition phase to remove the old to make room for the new.  There is no other way to put it: demolition is messy, dirty, and hard work!  When we undertake to remodel our spiritual growth infrastructure, we find demolition of old attitudes, habits, misbeliefs, unbelief, laziness, and corner-cutting to be just as messy, but just as necessary.  The flesh does not go down without a fight!  But fresh fruit will not grow on dried and shriveled vines that have not been pruned.  Jesus warned us about this painful pruning process in **John 15:1-2**:

$^1$"I am the true vine, and My Father is the vinedresser. $^2$Every branch in Me that does not bear fruit He takes away; and every branch that bears fruit He prunes, that it may bear more fruit.

In the midst of painful pruning, it is comforting to know Who is holding and expertly wielding the shears. And, it is sobering to know that there is no such thing as abiding in the vine without attracting the shaping attention of the vinedresser. He is after the fruit, and He knows just how to bring it forth.

After making a plan and counting the cost, it is time to gather materials. There are few things more exciting to me than a stack of fresh lumber primed and ready for construction! Tools are prepared, the plan is reviewed, say a prayer, and the work begins! All constructing ultimately comes down to doing the stuff. It does no good to stand and stare at a stack of lumber, just as it does no good to read Papa's word or listen to an anointed sermon, then go about your Independent Self business while ignoring the Father's business stuff. It would be better never to have heard than to hear and set it aside or ignore it.

## Discipleship Plan: Defining the Process

We often speak about God's plan for us; but what about *our* plan? Is it enough for Him to have an over-arching Plan that covers us and our responsibilities for growth when we fail to enact our own follow-through to connect our intentional actions to His purposes? I think it is not. God's Plan presupposes that we will take the framework He has ordained, embrace it as motivation for our prioritized actions, then customize and make a specific application to our own circumstances and development. Making and having a plan for our own discipleship can be the difference between meaningful progress and drifting through life, directed by the eddies and currents of the world system instead of the River of Life.

One of my favorite sayings is, "Do not get taken where you do not want to go." But "not getting taken" presupposes that I have *defined* where I don't want to go, and hopefully where I *do* want to go; those two working together constitute at least *some level* of planning. I am convinced that many Christians today do not make the spiritual progress for which they hope because they fail to make provision to focus both attention and effort. Planning enables focus and encourages diligence. Diligence is a character quality that does not usually come naturally to us; it *must* be cultivated to be experienced. It is not a word we hear used much

> **Proverbs 12:27**, "The lazy man does not roast what he took in hunting, but diligence is man's precious possession."

these days outside of Christian circles; but whether in Kingdom or secular application, diligence is a fundamental ingredient of success. The key ingredients for diligence are applied energy, care, direction, and thoroughness. An effort that is missing any of these four falls short of full potential. **Proverbs 12:27** implies that initial action is good, but diligence is identified by perseverance and follow-through. In other words, our initial intention is only as good as our subsequent *accomplishment*; and that is where making a plan comes in.

## Anatomy of A Plan

Applying emergency management planning principles to solve spiritual challenges makes *really* good sense. Many believers remain spiritual babies, sipping the "milk" of the word, undeveloped, and easy prey for the enemy's schemes, not because they are apathetic, unresponsive, or disinterested, but because nobody ever sat down with them and led them through a comprehensive and deconstructionist exercise to plan a clear path ahead. No one ever helped them organize their approach and efforts. No one had the requisite knowledge or cared enough to construct and record a plan that maps out "how to get from here to there." In sum, no one ever *discipled* them. This kind of discipleship happens at the coffee shop, not from a pulpit; it happens with pen and paper, not PowerPoint slides; it happens sitting across the table, not across the room.

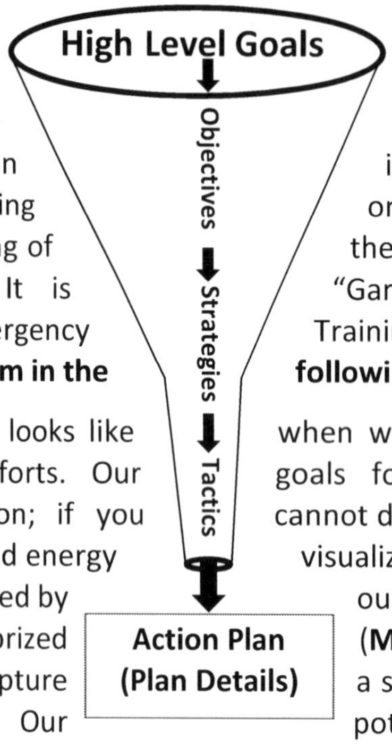

The following terms are indispensable to constructing a workable, balanced discipleship plan in one's life. There are a number of definitions for these terms depending on the school of thought to which one subscribes. A sloppy understanding of the components of a Discipleship Plan will result in sloppy execution. It is "Garbage-In-Garbage-Out" (GIGO) in action. I was taught by the National Emergency Training Center (NETC) in Emmitsburg, MD, so I define them here and will use **them in the following context:**

*[Diagram: an inverted funnel labeled "High Level Goals" at top, flowing downward through "Objectives → Strategies → Tactics", into a box labeled "Action Plan (Plan Details)".]*

- Goal—What the end state looks like when we are *completely* successful; the ideal, desired outcome of our efforts. Our goals for our spiritual development should include a word description; if you cannot describe your goal in detail, you have not yet spent sufficient time and energy visualizing it! Goals are our "dream-big-end-in-mind" mental picture inspired by our child-like imagination that Jesus declared to be highly-prized (**Matthew 19:14**). We access our Holy Spirit-inspired vision and capture a spiritual dreamscape of our full potential (i.e., "His fullness"). Our potential already exists in the eternal as a factor of our true identity. Our written goal translates it to T/S/M action. Formulating a goal is where the "If you can see it, you can be it" begins. Given the nature of our citizenship, our goal(s) should always relate to the person we are and shall be in the eternal realm.

- Objectives—Time-limited components for dividing goals into manageable components and segments. Accomplishing objectives is set for a specific targeted time period to encourage diligent effort and evaluate progress. Writing good, clear, concise objectives is both a skill and art; good objectives are <u>SMART</u>: <u>S</u>pecific, <u>M</u>easurable, <u>A</u>ction-oriented, <u>R</u>ealistic, and <u>T</u>ime-limited. Objectives answer the question, "*What* do we wish to accomplish *in the time prescribed*?" I find that my Discipleship Plan objectives do not change as frequently as, say, the Incident Action Plan and daily Situation Report operational objectives at an emergency incident, mainly because the transformation we seek takes time. Discipleship Plan objectives tend to not be "one-and-done" tactics, but repeated spiritual mind choices over weeks, months, or even years. However, included in our daily objectives review is time to evaluate immediate past performance, and routinely asking, "How am I doing with this objective." Since they are ultimately time-limited, objectives should be related to our T/S/M existence, though they have their end result in the eternal.

- Strategies—The methodology or series of maneuvers employed to accomplish an objective. Methods are typically groups of specific actions with a common theme, toolset, or repeatable steps that guide our approach to overcoming obstacles and accomplishing benchmarks. Strategies tend not to change much as we settle into those that work well for us. Principles of Scripture are often applied in us on the strategic level. My experience has been that, of all of the components of a plan, strategies are one of the most misunderstood; at the very least, the terminology misapplied. If a particular strategy is not yielding the results desired, our objectives review should reveal it and a new set of strategies may be adopted.

- Tactics—Answer the question, "How?" or, "In what manner?" Tactics differ from strategies in the level of detail. They are detailed steps that break strategies into specific activities or responses.

Much of the time, our good intentions are dissipated for lack of specific, "What do I do today?" actions. Tactics are the layer where accountability is best both defined and applied, frequently because the answer to, "Did you perform this tactic?" is, "Yes," or "No," not "Sort of."

- Action Plans—Answers the questions, "Who?" and, "When?" Action Plans are the finest level of planning detail; they are the rubber-meets-the-road (performance) aspect of the Choice Space! When Goals, Objectives, Strategies, and Tactics are clearly understood and written down, Action Plans become almost perfunctory—because the hard work is done! *Doing* is frequently far easier than *knowing what to do*. Once a Discipleship Plan is prayerfully considered and thoughtfully constructed, the prospect of our successful struggle in the Choice Space is greatly boosted!

A lot of published Christian literature these days targets the strategic or tactical level of life in the Spirit. That is, they address what method do I use or how do I accomplish a particular feature of my Christian walk (e.g., prayer, worship, healing, trauma, emotional, etc.). Certainly, such information is valuable for study; but this book shoots for understanding at a higher level—the goal level. Starting with the *purpose* of our pilgrimage and Papa's Program for preparing the Bride of Christ as gaining understanding enables us to align *all* of our discipleship planning efforts—goals, objectives, strategies, tactics and actions—from top to bottom; and this organizational framework keeps our vision in front of us, always in our view, to continually motivate and guide.

## Plan Components

There are standard, professional components of an Emergency Operations Plan (EOP). Having a comparison standard is helpful when beginning a new endeavor. However, the bottom line of the best plan is the one that works for you. No one else can or will ensure your development to match your potential, that is, the *full* potential that is endemic to the seed of the Kingdom Papa plants in us.

Aspiration, ambition, and even aggression are not inherently evil concepts in the Kingdom, as Jesus' words in **Matthew 11:12** indicate. Those things only serve an evil purpose when they are employed to promote self, even if disguised and downplayed as a ministry. Further, Jesus did not come to promote an egalitarian system where all men have equal access to the Father. He had no delusions about the fact that His message was not for everyone, and stated that plainly. He came speaking to sheep that would hear their Shepherd's voice, and who would commit themselves to wholehearted obedience; sheep that would not dedicate themselves to their own plans and interests, but would recognize and align theirs with His. What Jesus knew was that the Father had not only given all things into His hands (**John 13:3**), but He has likewise *put all things into our hands* with respect to our maturity and development in the Spirit.

> **Matthew 11:12**, "And from the days of John the Baptist until now the kingdom of heaven suffers violence, and the violent take it by force."

I have included a copy of my current personal Discipleship Plan in the Appendix for your reference. What makes your plan valuable and makes it your own is the time, thought, effort, and prayer *you* put into its development. The purpose of this section is to provide further description and detail to various components that may add value. Here are the components we will summarize:

> Remember: Plans are nothing; but planning is everything!

1) Personal Mission and Values Statement

2) Life Goal

3) Daily Strategic Prayer

4)     Legacy Scriptures
5)     Identity Statement
6)     Key Concepts of Operation
7)     Principles of Application
8)     Resources Inventory: Gifts, Talents, Knowledge, Skills, Abilities
9)     Objectives, Strategies, Tactics, Action Plans

## Personal Mission and Values Statement (PMVS)

After you have done the hard work of seeking your true identity through the clamor and fog of input from your flesh, that information is made more practical and useful to your discipleship efforts by crafting a Personal Mission and Values Statement. Once again, that means writing it down! A PMVS serves as a broad vision to keep you on task, on point and moving in the direction that the Holy Spirit has identified to you as your best self, your eternal self. The elements of a good PMVS often reflect the interests of spiritual gifting. For example, a person with a spiritual gift of exhortation and an office gift of pastoring would almost certainly include some element of listening, encouraging, and comforting others as a life purpose. PMVSs need to be succinct—you will have the opportunity to go into as much detail as you want in your Identity Statement. Like the curbing keeps us on the roadway and between the ditches, a PMVS acts in the place of an "elevator speech"—an easily memorized, easily shared summary of your *Last 15-Minute Self*.

## Life Goal

The Apostle Paul endorsed the concept of being goal-directed in **Philippians 3:12-15**:

> [12]Not that I have already attained, or am already perfected; but I press on, that I may lay hold of that for which Christ Jesus has also laid hold of me. [13]Brethren, I do not count myself to have apprehended; but one thing I do, forgetting those things which are behind and reaching forward to those things which are ahead, [14]*I press toward the goal* for the prize of the upward call of God in Christ Jesus. [15]Therefore let us, as many as are mature, have this mind; and if in anything you think otherwise, God will reveal even this to you.

Consider these statements regarding goal-setting and spiritual growth:

- A goal is a paidion-accessed dream reduced to writing, and answers the question, "What does it look like when I am completely successful?"
- If you do not have a primary goal that is *spiritual*—not career, money, family, etc.—you have *not* selected a *spiritual growth* direction, and are likely, therefore, easy pickings for the flesh.
- If your financial, career, and family goals have the same standing/priority as your spiritual goal(s), you are being controlled by your carnal mind.
- If you have not written down your overarching goal, but it remains, "in there somewhere," it is probably because you have yet to understand the power of focus, the power of "this one thing I do" (**Philippians 3:13**).
- If you are having trouble writing a goal on paper, you do not yet know what you want to accomplish.
- If you have intended to write down your goals but have failed to do so, you probably do not understand how important they are to the process of transformation.

I find it very helpful in this kind of goal-setting to take an inventory of what I like to do, what I do well, what I do naturally (not necessarily the same thing), what my resources are, and what gifts—spiritual and natural—do I have? Said another way, we do not set goals in order to know our own heart, we know our own heart in order to set goals. Picking out some ostensibly worthy goal without knowing your particular destination would be like buying an airplane ticket for Chicago because it is on sale, and hoping to end up in Dallas. Good luck with that!

One may have multiple goals in different areas of life, but the one in your Discipleship Plan here should be pertinent to your spiritual development. One mistake that some make is to make their goal too narrow. This is the venue to dream big! For sure there will be opportunities to amend and enlarge your goals in the future; but a goal should be challenging enough to require considerable effort, concentration, and, skills improvement.

## Strategic Prayer

Prayer is not just a "bow your head and close your eyes" activity. We are intended to be frequently—if not continuously—in communication with Papa. We are, after all, seeking union with Him. Communication with God in all of its forms is prayer. Paul called this connection to Papa "Praying without ceasing," and associates it with continuous rejoicing and giving thanks (**1 Thessalonians 5:16-18**). But there is another form of prayer that I have included in the Discipleship Plan format because it is integral to your spiritual growth: A Strategic Prayer that guides your development toward your goal.

> **1 Thessalonians 5:16-18**, "¹⁶Rejoice always, ¹⁷pray without ceasing, ¹⁸in everything give thanks; for this is the will of God in Christ Jesus for you."

Strategic Prayer is an expression of our identity and is as much a gift from Papa as any other part of our inheritance. Being strategic, it should be well-considered, and not change frequently. Recall that a strategy is a methodology to accomplish a goal or objective, so a prayer that is part of your growth strategy should be high-level and avoid the weeds. It is more appropriate for this purpose to pray for a means rather than an end; "teach me to" rather than "give me." It is a cry in your spirit, a longing placed there by the Holy Spirit. It is a prayer that is crafted—not popped off of the top of our head like blessing a meal.

A Strategic Prayer is life-directing. Papa delights to give good gifts to His children (**Matthew 7:11**), and He really likes it when we Him ask the right questions. **James 4:2** chides us by saying, "You do not have because you do not ask." But the verse following goes further, saying, in effect, "You don't get an answer because you ask the wrong things and for the wrong reasons." It seems apparent that, if we take the time and spiritual energy to figure out the right questions and stuff for which to ask, Papa guarantees an answer and positive growth that does not feed our Independent Self, our flesh, or carnal mind.

Just like the selection of Legacy Scriptures (next section), and just as carefully as we set our goals, we need to carefully compose a prayer that asks Papa for *exactly* what we are seeking to know and be. I am convinced that these prayers, when wisely chosen, are pleasing to the Father because they arise in Him, pass through us, and go back to Him by our lips. An example of a Strategic Prayer would be Solomon's request for wisdom when he was anointed King of Israel. Jesus tells us in **Luke 12:32**, "³²Do not fear, little flock, for it is your Father's good pleasure to give you the kingdom." He *has not* committed Himself to take "good pleasure" in giving us the kingdom of this world or things that feed our bloated self-interest. But He delights to show us glimpses of the Kingdom that reveal our future life together as Bride and Bridegroom.

I have personal experience that confirms Papa's delight to give us the Kingdom in the form of answering our Strategic Prayers. It is important when formulating your strategic, daily prayer that you

> **John 16:24**, "Until now you have asked nothing in My name. Ask, and you will receive, that your joy may be full."

take into account James' warning in **James 4:3**: "³You ask and do not receive, because you ask amiss, that you may spend it on your pleasures." It is *at best* ill-informed and immature to incorporate desires of your flesh in your Strategic Prayer. To be free from such influence, after all, is the objective of Strategic Prayer in the first place!

## Legacy Scriptures

Legacy Scriptures are those that Papa has impressed on you as specifically applicable to your experience of life; sometimes they are therefore called "life Scriptures." Graham Cooke says that Legacy Scriptures are those that jump off of the page and wrap themselves around your face! That is a great visual, and pretty much what if feels like when God assigns a Legacy Scripture to your future. They are an important part of your Discipleship Plan because they are important to your identity. Legacy Scriptures are one unique aspect of how you are known in heaven, because they indicate your spiritual DNA and growth and development potential. God knows each of us individually, and He reveals portions of His word to us as a prophecy about our identity and development. Often, they form a picture of who He is making you and what you want to be. He gives us big shoes, then teaches us to fill them! Legacy Scriptures are a portion of our inheritance—the gold that we are advised to purchase in **Revelation 3:18**. Papa offers the gold to us freely: He has provided our access, prospector's claim, and our digging tools; He has secured our mineral rights. But then it is up to us to do the mining, the exploration, the digging—the *sweating*! The work of excavating the promise of each Scripture establishes our claim and makes it ours. That is the "buy from Me" process. Each Legacy Scripture is a vein of pure gold to be excavated in careful detail in order to get the absolute maximum value from each vein.

If you looked at my example Discipleship Plan in the Appendix, and read the Legacy Scriptures Papa has assigned to me, you would find that the Scriptures there are featured prominently throughout this book. That is not a coincidence. You would have to be me to fully understand, but my Legacy Scriptures weaved together into a tapestry form an accurate picture of what I understand to be true about me and what I understand about His Kingdom. Just as He can and will do in you, He has concentrated a curriculum in my experience based on related Scriptures and personal coaching by the Holy Spirit. No one of us can embody the whole truth of the Kingdom, and our Legacy Scriptures frequently outline an area of specialized knowledge. This principle is sometimes known as a "life message." When a believer has a life-message from Papa, it is frequently what we see best in Scripture and primarily what we want to talk about. There is wisdom in knowing and sticking closely to what one knows best!

So, what comes first, the Legacy Scripture or its fulfillment? Are we led by Legacy Scriptures in God's word on our particular path across the wilderness? Or, as we are crossing the wilderness, do you and I look to find His word to confirm and guide our experience? The answer is, "It is both." I know this because from time-to-time Papa adds a new Legacy Scripture to my repertoire/collage and sends me off in a new direction. I am convinced that, "Strategy-by-Legacy-Scripture" is one essential of knowing and being known by Him, and the opposite of the relationship portrayed in **Matthew 7:22-23**:

> ²²Many will say to Me in that day, 'Lord, Lord, have we not prophesied in Your name, cast out demons in Your name, and done many wonders in Your name?' ²³And then I will declare to them, "I never knew you; depart from Me, you who practice lawlessness!"

One does not have to be known by the Bridegroom to prophesy in His name, cast out demons, do wonders, do other displays of power, or religious activity. It is sobering that the evidence factors by which many declare a particular ministry to be "anointed" are included in Jesus' "Get away from Me!" list. What *does* require personal knowledge is for Papa to select custom-fit portions of His word to light your way ahead, and prepare you for Kingdom responsibility. If the choice is between the goosebumps of power religion or faithful one-foot-in-front-of-the-other performance in tough circumstances and in the mundane affairs of life, I will choose faithfulness *every time*.

## Identity Statement

An Identity Statement (IS) is an important declaration of characteristics that are *"true about me."* But the "true about me" self you are describing in this is the "you" that you want to be, the one Papa shows you. It is your *Last 15-Minutes* Self-described in words, and it encapsulates and encompasses the person you envision laying on your deathbed, having completed your training course. As we discussed with Legacy Scriptures, each of us is known differently to Papa. Just as we all have a different blend of physical DNA, likewise, we have a highly individual fusion of spiritual DNA that governs who we are, what we do, what we value, and how we serve. And just as our children are all different in characteristics, attitudes, desires, and expressions, so are the individuals in Papa's family. We are all a mix of motivational, ministry, and office gifting in various combinations. **Proverbs 18:16** tells us, "A man's gift makes room for him, and brings him before great men." In the same way, our spiritual gifting makes a niche for us in the Church and in the Kingdom. Unfortunately, many believers never seem to know themselves well enough to know the gifts and resources with which they have been entrusted. A good Discipleship Plan can fix that!

Your Discipleship Plan Identity Statement is designed to encapsulate the character and identity that is uniquely you. That does not mean you are the only one with these character qualities, traits, and gifts, but likely you are the only one with them in your particular balance. However, it may *legitimately* contain characteristics of which you are currently unaware or in which you may not yet be fully functional, but to which you aspire. A declaration is a powerful tool in the spiritual realm! Your Identity Statement is a vision of the eternal you as much or more than it is current reality. "If you can see it, you can be it!" is a statement of faith with regard to becoming who you already are in the eternal. Bob Mumford has said, "It is more important to God what we *want to be* than *what we currently are*." That is in large measure true because our eternal identity is the real us, and our desire to grow connects us inter-dimensionally to the real us. The only caution that is appropriate, however, is to be sure that the qualities to which you aspire are *actually for you*, not some performance expectation pushed on you by others, or by some "the way it's done" system. If you find yourself easily influenced in this manner, the saying we have in Texas, "Go slow and watch for snakes," is literally and spiritually applicable.

Your Identity Statement is written down in order to serve as a daily reminder of what is true concerning you, and that is particularly useful under withering attack. Identity statements are useful for shutting down the accusations of the enemy, to inspire us to fulfill our spiritual destiny, and walk in our inheritance. They are very useful in correcting misbeliefs we have collected over the years. Remember: You are not your body, and your Identity Statement has nothing to do with your flesh! Further, it has nothing to do with anything anyone thinks or identifies with you other than Papa.

**James 1:23-25** makes an interesting statement about our ability to fixate a correct perception of our identity in our thinking:

<sup>23</sup>For if anyone is a hearer of the word and not a doer, he is like a man observing his natural face in a mirror; <sup>24</sup>for he observes himself, goes away, and immediately *forgets what kind of man he was*. <sup>25</sup>But he who looks into the perfect law of liberty and continues in it, and is not a forgetful hearer but a doer of the work, this one will be blessed in what he does.

One purpose for our reflection/meditation time throughout the day is to constantly refresh our memory about who we are, enabling us to be a doer, not a forgetful hearer. Your Discipleship Plan can be an invaluable tool for refreshing your memory, and your Identity Statement a faithful look in the mirror! Remember: You become most like what you most look at! After writing out the statement, we can recite it to the enemy any time he brings a charge against God's elect (that is you, dear). I often read my statement aloud as a declaration to the principalities, powers, and spiritual wickedness in the heavenly places. Why? I want them to know that I know who I am, and Whose I am.

## Key Concepts of Operation

Concepts of Operation (CONOPS) are broad statements of truth that form a framework of thought and philosophy. They serve as the skeleton on which the muscles of individual objectives are held together in a coherent framework. In a Discipleship Plan, CONOPS are often select, appropriate foundational truths of Scripture as they apply to your goal and personal mission. The CONOPS you select for your Discipleship Plan should have some connection that you can articulate to the goal toward which you are working.

The term, "Concept of Operation," is borrowed from emergency planning/operations and military operations, where they briefly outline what the commanding officer intends to accomplish, and often in what methodologies are appropriate for the operation. Perhaps you are recognizing at this point that a Discipleship Plan is a *strategic document*, and its strategic nature applies to the most important life-pursuit—transformation into the image of Christ. As an element of a Discipleship Plan, I use a CONOPS in a slightly different manner than they are often employed in an Emergency Operations Plan. The CONOPS in my Discipleship Plan describes important elements of success and anchoring truths; that is, "stuff I need to know to understand the plan"; and sometimes, "stuff I need to know to understand me." The components of a Discipleship Plan CONOPS section are statements that are comparable to elements of a Statement of Faith, or doctrinal affirmation. The difference is that in this application, the statements are highly personalized and customized to the framework of thought and spirit for the person writing the plan, not a broad statement as they are frequently applied to organizations, churches, or denominations.

A CONOPS section serves as a summary statement of my assumptions. At this point, it may be helpful for you to review the previous sub-chapter entitled *Examining Assumptions and Misbeliefs* if both their positive and negative functions are not clear in your thinking. Assumptions may be thought of as *pre-made choices.* They are learned responses that shortcut and bypass decision-making by storing up ready responses to particular circumstances or perceived facts. We are all likely familiar with the saying, "When you <u>assume</u>, it makes an <u>ass</u> out of <u>u</u> and <u>me</u>." While you may or may not find the implications of being called an ass amusing, it is the case that everyone assumes as a regular practice. Every person on the planet operates with a collection of assumptions, schemas, and understandings that run in the background of our conscious mind. The difference between disciples and others is not whether we make assumptions, it is whether we are self-aware enough to know what they are, and control them in a manner that they do not become an automatic open door to the flesh.

Every person alive acts according to assumptions about the world and how it works on a daily, even minute-by-minute, basis. Because so much of what we think we know comes to us because of our assumptions, it is really important to uncover them and evaluate whether they are helpful or working against our discipleship efforts. Think about this: An assumption is similar to a vow in that each is the direct result of experience, often a negative one. A *vow* shapes our future thinking by binding it to words from our mouth reflecting a declaration in our heart. An *assumption*, on the other hand, is also the result of experience but takes the form of a "software program" running in our unconscious mind. It says, in effect, "Do *this* when you encounter *this*," or, "When you see *this* it always means ____." As a *pre-made choice*, an assumption is prescriptive and can promote negative or hinder positive decisions in the Choice Space. They are often anti-choice in the sense that, once formed, we move on to our next assumption without actually choosing, and that is a pretty good identifier of growth-stagnation. Their identification is *extremely* important in planning, because hidden, underlying assumptions can wreck your plan if you do not know they are there, or if you are aware of them but take no action to correct those working against your plan. Finding and stating your assumptions upfront helps your clarity of focus, and helps others understand you.

Pre-made choices limit or block understanding by shutting our minds to truth from the Holy Spirit before it is fully heard. Two Scriptures from Proverbs help us to understand the effect of negative assumptions.

1) **Proverbs 18:13**: "He who answers a matter before he hears it, it is folly and shame to him." "Answering-before-hearing" is assumptive. It is getting just enough information to trigger what I already think about the topic that I think you are addressing. Answering before hearing locks out new information, new thinking, new perspective; and such closed thinking results in our folly, and to our shame. Acting on your old assumptions is tantamount to a six-year-old putting their fingers in their ears and singing, "La la la la la" to prevent hearing when their parent (Holy Spirit) is trying to teach them. It also results in us being imprisoned in our present perspective without the possibility of parole (transformation). If the goal of discipleship is transformation (and it is), it seems apparent that negative assumptions are *anti-choice*.

2) **Proverbs 18:2**, "A fool has no delight in understanding, but in expressing his own heart." Assuming what another is about to say and jumping into a preemptive strike is not only making an assumption, it is *anti-understanding*. Recall that in Chapter 4, we established that wisdom is an important prerequisite, but that understanding is the highest form of transformation because understanding morphs wisdom and information into big-picture, goal-level consciousness. Negative assumptions prevent transformation by circumventing the learning process in its early stages. Assumptions are your subconscious mind bullying your conscious mind by saying, "We have already learned that—move on!" Stephen Covey's 5th Habit, [20]"Seek first to understand, then to be understood," puts assumptions in their correct place: serving your consciousness, not bullying it.

It may be helpful to your own assumption discovery process if I give some examples. Often, assumptions are the master key to understanding your own perplexing behavior, your "that which I do not want to do" (**Romans 7:19**) choices. They govern the way we perceive the world (our "world view"), what we accept or reject as true, and what we receive as real. Here are some examples of unhelpful assumptions, their effects, and evidence that they exist whether known or unknown to the host:

- Racism, sexism and all forms of prejudice
- Stereotyping, including behavioral stereotyping

---

[20] http://www.quickmba.com/mgmt/7hab/

- Irrational feelings, and flash emotions inappropriate for the circumstances
- Inability to hear and summarize accurately what others are saying
- Negative projections not based on clear evidence ("Assuming the worst")
- Finishing another's sentences before they have an opportunity to be heard (ouch!)
- Thinking up your answer before another is finished presenting their perspective
- Snap judgments about other people or groups

The saying, "The unexamined life is not worth living," is nowhere truer than in our unconscious and subconscious thinking, and that means assumptions. Self-examination without a heroic attempt to know our below-awareness factors is an incomplete effort. I use the word "heroic" with intent because it can be scary to uncover and root out our motivations and assumptions. In an exercise to write a CONOPS section for our Discipleship Plan, it may become apparent that our assumptions do not match up with what we proclaim to believe. For example, frequently our proclamation that "Jesus is King and Lord of All," does not pass muster when an honest appraisal and focused introspection does not even reveal Him to be "King and Lord of Me"! Sometimes we have to hold our nose as we uncover them, and sometimes the experience seems too overwhelming. But understanding the corrective lenses (read: rose-colored glasses) through which we view the world is absolutely essential to the discipleship processes because it gives us an accurate origination point for pilgrimage.

## Principles of Application (PoA)

The Principles of Application is a section that should continue to grow through the rest of your life-long training. Two things to remember when adding PoA to your plan: 1) Your Discipleship Plan should function in much the same way a set of architectural blueprints function in the construction of a building. 2) One of the objectives for making a plan in the first place should be to organize your efforts to *learn God's ways,* and in doing so, prepare to rule beside our Bridegroom. PoA describe universal principles that Papa has built into His Program of Operation; they constitute the "way He does things" as we understand them. PoA are the anti-type of the specifications section in a building plan. They provide:

1) An in-depth description of what the building process looks like;
2) A detailed description of the manner in which the work should be done;
3) What quality standards must the building materials meet;
4) What the work process is intended to produce;
5) How to resolve seeming conflicts;
6) How the project should be approached;
7) Planning benchmarks;
8) How to know when you are finished with sections of the work.

The list of principles should be a permanent part of our plan because His *ways* never change, though His *dealings* with us and the *lessons* He is teaching us change as He leads us from glory to glory, from strength to strength, etc. The PoA should also grow as we move from milk to solid food. The list should grow as we discover more and more about His approach to governing, His dealings with His children, the inner-working of how He transforms us, characteristics of the Kingdom, and how He presents Himself in the world, to name only a few. They describe in detail the work and the workmanship we should embrace as we progress on our pilgrimage.

I propose that your PoA section should represent the "refined gold" you have purchased to date from Jesus, as He urges the Lukewarm Church (us) in **Revelation 3:18**. In **Psalm 19:7-10**, David breaks down the gold that we should desire as the law, testimony, statutes, commandments, fear (in the sense of veneration), and judgments of the Lord. These six factors roughly constitute what Scripture in other places refers to as, "His ways":

> **Revelation 3:18**, "I counsel you to buy from Me gold refined in the fire, that you may be rich."

> [7]The law of the Lord is perfect, converting the soul; the testimony of the Lord is sure, making wise the simple; [8]the statutes of the Lord are right, rejoicing the heart; the commandment of the Lord is pure, enlightening the eyes; [9]the fear of the Lord is clean, enduring forever; the judgments of the Lord are true and righteous altogether. [10]*More to be desired are they than gold; yea, than much fine gold.* Sweeter also than honey and the honeycomb.

David concludes this section, saying, "Moreover by them Your servant is warned, and in keeping them there is a great reward," (**Psalm 19:11**) reminiscent of the fact that Jesus' message to the Laodicean Church can only be interpreted as a warning. But the warning includes a message of hope immediately following (**Revelation 3:19-22**) to those who heed His advice and thereby experience the same great reward that David promises:

> [19]As many as I love, I rebuke and chasten. Therefore, be zealous and repent. [20]Behold, I stand at the door and knock. If anyone hears My voice and opens the door, I will come in to him and dine with him, and he with Me. [21]To him who overcomes I will grant to sit with Me on My throne, as I also overcame and sat down with My Father on His throne. [22]"He who has an ear, let him hear what the Spirit says to the churches."

The PoA section of your Discipleship Plan should serve as an archive-of-sorts, where the principles summarizing Papa's law, testimony, statutes, commandments, fear, and judgments are recorded for your daily review. It is a, "Here is what we know so far," brief; and the continuous review drives the lessons deep into our consciousness.

So, from where is this list of principles derived? Where can they be found, and how do you discover them? What function do they serve once constructed? As you probably already have concluded, the ultimate building plan is *God's revealed word* in Scripture. He supplements His written word by constant coaching of the Holy Spirit. The bulk of the specification for His building on the foundation (**1 Corinthians 3:10-13**) is usually derived directly from Scripture, and *always* consistent with (i.e., "authorized by") written Scripture. Even in those instances where the Holy Spirit reveals a principle directly to your spirit, the new specification *must be consistent* with the written specs to be valid. One very effective strategy for reading the word is evaluating each verse or passage by asking the question, "Does this verse reveal a principle of Papa's ways?" When we have that level of involvement with what we are reading, and we archive the lessons we are discovering, we have a good probability of being a doer of the word and not merely a hearer. All that remains, then, is to add our action.

Once Papa has revealed a principle in Scripture and we add it to the archive of our Discipleship Plan, it becomes a permanent part of our learning. The principles that have been revealed to us become part of our regular review of our plan. They serve as a permanent reminder to prevent us from, "Forget[ing] what manner of man [we are]" (**James 1:24**). Daily review of your plan is a powerful tool for, "stir[ring] up your pure mind by way of reminder" (**2 Peter 3:1**).

# Resources Inventory:  Gifts, Talents, Knowledge, Skills, Abilities

When considering our Resources Inventory (RI), it is important to first review the spiritual principles apparent in **Matthew 25:14-30**:

> [14]"For the kingdom of heaven is like a man traveling to a far country, who called his own servants and delivered his goods to them.  [15]And to one he gave five talents, to another two, and to another one, to each according to his own ability; and immediately he went on a journey.  [16]Then he who had received the five talents went and traded with them, and made another five talents.  [17]And likewise he who had received two gained two more also.  [18]But he who had received one went and dug in the ground, and hid his lord's money.  [19]After a long time the lord of those servants came and settled accounts with them.  [20]"So he who had received five talents came and brought five other talents, saying, 'Lord, you delivered to me five talents; look, I have gained five more talents besides them.'  [21]His lord said to him, 'Well done, good and faithful servant; you were faithful over a few things, I will make you ruler over many things.  Enter into the joy of your lord.'  [22]He also who had received two talents came and said, 'Lord, you delivered to me two talents; look, I have gained two more talents besides them.'  [23]His lord said to him, 'Well done, good and faithful servant; you have been faithful over a few things, I will make you ruler over many things. Enter into the joy of your lord.'  [24]"Then he who had received the one talent came and said, 'Lord, I knew you to be a hard man, reaping where you have not sown, and gathering where you have not scattered seed.  [25]And I was afraid, and went and hid your talent in the ground. Look, there you have what is yours.'  [26]"But his lord answered and said to him, 'You wicked and lazy servant, you knew that I reap where I have not sown, and gather where I have not scattered seed.  [27]So you ought to have deposited my money with the bankers, and at my coming, I would have received back my own with interest.  [28]So take the talent from him and give it to him who has ten talents.  [29]'For to everyone who has, more will be given, and he will have abundance; but from him who does not have, even what he has will be taken away.  [30]And cast the unprofitable servant into the outer darkness.  There will be weeping and gnashing of teeth.'

I am including this parable in its entirety because it is *that* important when considering our discipleship task. (I also admit that it is my favorite of all of Jesus' parables.)  There is enough in this parable to easily be the subject matter of an entire book, but we will concentrate on only a few principles. **Luke Chapter 19** contains a similar parable with a slightly different emphasis (minas instead of talents). Taken together, they form a *clear* picture of our responsibility in the Master's absence.

We are told that when the Master returns from acquiring a Kingdom, He will require an accounting from His servants (us!) of how we have stewarded His entrusted resources.  It is noteworthy that the Master in the Parable of the Talents pronounced a blessing or cursing upon the servants, not based on the amount of profit, but on *their faithfulness* in transacting with what they are given.  That is the key principle in understanding the importance of a Resources Inventory in our Discipleship Plan.  I have heard many sermons over the course of life about the words, "Well done, good and faithful servant.  Enter into the joy of your Lord," but I have heard far fewer sermons on what it takes to be in a position to hear those words!

When the Master shows up, He is looking for fruit.  In His absence, it is our responsibility to cultivate that fruit to have an offering in return for His trust.  Our Discipleship Plan is a place where we may take inventory of all with which we have been entrusted.  It is common sense that until we take inventory, we do not have a complete grasp of what we have to offer.  Another reason to take inventory is that we want to give the Master an increase from *all* that He has given us, with nothing falling through the cracks—we love Him that much!

Resources are the *personal* areas and expressions that you have to offer and with which you are able to transact the "Father's business" to expand the Kingdom. We all share the resources of time, identity, and choice; but personal resources are particular gifts, talents, knowledge, skills, and abilities that Papa has invested in you for your **Matthew 25/Luke 19** transactions. They fall into at least three categories: Spiritual, Professional, and General. Remember the "Cup of cold water shall not lose its reward" principle in (**Matthew 10:42**)? Your gifts and talents need not be huge or profound to be valuable. It is not the amount of increase at issue, but rather the principle of being faithful with that which you have been given.

Many Christians have never taken inventory of the spiritual gifts Papa has invested in them. Details concerning motivational, ministry and office giftings given to the Church is beyond the scope of this book, and many good studies exist to help you discern what spiritual gift DNA Papa has put into you. My contribution here is to encourage you to mine the gold of spiritual gifts in order to be able to make their use a part of your Discipleship Plan.

It is important that we drop the false, superficial humility and denial that we have anything unique or special to offer. Being unique or special is overrated in the first place. If He has chosen you, then He has also equipped you for every good work (**2 Timothy 3:17**), that is, *the good work He has prepared for you!* When we deny His equipping work in us or His gifts active within us, we are in essence saying that He is not powerful enough to reach *me*. Consider the arrogance of that statement. Such thinking is a version of the "not chosen" lie from which I had to be delivered (see Chapter 1). It is a lie of the enemy and a tragic position from which believers conduct affairs of the Kingdom. Not-chosen-thinking is an excuse born out of self-pity; I know that because I was one, and still fight it from time-to-time.

Once you have taken inventory, you are in a position to formulate some objectives to transact Father's business with those resources. To be most effective and most faithful, spiritual gifts, natural talents, knowledge, skills, and abilities are weaved together in a service and growth plan; and that brings us to our final section.

## Objectives, Strategies, Tactics, Action Plans (OSTAP)

Objectives, Strategies, Tactics, and Action Plans (OSTAP) are the guts, the rubber-meets-the-road portion of the plan. The OSTAP section answers the question that is a primal question of life: "What am I going to do **today** to make progress in transformation?" We are responsible to transact in this world with our time, identity, and resources He has placed in our inventory, and the OSTAP section is where we make it happen.

Recall that objectives break the goal into manageable bites. Recall as well that Papa is simultaneously accomplishing "being" and "doing" objectives in us—that is, He is transforming us (our character) and He is giving us things to do (good works to walk in). Recall that we are "God's field, God's building," therefore we should have objectives that address both our service and our development.

Multiple objectives are often connected together to describe what you hope to accomplish in a specific time period. Sometimes they describe activities in which you are already engaged and/or wish to make part of your ongoing service. Sometimes they describe new activities that Papa is developing in you. In any case, forming objectives require accessing your *spiritual inner vision* to capture the possibilities that Papa is holding for you.

In setting objectives, you may find it useful to review the "Frustration to Focus Cycle" from Chapter 4. Too many objectives can be as daunting as having none is malnourished! I suggest starting with 3-5 and see where Papa takes you from there. Each objective is listed with its own strategies, tactics, and action plans to provide a detailed mind map. When setting objectives, recall **Psalm 37:4**, "Delight yourself also in the Lord, and He shall give you the desires of your heart." That means that *not only does He fulfill your desires, but He puts them there in the first place!* So, it is important to listen to your heart and consider your personal resources when forming objectives. You may find that what He has for you to do is also what you *want* to do (i.e., "your heart's desire")! I have found it is useful to categorize my objectives in terms of connecting them to my Personal Mission. That way I can ensure that all aspects of my PM are being addressed in the plan.

## The Frustration-to-Focus Cycle

- God gives you a frustration to inspire you to dream. *A frustration without a dream is vanity;*
- He gives you a dream to inspire a vision. *A dream without a vision is fantasy;*
- He gives you a vision to inspire you to set goals. *Vision without a goal is purposeless;*
- He provides you a goal in order to inspire you to make a plan. *A goal without a plan is wishful thinking;*
- God gives you a plan to give you focus. *A plan without focus is unworkable.*
- God gives you focus to see your mission clearly and stay on task. *Focus without a mission is myopic.*

Recall that strategies are methods by which objectives are accomplished. For example, an objective "Develop outlets for my gift of serving in the next six months" (the "What?") might have a strategy like, "Join with a few friends to form a ministry to homeless," or "Develop ways to assist disaster victims" (the "method"). There can be a number of strategies to accomplish each objective. Developing strategies and tactics to accomplish your objectives is an excellent opportunity to develop and apply your spiritual inner vision to creatively express the resources He has put in you! It is also an excellent way to compare and find opportunities with like-minded others to dream big. Go for it!

Tactics break strategies into more detailed steps, and they answer the question, "How am I going to accomplish this strategy?" Without tactics to give it legs, a strategy just sits there, unaccomplished, ready for the trash heap along with other unfulfilled wishful thinking. It helps to have some expertise in the area of the particular tactics to support your strategy, but is it is not essential initially, and can often be developed along the way. The main thing is to get started and make incremental, *faithful* progress.

Action Planning is the finest level of planning detail. Action Plans answer the specific questions of "Who?" and "When? " They help us get past procrastination, past the inertia that holds us in our comfort zone. Action Plans put your Discipleship Plan on your itinerary and your calendar; they align your daily schedule with your *Last 15-Minute Self* goals. It is probably an overstatement to say that Action Planning is the most important step of discipleship; but it is not an overstatement to say that without Action Planning, discipleship is unlikely, at least, in the sense of fulfilling your entire potential.

## Revelation and Your Discipleship Plan

The only thing that any person can legitimately claim to know is what they themselves have discovered, and discovery in the realm of the Spirit only comes by revelation. Everything else that comes to us as so-called knowledge is, in reality, someone else's interpretation of events through the filter of their experience and belief. We are all subject to a particularly insidious form of bias: we see best what we expect to see, and we see least well or not at all that which we do not expect, or that which does not agree with our assumptions—our "Confirmation Bias." Think about it this way: *Conventional wisdom is only considered true because others say it is.* But those same others are only repeating what they were also told was conventional. Small errors over time can accumulate to constitute large errors and are then perpetuated through the instruction process.

The concept of what is a "fact" is massively and manipulatively overused today; most things purported to be fact are not, they are filtered opinion. Here are the first four meanings listed under the definition of fact: 1) Something that actually exists; reality; truth. 2) Something known to exist or to have happened; 3) A truth known by actual experience or observation; something known to be true; 4) Something said to be true or supposed to have happened.[21] The problem with all of the above is that it ultimately depends on relying on the word, testimony, teaching, and subjective interpretation of another person. Jesus' words recorded in multiple places in the Gospels and Revelation, "He who has ears to hear, let him hear," strongly implies that some are not equipped to hear His words. Likewise, I am not equipped to hear so-called "facts" promoted by some because of the filters, assumptions, and values the Holy Spirit has taught me. Ask yourself, "How are non-believers supposed to present so-called relevant 'facts' when the wisdom of God is foolishness to them?" The biggest "Emperor's New Clothes" issues in today's society have to do with contradictions to God's word. Believers who are intimidated by name-calling, mud-slinging, being accused of archaic or "fairy tale" beliefs have clearly never thought deeply about the nature of truth and revelation.

An infinitesimally small percentage of what we think we know has come to us by revelation; and yet any other source in the spiritual realm is suspect and to be held loosely. Just because a claim masquerades as fact does not mean it is; it just means that someone else has said it is. But revelation goes beyond knowledge and facts to synthesize meaning—and that is where the "still, small voice" of God is indispensable. Until we leave the realm of T/S/M perception and venture into the dimension of revelation and creative imagination, we remain a slave of the flesh. Our five senses enslave us by convincing us that what they are able to measure and observe is all there is. Freed from the enslavement of our senses we are able to observe the Kosmos (the Greek word for the world system as Papa created it) and imagine and discern the Father that created it. That is vital because the Fruit of the Spirit that we seek to assimilate is His character and nature. He does not love, He *is* Love. He does not give us peace; He is *our* Peace. There is no one good but Him, so without Him, there is no Goodness to emulate. His faithfulness is the standard by which all other Faithfulness is judged.

Why is the foregoing relevant to Discipleship Planning? Because Discipleship Planning is about forming and organizing the resources you have been given into the most effective Kingdom and character-growing plan you can muster. To make your Plan, you *must* hear directly from the Master Planner. You *have* to have ears to form a perception of the eternal realm. You *have* to think for yourself and filter the carnal mind from the stream of religious and fleshly "fact" and opinion flying in your direction. You *must* develop the skill to see the enemy's intimidation and lies for what they are. You *must* stand toe-to-toe with those spouting opinionated, flesh-based nonsense and be able to say in a child-like manner, "The Emperor is naked!"

Revelation is indispensable in developing your Discipleship Plan, and it is indispensable in executing it. We have to hear from Papa by revelation to know the identity for us that He sees. We are cast upon the Holy Spirit to interpret for us the wisdom that is foolishness to the world. We cannot experience union with our Bridegroom without knowing and being known. Now we turn to an in-depth study of the Fruit of

---

[21] https://www.dictionary.com/browse/fact?s=t

the Spirit, the commodity that is the product of all of our seeking and planning.  It is the product of all of our *abiding*.

## Writing it Down...

A good use of this space would be to make notes, record insights, ask questions, etc.

# Chapter 8: The Fruit of the Spirit Continuum

<sup>18</sup>For I know that in me (that is, in my flesh) nothing good dwells; for to will is present with me, but how to perform what is good I do not find. <sup>19</sup>For the good that I will to do, I do not do; but the evil I will not to do, that I practice. <sup>20</sup>Now if I do what I will not to do, it is no longer I who do it, but sin that dwells in me. <sup>21</sup>I find then a law, that evil is present with me, the one who wills to do good. <sup>22</sup>For I delight in the law of God according to the inward man. <sup>23</sup>But I see another law in my members, warring against the law of my mind, and bringing me into captivity to the law of sin which is in my members. (**Romans 7:18-23**)

## What Can We Learn from A Fig?

A fig is a fruit. A fruit by definition is the seed-bearing structure of a plant and can be eaten for food. We will not get hung up in the "botanical vs. culinary" argument between fruit and vegetables; rather, I will go with the designation indicated by **Genesis 1:29**. Jesus used the seed to talk about the Kingdom and the way it is propagated in and through us. In the Parable of the Sower in **Matthew 13:23**, He indicates that all believers are not equal with respect to fruit-production, in either potential or quantity: "But he who received seed on the good ground is he who hears the word and understands it, who indeed bears fruit and produces: some a hundredfold, some sixty, some thirty." The potential of a hundredfold, sixty, or thirtyfold is in the ground itself.

> **Genesis 1:29**, "And God said, 'See, I have given you every herb that yields seed which is on the face of all the earth, and every tree whose fruit yields seed; to you it shall be for food.'"

We are the field, and the character of our ground is determined by the choices we make and our decisions in the Choice Space. Having read this far into a book about discipleship, you are likely a person who is interested in maximizing their spiritual production potential; and that means maximizing the Fruit of the Spirit (FOTS) in you.

Clearly, not all seed produces good fruit, and not all fruit is good for food. **Matthew 13:37-40** differentiates between the seed produced by the sons of the Kingdom, and those masquerading as sons but are actually imposters acting to spoil the produce:

> <sup>37</sup>He answered and said to them: "He who sows the good seed is the Son of Man. <sup>38</sup>The field is the world, the good seeds are the sons of the kingdom, but the tares are the sons of the wicked one. <sup>39</sup>The enemy who sowed them is the devil, the harvest is the end of the age, and the reapers are the angels. <sup>40</sup>Therefore as the tares are gathered and burned in the fire, so it will be at the end of this age.

Further, Jesus indicates in **Matthew 7:15-20** that the responsibility for discerning good or bad fruit falls to us:

> <sup>15</sup>Beware of false prophets, who come to you in sheep's clothing, but inwardly they are ravenous wolves. <sup>16</sup>You will know them by their fruits. Do men gather grapes from thornbushes or figs from thistles? <sup>17</sup>Even so, every good tree bears good fruit, but a bad tree bears bad fruit. <sup>18</sup>A good tree cannot bear bad fruit, nor can a bad tree bear good fruit. <sup>19</sup>Every tree that does not bear good fruit is cut down and thrown into the fire. <sup>20</sup>Therefore by their fruits *you* will know them.

What can we learn from a fig? Figs don't grow on thistles. Grapes don't grow on thorn bushes. To produce figs or grapes, we have to stay connected to the correct plant. Further, the plant to which we are attached determines what we are and what we produce. Jesus plainly tells us that *He is the true vine*, and our abiding in Him in union is the life-giving connection that produces good fruit (**John 15:1-5**). Using the phrase "true vine" implies that there is such a thing as a "false vine," and we need to be on the alert for it as a matter of deception defense. Fruit that results from our Independent Self efforts is dead works and false fruit whose future is in the fire. As we turn our attention in this chapter to maximizing our fruit production, recall that we are designated as "God's field" (**1 Corinthians 3:9**) and that we are engaged in growing the Kingdom from seeds. Recall that He has placed His seed within us in the form of "all things that pertain to life and godliness...by which have been given to us exceedingly great and precious promises" (**2 Peter 1:3-4**). That means that the FOTS already exists in us in promise form; it is up to us to fertilize, weed, and water the seed until it reaches its maximum potential—a hundredfold!

The parables of **Matthew 13** and the lessons of Jesus' Sermon on the Mount are *really* important in discerning the mysteries of the Kingdom of God and our priorities and conduct in this life. The tares and false fruit share the same fate at the end of the age. Knowing that, doesn't it make sense to dedicate ourselves to understanding the fruit the Master looks for when He comes to inspect the produce?

## The Relational Power of the Continuum

We have shifted in this chapter from the Discipleship Plan to another tool useful for practical discipleship. The tool is a *visual* depiction of *invisible* concepts; I call it the Fruit of the Spirit Continuum. People have relationships, and so do words and ideas. Leonardo Da Vinci's famous quote, "Learn how to see. Realize that everything is connected to everything else," is a dynamic statement regarding the power of the relational thinking. The continuum concept is that power depicted visually. A relationship is defined as "a connection, association, or involvement." In common use, "relationship" is often taken to have the positive connotations of partnership. But the word relationship itself does not imply a positive affinity; the word is *neutral*, which allows us to show ideas—things that cannot be seen—in association with one another even when it is not a positive relationship.

As I have watched friends and church members, and struggled myself, against "that I would not do" behaviors to little or no avail, it became clear to me that we are sometimes ineffective because we fail to make the relationship connection between positive and negative actions and their consequences. Little things that seemingly count for nothing often accumulate to cause devastating effects. That is the way it happens with emotional pain and trauma, and that is the way it happens with the choices that we make for good or ill. No single raindrop believes it is responsible for the flood!

> "I believe that imagination is stronger than knowledge, that myth is more potent than history; that dreams are more powerful than facts, that hope always triumphs over experience; that laughter is the only cure for grief, and I believe that love is stronger than death." — Robert Fulghum, *All I Really Need to Know I Learned in Kindergarten*

Many of us have been taught all of our lives the "good that I will do" behaviors and attitudes to which Paul refers in **Romans 7:19**. Others may not have grown up in that environment; but as Robert Fulghum wrote in *All I Really Need to Know I Learned in Kindergarten*, the basics of positive and negative behavior ("that which I would not do") are all around us from an early age. It is up to us to choose wisely in *moments of truth*. The Choice Space is a mental model and tool that is about the proposition that only those persons that recognize, prepare, plan for, and routinely practice will experience consistent success in the transformation process. Envisioning our choices as a virtual space between a group of potential behaviors called the carnal mind and a group called the spiritual mind can help us grasp the life-drama that plays out in our experience daily. Seeing from this and from a "one step back" perspective can help simplify complex ideas.

## Opposites Define One Another

Norman Grubb wrote, "Now we can see that a universal [reality] of any kind is invisible and meaningless unless it has its manifest form, for any universal reality can only be known by its manifested form."[22] That is a primary reason Jesus came incarnate in the flesh—to show us the Father. As long as He remained "invisible God" our eyes could not "[behold] His glory" (**John 1:14**) in its fullness, but only that manifested in creation. Once visible in a

> **Colossians 1:15**, "He is the image of the invisible God, the firstborn over all creation."

*Person*, we obtain the ability to observe and imitate. This points out one of the chief differences between Law and Grace—in the Law, we had a commandment, *but in Grace, we have an example.* Additionally, Grubb writes,

> We come now to another Total Truth—that nothing can be known except by its opposite. There could not be light in the first chapter of Genesis without, in verse 2, "darkness on the face of the deep." This is a fundamental law of manifestation. Light cannot be known except by contrasted darkness, sweet by bitter, hard by soft, truth by a lie, and so on down the list. A thing is only to be known as a thing because it has an opposite. So, all conscious life is a recognition of opposites, and then their rightful combination, so that one is built upon the other and one swallows up the other...One has said that all life is the "rhythmic balanced interchange of opposites."[23]

If all life is "the rhythmic balanced interchange of opposites," then *transacting life is making choices between competing alternatives.* For that reason, I have designed a navigational aid diagram (model) that is a representation of the law of manifestation—the Choice Space Continuum. In the following pages, we will explore how a model like the Continuum can help to make sense of abstract concepts like the Fruits of the Spirit. Once the abstract is made visible, it can be imitated; once imitated, it can be assimilated. To add detail and richness, it turns out that polar opposite ideas can frequently be described as the sum of incremental actions, the performance of which results in movement in the direction of either extreme. Thus, the Choice Space Continuum (pictured below) was born to help understand, not only the individual Fruits of the Spirit but also specific behaviors that help us produce them or avoid their opposite.

In the dictionary, we list both the *synonym* and the *antonym* of words since ideas frequently can best be fully understood in association with their opposite. That, in a nutshell, is what the Continuum does for us visually. It helps us to understand root causes, it helps to identify intermediate steps between polar opposite ideas when the objective is to move away from the carnal mind negative and toward the spiritual mind positive. The Continuum, by showing a positive desired effect and the negative undesirable natural tendency, challenges us with choices of actions and behaviors. By writing it down we are forced to see how constructive certain behaviors can be while identifying the power of destructive behaviors in preventing our progress into the person we want to be.

---

[22] Grubb, Norman P., *Yes, I Am*. Zerubbabel Press, Blowing Rock, NC. 1982, pg. 21.

[23] Ibid, pg. 27.

Another advantage of the continuum concept is that, not only can the polar ends be identified in relation to one another, but it also identifies the component choices that accumulate to move us toward the positive or negative. These components can be identified as steps to perform, and therefore give us specific and helpful, *"What do I do today?"* or, *"What do I work on today?"* ideas. As we have discussed previously, until behaviors, attitudes, activities, and goals get translated from ethereal "that's nice" concepts to, "What do I do right now?" responses, they will forever remain an elusive and unattainable carrot tied to an arm's length stick. It may or may not keep our mule moving down the road, but it will not provide any direction, nor will it reward attainment.

The Continuum helps provide a roadmap out of the disciple's dilemma. It empowers us by putting specific names on "the good that I will to do," and on the "evil that I will not to do" (**Romans 7:19**). Identifying these helps us to define and clarify the competing minds, carnal and spiritual. By displaying desirable and undesirable traits, characteristics, behaviors, and attitudes as component parts of the Fruit of the Spirit or its corresponding opposite spirit, we can make choices at decisive moments of truth. When we know what the negative looks like, we can avoid it; and, when we know what positive energy and action can move us toward transformation and renewal, we can choose it and prosper. We have identified "Stop doing dumb stuff" as one of our Discipleship Rules list. The first step in continuous improvement is to stop doing dumb stuff; *then* we can start doing smart stuff, helpful stuff. The Fruit of the Spirit Continuums help us identify behaviors that constitute each—the dumb and the smart!

## The Choice Space as a Mental Model

The pieces of a puzzle assembled constitute a "manifested form" referenced by Mr. Grubb as quoted above. For example, our concept of love may remain a nebulous idea of a squishy emotion until, by breaking the concept into component parts reproducible by a repetitive process, we can establish that love is more about *doing* than *doting*. That is what the Apostle Paul did when he listed his, "Love is…" and "Love does not…" statements in **1 Corinthians 13**—he made a word model for us. Similarly, a visual model of "Joy" can be shown to be more the product of intentional choice than fickle feelings. The writer of Hebrews recognized the value of a word model when he gave us the definition of faith in **Hebrews 11:1**; he used words like "substance of things hoped for" (an abstraction) and "evidence of things not seen" (another abstraction). He triangulates and defines one abstract concept in terms of two others that, in combination with one another, give us a word picture of faith. Genius! Until an abstract universal reality is made manifest, it cannot accurately enter our world and have its most beneficial impact. That is why Jesus said, "If you have seen me you have seen the Father." It is why Paul said, "Imitate me as I imitate Christ." When faith is modeled, I can grasp its intent; I can understand its context, and I can take intentional action to go beyond the veil of the flesh into the realm of the Spirit.

The concept of a model is no more complicated than a representation of an idea or collection of ideas in relation to one another. If I make a model of an airplane, I may take plastic pieces that, in miniature, look like and represent an actual airplane, but they also serve the dual purpose of representing a visual result of all of the thought and design that went into the airplane's creation. The model is not the thing, it represents the thing. A model for a non-tangible idea—for example, any one of the nine Fruits of the Spirit as recorded in the following pages—can prove very helpful in our understanding because so many of us are *visual learners.* In cases like these, models help us shape ideas by presenting them with tangible form. That, in turn, helps us to understand the relationship between the puzzle pieces, how they interact, and how one affects another. In short, a model can help us make order out of what otherwise might remain chaos—our lives, for example.

As an example, imagine with me (if you will), a line—a continuum—that begins with you as the midpoint, and has two infinite rays in opposite directions on each side, right and left. On the (theoretical) right end is complete union with God in spirit and soul. On the left (theoretical) end is the absolute position

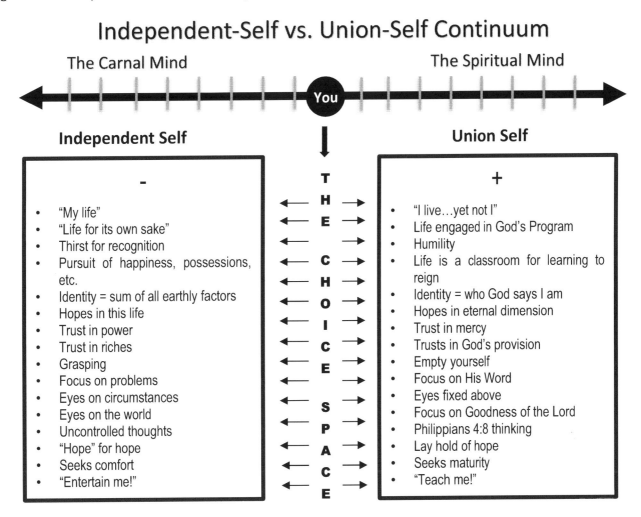

# Independent-Self vs. Union-Self Continuum

**The Choice Space as a Discipleship Tool**

of Independent Self. Let's call the model the "Independent-Self vs. Union-Self Continuum." This model is the most basic application of the fundamental law of manifestation. It demonstrates the basic conflict of independence vs. union that is the initiation of all of our discipleship activities, and our struggle against the carnal mind in favor of the spiritual mind. The principal feature of this model is the prominent Choice Space between the positive and negative extremes. Also prominent is a listing of potential positive and negative (or, helpful and unhelpful, if you prefer) actions that serve as, and mark, the hash marks between the polar ends. Notice that each choice listed on the right of the Choice Space has a corresponding choice to the left. They are, for all intents and purposes, opposites (what Graham Cooke calls, "responding in the opposite spirit") and determine both our response and the direction of our subsequent growth or deterioration. In other words, a choice from the negative list moves us toward the left end of the continuum and increases our trust in our own strength and abilities. A choice from the positive list moves us toward the positive of abandoned trust in the Lord.

Below is another related example of a continuum called the Locus of Trust. On the theoretical left end is self-trust, a categorical rejection of trust in God. On the right is the positive ultimate position of complete and abandoned trust in the Lord. Throughout life, unless actively opposing the pull, individuals gravitate naturally and progressively in the direction of the "self-trust," "trust in man," and "flesh-trust"

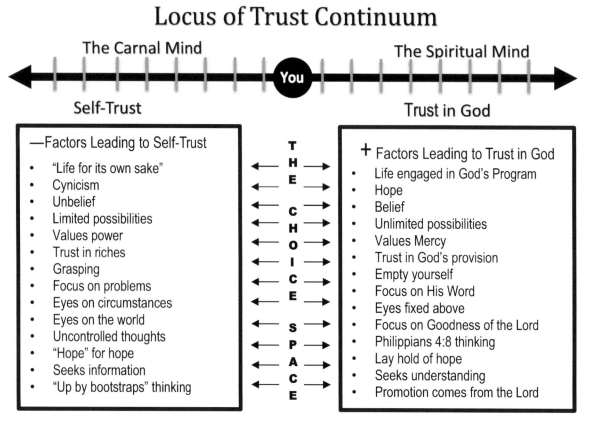

# Locus of Trust Continuum

The Carnal Mind — You — The Spiritual Mind

Self-Trust — Trust in God

—Factors Leading to Self-Trust

- "Life for its own sake"
- Cynicism
- Unbelief
- Limited possibilities
- Values power
- Trust in riches
- Grasping
- Focus on problems
- Eyes on circumstances
- Eyes on the world
- Uncontrolled thoughts
- "Hope" for hope
- Seeks information
- "Up by bootstraps" thinking

THE CHOICE SPACE

+ Factors Leading to Trust in God

- Life engaged in God's Program
- Hope
- Belief
- Unlimited possibilities
- Values Mercy
- Trust in God's provision
- Empty yourself
- Focus on His Word
- Eyes fixed above
- Focus on Goodness of the Lord
- Philippians 4:8 thinking
- Lay hold of hope
- Seeks understanding
- Promotion comes from the Lord

perspectives. (I use the word "gravitate" intentionally because, like gravity, the pull toward the negative is continuous and absolute unless we actively oppose it.) The practice of mistrust is itself a form of trust relationship that has the effect of searing and hindering our future ability to trust positively. People who seem never to trust anyone or anything are declaring their own form of trust relationship—in their own abilities (flesh), and in their assumed capability to recognize and know the heart and motivation of others (false discernment). Moving toward the right (positive end) on our trust continuum is *always* initially an intentional action based on choice. Trust in God is *always perceived* as a risk in our T/S/M reality, at least and until we faithfully persevere to build the strength of our grip on the eternal. Until the ability to see behind the veil of the flesh becomes our go-to skill, we vacillate between trust in the flesh and trust in the Spirit. The Choice Space is about developing the skill to, first, recognize when choice opportunities exist; and second, see the choices from both the flesh and spiritual mind; and third, habitually choose the positive action. We do not need to be evil, depraved, or atheistic to live under the life curse of self-trust; we just have to be unintentional, unplanned, or apathetic in our response to God, and we will naturally gravitate toward the negative. Such is the nature and influence of the flesh—its natural activity is to corrupt, its natural interest in all things egocentric, its natural state is weakness.

## The FOTS as Steps on the Journey

Earlier we identified our recognition of the fact that we have died, and our life is hidden with Christ in God (**Colossians 3:3**), as the beginning point—start line, if you will—of our discipleship pilgrimage. But then the starter's pistol goes off, and our problem becomes a very different one: The problem of *wanting* to move forward versus *actually* moving forward kicks in. I have proclaimed that I am a guy pretty much like you, and I understand this problem very well: "What do I do first/now?" An undertaking as daunting as transforming all of our natural tendencies and substituting in their place things unseen and character qualities that are foolishness to the world can be mind-boggling. When we engage a task where there is seemingly no hope of success, our tendency is just to sit and stare straight ahead. When there are too many decisions to make, and too much stress associated with all of them, we tend to simply shut down. At that point, we rightly ask the question, "Where do I even begin?" The answer returns to us in Paul's epistle to the **Galatians, Chapter 5, verses 22-24**:

> [22]But the fruit of the Spirit is love, joy, peace, patience, kindness, goodness, faithfulness, [23]meekness, self-control. Against such, there is no law. [24]And those who are Christ's have crucified the flesh with its passions and desires.

Paul gives us nine FOTS to imitate, emulate, and ultimately assimilate. We begin there. We begin by asking the Holy Spirit to illuminate these qualities to our heart and mind. We begin by meditating on the true nature of each quality, not a surface understanding, but what each looks like in practice. We go to the word and seek out the definition of each and their relation to other Scriptural concepts. There is a bonus in this passage of Scripture: Not only does it boost our planning by listing for us a model of *character qualities* from which to shape our goal, it further gives us the *strategy* for pursuing it in **verse 24**: "[crucifing] the flesh." That sounds remarkably similar to Jesus' declaration that, if we want to follow Him, it requires denying self and taking up our cross daily (**Matthew 16:24**). By continuum modeling and a dogged determination to take up our cross daily, we learn what the manifested form of the abstract concepts "deny self" and "take up your cross" are, what the components are, and what decisions in the Choice Space we must make to progress. By studying and defining them by Scriptural principles, we gain depth of understanding into component parts of each Fruit. We learn the nuanced differences that circumstances make in our choices. We learn that the elephant-sized problem breaks down into manageable bites. We learn that we can fertilize and facilitate our fruit-bearing depending on our focus and our choices. In essence, we identify the "the good that I will to do" and "the evil I will not to do" (**Romans 7:19**). By identifying it, we give it a name; and by naming it, we gain power over it. By listing the component positives and the component negatives of the manifestation of each FOTS, we clarify our choices, limit deception, and take responsibility for our own growth.

## The Continuum: Cultivating Love

It is difficult to imagine any discussion of Agape Love without Paul's famous chapter in **1 Corinthians**. If you have accepted the Bible as the word of God (as I have), there are conclusions about the Love of God[24] that are inescapable from plain reading; and our first duty in cultivating Love as a Fruit of the Spirit is to understand what it is in Scriptural terms. That quest will necessarily include much of what it is not since we have so much "love insight" thrown at us from other sources these days. From pop music to movies, to high school dating and beyond—the world attempts to force upon us a carnal, self-centered, selfish view of love, and what it looks like in practice. Our interest in cultivating Love in the Choice Space

---

[24] As you probably know, there are a several Greek words in the New Testament that are translated "love." Our references here are to Agape love, or the love that expresses the nature and essence of the Father.

is narrow, confined to the question, "How can I understand the components of Agape Love in a manner by which I can grow it as a fruit in my Discipleship Plan?"  Since Love is an abstract concept, we must rely on Paul's "Love is…" and "Love does not…" word model in **1 Corinthians 13:4-8** as a jumping-off point:

> [4]Love suffers long and is kind; love does not envy; love does not parade itself, is not puffed up; [5]does not behave rudely, does not seek its own, is not provoked, thinks no evil; [6]does not rejoice in iniquity, but rejoices in the truth; [7]bears all things, believes all things, hopes all things, endures all things.  [8]Love never fails.

The *first* building block on which we must agree—or else nothing that follows will make sense—is that the Love of God is *not primarily an emotion*.  There is no doubt that we all need to *feel* the emotion of love to live a well-rounded life.  Persons who are sociopathic lack the empathetic connection with others that comes from love.

"God *is* Love" (**1 John 4:8**).  "God *is* light" (**1 John 1:5**).  What are we intended to understand from John's metaphors for Papa?  What if, rather than one of many individual characteristics, Love is the

> **1 John 4:8**, "He who does not love does not know God, for *God is love*."

compilation of *all* the attributes of God as a sort of "master attribute?"  What if, rather than merely loving as an act/activity, Love is His essence and being?  And if that is true, what does it mean for us and our discipleship?  How does it change the way we express Love?  Is it even possible to Love in the absence of knowing Him, or, is the best we can muster the self-centered/erotic love worshiped in today's culture?  The "$7 bill" example we discussed previously (pg. 69) is on-point and relevant to our quest for Love.  After all, what more germane counterfeit (there are two words that are strange bedfellows!) could be proffered than to obscure the path to Papa by counterfeiting His Nature and essence?

What if there are other characteristics of Love and Light that can help us understand how to express His life?  In the same way that white light is the sum of all light wave frequencies, what if God's Love is the aggregation and coalescing of all of His individual attributes, united in One Being?  What if, in the same manner a prism divides light into color bands specific to a particular wavelength, the Holy Spirit's capabilities include breaking the Love of God into "frequencies" that we recognize as His mercy, His grace, His compassion, His loving-kindness, His care, His justice, His giving, etc.  What if the Fruits of the Spirit are actually the various wavelengths of the Master-Fruit, Love?  And, what if these frequencies can be coalesced and re-combined in us as we are discipled and transformed by the Holy Spirit?

In the context of these questions, we can clearly see that Agape Love is much more than a squishy emotion, and bears no resemblance to the pop-culture version.  When we aspire to Love, we aspire *to be God in His full nature and glory*.  Notice at this point that the serpent's lie to Eve in the Garden of Eden was, "You shall be *like* God."  *Like* God is Independent Self.  *Like* God maintains a separation between His Person and my person.  *Like* God is me making my best effort to imitate Him—a good starting point, but not the desired end result!  Agape Love cannot be impersonated or duplicated; it can only be channeled.  Becoming an open, unobstructed channel of His Spirit and essence takes union.  It takes suppressing and killing of our selfish-love instincts.  It takes whatever is necessary to remove our flesh as an impediment.  And, it sounds remarkably like "Abiding in the vine" (**John 15:4**).

If Agape Love is the amalgamation of all of Papa's attributes, the question arises of whether we can claim to Love if we lack some portion of those qualities in our own character.  What if I am not very good at the patience thing?  What if I have anger issues but really have a heart of compassion for people?

Can I still Love if some important frequency is missing? Actually, it is something of a trick question, because it assumes that we have some right or ability to claim to Love in the first place! The real question would be, "Is it possible for me to channel the Love of God on some occasions, and fail to channel it on others?" The answer is, "Of course!" That is the very definition of spiritual growth: Increasing the amount and percentage of the time, and the completeness with which I channel the Love of God when called upon. The objective is to do so more today than I did yesterday, and more still tomorrow.

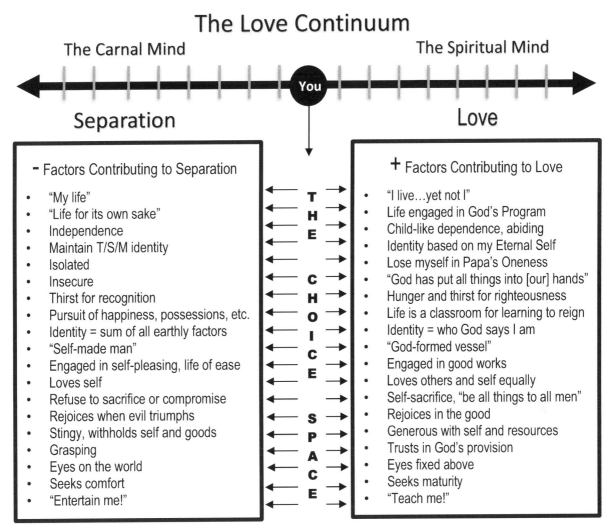

# The Love Continuum

The Carnal Mind                     The Spiritual Mind

Separation                                          Love

THE CHOICE SPACE

**− Factors Contributing to Separation**

- "My life"
- "Life for its own sake"
- Independence
- Maintain T/S/M identity
- Isolated
- Insecure
- Thirst for recognition
- Pursuit of happiness, possessions, etc.
- Identity = sum of all earthly factors
- "Self-made man"
- Engaged in self-pleasing, life of ease
- Loves self
- Refuse to sacrifice or compromise
- Rejoices when evil triumphs
- Stingy, withholds self and goods
- Grasping
- Eyes on the world
- Seeks comfort
- "Entertain me!"

**+ Factors Contributing to Love**

- "I live...yet not I"
- Life engaged in God's Program
- Child-like dependence, abiding
- Identity based on my Eternal Self
- Lose myself in Papa's Oneness
- "God has put all things into [our] hands"
- Hunger and thirst for righteousness
- Life is a classroom for learning to reign
- Identity = who God says I am
- "God-formed vessel"
- Engaged in good works
- Loves others and self equally
- Self-sacrifice, "be all things to all men"
- Rejoices in the good
- Generous with self and resources
- Trusts in God's provision
- Eyes fixed above
- Seeks maturity
- "Teach me!"

Dying to self is a prerequisite to growing in Love, and there is an inverse relationship between the two: When one increases the other decreases. That means that the more dead we are, the freer we are to flow His love. Dying to self (more accurately, growing in the reality that we have already died) is the bottom-line *primary* task of discipleship. The major activity is getting self out of the way ("crucifying the flesh") as an impediment to the Spirit's flow through us, and any discipleship model or system has to facilitate that process to be legitimate. We are intended to channel His life in the way the banks of a river channel water and be transformed in the process. But, the *banks* of the river are not the *river*—the water is the river. In the same way, our vessel of flesh is not the "lover," nor is the soul (mind, will, or emotions) living in the vessel—they only channel the flow of Love (living water) from the source to the point of need. Independent Self dams up the flow. Independent Self restricts the living water movement. Independent Self skims a big cut for itself. Even when the River of Life is flowing, Independent Self interjects itself and causes the eddies, whirlpools, and rocky rapids that make navigation dangerous. So, when we make a visual model of Agape Love and its opposite, the negative end of the continuum is Separation; i.e., full devotion and entrenchment in Independent Self.

Remember, Independent Self is separated self. Independence severs the life flow that comes from union, and separation shrivels the branches and makes them fit only to be burned. Healthy branches only result from abiding in the vine (i.e., living attached) as Jesus requires of us in **John 15:4-8**:

> [4]Abide in Me, and I in you. As the branch cannot bear fruit of itself unless it abides in the vine, neither can you, unless you abide in Me. [5]I am the vine, you are the branches. He who abides in Me, and I in him, bears much fruit; for without Me you can do nothing. [6]If anyone does not abide in Me, he is cast out as a branch and is withered; and they gather them and throw them into the fire, and they are burned. [7]If you abide in Me, and My words abide in you, you will ask what you desire, and it shall be done for you. [8]By this My Father is glorified, that you bear much fruit; *so you will be My disciples*.

I have been in the Church since I was a newborn, and have seen many versions of the gospel over the course of 66+ years, many of them bearing no resemblance to Jesus' requirements for friendship, much less discipleship. When our conduct of the Gospel does not match our preferred proclamation of it, we fall back on a strategy of blurring, questioning, obfuscating, and saying things like, "I don't think that is what that means," or, "Did God really say that?" in much the same way the serpent deceived Eve in the Garden. Here is a "great evil that I have observed under the sun" (forgive me, Solomon!): ***We read phrases like, "Abide in Me," and automatically include ourselves among those actually abiding.*** But abiding is the state of living attached, and it is absolutely impossible to claim attachment while actively living according to the carnal mind and Independent Self. That is why I have taken every opportunity to hammer the Independent Self as a lifestyle—it dwells unattached from the vine.

The Independent Self wants to draw near to God, but preserve the distinction that is lost in union. "Right next to" is not the same as "abiding in." In the same way, we tend to automatically assume abiding status, we confer on ourselves "disciple" status, even in the absence of fruit (**John 15:8**)—or worse, in the presence of negative fruit! Here is the unvarnished truth: Without *verifiable* (not fudged!) evidence of Love, Joy, Peace, Patience, Kindness, Gentleness, Faithfulness, Goodness, and Self-Control you are not entitled to claim to be a disciple! You do not need to provide verification to me, but there will come a day when the Master will come looking for figs, and it is in your best interest to have some on hand.

We have a propensity to gravitate toward easy, pat answers. So, when the question is, "What is the opposite of Love?" we pop "hate" off of the top of our head. But Agape Love is a person, not an emotion. Further, it is a particular person—Papa Himself. Therefore, the opposite of Love is also a person—you and I acting out of Independent Self, and reflecting our separated status. It is us doing our, "There is a way that seems right to a man, but its end is the way of death" (**Proverbs 16:25**) caricature. We are not capable of loving Agape-style without His living water flowing through us. When we abide in Him, we "flow" Him, and the world receives it as Love. When we abide separated, we flow something else entirely. It may be concern, attraction, infatuation, "like," but it is not Love! Therefore, the incremental positive Choice Space activities that lead us toward Love also inevitably lead us *away from self and separation*. Following our natural instincts—the flesh—moves us away from Love, gives us many obstructions to the smooth, peaceful flow of the Spirit, and leads ultimately to fully entrenched independence. At that point, we are positioned to hear the Master's, "I never knew you, depart from me..." pronouncement (**Matthew 7:23**). The work of the spiritual mind is to dredge the River; the work of the carnal mind is to fill it with rocks, trash, dead branches, dead works, and religious pursuits.

Your Love Continuum might look something like mine (above). It should be clear that many of the Love Continuum activities are also included in the other models as we progress through the Fruit of the Spirit. That is one of the ways we know that Love is the Master-fruit, with all others being sub-components. Also, it should be readily apparent that there are many other activities that could be listed in contrast to one another on each side of the Choice Space. That brings us to an important point about your pilgrimage, constructing your Discipleship Plan, and making your models for study: It is *your* "salvation-working-out" process to make of it what you will, and what you are able. There is no prescribed method, no right way, no "my way or the highway." One of the most precious and valuable benefits of adopting this methodology is the time it takes sitting in Papa's Presence, at His feet, discussing with Him your own plan according to His advice, and according to the identity He sees. I make it a practice to do that every morning and again every night—and hopefully, many times in between. As my dad used to say, "It's your goat, you milk it!" This is the point where you warm your hands and get busy!

## The Continuum: Cultivating Goodness

Next, we will look at Goodness, out of order of its place in Paul's FOTS list, because of its overlapping similarity with our discussion of Papa's Love. Recall that we began the Love discussion with two declarations from John: "God *is* Love" (**1 John 4:8**), "God *is* Light" (**1 John 1:5**). These are remarkable for what John did not write. He did not write, "God is *like* love," or, "God is *like* light." No, he claimed that these two things are His *essence,* His *nature.* The way we experience the FOTS Agape Love is by channeling Papa's nature through us as the banks of a river channel the flow of water. Our part is to stay connected to the headwaters (the source, the "vine," **John 15:1, 5**) and that connection results in fruitfulness.

Cultivating Goodness is a similar process with unique results. As Agape Love is our channeling of Papa's Love nature, *Goodness is the shining of His Light nature through us.* Near the beginning of His Sermon on the Mount, Jesus' declaration concerning us is recorded in **Matthew 5:14-16**:

> [14]You are the light of the world. A city that is set on a hill cannot be hidden. [15]Nor do they light a lamp and put it under a basket, but on a lampstand, and it gives light to all who are in the house. [16]Let your light so shine before men, that they may see your good works and glorify your Father in heaven.

Why should *our* shining result in *God's glorification*? If they are our good works, how does that transaction take place? We are all well familiar with observing and admiring the moon in the night sky. We know, of course, that the moon has no incandescence or luminescence of its own. The moon's only ability to "shine" is attributable to its ability to reflect from a true light source. Imagine yourself as the moon, your natural habitat is a sky full of darkness (that will preach!). Think of the migration of the moon's glory from the New Moon to fullness as the cycle of our pilgrimage in the Spirit from first breath to last. We begin our journey as fresh as the barely visible New Moon, with glorious aspirations of full reflection and the beauty of brilliant reflection of the face of Christ (oneness). The light "shin[ing]

**2 Corinthians 4:6**, "For it is the God who commanded light to shine out of darkness, who has shone in our hearts to give the light of the knowledge of the glory of God in the face of Jesus Christ."

out of darkness" represents our progressive spiritual reflection of the glory of the Son of God (**2 Corinthians 4:6**) as we learn and grow, as dead parts are regenerated, as we are transformed into His image, and renewed in the spirit of our mind. Additionally, we know from **Ephesians 2:10** that, not only do we reflect His light (glory) having none of our own, but the good works themselves were prepared by

Papa before we were around before we had input to mess them up! Our task is to stay in His orbit, follow Him wherever He goes, doing whatever He does, reflecting His light on all around.

Here is a paradox with which we strive: Our view from the earth appears as a partial representation of His glory; yet, the moon (us) remains complete and has the full moon potential at all times as the shadow of the flesh progressively moves out of the way. As we move ever more completely into union with Him, our "hearts [reflect] the light of the knowledge of the glory of God in the face of Jesus Christ." It is a matter of better and more completely reflecting His glory *as we move in relation to His radiance.* The partial reflection we see in the night sky is only a representation of that work of the Spirit (our transformation) in progress. In addition to the face of the moon we see from our earth-bound vantage point, there is another face that is just as much a part of the moon, but remains unseen as the "back" or "dark side." The backside of the moon is that portion that is real-but-not-apparent and is analogous to our eternal, *real* self. Beyond today's partial reflection is a moon that is, outside of our perception, "perfect and complete, lacking nothing" (**James 1:4**). Our T/S/M limitation is eclipsed by a greater reality, and it is from this perspective that our Father views us! From His perspective in eternity—outside of the T/S/M limitations—He already sees the full moon *and* the *whole moon*, the full and complete reflection of the Son of God, and our face fully reflecting His face in all of its luminescent glory.

What are the functions of light? We must understand this if we are to know if we are being true to *our* intended function, and what should be the effect of our shining of Papa's light on each other and the world around. Some of the functions are:

1) Light *dispels* darkness;
2) Light *reveals* the path ahead;
3) Light *attracts* the sighted;
4) Light *illuminates* your destination;
5) Light *enables* movement and *empowers* good works;
6) Light *glorifies* the Father;
7) Light *reveals* the hearts of men.

**Psalm 36:9** tells us that, "In [His] light we see light." As a function of His Light shining on us, we are able to see all of the manifestations of Papa that are so precious to us: His mercy, His compassion, His loving kindness, forbearance, favor, etc. Yes, His light is *that important*; and it is *that important* that we embrace our commission to shine it purely on all around.

In **John 8:12**, Jesus *calls Himself* the light of the world: "Then Jesus spoke to them again, saying, "I am the light of the world. He who follows Me shall not walk in darkness, but have the light of life." "Now wait

| **John 9:5**, As long as I am in the world, *I am the light of the world."* | just a doggone minute. How can *He* be the light of the world after He called *us* the light of the world? How can He and I be the light of the world at the same time unless we are the same expression of the Father?" *Exactly!* Jesus was not sloppy with His word choice here, or anywhere else. We are intended |

to read these Scriptures and equate His experience with ours, His role with ours, His *Person* with ours. When He left to go receive His Kingdom from Papa, we are intended to assume His role as shining the "True Light" (**John 1:9**) into the world to dispel darkness. Our ability to fulfill that function is dependent on our efforts to overcome Independent Self and stay connected to the Vine.

**Psalm 53:2-3** sets the tone for our discussion of the source of Goodness. It is quoted in **Romans 3:12**, and is the idea presented by Jesus in His discussion with The Rich Young Ruler (RYR):

- **Psalm 53:2-3**, "[2]God looks down from heaven upon the children of men to see if there are any who understand, who seek God. [3]Every one of them has turned aside; they have together become corrupt; there is none who does good, *no, not one.*"

- **Romans 3:12**, "They have all turned aside; They have together become unprofitable; *There is none who does good, no, not one.*"

- **Matthew 19:16-17**, "[16]Now behold, one came and said to Him, "Good Teacher, what good thing shall I do that I may have eternal life?" [17]So He said to him, *"Why do you call Me good? No one is good but One, that is God."*

Like me, you may have seen the videos of random interviews conducted with people on the street, asking, "If you died today would you go to Heaven, and why?" A large percentage of the interviewees answer, "I think so. I try to live a good life," or similar. This answer stems from a *purely* transactional mindset—earning the "Heaven" merit badge. "I try to live a good life" fails to pass the "notional vs. motivational" test because it is easy to claim to try without ever having to provide any actual evidence.

This becomes a thorny problem: There is none good. David seemed thoroughly convinced of it, having used the same phrase, "there is none good" five times in his Psalms, and on three occasions adding the zinger "no, not one" for emphasis! Dissonance arises in our brain when we are told by Paul in Romans that there is no one who qualifies as good, then he encouraged us in Galatians to develop the Fruit of the Spirit "Goodness." Jesus contributed to our conundrum with His answer to the RYR's greeting, "Good Teacher." For Jesus to decline to be identified as "Good Teacher" flies in the face of our Church tradition! Moreover, His "Why do you call me good?" question was not even the substance of His answer to the RYR's question, so it is curious why He would respond in that manner. He calls Himself the "Good Shepherd" in **John 10:11, 14**, and He did not display a habit of self-deprecation in other places, so why would He object to being known as "Good Teacher"? It must have been to convey an important message about the source of *all* Goodness, and also to deal with a specific problem He recognized in the RYR.

The message Jesus was reinforcing is that there is *no such thing as good* apart from the nature and being of the Godhead. It is God's prerogative to define good and evil, and only He can define it accurately because it is bound up with His nature. So, when Jesus said, "No one is good but One, that is God," He was telling us plainly the source of His own Goodness; and consequently, the *only* source of Goodness available to us: not behavior, not rules, not law, but a relationship. That brings us to this pivotal understanding: Our degree of attainment of the Fruit of the Spirit Goodness is a reflection and measure of our attainment of soul union with Him, and therefore our abandonment of the Independent Self! Further, the "One" to which Jesus refers to here is the same "one-ness" that Jesus prays for us in **John 17:21**. When we read Jesus' priestly prayer for us, we see that He was good because He and the Father were One; yet the Goodness was not His own, that is His to "possess," only to channel; and it is the only way we achieve Goodness as well. That should not be at all surprising since Paul plainly tells us in **Philippians 2:7** that He emptied Himself of self and of His divine prerogative.

The answer to our problem begins to come into greater focus when we realize that Jesus makes a clear distinction between good as an activity or behavior, and Good as an attribute of nature:

> [20]I do not pray for these alone, but also for those who will believe in Me through their word; [21]that they all may be one, as You, Father, are in Me, and I in You; that they also may be one in Us, that the world may believe that You sent Me. [22]And the glory which You gave Me I have given them, that they may be one just as We are one: [23]I in them, and

You in Me; that they may be made perfect in one, and that the world may know that You have sent Me, and have loved them as You have loved Me. **(John 17:20-23)**

Clearly, we are able to do good things. We are even capable of good behavior for short periods of time—some shorter than others! But the Goodness to which Jesus refers and about which Paul writes as a FOTS is a permanent, indwelling change in our soul's precious life, and is the "good treasure" that Jesus spoke of in **Matthew 12:35** and appears in other Scriptures:

- A good man out of the good treasure of his heart brings forth good things, and an evil man out of the evil treasure brings forth evil things. (**Matthew 12:35**)

- A good tree cannot bear bad fruit, nor can a bad tree bear good fruit. (**Matthew 7:18**)

- [10]Out of the same mouth proceed blessing and cursing. My brethren, these things ought not to be so. [11]Does a spring send forth fresh water and bitter from the same opening? [12]Can a fig tree, my brethren, bear olives, or a grapevine bear figs? Thus, no spring yields both saltwater and fresh. (**James 3:10-12**)

- [16]You will know them by their fruits. Do men gather grapes from thornbushes or figs from thistles? [17]Even so, every good tree bears good fruit, but a bad tree bears bad fruit. [18]A good tree cannot bear bad fruit, nor can a bad tree bear good fruit. (**Matthew 7:16-18**)

It is apparent from the foregoing that behavior derives from nature, so the essence of a person's core being (identity) is discernable by what they do, what they say, and their labor's fruit.

Our efforts to cultivate Goodness become an exercise to shine the cleanest, clearest, most unfiltered light into the world. Any filtration of that Light from Independent Self pollutes and degrades it. Therefore, to derive the opposite of Goodness we conclude it is the absence of light—darkness. But, for the purposes of our Goodness Continuum, there is a *particular kind* of darkness that is usually the issue for those who would count themselves as religious and is *always* a manifestation of the flesh tugging at those spiritually minded: self-righteousness. That is the form of darkness that Jesus identified in the RYR—the religious pride that boasts, "These things have I done from my youth." I think the RYR was probably shocked by Jesus' answer because he most likely expected Him to say some variation of, "Look, dude, you don't need to change *anything*. You've got it going on!" I think that as soon as Jesus saw him, He knew from the RYR's bearing and boasts that self-righteousness and position consciousness was strong in him; and He tailored His "everlasting life" prescription accordingly.

Jesus used a fascinating phrase in **Matthew 6:23**: "If therefore the *light* that is in you is *darkness, how great is that darkness*!" In this teaching, we have a premonition of the scourging criticism that was to

> **Matthew 6:23**, "But if your eye is bad, your whole body will be full of darkness. If therefore the light that is in you is darkness, how great is that darkness!"

follow for the Pharisees and others whose self-righteousness was not from Papa's Light source, but from their own efforts to shine. Only someone standing in complete darkness could mistake a pile of filthy rags (our righteousness, **Isaiah 64:6**) for a white linen wedding garment (**Revelation 19:8**). Only one entrenched in self-delusion could show up to a wedding in rags of their own stitching and expect to be admitted to the feast (**Matthew 22:11-13**). Solomon tells us, "There is a way that seems right to a man, but the end is the way of death" (**Proverbs 14:12, 16:25**). We do not want to share that fate, so it is important that we emphatically reject all Independent Self urging to shine any light other than the "True Light that has come into the world" (**John 1:9**).

With the foregoing in mind, I have chosen for my Goodness Continuum not to feature darkness, but "Self-righteousness" on the negative end of the spectrum. You may come to a different conclusion and feature "darkness" in that position—both would be accurate. But I find Jesus' pronouncements against self-righteousness to be very persuasive, and worthy of significant effort against which to guard. The diagram following is the Goodness Continuum that I use in my Discipleship Plan and studies:

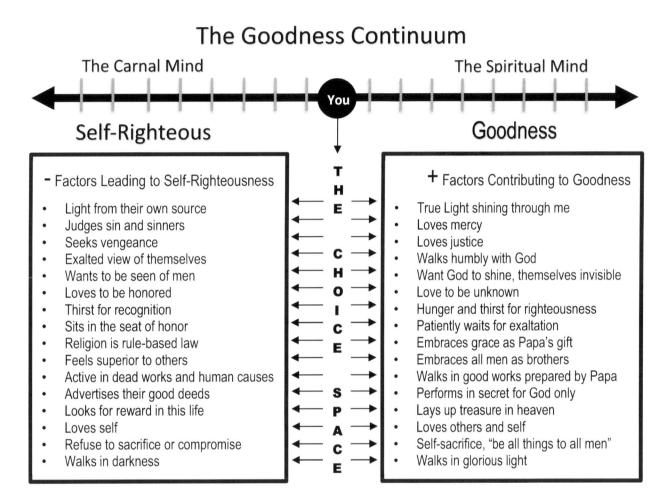

# The Goodness Continuum

**The Carnal Mind**      **The Spiritual Mind**

**You**

**Self-Righteous**      **Goodness**

| **– Factors Leading to Self-Righteousness** | **THE CHOICE SPACE** | **+ Factors Contributing to Goodness** |
|---|---|---|
| • Light from their own source | | • True Light shining through me |
| • Judges sin and sinners | | • Loves mercy |
| • Seeks vengeance | | • Loves justice |
| • Exalted view of themselves | | • Walks humbly with God |
| • Wants to be seen of men | | • Want God to shine, themselves invisible |
| • Loves to be honored | | • Love to be unknown |
| • Thirst for recognition | | • Hunger and thirst for righteousness |
| • Sits in the seat of honor | | • Patiently waits for exaltation |
| • Religion is rule-based law | | • Embraces grace as Papa's gift |
| • Feels superior to others | | • Embraces all men as brothers |
| • Active in dead works and human causes | | • Walks in good works prepared by Papa |
| • Advertises their good deeds | | • Performs in secret for God only |
| • Looks for reward in this life | | • Lays up treasure in heaven |
| • Loves self | | • Loves others and self |
| • Refuse to sacrifice or compromise | | • Self-sacrifice, "be all things to all men" |
| • Walks in darkness | | • Walks in glorious light |

## The Continuum: Cultivating Joy

The next attribute in the Fruit of the Spirit basket is "Joy." As with Love, the first building block on which we must agree is that Joy is not an emotion, at least not initially until it matures into fullness. Many people mix and intermingle "happiness" and "Joy" inappropriately; often they spring up at the same time, but not always. Many people believe that Joy and happiness are the same things, only one experienced to a greater degree. Again, not true. Happiness is the pleasurable lift and sense of well-being we feel when the hormone, serotonin, is released into our body. But Joy is not the product of body chemistry, but rather the product of our internal vision. Joy is a response of our spirit to a future hope. It is seeing an inevitable recompense, anticipating it, and basing our response on it rather than on present circumstances. **Hebrews 12:2** tells us that is the process Jesus experienced concerning His suffering and crucifixion:

> Looking unto Jesus, the author and finisher of our faith, *who for the joy that was set before Him endured the cross*, despising the shame, and has sat down at the right hand of the throne of God.

Jesus was not giddy about His crucifixion, but looked past pain to fulfillment; and in so doing, counted it joy. That makes Joy equivalent to an inspired decision rather than an emotion, which explains how we can *choose* Joy in circumstances that do not seem to merit a *feeling* of joy. It makes rejoicing the result of the fulfilled promise, and a decision to "count it all joy" a precursor to the fullness of Joy. And it makes it another spiritual fruit we must understand in context, that is, in the context of the promises Papa has given us, and the context of hope and certainty of their fulfillment.

The writer of Hebrews praised the Church for its joyful acceptance in response to persecution and tribulation. It is difficult to imagine the Hebrews dancing around, excited and grinning from ear-to-ear as possessions were plundered and tribulation made life miserable:

> [32]But recall the former days in which, after you were illuminated, you endured a great struggle with sufferings: [33]partly while you were made a spectacle both by reproaches and tribulations, and partly while you became companions of those who were so treated; [34]for you had compassion on me in my chains, and *joyfully accepted the plundering of your goods, knowing that you have a better and an enduring possession for yourselves in heaven.* (**Hebrews 10:32-34**)

"I can't imagine being joyful about being 'plundered'! Maybe the writer got it wrong, and they really did not have it that bad." Could it be, rather, that we have misunderstood the basic nature of Joy? Perhaps we have made wrong assumptions about the source of Joy and have mistaken it for happiness? Maybe

| Gratitude + Hope = Joy |

Joy has less to do with present circumstances, and more to do with the promises of hope in which we anchor our heart and the faith by which we establish it? We know from the account of His Gethsemane experience that Jesus' Joy was not euphoric, and was so stressful that He sweated drops of blood. That is some pretty tough love and some very intense Joy!

A primary background component of Joy is an "attitude of gratitude." Gratitude is a life-characteristic that separates the joyful from others. We are grateful for what Papa has done, is doing, and will do. We have an internal paidion vision of the Kingdom and our place in it, and that vision inspires overwhelming gratitude from those who know they do not deserve His consideration, much less His kindness. That makes hope a second primary component of Joy because hope is that internal vision that looks past pain to fulfillment. So the equation for Joy is, "Gratitude + Hope = Joy." The foregoing brings us to the mechanics of the process of cultivating Joy, and for that, we turn to **James 1:2-4**:

> [2]My brethren, *count it all joy* when you fall into various trials, [3]*knowing* that the testing of your faith produces patience. [4]But let patience have its perfect work, that you may be perfect and complete, lacking nothing.

Do you know how sometimes you have a "love-hate" relationship with certain Scriptures? Well, that is the type of relationship I have with this verse—my flesh *hates* what it requires of me, and my spirit *loves* the result when I am obedient. Here is the point: James did not write, *"feel* it all joy," he wrote, *"count* it all joy." What is the difference? Disciples are not among those that have abandoned self-control to the whims and wishes of fickle, self-centered, enemy-stirred emotion. They *are* those that understand that emotions are only one aspect of our soul (with mind and will), and are *not* intended to drive the bus, only enrich the ride. When self-control is abandoned to serve emotions, an "If it feels good, do it" mindset takes over, and my will becomes dedicated to searching for the next emotional rush. In short, the quest to save your soul is abandoned in deference to a feast of emotional flesh.

When we *learn* to count it all joy instead of feeling it all joy, we purposely subject our emotions to the guidance of mind and will—that is, we make an affirmative choice based on truth, based on an understanding of God's process, and based on obedience to His commands. Sometimes our emotions come around to the correction of our mind and will, sometimes they don't. But, because we have "count[ed] it all joy," we still get to experience the by-product of patience (**verse 4**). The objective of "count it all" is not the transitional state of joy itself, but the mature, settled state of "perfect and complete, lacking nothing." James tells us that the *gateway* to soul-perfection is *patience*, and patience begins with "counting." And, the key to "count[ing] it all joy" is *reframing* our thoughts to bring our flesh and carnal mind into subjection to the spiritual mind. That brings us full-circle back to the Choice Space and the Joy Continuum!

How does this view of joy mesh with our premise that the prime work of discipleship is choosing to free ourselves of self? I find it helpful to understand that the opposite spirit of gratitude is an arrogant expectation of entitlement. Where gratitude says, "Thank you!" entitlement says, "I deserve…," even, "It's about time!" The companion response of frustrated entitlement is anger. So a person who has not cultivated gratitude encounters the various trials of **James 1:2** and typically responds with anger. When I don't get what I want, I get angry. When I don't get what I deserve, I get angry. Rhetoric from the "war on drugs" or those programs opposing alcohol and tobacco notwithstanding, our society's most pervasive, alluring, and debilitating addiction is not smoking, alcohol, or drugs, or even pornography, it is to *anger*. People—regular people, "salt of the earth" people—who would never consider snorting meth or shooting up with heroin are caught up in the tidal wave of rage prevalent today and feel perfectly justified. And not only justified, but we are told through multiple media (including a popular bumper sticker) that to be offended, enraged, and appalled is the appropriate mindset for those who are "paying attention." Needless to say, the first internal victim of our offense and outrage is Joy.

If gratitude is a precursor to joy, and if the opposite spirit of gratitude is anger and resentment, then it stands to reason that anger and resentment would be the precursor to the opposite of joy and the negative (left) end of our Joy Continuum. As it turns out, that is the case. Anger and resentment nursed and coddled over time convert into a root of bitterness that defiles us (**Hebrews 12:15**). Bitterness is the terminal state of anger. I can think of no more distasteful outcome for my *Last 15-Minute Self* than to end up a bitter, complaining old man full of resentment, self-pity, and seething anger, blaming everyone and everything for my failure to choose wisely.

Separation gives rise to the Independent Self, that much we have established. The Independent Self, then, pronounces itself the sole and authoritative arbiter of good and evil—that is the carnal mind in action! The carnal mind *only* considers the effect of events and circumstances in terms of their effect on itself! Therefore, good

> **Hebrews 12:14-15**, "[15]looking carefully lest anyone fall short of the grace of God; lest any root of bitterness springing up cause trouble, and by this many become defiled."

becomes "whatever is good for me, and results in my pleasure"; and evil becomes "whatever thwarts or interferes in my experience of pleasure and self-gratification." In its role as god, the Independent Self usurps prerogatives reserved for God the Father, and in essence, becomes the center of the universe. As the center of its own universe, it has these unconscious thoughts in residence at all times:

- "My life should be smooth and trouble-free."
- "I deserve to get what I want."
- "My comfort is the highest priority."
- "Others must adapt to my personality."
- "My perspective is always the right one."
- "I must be the center of attention."

- "I should always be celebrated."
- "I should always be the star."
- "I want it *now*!"
- "Entertain me *now*!"

Our unbridled Independent Self is something of an amalgamation of the four unruly children (not Charlie!) touring Willie Wonka's chocolate factory! When our Self-Control is non-existent, and our self is in control, we become Violet, Veruca, Mike, and Augustus all rolled into one consciousness—and that makes it a bad egg! As this world's "golden ticket holders," we feel entitled to all access—even Charlie and Grandpa Joe fell victim to this thinking. When our unconscious entitlement is thwarted—or even challenged—the result is anger, and anger precludes Joy. Therefore, the primary mechanism for cultivating Joy is to understand from where our anger and resentment originate (e.g., self-centered roots) and how to deal with it at the source *before* it converts into bitterness.

Anger may not be as body-wrecking as *some* substances, but it is definitely soul-wrecking. Like other addictions, anger alters our perception of reality to the degree that we stop perceiving accurately, and see and hear only what we expect to see and hear. Instead of Love, anger forms the filter through which we see the world. Like other addictions, anger has become a go-to strategy for many to deal with their daily circumstances. Like other addictions, addicts make friends with their anger as a comforter and crutch to get from today's stress to tomorrow's train wreck. Here is a short list of life wreckage strewn along the path and in the wake of anger:

> The path from today's stress to tomorrow's train wreck is *anger*!

- Severe depression and suicide
- Divorce
- Political in-fighting, and public displays of uncivilized, even egregious behavior
- Epidemic and endemic violence
- Lashing out, revenge and reprisal, including oppression and misuse of authority
- Relationship severance
- Oversensitivity, and a condition of being perpetually and easily offended
- A cluster of negative attitudes that alter the outlook, and even the personality (e.g., contentiousness, petulance, surliness, brooding, hypercritical, and cynicism)

We come now to a discussion of a topic that is often a major fork in the road in our experience of life: Grief. All of us experience grief at some point, and nothing tests our orientation to self as does our experience of profound loss. Loss of a child, loss of a spouse or other family member, financial ruin, even loss of a beloved pet can all be occasions that upset our apple cart in the extreme. An occasion of grief is one of the "big hairy deals" (BHDs) we referenced earlier. It is really difficult to keep at the forefront of our consciousness in grief is that we have a choice in our response. It is difficult because we feel so bullied by the circumstances and emotions that we feel absolutely powerless to do anything besides sitting alone in a dark place. I get it. It hurts. Bad.

I have a good friend that recently had major back surgery. After the successful procedure, the nursing staff insisted that he get out of bed and walk (with assistance, of course) *within a few hours* of the procedure! Needless to say, my friend didn't feel like getting out of bed. If I know him, he directed some good-natured barbs in their direction as he complied with their instruction. But the point is, *he did comply*—contrary to his feelings, and rather than take the "comfortable" (!) path of remaining motionless.

Anyone who has had major surgery understands that the earlier one gets out of bed the faster full recovery typically follows.  Hopefully, the meaning of recovering from major surgery compared to an episode resulting in grief is apparent.  In each case, the decision to *move* is critical to eventual recovery.

The BHD's Choice Space is as real as it gets in this life.  The pain—emotional, and often physical—is

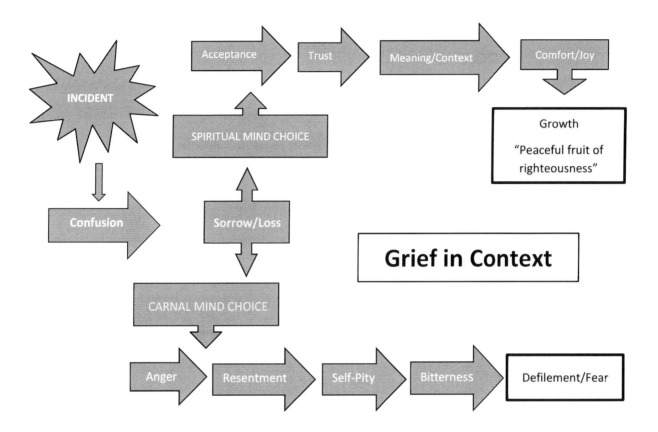

overwhelming.  Making choices and moving forward is contrary to every carnal mind instinct.  But at some point, we will have to realize that we do have a *response choice*; and that refusing or failing to make one between a carnal mind or spiritual mind is in itself a negative choice.  Once we choose acceptance of our emotions, of the circumstances, and of the loss we have experienced, we can move on—not without pain—to acknowledge our affirmative trust in Papa's care and love for us.  We can reframe our feelings in the context of our growth and look for meaning—not necessarily in the loss itself, but in our ability to overcome and grow with His assistance.  At that point, we are in a place to access His comfort, and begin to count it all joy.  Whether this process takes hours or years is up to us; but it is the only way to avoid the negative track and inevitable domino effect that results in bitterness, defilement, and fear.

What makes this understanding of grief and loss so important is that anger, self-pity, and resentment are not only *bitter* pills but also *anti-discipleship* pills.  We will see in later sections that anger destroys not only Joy, but Peace, Patience, Kindness, and Self-control as well.  As long as we nurse our friendship with anger—and the Independent Self that is its growth medium—we have chosen bitterness as a dance partner.  Bitterness then defiles us, and we have no chance to make meaningful progress on our discipleship pilgrimage.  Therefore, bitterness has earned its place of negative prominence on The Joy Continuum as the "opposite spirit."  The following is my Joy Continuum, and the choices—both positive and negative—that move me left and right:

# The Joy Continuum

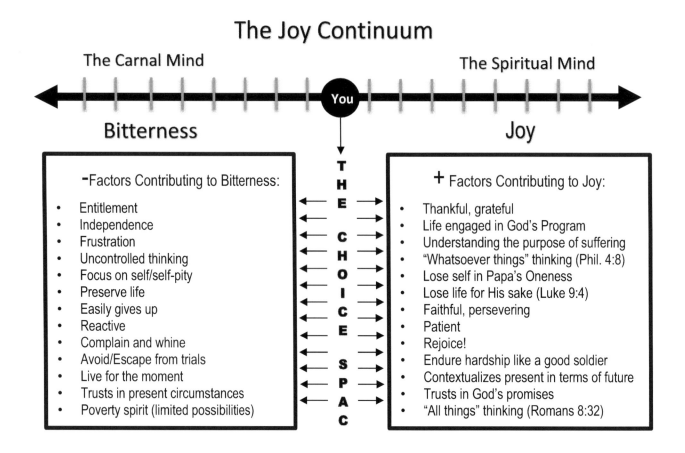

The Carnal Mind | The Spiritual Mind

← Bitterness | Joy →

THE CHOICES PACC

**−Factors Contributing to Bitterness:**

- Entitlement
- Independence
- Frustration
- Uncontrolled thinking
- Focus on self/self-pity
- Preserve life
- Easily gives up
- Reactive
- Complain and whine
- Avoid/Escape from trials
- Live for the moment
- Trusts in present circumstances
- Poverty spirit (limited possibilities)

**+ Factors Contributing to Joy:**

- Thankful, grateful
- Life engaged in God's Program
- Understanding the purpose of suffering
- "Whatsoever things" thinking (Phil. 4:8)
- Lose self in Papa's Oneness
- Lose life for His sake (Luke 9:4)
- Faithful, persevering
- Patient
- Rejoice!
- Endure hardship like a good soldier
- Contextualizes present in terms of future
- Trusts in God's promises
- "All things" thinking (Romans 8:32)

This is a pretty decent start but is by no means complete. As with the Love Continuum, The Joy Continuum should become your own, reflecting your own thoughts, your own challenges, and your own Discipleship Plan. By making *your* list of positive/negative behaviors, you can understand some of your more perplexing responses to circumstances, and learn to, "Count it all joy."

## The Continuum: Cultivating Peace

Peace is the absence of conflict—at least, that is the common usage. But the absence of conflict, when and if it is present, is only a collateral benefit of peace, not its definition. Additionally, it is possible for those who have cultivated peace to remain at peace *even in the middle of a conflict*. How is that possible? It is possible because our misunderstanding and mis-definition come from a lack of comprehension of Peace's root source. Peace comes from strength, and strength flows from security. There are many life implications and behaviors that are the result of our of personal security; a few are:

- Our ability to trust
- Our view of ourselves
- Our ability to be content with our own company
- Our ability to take risk
- Our ability to calm ourselves, relax and rest

- Our ability to resist inappropriate performance expectations
- Our ability to be "real" and vulnerable
- Our ability to be content with possessions and circumstances
- Our ability to not always be right, and even to admit that we are wrong
- Our ability to humble ourselves
- Our ability to apologize when it is the right thing
- Our ability to be "comfortable in our own skin"
- Our ability to repent
- Our ability to let other people be who they are
- Our ability to make choices and own the consequences
- Our ability to know from where we have come and where we are going
- Our ability to be weak
- And, yes, our ability to be "at peace"

These are but a few examples, but from these, we can see that the implications of our security largely shape our identity, and our identity either frees or enslaves us. Notice that each of these is an ability/skill to be developed. None of us are born secure, and many of us have good reasons for our feelings of insecurity from a natural perspective. But security does not come from within us. The secret of a secure identity is to hear and embrace what Papa says is true about us. It is connecting with His Love for us and wrapping up in it like a blanket. That is bedrock security, and it is bedrock, un-disturbable peace.

When I was trying to learn to play the piano as a child, I hated to practice scales—which is probably why I never learned the piano! It was the repetitive, muscle-memory movements that I simply could not master—probably because of my attitude. I have never liked the details of any endeavor because they slow me down and force me to concentrate. Like you, I would rather play video games. But in the detail of discipleship is where life and transformation happen. We lose our battle to maintain our Peace, not in the middle of major conflict, but when we surrender it in the tens and hundreds of frustrations that we experience daily.

There are two aspects of experiencing Peace with which we should become very familiar. The first is how to find our place of Peace and security in this T/S/M dimension. That requires being able to see into the eternal, embrace who we already are in God's eyes, and living in union with our true self. The second aspect is just as important: how to return to Peace and security when you lose your way and forget. Our safe place doesn't move—it never moves—but sometimes we have difficulty finding it. That is why Paul tells us in **Colossians 3:15**, "And let the peace of God *rule in your hearts*, to which also you were called in one body; and be thankful." The phrase, "let peace…rule in your hearts," is an interesting one. It means (paraphrased), "let Peace be the referee," or, "let Peace be moderator/adjudicator." Peace, or lack thereof, lets you know if you are in the right place and the right Choice Space. Peace is like a radio compass direction-finder and Geiger counter all rolled into one, and it "beeps" louder and more frequently as we approach nearer to the source. It is the referee that lets us know when we are on course, and when we are wandering off of the path of our pilgrimage. And when necessary, Peace informs us when we have committed a foul! The nearer to our security source we approach, the more we are aware that we are covered by His wings, we are cared for by His love, we are protected by His favor, and we are shielded from enemy attack. In short, we can relax and trust Him.

Our discipleship strategy for cultivating Peace is fundamentally the pursuit of the security of which it is a product. Since Peace is a natural outgrowth, and the benefits from connecting with our secure identity are myriad, a razor-sharp focus on the root source makes perfect sense. That means that the positive factors for our Peace Continuum should be activities and attitudes that acquaint us better with Papa's perspective of us. God does not give us peace, He *is* our Peace! Therefore, we are only as peaceful as we are secure in our knowledge of our identity and His thoughts toward us.

On the opposite end of the spectrum is insecurity. When we are insecure, we feel exposed, unsafe. We have to compensate for our lack of covering by "making aprons of fig leaves"—and they are never

> **Philippians 4:13**, "I can do all things through Christ who strengthens me."

adequate. We have to attempt to control our environment, control others' behavior, protect ourselves from real or potential pain, insult, injury, and attack. Even the best of us know down deep that we are inadequate for life's challenges, and that knowledge results in anxiety and fear. Fear debilitates and makes us zombies. We lose the ability to love, the ability to risk, the ability to be vulnerable. We lose the ability to be real because we do not know what "real" looks like. We cannot be weak or let people into our hearts because to expose our soft underbelly is a sure and certain catastrophe. We cannot commit, because what if a better offer comes along? Ultimately, we cannot know Peace because we do not know what it is to have our feet planted on the Rock.

Being free from Independent Self in the environment of insecurity is difficult-to-impossible. We cannot risk embracing Jesus' 2nd Great Commandment ("You shall love your neighbor as yourself," **Matthew 22:39**) because we cannot let down our guard for even one minute. Because Independent Self is inadequate for the task of life, it is full of anxiety and stress, control and performance standards, rules and emotional pain. But even in this seemingly hopeless condition, we can choose the spiritual mind; and we can be liberated from independence choice-by-choice. We can inch our way toward Peace and security. We can recognize the independence that enslaves us and choose a new basis for our trust and security. Such a re-training of our soul is a complete overhaul of how we perceive ourselves in the world, and "complete overhaul" is another way to say "transformation." "Make-over" is one of the concepts that completely fascinates us these days—to the degree that television producers have recognized it as a money-in-the-bank strategy for entertainment. From flipping houses to hair/makeup/fashion changes, to radical weight loss, we are enamored with change, even as we proclaim our dislike and fear of it. But contrary to common opinion, people don't fear change, they actually crave it. What they fear is *loss*, and our insecurity and inability to risk are tied up in the bundle of insecurity. Papa offers us His Peace to counter our insecurity. With our insecurity settled, we can accept—even crave—the His transformation.

My Peace Continuum model looks like the diagram below. Paul makes a statement in **2 Corinthians 12:10** that is absolutely ludicrous to our flesh. He wrote, "Therefore I take pleasure in infirmities, in reproaches, in needs, in persecutions, in distresses, for Christ's sake. For when I am weak, then I am strong." The pursuit of Peace is the embracing of personal weakness so that we may know His strength. "The way up is down," "The way to find your life is to lose it," "The way to life is through the eye of a needle," and, "When I am weak, then I am strong." We use paradoxical phrases all the time to describe our Christian journey. Only the spiritual mind can make sense of such seemingly conflicting truths, and only the spiritual mind choice is discipleship.

# The Peace Continuum

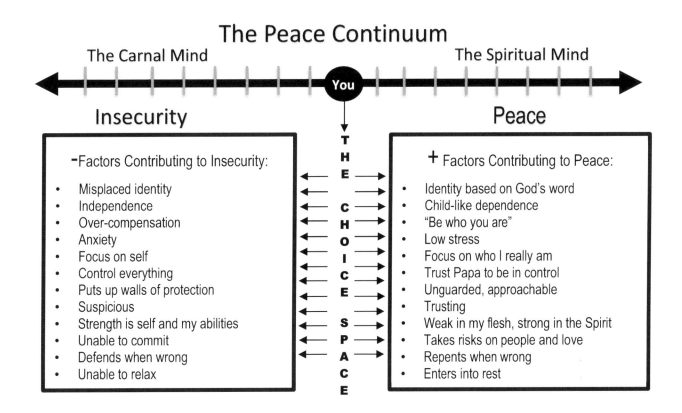

The Carnal Mind / The Spiritual Mind

You

Insecurity / Peace

**THE CHOICE SPACE**

-Factors Contributing to Insecurity:

- Misplaced identity
- Independence
- Over-compensation
- Anxiety
- Focus on self
- Control everything
- Puts up walls of protection
- Suspicious
- Strength is self and my abilities
- Unable to commit
- Defends when wrong
- Unable to relax

+ Factors Contributing to Peace:

- Identity based on God's word
- Child-like dependence
- "Be who you are"
- Low stress
- Focus on who I really am
- Trust Papa to be in control
- Unguarded, approachable
- Trusting
- Weak in my flesh, strong in the Spirit
- Takes risks on people and love
- Repents when wrong
- Enters into rest

## The Continuum: Cultivating Patience

The unvarnished truth is that lack of patience is the demand of our flesh for immediate gratification. Perhaps you have heard the Patience Prayer, "Lord, give me patience, and give it to me now!" Another word sometimes translated for "Patience" is "longsuffering," and that is tell-tale in itself about the gut-wrenching involved in its development. *None* of us are born patient because *all of us* are born as Independent Selves! The inconvenient truth is that Independent Self *never* goes down without a fight, and a corollary truth is that Independent Self *always* has a rationale, an explanation, and an excuse to justify its existence. Our addiction to impatience is no different!

Most deadlines set by impatient people are not real, that is, there is no horrible pending consequence if it is not met beyond what we inflict on ourselves and each other. Yet, we act like they are not only real but a matter of life and death. In fact, we often define compliance with an artificial deadline as the barometer of success or failure. *How goofy and self-centered is that?* The only non-negotiable deadline is our *Last 15-Minute Self*—and even there we *may* have 14-or-so minutes to play with!

Some are squirming right now, wondering to themselves how they would cope with life without deadlines. How would I make myself do anything if I didn't have an artificial cattle prod waiting to zap me? How would I blast myself out of my complacency if I did not have the "security" of a deadline that I can meet? Why would I work 60 hours per week if I didn't have to meet the quota? Tracing this line of thinking back to its logical source, it leads to, "How would I ever choose Heaven without the punishment of Hell hanging over my head?" That is Pavlov's Dog thinking ("When this bell rings, I have to eat!"). That is Independent Self thinking. Where Patience is lacking, there is *always* Independent Self in control.

> **James 1:4**, "But let patience *have its perfect work*, that you may be perfect and complete, lacking nothing."

Impatience in the spiritual realm is, by its nature, dissatisfaction with the process. We cannot be impatient without an underlying motivation of discontent. We cannot be patient without underlying security. Any process of lasting growth takes time to develop: it is what it is, and it takes what it takes. When we have an impending test, we have two preferable strategies: 1) avoid it altogether, or, 2) get it over as quickly and painlessly as possible. But pursuing our preferences shortcuts the process of perfection. **James 1:4** reminds us to, "Let patience have its perfect work." When we choose Patience in the midst of the Choice Space, we are engaging in the perfection process. Paul bundled "patient in tribulation" with other attributes in his exhortation in **Romans 12:9-14**:

> [9]Let love be without hypocrisy. Abhor what is evil. Cling to what is good. [10]Be kindly affectionate to one another with brotherly love, in honor giving preference to one another; [11]not lagging in diligence, fervent in spirit, serving the Lord; [12]rejoicing in hope, ***patient in tribulation***, continuing steadfastly in prayer; [13]distributing to the needs of the saints, given to hospitality.

Think of the occasions when you feel impatient. What do they have in common? I submit that careful consideration will reveal that impatience results when something I want or want to happen is frustrated—i.e., when the meeting doesn't start on time; when the toddler doesn't respond quickly to potty training or won't sleep through the night; when your friend keeps canceling on you; when your car breaks down for the second time in a month, etc. The impact of all of these circumstances (and many, many more) is how they affect me, and my companion, my Independent Self.

It is tempting to define the opposite spirit of Patience as "impatience." But though impatience is a term for the lack of Patience, it is not the root cause; and root causes are what we want to record on the negative end of the continuum. One the left end of the Patience Continuum is *the flesh's demand for*

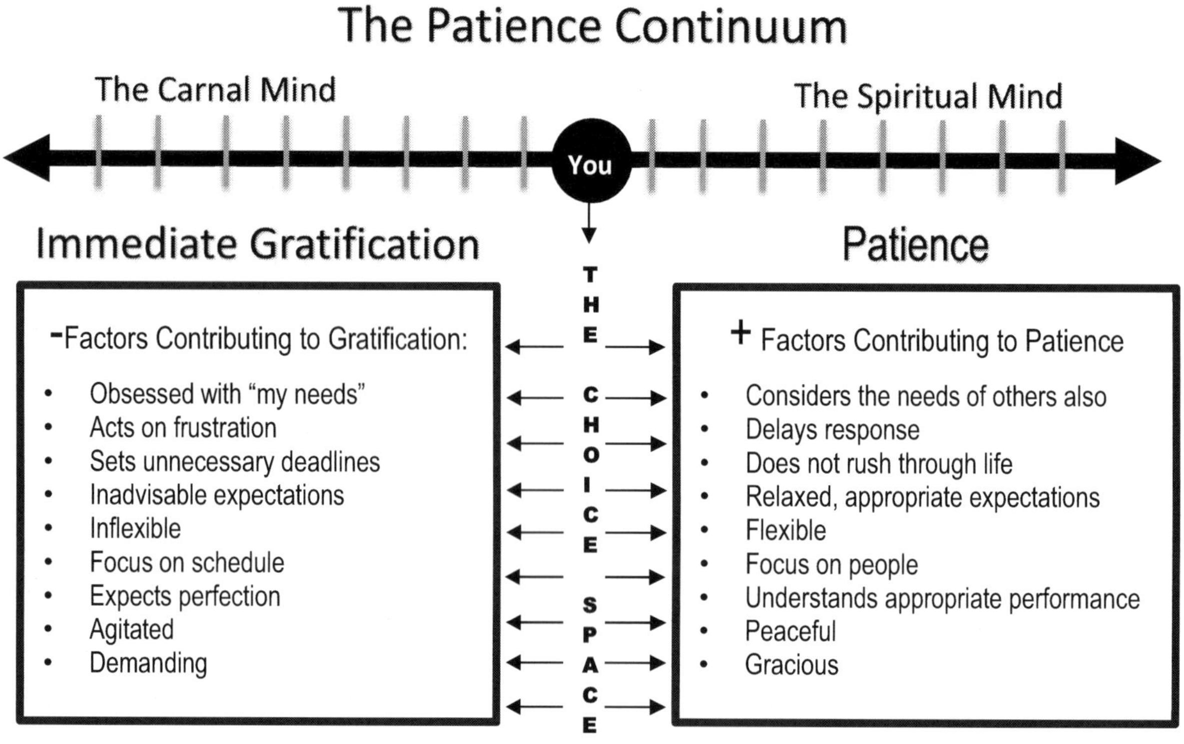
The Patience Continuum
The Carnal Mind
The Spiritual Mind
You
Immediate Gratification
Patience
THE CHOICE SPACE
-Factors Contributing to Gratification:
Obsessed with "my needs"
Acts on frustration
Sets unnecessary deadlines
Inadvisable expectations
Inflexible
Focus on schedule
Expects perfection
Agitated
Demanding
+ Factors Contributing to Patience
Considers the needs of others also
Delays response
Does not rush through life
Relaxed, appropriate expectations
Flexible
Focus on people
Understands appropriate performance
Peaceful
Gracious

*immediate self-gratification*. In tribulation, that gratification looks like escape; in irritation, it looks like the release of frustration directed at the offending party; in response to perceived affront or inconsideration, it looks like anger. *Always*, it begins with a performance expectation that is not met.

Cultivating Patience, then, becomes an exercise in choosing to deny self-centered interest, consider the interests of others, and suppress the impatient response. It is learning to control my expectations. It is embracing the fact that Papa has ordained a learning process for us, and that process should not be circumvented. It often involves intentionally taking our feelings in hand, delaying our immediate flesh response, and making a thoughtful, conscious Choice Space decision in favor of the spiritual mind option. For Patience to have its perfect work, we have to choose it when it is time to choose it. If Patience is not chosen at the moment it is called for, it is not Patience, but repentance. With that in mind, the Patience Continuum looks like the above model.

## The Continuum: Cultivating Kindness

Kindness goes way beyond being nice. When we settle for being nice instead of dealing with the root problem that causes our abuse of fellow travelers, we fall into the category of those admonished by Paul when he wrote in **Romans 12:9**, "Let love be without hypocrisy." Kindness differs from niceness in the same qualitative way that Joy differs from happiness. Though often confused, they are not the same. Although not the only FOTS that affects our interpersonal dealings, it is unique in that it expresses a response to an understanding of the lengths to which Papa has gone and the depths to which He has reached to embrace us with His Love and Kindness.

> **Romans 12:10**, "Be kindly affectionate to one another with brotherly love, in honor giving preference to one another."

Kindness flows from genuine affection, and affection flows from a source of respect and care. I do not have to know you to be Kind to you, because I respect and care for Papa's creation. Respect in this usage differs from, say, professional respect, or what one may earn from what they know. The respect of Kindness is more basic: respect for one another as a brilliant expression of our common Creator. In the same way that we "love God because He first loved us" (**1 John 4:19**), we respect and value one another because Papa first respected and valued us. From when we were knit together in our mother's womb (as David tells us in **Psalm 139:13**), each of us has been a member of God's chosen creation, a family with different moms and dads, but the same Father. When we lose sight of that—or worse, we never develop that perspective—niceness is a stretch, and Kindness is all but impossible. It is possible to be nice to someone without really caring for their well-being, and it is conceivable to be episodically nice to someone you neither value nor respect. However, in both instances, you cannot be consistently Kind because Kindness requires the sacrifice of our autonomous, self-centered position. It requires the 2nd Commandment (**Matthew 22:39**).

Because we were first valued and respected by Papa, providing that same courtesy and deference to one another is an exercise of The Golden Rule: "Whatever you want men to do to you, do also to them" (**Matthew 7:12**). That is a *great* guideline for the treatment of your spouse in a marriage, and it is a *great* guide for relating to others. The purest motivation for responding to one another in this way is that it is an expression of love for God, and admiration for His creation. If you have not yet grown to appreciate that, then at least do so for the promise of your own well-treatment (that would be an Independent Self motivation). Another principle of Scripture is that you reap what you sow (**Galatians 6:7**). We should, therefore, be constantly motivated to sow good seeds of Kindness, again, if for no other reason than our own well-treatment. Value-and-respect-given as a response to value-and-respect-received is one form of showing the same mercy and debt-forgiveness of which we have been a recipient.

Jesus gave us a brilliant parable to illustrate the principle in **Matthew 18:21-35**:

> $^{21}$Then Peter came to Him and said, "Lord, how often shall my brother sin against me and I forgive him? Up to seven times?" $^{22}$Jesus said to him, "I do not say to you, up to seven times, but up to seventy times seven. $^{23}$Therefore the kingdom of heaven is like a certain king who wanted to settle accounts with his servants. $^{24}$And when he had begun to settle accounts, one was brought to him who owed him ten thousand talents. $^{25}$But as he was not able to pay, his master commanded that he be sold, with his wife and children and all that he had, and that payment be made. $^{26}$The servant, therefore, fell down before him, saying, 'Master, have patience with me, and I will pay you all.'
>
> $^{27}$Then the master of that servant was moved with compassion, released him, and forgave him the debt. $^{28}$"But that servant went out and found one of his fellow servants who owed him a hundred denarii; and he laid hands on him and took him by the throat, saying, 'Pay me what you owe!' $^{29}$So his fellow servant fell down at his feet and begged him, saying, 'Have patience with me, and I will pay you all.' $^{30}$And he would not, but went and threw him into prison till he should pay the debt. $^{31}$So when his fellow servants saw what had been done, they were very grieved, and came and told their master all that had been done. $^{32}$Then his master, after he had called him, said to him, 'You wicked servant! I forgave you all that debt because you begged me. $^{33}$Should you not also have had compassion on your fellow servant, just as I had pity on you?' $^{34}$And his master was angry and delivered him to the torturers until he should pay all that was due to him. $^{35}$"So My heavenly Father also will do to you if each of you, from his heart, does not forgive his brother his trespasses."

**Matthew 7:2**, "For with what judgment you judge, you will be judged; and with the measure you use, it will be measured back to you."

*Wow.* It boggles the mind how the wicked servant could engage in such egregious and selfish behavior. But we see it all the time in Church and in the world—refusal to forgive and show mercy from the very ones who should most appreciate it. Forgiveness and mercy are not on the list of Fruits of the Spirit, but they do qualify as expressions of Kindness, as well as "refractions" of the Master-fruit of Agape Love. They both begin with deep humility and appreciation for the Kindness Papa has extended to us.

Enthroned self can be a mean, tyrant-god, ready to take us by the throat and dispense fury when challenged or things do not go his/her way. When Independent Self rules, Kindness is at best erratic and moody, because the standard of measure that it applies to all situations and relationships is, "How does this affect and benefit me?" By now you should be noticing a consistent theme: The underlying struggle to cultivate all Fruit of the Spirit is against enthroned Independent Self. Further, if you can see and accept it, it is, "Self as god." Here is the distilled truth: Papa has already dealt with one rebellion (Lucifer's—**Isaiah 14:12-15**) based on self, and I am confident He does not intend to undergo a 2$^{nd}$. Could that be why He has given us such a brilliant classroom and internship opportunity to learn to crucify the flesh and abandon Independent Self before He returns Jesus' Kingdom to Him? Could it be that for those who will live and serve there, unswerving loyalty (*even over our Independent Self interests*) is a qualifying leadership trait for the Bride of Christ? Is it possible that He wants us to learn in this T/S/M experience the uber-qualitative difference between "I will be like the Most High" (**Isaiah 14:12-15**) and "that they may be One just as we are one" (**John 17:22**). Can you see it? Can you catch a glimpse of why overcoming self is so important? It is because the self is at the heart of rebellion!

When we figuratively take one another by the throat and make demands as the wicked servant did, we forfeit our own access to the Master's Kindness toward us. Jesus told us in His Sermon on the Mount that we determine our own standard of judgment by what we dispense to others. Kindness begins with reciprocal respect and appreciation for what Papa has extended toward us. Therefore, we can understand the opposite spirit of Kindness to be disrespect, which includes lack of appreciation and value. Many selfish behaviors fall into the negative contributors to a state of fixed disrespect, and all of them have a strong element of selfishness and/or disdain. They include a lack of respect and value for life itself. The wicked servant in Jesus' parable is disrespect personified. The wicked servant views all of humanity as tools to meet his needs, and cogs in the great machine of daily self-indulgence. The following model is a beginning point for your construction of a Kindness Continuum to suit your own pilgrimage.

Cultivating Kindness begins with exploring a deep understanding of the mercy and grace that has been extended to us. Our thoughts and meditations should rightfully begin with the sacrifice that both the Father and the Son have made to elevate Man from dust status to "a little lower than the angels" (**Hebrews 2:7, 9**). When we receive His care for and Kindness toward us, it is all-but-impossible not to melt into His arms and reciprocate. Like joy, it develops a deep appreciation and *profound* sense of gratitude. It embraces humility because we affirmatively know that we did nothing to deserve His gift. We progress in Kindness as we guard our heart against the intrusion of Independent Self, against over-valuing our own worth apart from His Love, and against the flesh's constant rancor to "pay me what you owe."

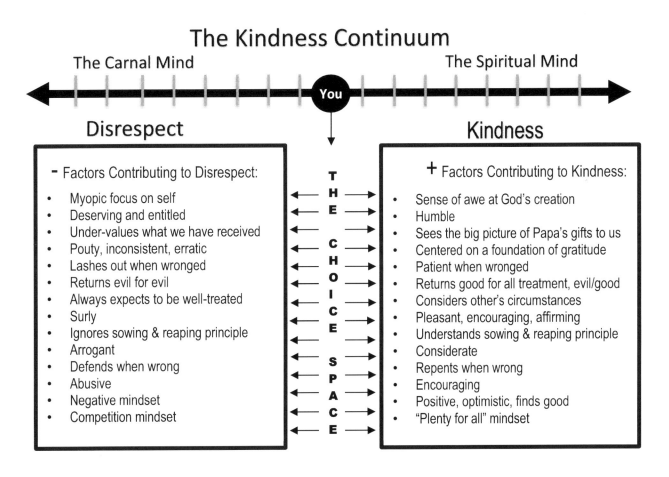

# The Kindness Continuum

The Carnal Mind — The Spiritual Mind

You

## Disrespect

**– Factors Contributing to Disrespect:**

- Myopic focus on self
- Deserving and entitled
- Under-values what we have received
- Pouty, inconsistent, erratic
- Lashes out when wronged
- Returns evil for evil
- Always expects to be well-treated
- Surly
- Ignores sowing & reaping principle
- Arrogant
- Defends when wrong
- Abusive
- Negative mindset
- Competition mindset

THE CHOICE SPACE

## Kindness

**+ Factors Contributing to Kindness:**

- Sense of awe at God's creation
- Humble
- Sees the big picture of Papa's gifts to us
- Centered on a foundation of gratitude
- Patient when wronged
- Returns good for all treatment, evil/good
- Considers other's circumstances
- Pleasant, encouraging, affirming
- Understands sowing & reaping principle
- Considerate
- Repents when wrong
- Encouraging
- Positive, optimistic, finds good
- "Plenty for all" mindset

# The Continuum: Cultivating Faithfulness

Consider the following Proverbs:

- **Proverbs 27:2**, "Let another man praise you, and not your own mouth; a stranger, and not your own lips"; and,
- **Proverbs 20:6**, "Most men will proclaim each his own goodness, but who can find a faithful man?"

Solomon reveals his genius in these two Proverbs. I am struck by the juxtaposition of these two ideas: 1) not proclaiming your own goodness, i.e., "praising yourself"; and, 2) faithfulness. So, how do these two ideas mesh into one piece of good advice?

I have a son to whom I had to routinely say during his formative years, "Don't *tell* me, *show* me!" This was frequently necessary because of, at least in part, the constant barrage of negative example proliferating in the world around us. We live in a time of arrogance, of proclaimed self-aggrandizement, of blustering, of "cheap-and-easy talk." All of these characteristics have something in common: They proceed from an inner core of insecurity. When I am insecure, I must make it my business to point out to you my worth to compensate for my self-doubt. When one combines self-doubt with an uncontrolled tongue, the result is arrogance. We have a phrase for it: "trash talk." I'm not addressing the trash talk that is nothing more than light banter between friends. I'm talking about the mean-spirited, over-compensating self-aggrandizement that we see in so many arenas today, from politics to sports, to the dining table.

In light of the foregoing discussion, we have Solomon quietly telling us, "Don't *tell* me, *show* me!" Though the words are different, the meaning is clear. This world is full of "one-and-done" one-hit wonders proclaiming each their own goodness; but who can find a *faithful* man? Faithfulness means to keep on keeping on. It means consistency. It means showing up, ready to perform, ready to work, ready to sweat. It means, "I will be here tomorrow, same place, same time, to do the same thing." Faithfulness is the antithesis of a participation trophy. Our *rock stars* should be the faithful among us, not the flashy, arrogant, boasting, or attention-seeking. Of course, these, too, need attention; but it is the attention of *healing*, not the attention of admiration.

Faithful men and women are committed to a vision, and are mission-minded; that is, they keep whatever mission Papa has assigned them in the forefront of their thinking. The FOTS Faithfulness focuses us, and focus multiplies our effectiveness. Because of a lack of vision, people who wander through life directionless do not qualify as faithful. They may qualify as persistent, even stubborn, but stubborn is not Faithful. Faithfulness means persistent, unrelenting righteousness. Wrapped up in the attribute is a whole cluster of qualities that each contribute their own puzzle piece: steadfastness, tenacity, perseverance, loyalty, resoluteness, undeterrable, energetic, and trustworthy. Faithfulness is the result of an internal fire that cannot be extinguished. Our quest to identify the negative end of the Faithfulness Continuum needs to encompass the opposite spirit of as many of these as possible. For my continuum, I considered several concepts: immature, unreliable, disloyal, untrustworthy, lazy, and "in-too-much-pain-to-move."

There are no warriors on the negative end of Faithfulness, only those that are constantly victims because they lack what it takes to climb out of the pit. On the negative end of the continuum are people without spunk, no grit. They give up easily. For that reason, I have chosen "broken" as the negative terminus because those that dwell here are not only broken but will always be so until they find the courage to be faithful. I am not using broken here in any *good* sense that we might employ the term, to indicate a dependence on God, or humble, for example. I mean non-functional, and lost in a stew of self-pity, bewilderment, nursed pain, and lack of resolve of their own making. As you may recognize from my story in Chapter 1, I have been there. There is no cure for broken except for the discipleship process.

It may sound as if I have no compassion for brokenness, but that is not the truth. Having been there in spades, I recognize that gushing compassion is the *last thing needed*. A broken person needs a strength infusion. Gushing compassion has the effect of anchoring the broken in their current estate. But what they need a vision of continuing life as a healed and whole person. They need to do the things to move them "to the right" toward Faithfulness until the ideal comes back into view. The following Faithfulness Continuum may help map the way from broken to Faithful function once again:

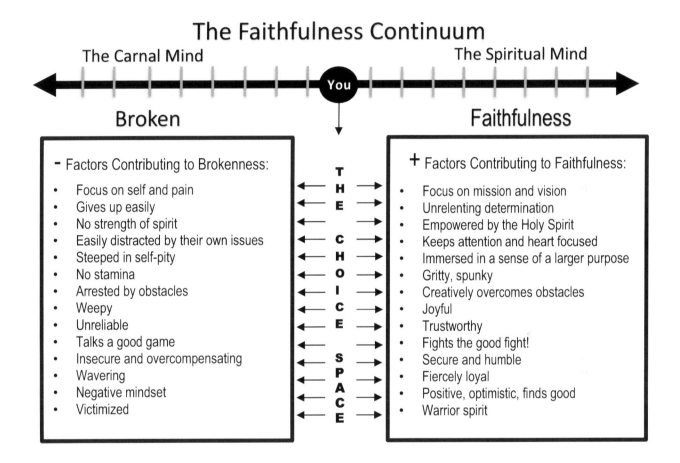

## The Continuum: Cultivating Meekness

The dictionary definition of Meekness highlights the problem with going to a worldly source for a spiritual definition, at least in the absence of confirming understanding from Scripture. Doing so yields a pejorative view of meekness as "humbly patient or docile, as under provocation from others"; or "overly submissive or compliant; spiritless; tame."[25] Docile? Overly submissive? *Spiritless*? **Tame**? Here is a question for you: In what universe would being in union with the "Lion of the Tribe of Judah"—our goal in this life—yield a docile, spiritless, *tame* disciple? While you are contemplating that dichotomy, I will quickly add that **Revelation 5:5-6** reveals the answer to the mystery, the spiritual bridge that spans the paradox and conflict between the polar ends of the question: The *Lion* and the *Lamb* are the same Being!

---

[25] https://www.dictionary.com/browse/meekness

The world's dictionary does not comprehend the dichotomy because its writers did not understand the connection between the Lion and the Lamb, nor do they account for the union life of Christ to overshadow and express itself in our human existence. The worldly system frequently confuses behavior or appearance as nature—and that is a grave mistake! There is nothing docile, spiritless, or tame about the Lion, the Lamb, or the disciple through whom His life is being expressed.

> **Revelation 5:5-6**, "But one of the elders said to me, 'Do not weep. ***Behold, the Lion*** of the tribe of Judah...' ⁶And I looked, and ***behold... stood a Lamb...***"

What is an accurate understanding of Meekness as Paul lists it in the Galatians 5:22? To get it, we must look to Scripture for context, and that means **Numbers 12:3**: "Now the man Moses was *very meek*, above all the men which were upon the face of the earth." The Meekest man on earth. What does that look like, and would we receive that as a compliment if said about us? What do we know about Moses, his calling, and how he dealt with both Pharaoh and the Israelite nation that would qualify him as "most Meekest"? First and foremost, we know that God provided Him powerful tools and an assurance that He would act on his behalf, as recorded in **Exodus 4:1-8**:

> ¹Then Moses answered and said, "But suppose they will not believe me or listen to my voice; suppose they say, 'The Lord has not appeared to you.'" ²So the Lord said to him, *"What is that in your hand?" [Moses] said, "A rod." ³And He said, "Cast it on the ground."* So, he cast it on the ground, and it became a serpent; and Moses fled from it. ⁴Then the Lord said to Moses, "Reach out your hand and take it by the tail" (and he reached out his hand and caught it, and it became a rod in his hand), ⁵"that they may believe that the Lord God of their fathers, the God of Abraham, the God of Isaac, and the God of Jacob, has appeared to you." ⁶*Furthermore the Lord said to him, "Now put your hand in your bosom." And he put his hand in his bosom, and when he took it out, behold, his hand was leprous, like snow.* ⁷And He said, "Put your hand in your bosom again." So, he put his hand in his bosom again, and drew it out of his bosom, and behold, it was restored like his other flesh. ⁸"Then it will be, if they do not believe you, nor heed the message of the first sign, that they may believe the message of the latter sign."

God *did not* turn Moses' shepherd staff into a magic wand for doing tricks. He *did* make it a symbol and tool of His assurance to Moses, and a symbol of both His power and Moses' commission to Pharaoh. Moses' hand was part of him, and the rod the tool of his trade. He said to Moses, in effect, "Whatever you have, I will take and transform to accomplish my will." We have the same assurance from Papa today. He takes whatever we have ("What is that in your hand?" **verse 2**) and turns it into something mighty. He takes that which we carry with us all the time and says, "Be prepared to throw it down and watch it transform!" Meekness is not a milk-toast demeanor, it is stepping out of the way and letting God fight your battles for you!

While true that Moses objected to his spokesperson status because his perceived "slow[ness] of speech and...of tongue" (**Exodus 4:3**), he also had a knowledge of another secret weapon that Papa put at his disposal (**Exodus 4:11-12**):

> ¹¹So the Lord said to him, "Who has made man's mouth? Or who makes the mute, the deaf, the seeing, or the blind? Have not I, the Lord? ¹²Now therefore, go, and I will be with your mouth and teach you what you shall say."

If I may paraphrase, Papa is saying in His, "Who made man's mouth?" rhetorical question, "If I made your mouth—and I did—and if I am God—and I am—doesn't it make sense that it came out just the way I wanted? What if I don't want a smooth-talker, but rather a smooth-listener?" In God's promise to Moses, we glean yet another lesson: Whatever we perceive our weaknesses to be, they become strengths when submitted to Papa's control. When Moses faced Pharaoh, he said all he needed to say; he had all the words required to get the job done. *We* are the tragic losers when we allow our weaknesses, perceived lack, and inadequacy to stop our participation in building the Kingdom. Papa will build His Kingdom with or without us, and it is greatly to our advantage to be heavily invested in the building process. To do less is unbelief and to lose out big-time.

Meekness and humility are *not* synonymous with shyness and introversion as they are understood by the world. They are companion terms to one another, and a deep understanding of either usually leads to the character development of the other. Humility is "Choosing the lowest place," and Meekness is "Letting God fight your battles for you!" That is *precisely* what Moses did, and the secret he learned from carrying what appeared to the world as a shepherd's staff, but was, in reality, the Rod of the Lord anointed by *His* power.

> **Luke 12:11-12**, "11Now when they bring you to the synagogues and magistrates and authorities, do not worry about how or what you should answer, or what you should say. 12For the Holy Spirit will teach you in that very hour what you ought to say."

Moses understood the dynamic, "Speak softly and carry a big stick!" He showed up before Pharaoh, then stepped back and let the power of God speak on His behalf. Meekness is not acting in your own power, but releasing the authority and channeling Papa's strength. It is fighting battles in the spiritual realm while others are fighting in the power of darkness; or at the very least, in the power of the flesh.

When we present ourselves in the appearance of the Lamb, the Lion works on our behalf. The New Testament equivalent of Moses' experience is Paul's message in **2 Corinthians 12:9-10**:

> 9And He said to me, "My grace is sufficient for you, for My strength is made perfect in weakness." Therefore, most gladly I will rather boast in my infirmities, that the power of Christ may rest upon me. 10Therefore I take pleasure in infirmities, in reproaches, in needs, in persecutions, in distresses, for Christ's sake. For when I am weak, then I am strong.

In this context, then, Meekness may be understood as, "Perfect strength replacing and operating through my infirmities." It is, "The Power of Christ, resting."

There is another aspect of Meekness as it impacts our preparation to rule with our Bridegroom—it is a major component of our leadership capability. Recall that we have said that good leadership in the Kingdom is reflected in good leadership on earth. Few things define our leadership style and capability as our willingness to intentionally take self out of the way and access Papa's work and strength on our behalf. Many today confuse aggressive self-assertiveness and self-promotion as the mark of a true leader. That is a lie from the pit of hell. Strong leadership sometimes calls for a heavy hand—as Moses demonstrated to Pharaoh. But it was God's heavy hand, not Moses'; and if you do not know the difference, you still have a few more things to learn about leadership. Unfortunately, those who adopt such a style are least able to hear because listening is not part of the flesh's typical strong leader persona.

How does the Meekness Continuum apply to grow the character quality in us? The essence of the Choice Space dilemma is dwelling between the spiritual mind and the carnal mind. And choosing Meekness is to choose the spiritual mind when faced with the dilemma of rising up in our own strength, or stepping aside for Papa's Perfected Strength. It is the choice not to defend yourself. In fact, it is the choice not to consider Independent Self at all, but to abandon independence for the strength of union.

In light of the foregoing, it is reasonable to place "the assertion of self'—or Self-Assertive—in the place of the opposite spirit of Meekness on our continuum. As we have done with other Fruits of the Spirit, once we understand the true meaning of Meekness, and the opposite spirit and motivation, we should be able to list spiritual mind behaviors that contribute to growing meekness as a character quality, and carnal mind behaviors that contribute to our independence and self-assertiveness.

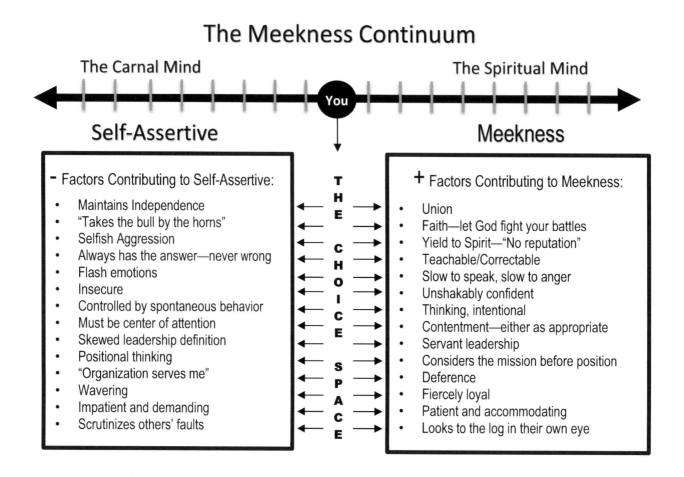

# The Meekness Continuum

The Carnal Mind | You | The Spiritual Mind

Self-Assertive | Meekness

THE CHOICE SPACE

**− Factors Contributing to Self-Assertive:**

- Maintains Independence
- "Takes the bull by the horns"
- Selfish Aggression
- Always has the answer—never wrong
- Flash emotions
- Insecure
- Controlled by spontaneous behavior
- Must be center of attention
- Skewed leadership definition
- Positional thinking
- "Organization serves me"
- Wavering
- Impatient and demanding
- Scrutinizes others' faults

**+ Factors Contributing to Meekness:**

- Union
- Faith—let God fight your battles
- Yield to Spirit—"No reputation"
- Teachable/Correctable
- Slow to speak, slow to anger
- Unshakably confident
- Thinking, intentional
- Contentment—either as appropriate
- Servant leadership
- Considers the mission before position
- Deference
- Fiercely loyal
- Patient and accommodating
- Looks to the log in their own eye

## The Continuum: Cultivating Self-Control

It is no accident that the last FOTS in Paul's list sums up the previous eight. Self-Control is the key that unlocks the release of the entire fruit basket into our experience. That is absolutely true—but, it may not be true in the way you are currently thinking about it. Self-Control as a discipleship catalyst does not mean "behavior control" *per se*. Settling for behavior control is treating symptoms and not dealing with root causes and problems at their source. Self-Control as a FOTS means "Control of Self"! It means putting and keeping Independent Self in check, out of the pilot's seat of life. It means taking the unnatural step of denying the instincts that accompany separation from God. It is the rejection of living life for the sake of living life, and what we can accumulate and experience ("Life for its Own Sake"). As we have explored each of the FOTS continuums, we have been careful to point out the Independent Self component and the opposite spirit of each. We have defined life's goal as increasingly coming into Oneness with Papa and our Bridegroom in our mind, will, and emotions. We have explored the virtues of learning His ways, and abandoning our own separated, independent ways—the "way that seems right to a man" but ends in death (**Proverbs 14:12**). Independent Self is separated self, and separated self by definition cannot abide in the vine because it does not know union or even how to connect on the organic level.

There are three Scriptures that are virtually identical in each of Matthew, Mark, and Luke's Gospels. Jesus' words on this occasion were so impacting that they made all three disciple's sermon notes that day! (Luke was not one of the Twelve, but he definitely qualifies as a disciple.) Here is the **Matthew 16:24** version: "Jesus said to His disciples, 'If anyone desires to come after Me, let him deny himself, and take up his cross, and follow Me'" (also **Mark 8:34**, **Luke 9:23**). Jesus boils it down to a simple summary of day-to-day action, no words about church attendance, nothing about taking communion, nothing about baptism or any religious activity. Just "deny yourself [today], follow me." Controlling our self-centered interests is the work of the cross in us. What Paul called "controlling" self, Jesus called "deny[ing]" self. Deny means to oppose, refuse, rebuff, renounce, and a whole bunch of other synonyms that convey the message of abject rejection. Jesus' simple formula meshes nicely with the central message of the "Control of Self" in FOTS #9. In fact, Paul's use of the term self-*control* seems to be an understatement in light of Jesus' commandment to renounce and crucify self every day. Crucifixion is brutal; crucifixion is ferocious, messy, calloused, and merciless. We may conclude therefore that the only way to control self is to kill it, and to kill it in the most ruthless way—to drive spikes through your metaphorical hands (what you do) and feet (where you go) every day and hang it out to die a slow, agonizing death. Jesus is not interested in making a nicer, more compliant, more polite, sweeter smelling version of your Independent Self. *He is interested in taking over*, and that requires your death.

Displacing Independent Self is completely foreign to our world-orientation, and to what we call "our life." Our normal expectation—whether we are honest enough to admit it or not—is to treat ourselves, and be treated, as "gods-with-a-little-g," like rock stars. Recall in Chapter 1 I made the statement, "It is a strange orientation to life when you spend your entire waking day *not doing* something"? It is time now to explore more fully what that phrase means, and how it impacts our quest for Control of Self. This time, the "not doing something" that we are shooting for is not indulging Independent Self.

The central feature of God's Program on earth is the restoration of a Kingdom to His Son. Papa has already dealt with one rebellion based on an exaltation of self (Lucifer's), I'm quite sure He is taking the action necessary to prevent a repeat of Lucifer's **Isaiah 14:12-14** declarations in the coming Kingdom:

> [12]How you are fallen from heaven, O Lucifer, son of the morning! How you are cut down to the ground, you who weakened the nations! [13]For you have said in your heart: "I will ascend into heaven, I will exalt my throne above the stars of God; I will also sit on the mount of the congregation, on the farthest sides of the north; [14]I will ascend above the heights of the clouds, *I will be like the Most High*."

One aspect of God's Program of rebellion-prevention in the Kingdom is training Self-Control on earth as a FOTS in the Bride of Christ—teaching us to reject self-exaltation and separation at its source. You may recognize Lucifer's "trash talk" about his intention to take over and usurp the glory of the Most High. ("Most High God" is a title for the Son of God in His office of "Possessor of Heaven and Earth.") Before you direct ridicule and contempt in Lucifer's direction, you should take a moment to pause and think how you (and I) do *exactly* the same thing every day. He did in macro what we naturally do in micro daily. Unless we are *actively, intentionally* denying self and taking up the *humility* of the cross *daily*, we will always find ourselves repeating the same pattern. We have the perfect example in Jesus, who:

> [6]Exist[ed] in the form of God, did not count equality with God a thing to be grasped, [7]but *emptied himself*, taking the form of a servant, being made in the likeness of men; [8]and

being found in fashion as a man, he *humbled himself*, becoming obedient even unto death, yea, the death of the cross. (**Philippians 2:6-8)**

For sure, we are not *guilty* of the same rebellion as Lucifer, but only because Jesus has paid the price to redeem our rebellion—that is justification. But, like Paul, we "press on, that [we] may lay hold of that for which Christ Jesus has also laid hold of [us]" (**Philippians 3:12**). Our justification removes the guilt of our separated self, our salvation process moves us on to root out the vestiges of Lucifer's offensive rebellion in us—Independent, Separated Self.

One of the fascinating things about Jesus' command to, "[T]ake up [your] cross daily," is that in all three Gospels, it occurs before His own crucifixion! Matthew's quote, for example, occurs in **Chapter 16, verse 22**; but his account of the crucifixion doesn't follow until **Chapter 27**! Assuming the chapters are in chronological order, what must the disciples and the listening crowds have thought when well before the event, Jesus is talking about something as gruesome as crucifixion? They must have had a rude awakening, an "I don't think we're in Kansas anymore, Toto!" moment. Like cold water thrown in your face on a hot day, those that expected political and social deliverance/justice from His ministry must have been in shock. "What do self-denial and crucifixion have to do with being nice to everyone, and everyone being nice to me? Jesus, why are you talking about painful, brutal things when all we are looking for is fuzzy feelings, prosperity, and a better, more moral life?" No wonder so many turned around and followed Him no more (**John 6:66**)! As long as it was all about free wine, bread, healing, and other demonstrations of power, they were all in. But when Jesus' talk got offensive and personal, it was time to go. "Who does this guy think He is—He's just the carpenter's son!" (**John 6:42**).

> **Matthew 26:37-38**, "³⁷And He took with Him Peter and the two sons of Zebedee, and He began to be sorrowful and deeply distressed. ³⁸Then He said to them, 'My soul is exceedingly sorrowful, even to death. Stay here and watch with Me.'"

Jesus struggled mightily with His follow-through in submitting to the pain of the cross (**Matthew 26:37-38**). He did not relish *His process* any more than we relish our process of self-denial. But when it came time to perform, He rose up and embraced "the cup," the brutal challenge of pain and death. And that is the same self-denying, self-emptying, "no reputation" choice we face today in pursuing Self-Control:

- **Romans 8:13**, "For if you live according to the flesh you will die; but if by the Spirit you *put to death the deeds of the body,* you will live."
- **Colossians 3:5**, "⁵Therefore *put to death your members* which are on the earth: fornication, uncleanness, passion, evil desire, and covetousness, which is idolatry."
- **1 Peter 3:18**, "For Christ also suffered once for sins, the just for the unjust, that He might bring us to God, being *put to death in the flesh* but made alive by the Spirit."

Clearly, on the negative end of the Self-Control Continuum is "Self in Control." It is our T/S/M identity expressing itself in all of its dubious "glory." It is Independent Self doing what it does best—looking out for #1. That the plain meaning of Jesus' words escapes some believers is a testimony to the power of Independent Self's delusional capabilities. The Choice Space with respect to Self-Control begins narrow and is closing all the time as we concentrate on our interests and worldly responsibilities, and we get better and better skilled at being selfish. Is there any doubt that is what we are observing in the world today? In the course of just my lifetime, selfishness has accelerated and been perfected to the point of being practiced as a religion and art. As a religion, it is generally known as Humanism; as an art, it goes by many names, among which are the "American Dream," financial independence, self-actualization, Existentialism, and Rationalism, to name a few.

# The Self-Control Continuum

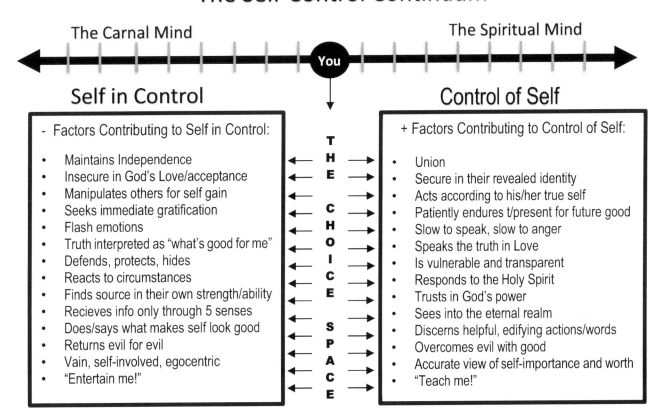

The Carnal Mind

The Spiritual Mind

**You**

## Self in Control

## Control of Self

- Factors Contributing to Self in Control:

- Maintains Independence
- Insecure in God's Love/acceptance
- Manipulates others for self gain
- Seeks immediate gratification
- Flash emotions
- Truth interpreted as "what's good for me"
- Defends, protects, hides
- Reacts to circumstances
- Finds source in their own strength/ability
- Recieves info only through 5 senses
- Does/says what makes self look good
- Returns evil for evil
- Vain, self-involved, egocentric
- "Entertain me!"

THE CHOICE SPACE

+ Factors Contributing to Control of Self:

- Union
- Secure in their revealed identity
- Acts according to his/her true self
- Patiently endures t/present for future good
- Slow to speak, slow to anger
- Speaks the truth in Love
- Is vulnerable and transparent
- Responds to the Holy Spirit
- Trusts in God's power
- Sees into the eternal realm
- Discerns helpful, edifying actions/words
- Overcomes evil with good
- Accurate view of self-importance and worth
- "Teach me!"

An interesting question is, "Is it possible to progress in the realm of the Spirit to the point that Independent Self is completely overcome and union is fully assimilated into union?" I confess that I do not know the answer from experience, no one I know has ever attained that status as far as I can tell. I know that Papa does not tease us, and if He gives us a vision of what is possible, He is also able to complete the work if I am of a mind to work. I am heedful-but-hopeful for myself in the ability of the Holy Spirit to coax me out of my independence and separateness to an enhanced degree; I know He is fully able, and am only wary about my ability to endure the cost, to "drink the cup." The only way is if I spend time meditating on what to emulate with Control of Self, and what to forsake with "self-in-control," to learn what it looks like, its early signs, and how it may be avoided. Only then can I intentionally work to control its ugliness *before it appears*, or repent and forsake *when it appears*. Only when I specify steps on the right side of the continuum to move me toward union and Self-Control as a component of my discipleship planning can I incrementally, but systematically, be emptied of what comes so naturally and readily to my flesh. It is a life-long quest, not an instantaneous work. It can't be an instantaneous work because we only see from horizon to horizon, and do not know what will be the character and nature of our Choice Space beyond today's horizon. The best we can do is walk in today's challenge, and pray for Papa's grace, mercy, and strength to embrace tomorrow's.

# Chapter 9—Epilogue: Where Do We Go from Here?

²Set your mind on things above, not on things on the earth. *³For you died, and your life is hidden with Christ in God*. ⁴When Christ who is our life appears, then *you also will appear with Him in glory*.
**Colossians 3:2-4**

## Minas and Talents—What Discipleship Is All About

It is not difficult to imagine traveling with Jesus, hearing the same basic message day after day, letting it soak into the core of our being. We discussed in Chapter 2 what that message was: the gospel of the Kingdom of God. Politicians running for office today are coached to, "select a message, then stay on it, and don't vary from it." Candidates are further counseled to keep it simple, and not to create controversy. Keeping it simple and avoiding controversy was not Jesus' style—but then, He was not running for office! He intentionally obscured His message so that only the motivated and the elect would understand and pursue the Kingdom. He expressly said, "I did not come to bring peace but a sword" (**Matthew 10:34**). Complexity, controversy, and conflict did not bother Him because He knew from where He had come, who He was, and to where He was returning—and He knew why He was sent. It is the same way with us—when we understand 1) from where we came, 2) who we are in Christ, 3) why we have been placed in these containers of flesh in this time and space dimension, 4) what we are to be about while we are here, and 5) what comes after this portion of our eternal journey is "in the books."

Matthew and Luke give us accounts of Jesus' Parable of the Talents and Parable of the Minas, respectively. The Parables are remarkably similar and are both "on message": The Master (clearly, Jesus) has gone on a journey to receive a Kingdom, and He has left us resources with which we are to be about transacting His business while He is away. And (drum roll please!) when He returns, our role in His Kingdom will be predicated on our faithfulness to transact business and increase the Kingdom in His absence. The primary difference is Matthew's use of "talents" (presumably talents of gold) and Luke's "Minas." Also, Luke adds a section about the citizen's response to the Master's servants, and His subsequent dispatch of their rebellion upon His return—clearly a reference to the persecution of the Church and Jesus' future dealing with those involved.

It is important to note that the Master's resources were entrusted to His *servants*, not just any old citizen that came along, or even a specialized group of investment professionals (read: pastors and evangelists). That is an important fact to remember when we later read of the two different accounting processes that took place. The citizens that hated Him and declared, "We will not have this man reign over us" (**Luke 19:14**), had their own accounting for their actions. But their accounting was not the same as that of the servants, nor was the standard of measure (faithfulness in the Master's business) the same. There is no indication that there was any positive outcome for non-servants, only a negative consequence for their rebellion. But, for the servants, their accountability was to be rewarded based on faithfulness, based on what they had done with the Master's resources. The acceptance range of their effort (or lack thereof) included both handsome reward and abject rejection. No one else can or will ensure your development to match your potential, e.g., the *full* potential that is endemic to the Seed of the Kingdom Papa plants in us. The seed itself has the intrinsic value of life, but is ours to tend, promote, transact, and increase. It truly is your goat to milk!

> **Luke 12:48**, "For everyone to whom much is given, from him much will be required; and to whom much has been committed, of him they will ask the more."

## Jars of Clay

Being at the top of the earthly food chain sometimes results in us egotistically regarding ourselves as more than we actually are. Israel is God's chosen people, and many in that culture have taken refuge in that status, even exult in it. But John the Baptist called out the people to whom he preached for attaching pride and status to their position of being sons of Abraham without accepting the responsibility connected to their position to bear fruit:

> [8]Therefore bear fruits worthy of repentance, and do not begin to say to yourselves, "We have Abraham as our father." For I say to you that God is able to raise up children to Abraham from these stones. (**Luke 3:8**)

There are great privileges and promise associated with being chosen by God, whether as a nation as Israel was, or "before the foundation of the earth" as was the Church (**Ephesians. 1:4**). But Paul reminds us in **Romans 11:17** that we were "grafted in," and have no special standing, abilities, or superior value apart from His choosing of us. Knowing that, our chosen status should have an effect in us of inspiring overwhelming gratitude toward Him who chose us and places us in the learning and production environment where we can be successful.

> **2 Corinthians 4:7**, "But we have this treasure in earthen vessels, that the excellence of the power may be of God and not of us."

Our bodies may only be earthen vessels, but we are earthen vessels that are filled with the treasure of the Spirit of God, and the promise of the Kingdom of God in seed form. One of the recurrent themes in

## "We Have This Treasure in Earthen Vessels" (2 Corinthians. 4:7)

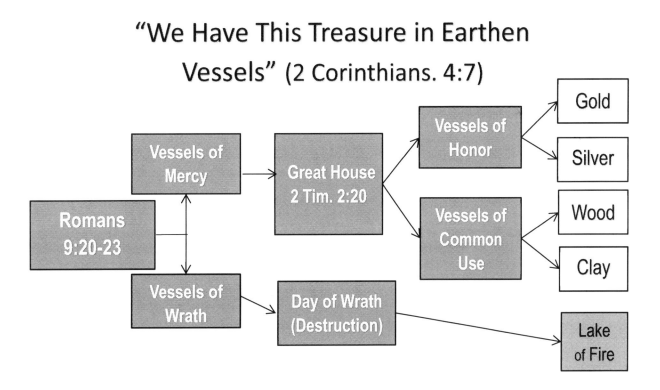

Paul's writing is that the Church, as a temple, is a container of His glory. As a vessel, the important thing is the essence inside (i.e., our "precious life"), not the covering outside. This fact is offensive to the world and its self-important viewpoint. **Romans 9:20-23** defines two categories of vessel into which all humanity is divided—vessels fitted for wrath, and vessels of mercy. The category of "vessels of mercy" is further subdivided into "vessels of honor" and "vessels of common use" in **2 Timothy 2:20**. (Note that *both* of the latter are still in the "great house.") We can readily understand this principle from our daily experience—we have one vessel in the house that contains the milk, and one into which we drain the used motor oil; both are necessary, but you wouldn't want to get them mixed up.

But "vessel of honor" and "vessel for common use" are not the final breakdown of Paul's vessel metaphor. He further divides vessels in the great house by the material from which they are made: gold and silver, wood and clay. The discipleship process has, as its goal, an alchemistical outcome: to turn clay pots into golden and silver bowls fit for display and service in the great house of the King of Kings. A really smart and astute request of Papa—and ingredient for inclusion in our Discipleship Plan—is, "Make me a golden vessel in Your Great House!"

## The Greatest Mystery of All

How does our oneness with Jesus and the Father cause the world to "...believe that [the Father] sent [Him]" as Jesus' prayer in the last half of **John 17:21** claims? To understand how Jesus thought about oneness, and to begin to understand what He meant by the phrase "make Us one," it is helpful to look at **John 14:8-10**:

> [7]If you had known Me, you would have known My Father also; and from now on you know Him and have seen Him. [8]Philip said to Him, 'Lord, show us the Father, and it is sufficient for us.' [9]Jesus said to him, "Have I been with you so long, and yet you have not known Me, Philip? He who has seen Me has seen the Father; so how can you say, 'Show us the Father'? [10]Do you not believe that I am in the Father, and the Father in Me? The words that I speak to you I do not speak on My own authority; but the Father who dwells in Me does the works."

Jesus seemed to be speaking in riddles. Clearly, Phillip did not understand that Jesus was declaring to the Disciples that to see His acts, hear His words, and observe His works is tantamount to "seeing" the Father. But such observation is only a part of the understanding equation. Observation is the "milk" relationship; "meat" requires mining our observations for deeper meaning. Observation must be followed by contextualizing the information in order to get past the time/space/matter dimension and to see behind the veil of our flesh. Our disbelief must be set aside before we can overcome our unbelief. Philip clearly saw Jesus' flesh manifestation by being in His physical presence day after day. He even observed Jesus' mastery over the time/space/matter material world in His miraculous works—which miracles were intended to direct his and the other observers to the truth of the eternal dimension.

But Jesus expected Philip (and the other disciples) to see more—He expected them to perceive the "there-but-not-there" world. You can hear Jesus' raised eyebrows as he said to Phillip the equivalent of, "I've been with you all this time and still you don't get it?" (**verse 9**). It seems that the sticking point with Philip and the other disciples is the same as we experience today: Jesus is referring to oneness on the level of our "precious life" (i.e., spirit and soul), while the disciples seemed to be expecting to see the Father appear in some manifestation with their physical eyes. Philip was still operating out of his Independent Self orientation and world view and therefore could not process the meaning that Jesus was conveying.

If oneness and being free from the Independent Self has a key principle that unlocks the union possibilities, it is *dependence*. Recall that we discussed that dependence is one of the characteristics that children share in their childlike-ness. As we progress in age from newborn to adulthood, our Independent Self grows until we become veritable islands of existence in terms of our dependence on others. Our culture even values and reinforces the motivation to stand strong and stand alone. We have also discussed how our flesh and carnal mind are hardwired to depend on our five senses to make sense of the world, and how Jesus' admonition to "be converted and become like little children" (**Matthew 18:3**) requires regressing to a pre-Independent Self childlike state where we can "see" the "there-but-not-there" world of the eternal. Jesus tells us that without that regression, we cannot enter the Kingdom of God (**Matthew 18:2-3**). That, in itself, should motivate us to empty ourselves of all independence in favor of dependence on the Father.

## What is Overcoming?

**Revelation Chapters 2 and 3** contain prophetic letters to the 7 churches of Asia Minor. The letter to the Church of Pergamos (the "Compromising Church") contains a passage that is obviously intended for the Church in general and through all time:

> He who has an ear, let him hear what the Spirit says to the churches. To him who overcomes I will give some of the *hidden manna* to eat. And I will give him a *white stone*, and on the stone a *new name* written which no one knows except him who receives it. (**Revelation 2:17**)

The remarkable aspect of this Scripture to me is that there is such a thing as hidden manna; there are white stones, and new names; and the existence of each of the above is significant and promised as a reward for those individuals in the churches that "overcome." The existence of these pending rewards for the Body of Christ begs an answer to the question of, "What constitutes overcoming?"

"Hidden manna" is intriguing to me—not that a white stone with a new name would not be very cool as well! But when the topic is mysteries, secrets, and hidden wisdom, the term "hidden manna" catches my attention. We have established that God reserves a certain understanding for those who search for it diligently. I do not think it is a stretch—nor does it do violence to the meaning—to equate that diligent search, intentionality, and the connection of all the mysterious dots with the struggle and overcoming process. Moreover, overcoming the world and the flesh are the principal battleground of the Choice Space. In all of this, it is vital to recognize the following: A casual, erratic, and unplanned (even serendipitous!) pursuit of our development in the Spirit will be ineffectual in establishing our status as overcomers, with all of the promised benefits.

In light of the promised reward of **Revelation 2:17** for overcoming, it is reasonable to consider the task in relation to the reward promised. That is, overcoming should bear some nexus to hidden manna and a new name. Consider Solomon's advice from **Proverbs Chapter 9**:

> [1]Wisdom has built her house, she has hewn out her seven pillars; [2]she has slaughtered her meat, she has mixed her wine, she has also furnished her table. [3]She has sent out her maidens, she cries out from the highest places of the city, [4]"Whoever is simple, let him turn in here!" As for him who lacks understanding, she says to him, [5]"Come, eat of my bread and drink of the wine I have mixed. [6]Forsake foolishness and live, and go in the way of understanding."

The hidden manna is bread eaten at wisdom's banquet table. It is revelation discovered in concealed, mysterious places—like deep in one's cave in silent meditation, sitting before the Holy Spirit in a position and attitude of reception! It is the result of labor in the Spirit until our new person is birthed. The hidden manna is that gold that must be mined from deep in the earth after hour upon hour of digging into Papa's mysteries. It is spending quality time in the place of *paidion vision*—seeing through from one dimension into another.  The hidden manna is the revelation of the Kingdom—and your place in it—and living life in that context while yet in this time/space/matter reality.

In previous pages, we have discussed our identity in Christ—who you and I *really* are, not who this world says we are, or who the enemy has tricked us into thinking that we are.  **Revelation 2:17** tells us what is waiting for those who overcome the fog of false identity foisted upon us by Satan and the world system that is under his influence.  The Spirit speaking to the Church through the ages tells us that, for those who overcome the fog of an obscured identity ("For now we see in a mirror, dimly" **1 Corinthians 13:12**), a white stone with our new name is waiting.  It is the name by which we are known in heaven; it is the name that captures the essence of the precious life that resides in this container of flesh, and the name attached to the spiritual authority that accompanies it.  It is the name associated with the person that remains following the purification of the Bema Seat judgment.  Our identity and name are intimately connected, and the Spirit in **Revelation 2:17** is telling us in the language of mystery that to overcome is to see through and to see ahead who we already are in the eternal.

> **Proverbs 9:4-6**, ""⁴Whoever is simple, let him turn in here!'  As for him who lacks understanding, she says to him, ⁵'Come, eat of my bread and drink of the wine I have mixed.  ⁶Forsake foolishness and live, and go in the way of understanding.'"

**Revelation 3:21** connects the act and status of overcoming with the right to rule with our Bridegroom: "*To him who overcomes* I will grant to sit with Me on My throne, as I also overcame and sat down with My Father on His throne."  A fair question is, "After Jesus' complete and vanquishing victory over sin, death, over the gates of Hell; after making a spectacle of the enemy, and overcoming the world system; after taking back His people and His creation—what is left for us to overcome?"  The answer is the heart of the issue for our *Last 15-Minute Self*.  In the Old Testament, God not only delivered Israel out of Egypt (a picture of sin/captivity), He also prepared a Promised Land for the Israelites to possess and in which they were intended to dwell.  However, He left it up to them to fight for and take possession of it.  Likewise, He has prepared an inheritance for us and now leaves it up to us to take possession of it through the "Every place on which the sole of your foot treads" pilgrimage process.  Our journey is through the wilderness, into our promised inheritance, and into battle with our carnal mind and flesh.  Identity is vital to overcoming; acting in this realm according to the new name we possess in the eternal realm is to overcome this world and the enemy's system of deception.  Acting according to our true identity and the authority associated with it—that name written on the white stone—is the consummate method of overcoming the flesh and the carnal mind.

> **Deuteronomy 11:24**, "Every place on which the sole of your foot treads shall be yours: from the wilderness and Lebanon, from the river, the River Euphrates, even to the Western Sea, shall be your territory."

The intent of **Revelation 2:17** is to inspire; that is, the Spirit intends to cast vision for those who are paying attention closely enough to catch that overcoming is not just passing one's time going about business as usual; nor is it about success in the realm of "life for its own sake."  It is a cloaked reference directed to those whose heart is set on pilgrimage to set them off in the direction of pursuing Papa's secrets and our true identity.  It is for those who have ears to hear, eyes to see, and the heart to follow.

## From Glory to Glory

We began with the concept of pilgrimage, and now we will end with the same.  **Psalm 139:3** tells us, "You comprehend my path and my lying down, and are acquainted with all my ways."  It strains our imagination and credibility to think about how our Father can simultaneously be intimately acquainted with untold millions of His children—and still have time to count the sparrows that fall to the ground! The point I make from verse **Psalm 139:3** is that you have a path, and it is uniquely yours. For all of its talk of diversity, the movement in today's society is just the opposite: to try to make men and women uniform, thinking alike, and boringly homogeneous. Nevertheless, David points out that there are as many paths in the Kingdom as there are believers. If there is any diversity, any creativity to be enjoyed—and there are beaucoups!—our Father is the author.

To have our own path means that we are each presented with challenges and puzzles, the combination and re-combination of which are specifically and carefully designed for who we are. God has provided us with an instruction manual (the Bible) and has assigned us a life-coach (the Holy Spirit). Embracing the process is up to us. There are for sure bumps and bruises involved. There are dead-ends and switchbacks. The Scripture does not teach

> In our similarities we can help one another; in our differences, we can complement one another.

that there is *one* right path for each of us; nor does it promise that it is linear or the shortest distance between two points! It teaches that our experience is a custom-designed classroom structured to bring each of us from beginning to end, from separation (Egypt) to Promised Land (inheritance/union), from glory to glory, from faith to faith, from strength to strength, and from pool to refreshing pool. One reason we are told not to judge one another's journey is that, being uniquely designed for us as individuals, to criticize the path and process is to criticize the path Designer. My path and challenges do not look like yours, though there are likely some overlapping similarities. In our similarities, we can help one another; in our differences, we can complement and encourage.

The "From—To Principle" is the journey of enlightenment from our present understanding of our identity to our final understanding. It is how we get from the present to our *Last 15-Minutes Self*. The "From—To Principle" implies movement, and it is ongoing and dynamic. It portends change and growth. It specifies progress from our point of departure to a successful destination. The From—To journey also implies an upward climb, an increase in revelation and maturity, not simply ground covered. In other words, we are intended not only to experience different forms of glory but also to progress from an initial state to a settled, mature state of glory! We experience multiple instances and applications of faith, but each instance is designed to be an improvement—an increased amount and quality—of faith.

In **Romans 5:17**, Paul tells us the objective outcome and the *full effect* of Papa's abundance of grace and gift of righteousness that should be in our experience:

> For if by the one man's [Adam] offense death reigned through the one, much more those who receive abundance of grace and of the gift of righteousness will *reign in life* through the One, Jesus Christ.

Here is an audacious-but-accurate statement: *Anything less than reigning in life is settling.* It is making a treaty with mediocrity, a non-aggression pact with this world and the carnal mind. It is, in effect, "You leave me alone and I'll leave you alone" compromise.

> Anything less than reigning in life is settling. Anything less than presiding over circumstances is acquiescing to living life as a victim.

To grasp this, we must understand that reigning means to "preside over your circumstances." Reigning is not ruling. Ruling is the prerogative to *change* your circumstances, and that prerogative will be ours eventually as joint heir to the Kingdom. But for now, Papa is teaching us that circumstances and challenges are subservient to our character and the Fruit of the Spirit in us. Circumstances and problems are what they are, but life is made manifest in our internal response, not in external experience. He is teaching us that we are *not* the sum total of what happens **to** us, we are the aggregation of His Life manifested **in us**, in royal character, vision, wisdom, and understanding; not a petty hand-to-mouth "gimme that" and "entertain me *now*" short-sighted outlook. *Reigning in life* only happens in moment-by-moment, choice-by-choice embracing of the spiritual mind. With each increase in our total faith comes an increase of risk to be embraced. It is not surprising, then, that our spiritual strength grows as a natural consequence. As we experience increased success in overcoming the flesh and in overcoming the enemy of our soul, we become a force with which to be reckoned, and we become recognized in the spiritual realm. That is the normal Christian life, and that is the dilemma we face every day in the Choice Space.

The Father has made the provision, and Jesus is watching and waiting for His Bride to emerge. The Holy Spirit is standing by, ready and willing to coach. We are surrounded by a great and auspicious cloud of witnesses to cheer us on. The rest is up to you. What will you choose today, at this moment? What will be the cumulative legacy of your *Last 15-Minute Self?*

This Circle Represents the Sum Total of Your Life.

This Is the Portion You Live on Earth In the Flesh.

Are You Circle Motivated, Or Dot Driven?

# Appendix — Discipleship Plan Example

| Discipleship Plan | Name: **Randy Templeton** | Last Update: 09/14/2019 |
|---|---|---|

| **Personal Mission** | To leave a legacy of integrity, wisdom, kindness, and accomplishment. To both BE and DO to present to the world an expression of Christ's life in this body. To live intentionally to become my envisioned Last 15-Minute Self. |
|---|---|

| **Goal** | To live in perfect union with the Father in soul and spirit, as Jesus did. To transcend the Time/Space/Matter life and live in the reality of the eternal. |
|---|---|

| **Strategic Prayer** | "Papa, teach me Your *Ways*, show me Your *Kingdom*, and reveal to me Your *Program*." |
|---|---|

| **Legacy Scriptures** | <ul><li>Job 13:15, "Though He slay me, yet will I trust Him."</li><li>Job 2:10, "'Shall we indeed accept good from God, and shall we not accept adversity?'" In all this Job did not sin with his lips."</li><li>Galatians 2:20, "I have been crucified with Christ; it is no longer I who live, but Christ lives in me; and the life which I now live in the flesh I live *by the faith of the Son of God*, who loved me and gave Himself for me."</li><li>Psalm 84:5-7, "⁵Blessed is the man whose strength is in You, *whose heart is set on pilgrimage.* ⁶As they pass through the Valley of Baca, they make it a spring; the rain also covers it with pools. ⁷They go *from* strength *to* strength; each appears before God in Zion."</li><li>John 13:3-4, "³Jesus, knowing that the Father had given all things into His hands and that He had come from God and was going to God, ⁴rose from supper and laid aside His garments, took a towel and girded Himself."</li><li>2 Peter 1:3-4, "³as His divine power has given to us all things that pertain to life and godliness, through the knowledge of Him who called us by glory and virtue, ⁴by which have been given to us exceedingly great and precious promises, that through these you may be partakers of the divine nature…"</li><li>Proverbs 25:2, "²It is the glory of God to conceal a matter, but the glory of kings is to search it out."</li><li>Revelation 3:18, "I counsel you to *buy from Me gold refined in the fire*, that you may be rich; and *white garments*, that you may be clothed, that the shame of your nakedness may not be revealed; and anoint your eyes with *eye salve*, that you may see.</li><li>Luke 9:23, "Then He said to them all, 'If anyone desires to come after Me, let him deny himself, and take up his cross daily, and follow Me.'"</li></ul> |
|---|---|

| **Identity Statement** | I am a man in **UNION** with God, thoroughly settled on who He has made me; therefore, I am unshakably **CONFIDENT**. I **RESPOND** to all situations with the Fruit of the Spirit, not works of the flesh reactions. God **TRUSTS** me to act on His behalf, and I **EXPAND** the Kingdom daily. I am **GRATEFUL** for all that comes from Papa's hand, and **SHARE** open-handedly with others. I **HEAR GOD** speak and **SEE GOD** act in daily circumstances. I wake up **FRESH** in Spirit every morning, and go to bed **VICTORIOUS** every night, having done all to stand. I enjoy Papa's **FAVOR**, His **REST**, and His **PEACE** in life's circumstances, and joyfully **ENCOURAGE** others. I am a **WORSHIPER** who loves God with my heart, soul, mind and strength, and my neighbor as myself. I am a **WARRIOR** that never gives up, never gives ground, never gives quarter to the enemy, and never gives less than Papa's best to those around. |
|---|---|

| | |
|---|---|
| **Principles of Application** | 1. "Add To" Principle<br>2. The inverse relationship between growth and comfort.<br>3. Reaping and Sowing Principle<br>4. From—To Principle<br>5. First Principles (milk, not solid food)<br>6. Vessel of Honor/Common Use Principle<br>7. "We become most like what we most look at"<br>8. What you take takes you.<br>9. The innocent must die for the guilty.<br>10. The Hope of Glory Principle (Christ in me, as me.)<br>11. Childlike Principle (dependence, imagination, etc.)<br>12. Life for Its Own Sake principle<br>13. "Opposites define one another" Principle<br>14. "That Which Every Joint Supplies" Principle.<br>15. Surrender Principle (You can't fix yourself)<br>16. Principle of Paradoxical Response<br>17. "Grasp the One Don't Let Go of the Other" Principle.<br>18. Good leadership Principle<br>19. Imitate, Emulate, Assimilate Principle<br>20. Foolish Things of the World Principle<br>21. Lay Up Principle<br>22. All Things in Your Hands Principle<br>23. Accumulated Value Principle: "Our life has only the accumulated value of all the character qualities of our Bridegroom that have been transformed in us and the good works (reward) that we have sent ahead into the Kingdom."<br>24. "Heart Co-locates with Treasure" Principle<br>25. "Strength in Weakness" Principle<br>26. If it is not intended, it cannot be allowed. If it *is* intended, it cannot be prevented"<br>27. Asymptotic Growth Principle<br>28. "Small Things Principle" Cup of cold water shall not lose its reward" (Matthew 10:42)—Your gifts and talents need not be huge or profound to be valuable.;<br>29. "Small Beginnings" Principle<br>30. The inverse relationship between our earthly *choice* conduct of leadership and our *conferred* Kingdom leadership status. We may have our reward here on earth, or have it in full in the Kingdom.<br>31. Confidence flows from security, arrogance from insecurity. |
| **Resources: Gifts, Talents, Knowledge, Skills, Abilities** | Spiritual<br>• Motivational Gift: Teaching<br>• Ministry Gift: Serving, Administration, Encouragement<br>• Office Gift: Pastor/Teacher<br><br>Professional<br>• Emergency Management, emergency response, planning<br>• Incident Command System knowledge<br>• Continuity of Operations<br><br>General<br>• Building trades<br>• Writing<br>• Moderate furniture craftsmanship<br>• Structured thinking, organizational skills |

| Objectives | Related Scriptures: |
|---|---|
| | • 1 Corinthians 3:9, "For we are God's fellow workers; you are God's field, you are God's building." |
| | • Revelation 19:7, "Let us be glad and rejoice and give Him glory, for the marriage of the Lamb has come, and *His wife has made herself ready*." |
| | • Matthew 6:20, "[B]ut lay up for yourselves treasures in heaven, where neither moth nor rust destroys and where thieves do not break in and steal." |
| | • Philippians 4:8, "Finally, brethren, whatever things are true, whatever things are noble, whatever things are just, whatever things are pure, whatever things are lovely, whatever things are of good report, if there is any virtue and if there is anything praiseworthy—meditate on these things." |

| Objective #1: (integrity, wisdom) | **Prepare to rule beside my Bridegroom by cultivating His character, values, ways in Our life together.** |
|---|---|
| **Strategy #1** | **Develop character by implementing the Fruit of the Spirit and other key character qualities.** |
| Tactics | 1. Understand thoroughly FOTS traits and their opposites. <br> 2. Continue to develop continuums for each FOTS and selected other qualities. <br> 3. Meditate on character qualities and how they are implemented. <br> 4. Review daily previous performance, and journal as appropriate. |
| Action Plan | 1. Focus on FOTS Patience. <br> 2. Focus on FOTS Kindness <br> 3. Focus on FOTS Control of Self |
| **Strategy #2** | **Review Discipleship Plan daily, update regularly.** |
| Tactics | 1. Maintain Discipleship Plan. <br> 2. Begin each day by reviewing the plan. <br> 3. Record character traits/issues on which I am working. *Be specific!* |
| **Strategy #3** | **Mediate on the nature of the Kingdom.** |
| Tactics | 1. Pray daily to be shown the nature of the Kingdom. <br> 2. Set aside time regularly to "think on these things"; keep the nature of the Kingdom at the forefront of my thoughts. <br> 3. Mediate on Union, particularly Galatians 2:20. Seek to understand "Christ *in* me, *as* me." <br> 4. Meditate on the shadow of reality, and the eternal dimension. <br> 5. Control my thought process, confine to Philippians 4:8 "things." |
| **Strategy #4** | **Develop leadership skills.** |
| Tactics | 1. Read selected leadership books and other materials. <br> 2. Consider writing about resilience and other leadership qualities related to the Kingdom. |

| Objective #2:<br>(kindness, accomplishment) | **Increase the Kingdom by laying up treasures in heaven.** |
|---|---|
| **Strategy #1** | Develop *The Last 1-Minutes* (L15-M) ministry. |
| Tactics | 1. Evaluate the need/possibility of a L15M Workbook.<br>2. Develop Logistical Plan/alternatives for multiple formats of L15M retreats.<br>3. Construct new PowerPoint slides for presentation opportunities of multiple lengths, venues, and formats. |
| **Strategy #2** | Daily/regular efforts to encourage others. |
| Tactics | 1. Continue daily Facebook posts, and "Morning Glory!"<br>2. Evaluate a daily blog post.<br>3. Continue to grow in Gift of Knowledge sharing/encouragement. |
| **Strategy #3** | Strategic volunteering. |
| Tactics | 1. Locate and adopt organization(s) that are a match for KSAs, interests, and needs, and also that are an efficient and effective investment of my time.<br>2. Donate *a minimum* of 4 hours per week. |
| **Strategy #4** | Strategic projects for others, using building and craftsmanship abilities. |
| Tactics | 1. Continue crib construction for children and selected others.<br>2. Continue finishing house projects and home maintenance as needed. |
| **Strategy #5** | Fund/Go on at least one mission trip annually. |
| Tactics | 1. Fund at least one freshwater project in India, Honduras or Guatemala each year.<br>2. Go on a mission trip annually, either service project or evangelism. |
| **Objective #3**<br>(Integrity, wisdom) | **Abandon the Independent Self in all of its forms.** |
| **Strategy #1** | Develop Hyper-sensitivity and hypervigilance to expressions of self. |
| Tactics | 1. Mediate on, study and read about independence, separation, union, and oneness.<br>2. Examine my motivations as a routine activity.<br>3. Think about a discipleship tool for overcoming Independent Self as the goal.<br>4. Memorize "Dying to Self" Poem. |
| **Strategy #2** | Begin research and writing on the topic of Independent Self as a new emphasis. |

# Dying to Self

When you are forgotten, or neglected, or purposely set at naught, and you don't sting and hurt with the insult or the oversight, but your heart is happy, being counted worthy to suffer for Christ, **THAT IS DYING TO SELF.**

When your good is evil spoken of, when your wishes are crossed, your advice disregarded, your opinions ridiculed, and you refuse to let anger rise in your heart, or even defend yourself, but take it all in patient, loving silence, **THAT IS DYING TO SELF.**

When you lovingly and patiently bear any disorder, any irregularity, any impunctuality, or any annoyance; when you stand face-to-face with waste, folly, extravagance, spiritual insensibility - and endure it as Jesus endured, **THAT IS DYING TO SELF.**

When you are content with any food, any offering, any climate, any society, any raiment, any interruption by the will of God, **THAT IS DYING TO SELF.**

When you never care to refer to yourself in conversation or to record your own good works, or itch after commendations, when you can truly love to be unknown, **THAT IS DYING TO SELF.**

When you can see your brother prosper and have his needs met and can honestly rejoice with him in spirit and feel no envy, nor question God, while your own needs are far greater and you are in desperate circumstances, **THAT IS DYING TO SELF.**

When you can receive correction and reproof from one of less stature than yourself and can humbly submit inwardly as well as outwardly, finding no rebellion or resentment rising up within your heart, **THAT IS DYING TO SELF.**

**Are you dead yet?**

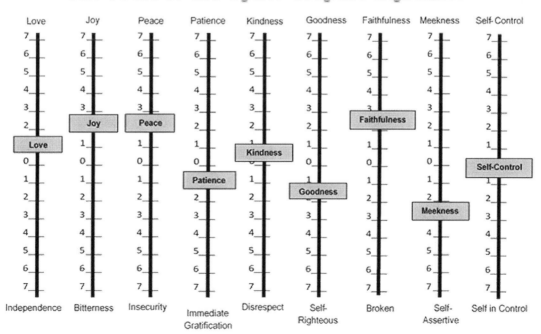

Made in the USA
Columbia, SC
09 October 2020